SHAKESPEARE IN COMPANY

for Nicola

from

Bart

P. 3. 2013

Shakespeare IN Company

BART VAN ES

OXFORD
UNIVERSITY PRESS

OXFORD
UNIVERSITY PRESS

Great Clarendon Street, Oxford, OX2 6DP,
United Kingdom

Oxford University Press is a department of the University of Oxford.
It furthers the University's objective of excellence in research, scholarship,
and education by publishing worldwide. Oxford is a registered trade mark of
Oxford University Press in the UK and in certain other countries

First Edition published in 2013

Impression: 1

British Library Cataloguing in Publication Data
Data available

Library of Congress Cataloging in Publication Data
Data available

ISBN 978-0-19-956931-1

Printed in Great Britain by
MPG Books Group, Bodmin and King's Lynn

for Josie

Acknowledgements

As this is a book about the creative outcome of fellowship it feels especially appropriate to begin by thanking the friends and colleagues who helped bring it to completion. The ideas behind *Shakespeare in Company* took shape in 2005 as I planned a series of lectures as a newly appointed post-holder at the Faculty of English in Oxford. Discussion with David Norbrook, Emma Smith, and Laurie Maguire made me reflect on the difficulty that many students have in relating Shakespeare to contemporary Renaissance writers. The literary objectives of poet-playwrights such as Marlowe, Jonson, and Fletcher can seem at variance with Shakespeare's. Yet, as I began my research, I was struck by early and late periods of close correspondence between Shakespeare's work and that of fellow playwrights, individuals with whom he sometimes co-wrote. It was on the basis of this observation that the argument of this book took shape.

At the early stage I found a number of existing studies especially helpful: James Shapiro's *Rival Playwrights*; Lukas Erne's *Shakespeare as Literary Dramatist*; Andrew Gurr's *The Shakespearian Playing Companies*; Tiffany Stern's *Rehearsal from Shakespeare to Sheridan*; and David Wiles's *Shakespeare's Clown*. Not all of these works feature regularly in my completed monograph, but I remain in their debt. It was initially in response to them that I developed my core thesis, which is that Shakespeare's dramaturgy can usefully be divided into four phases based on the professional company that he kept.

In 2007, at the invitation of Michael Caines, I published a Commentary piece in the *TLS* that sketched the opening stage of this argument: this was the claim that joining an acting company in the year 1594 had a transformative effect on Shakespeare's art as a playwright because from this point onwards he responded directly to the personal characteristics of his actors as he wrote. Counterblasts from established theatre historians Ros Knutson and Grace Ioppolo were salutary and intellectually productive. Still more so was my introduction to an extraordinarily generous body of Shakespeare scholars who engaged me in debate. This fellowship with other interested parties made research a productive, dialogic exercise. From the first, Tiffany Stern commented on the book in detail: without her incisive suggestions, encouragement, and scrutiny I could not have made the progress that I did. Over the years, Laurie Maguire, Katherine Duncan-Jones, Andrew Hadfield, David Scott Kastan, Patrick Cheney, Andrew Gurr, Stanley Wells, and Kirsten Shepherd-Barr have likewise taken time to read my work in progress: their generosity went well beyond what could reasonably be expected and helped a great deal. I also feel fortunate to have been able to discuss my work with other friends and scholars: Colin Burrow, Richard McCabe, David Norbrook, David Womersley, Emma Smith, Peter D. McDonald, Christopher Tilmouth, John Kerrigan, James Shapiro, Margreta de Grazia, Russ McDonald, Thomas Healy, Gordon McMullan, Lukas Erne, Tore Rem, Michael Suarez, Justine Pila, and Lara M. Crowley to name but some.

I have had many valuable conversations at seminars and conferences where I have presented my work on Shakespeare. These have included the University of Sussex Renaissance Seminar; the London Renaissance Theatre Seminar; the Oxford Theatre in Performance Seminar; and the meetings of the Shakespeare Association of America, Renaissance Society of America, and British Shakespeare Association. In 2010 Helen Cooper, Peter Holland, and Ruth Morse invited me to participate in a conference on Shakespeare and the Middle Ages at the London Globe. My contribution to its sessions (which relates to the final part of this monograph) is forthcoming in *Shakespeare's Middle Ages*, to be published by Cambridge University Press. An earlier paper, written for a seminar on the Queen's Men led by Helen Ostovich at SAA in 2009, came out in *Shakespeare Quarterly* in 2010 and overlaps with some of the material in the first part of this book.

Librarians have been unfailingly helpful; I am especially grateful to the staff of Dulwich College, the Folger Shakespeare Library, Alnwick Castle Library, the British Library, the Bodleian, and the Victoria and Albert Museum, where I conducted significant amounts of research. Over the course of many trips to London I stayed with my friends Nicholas Barber, Nicola Holloway, and Mabel: their hospitality was superb. This book was contracted to Oxford University Press in 2008 under the editorship of Andrew McNeillie, who gave inspirational support. Since then I have had equal enthusiasm, advice, and rapid practical aid from his successor, Jacqueline Baker, and her assistant, Rachel Platt. I am grateful to Malcolm Todd for his work as copy editor, and also to Rosemary Roberts for her attention to detail in reading the proofs. This project's completion was made possible through the award of a year's Arts and Humanities Research Council Fellowship, which ran from 2010 to 2011 and gave me invaluable time to write and think. I am grateful for the support of the Council's anonymous reviewers as also for the anonymous readers at the Press.

It has been a privilege to be able to write this book in the tranquil surroundings of St Catherine's College. Sincere thanks go to the Master and Fellows and especially to my colleagues in English: Jeremy Dimmick, Ben Burton, Paddy Bullard, David Womersley, and Kirsten Shepherd-Barr. Finally, thanks and love go to my family, starting with my parents, Henk and Dieuwke, and my brother Joost. Along with my wife, Anne Marie, and children, Josie, Beatrice, and Edgar, they have been the most important company of all.

Contents

PHASE IV. SHAKESPEARE IN THE COMPANY OF PLAYWRIGHTS AGAIN (1608–1614)

Conventions and references

The conventions and references used in this book are designed to make it as accessible as possible to the reader. In quoting from early modern texts I use modern editions where these are available. When a material detail or textual variant is at issue, however, I also refer directly to the original printed book or manuscript. Quotations have been modernized in their spelling, punctuation, and alphabetic conventions where possible; in cases where such modernization would significantly impair meaning I have retained original orthography and have supplied an explanatory note. A significant number of the plays I discuss have shared or disputed authorship. In these cases I explore issues of attribution in the main body of my argument and list the work in my bibliography under the name that is given in the text that I use. For works in Latin I largely use modern editions that supply a parallel translation. Early modern Latin texts are cited when Shakespeare's direct contact with printed books is under discussion and in these cases the translations given are my own.

For Shakespeare's work the standard editions that I quote are those of the Arden3 series, using Arden2 in the few cases where the new edition has yet to appear, but checking these against the Oxford Shakespeare in the footnotes. Where relevant, I also quote other Shakespeare editions, providing details in my notes. Unless otherwise stated, direct quotations from the First Folio and Quarto texts are silently modernized in accordance with the conventions outlined above. References to the Folio use Through Line Numbering (TLN) from *The Norton Facsimile* (New York: Norton, 1968); those to Quartos use signature numbers from the printed text. For ease of recognition I prefer versions of the Folio titles (for example, *Henry VI Part 2*) to those of the Quartos (such as *The First Part of the Contention of the Two Famous Houses of York and Lancaster*). Where these are available, I use Revels editions for other plays.

Dates of performance are based on a variety of sources and at certain junctures these are discussed in the main text and in the notes. Unless otherwise stated, for plays by authors other than Shakespeare dates are taken from Alfred Harbage, *Annals of English Drama: 975–1700*, third edition, revised by Sylvia Stoler Wagonheim (London: Routledge, 1989). Because of certain problems with this edition it has been checked against the second edition and its supplements. For works by Shakespeare dates are taken from Stanley Wells and Gary Taylor, *William Shakespeare: A Textual Companion* (Oxford: Clarendon Press, 1987), checked against the judgement of Arden3 editors and scholarly discussion elsewhere. The appendix consists of a table containing the date ranges for Shakespeare's works that are used in this study. I have been as cautious as possible in my assumptions on dating and in the few cases where I differ from Wells and Taylor an explanatory note is supplied in the appendix and in the main text. All dates are given in New Style (with the year starting on 1 January rather than 25 March). Discussion in the main text sometimes makes mention of a work's date of publication. Occasionally I also express a conviction about the likelihood of a particular moment of first performance, but this always falls within the date range of composition that the Appendix sets out.

The abbreviations used are listed on the following page.

List of abbreviations

Arden2	The Arden Shakespeare, 2nd series
Arden3	The Arden Shakespeare, 3rd series
Oxford DNB	*Oxford Dictionary of National Biography*
F	Folio
IND	Induction
OED	Oxford English Dictionary
Q, Q1, Q2	Quarto, First Quarto, Second Quarto
REED	Records of Early English Drama
SD	Stage direction
TLN	Through Line Numbering
TLS	*Times Literary Supplement*

List of illustrations

Prologue: Shakespeare's early life and the origins of commercial theatre (1576–1592)

I n 1576 William Shakespeare, eldest son of an alderman of Stratford, was studying Latin compositions; around eighty miles away, just north of the city walls of London, James Burbage (actor and joiner) was constructing the first permanent English playhouse.[1] Around fifteen years later their paths would cross. This book is about the meeting of a classically educated poet and a company of actors. That meeting was not unusual. As the commercial theatre expanded, many young men, primed with a command of rhetoric thanks to their training in the new grammar schools, made their way to the capital. Under-employed and highly literate, they were soon called upon to produce copy for the players, who (with large venues and longer periods of residence) were turning over material at an unprecedented rate. What was

---

1. The Theatre is generally credited as the first permanent purpose-built structure for perform-ance but, as I discuss below, there had been earlier theatrical constructions. Other claimants for the title of first playhouse are discussed by Herbert Berry, 'Playhouses, 1560–1660', in Glynne Wickham, Herbert Berry, and William Ingram, eds., *English Professional Theatre, 1530–1660* (Cambridge: Cambridge University Press, 2000), 285–674 at 290–387. For details on Shake-speare's life I am indebted to S. Schoenbaum, *William Shakespeare: A Documentary Life* (Oxford: Clarendon Press, 1975); E. K. Chambers, *William Shakespeare: A Study of Facts and Problems*, 2 vols. (Oxford: Clarendon Press, 1930; repr. 1988); and Peter Holland, 'Shakespeare, William (1564–1616)' in *Oxford DNB*. Shakespeare's father had been elected as an alderman in 1565, serving in various prestigious capacities. As such he was entitled to educate his sons free of charge at the grammar school (Schoenbaum, *Documentary*, 30). John Shakespeare finally lost his position in 1586, suffering financial problems that had begun to surface in 1576. On the stage of education the poet would have achieved in 1576 see Schoenbaum, *Documentary*, 56–7.

unusual about Shakespeare (aside from his genius) was that, in addition to being a writer, he became an investor and a performer. Twenty-three years after the construction of the Theatre he would, in fact, come to own a portion of the very timbers that James Burbage had erected in 1576. The argument of this book is that Shakespeare's decision to become a stakeholder in the theatre industry transformed and would continue to affect the way that he wrote his plays.

Shakespeare's background was entirely typical for a late-sixteenth-century playwright. His paternal grandfather was a successful tenant farmer whose son, John, had moved to the town as an apprentice whittawer, a craft that involved making and selling soft leather goods such as gloves, purses, and aprons.[2] This artisan parentage was the norm amongst Shakespeare's professional contemporaries: Christopher Marlowe's father was a shoemaker; Anthony Munday's a stationer; John Webster's was a prosperous cartwright; Henry Chettle's a dyer; Thomas Kyd's a scrivener; Robert Greene was the son of a cordwainer or saddlemaker—the list goes on.[3] If anything, Shakespeare's childhood was above average in its prosperity. His father thrived at business and also profited from dealing in wool, so that by the time of his eldest son's birth he was already the owner of several properties in Stratford. Shakespeare's mother, Mary Arden, was a wealthy farmer's daughter descended from venerable stock, able to trace her ancestry back to before the Norman Conquest. The simple fact of this marriage shows that John Shakespeare had done well. By the late 1570s he had not only become one of the town's fourteen aldermen, he had also been admitted to its highest elected office, serving as Bailiff and Justice of the Peace. This considerable status entitled the family to send its sons to the grammar school free of charge.

Shakespeare's education was, again, like that of other professional playwrights of the period. Christopher Marlowe, his exact contemporary, was the son of a Freeman of the Shoemakers' Company of Canterbury and

2. Details in this paragraph come from Schoenbaum, *Documentary*, 13–40. Schoenbaum (13–14) notes that the poet's grandfather left goods on his death valued at £38. 17s—nearly £5 more than what was left by the vicar of his parish, that of St James the Great, Snitterfield.

3. G. E. Bentley, *The Profession of Dramatist in Shakespeare's Time, 1590–1642* (Princeton, NJ: Princeton University Press, 1971), 27, lists the 'more or less professional' playwrights of the period. For the biographies of these and the other playwrights and actors discussed in this introduction I rely in the first instance on the articles in the *Oxford DNB*, making acknowledgement in the footnotes only when citing direct quotations and specific dates.

attended the grammar school. Thanks to a Parker scholarship Marlowe made it to Cambridge, but many comparable literary playwrights of his generation (such as George Chapman, Thomas Kyd, John Webster, Michael Drayton, and Ben Jonson) relied only on their schoolboy training.[4] A playwright's literary accomplishment was in practice little affected by attendance at university: Oxford and Cambridge specialized in the teaching of theology, philosophy, history, and similar branches of exact learning, and not in literature of a kind that a poet might readily apply. Self-consciously erudite poets such as Donne, Spenser, or Daniel were a little different (although Spenser was the son of a tailor).[5] These, however, did not deign to write their verses for the popular stage. While some playwrights (notably Robert Greene, who went to Norwich Free School and proceeded to take an MA at Cambridge) made great play of their academic credentials, the majority did not. Thomas Heywood, who attended Emanuel College, Cambridge, was like most of his contemporaries unashamed of his adoration of Shakespeare, considering his own poetry to be 'not worthy [of] his patronage'.[6]

Grammar schools, to which many successful artisans sent their children, were a breeding ground for poets. At Stratford's King's School, which was a highly regarded institution, Shakespeare would have received a thorough training in the rhetorical arts.[7] The template for his education had been set early in the century.[8] In effect, dialectic and rhetoric had fused in the programmes of humanist educators like Erasmus, who looked back to the oratorical model of Cicero and sought above all to make their pupils

---

4. Exactly half of those listed in Bentley, *Dramatist*, 37, as 'regular professionals' had a university background. The percentage of those thus educated increased as the century went on.

5. All these figures, of course, held a subtly different place on the social spectrum. Donne came from a substantial family, had private tuition before going to Oxford, and avoided even the stigma of print; Daniel, on the other hand, came closer to commercial employment through closet drama, the writing of masques, and his later association with the Children of the Queen's Revels.

6. Thomas Heywood, *An Apology for Actors* (1612), G4[b].

7. The standard account of the education system remains T. W. Baldwin, *William Shakspere's Small Latine and Lesse Greeke*, 2 vols. (Urbana: University of Illinois Press, 1944) and the following account is based largely on his study. As Baldwin observes, at the King's School Shakespeare would have had 'as good a formal literary training as had any of his contemporaries' (*Small Latine*, II, 663).

8. Desiderius Erasmus's *De copia verborum ac rerum* or 'Foundations of the Abundant Style' (1512) had been completed in England and was dedicated to John Colet, founder of St Paul's School, the institution that established the nation's grammar school system. In *De ratione studii* of the same year Erasmus set out the curriculum for St Paul's, which was thereafter adopted at Stratford as it was throughout the land.

competent in the fluent style. Verbal art thus constituted the main body of humanist pre-university education. All schools had a similar pedagogical setup, with an intense concentration on language. Having completed petty school, boys from the age of eight onwards spent around nine hours a day, six days a week, in all but seven weeks a year on literary exercises such as learning by rote, writing according to formulae, reproducing *sententiae*, imitating classical authors, and constructing arguments for and against set propositions.[9] Even if their range of independent reading might be relatively narrow, a student of such a system could not fail to be practised at the construction of arguments. Young scholars would be intimately acquainted with over a hundred and fifty literary tropes and figures, being trained to recognize and record them, and to deploy them in compositions of their own. That Shakespeare was a characteristic product of this system is a well-established fact of scholarship but it is sometimes neglected by biographers, who tend to favour projections of a natural love for the life of the stage.[10]

Up until 1576 the Shakespeare family were upwardly mobile, with John—a pillar of the community—even applying for a gentleman's coat of arms.[11] Thereafter, however, they became mired in financial problems and the poet's father rapidly withdrew from his role in civic affairs. Although we do not know their nature, such money troubles were not unusual in the period—indeed one could argue that many playwrights owed their choice of profession to losses of precisely this kind. George Chapman, for example, was the son of a yeoman and copyholder of Hitchin in Hertfordshire and the financial problems of his father sent him first into the household of Sir Ralph Sadler and thence to London for a career as a poet and playwright. Thomas Heywood, comparably, had his study at Cambridge cut short by the death of his father and went to the capital in

9. On pre-grammar school education see T. W. Baldwin, *William Shakspere's Petty School* (Urbana: University of Illinois Press, 1943). For a survey of the literary outcomes of the humanist exercises see Arthur F. Kinney, *Humanist Poetics: Thought, Rhetoric, and Fiction in Sixteenth-Century England* (Amherst: University of Massachusetts Press, 1986), 8 and *passim*.

10. The authoritative Park Honan, *Shakespeare: A Life* (Oxford: Oxford University Press, 1999), it should be acknowledged, gives an excellent account of Shakespeare's education at grammar school, but cannot avoid imagining that 'his alert impressionable nature, with his energy and agility, would have made him hope to prove his talent as a player' (92). Even the judicious Schoenbaum decides, on the basis of lines such as Romeo's 'love goes toward love, as schoolboys from their books' that 'Shakespeare does not seem to have cherished especially tender memories' of his days at school' (*Documentary*, 52). Mockery of school life, however, is a standard element amongst those who had undergone this education (witness, for example, the foolish schoolmaster of Sir Philip Sidney's *Lady of May*).

11. For details of this and the subsequent crisis see Schoenbaum, *Documentary*, 36–40.

search of the same kind of work. It is quite conceivable that an unspecified family crisis, much more than any initial passion for the theatre, had a pivotal influence on Shakespeare's career.

The poet was still young in 1576 and the impact of his father's problems was gradual rather than immediate, so he may well have continued for some time at school. In 1582, aged seventeen, Shakespeare married the already pregnant Anne Hathaway, the daughter of a local farmer. The following May saw the birth of their first child and February of 1585 the arrival of twins. The poet's name in the Parish Register recording their baptism is the last piece of documentary evidence confirming his whereabouts until the appearance of *Greenes Groats-worth of Wit*, which places him as an 'upstart crow' writing plays in London in 1592.[12] Gaps in the biographical record are not unusual in this period: we know virtually nothing, for instance, about the early years of other playwrights such as Henry Porter, William Rowley, or Richard Brome, and the career of Thomas Heywood has several lacunae of comparable length.[13] Some scholars believe that the 'lost years' were spent by Shakespeare as a travelling player.[14] Given his social and educational background I think this unlikely, but the possibility is there.[15] Alternatively he may, like Michael Drayton (another Warwickshire poet-playwright with a grammar school education) have spent a spell as a secretary in an aristocratic household.[16] There is also the story recorded by John Aubrey that Shakespeare worked for some years as 'a schoolmaster in the country'.[17]

12. Robert Greene (?), *Greenes Groats-worth of Wit* (1592), F1[b]. It is conceivable that Shakespeare was in London in October 1589 to press in person his family's claims in a property dispute, but the case remains speculative. On the order for trial see Chambers, *Facts and Problems*, II, 35–41.

13. See respective *Oxford DNB* articles. We know nothing certain about Heywood's life before his arrival at Cambridge and he 'drops virtually out of sight for nearly a decade' after 1612 (see David Kathman, 'Heywood, Thomas (c.1573–1641)', *Oxford DNB*).

14. The idea is a standard one, but Katherine Duncan-Jones in *Ungentle Shakespeare: Scenes from his Life* (London: Arden, 2001) and *Shakespeare: Upstart Crow to Sweet Swan, 1592–1623* (London: Arden, 2011) is an especially strong advocate.

15. For a statement of the case that the poet is much more likely to have begun earning his keep by means of the pen see Bart van Es, '*Johannes fac Totum?*: Shakespeare's First Contact with the Acting Companies', *Shakespeare Quarterly* 61 (2010), 551–77.

16. Drayton spent time as some kind of amanuensis to Thomas Goodere before pursuing a literary career in the capital—he can be placed there in 1585 because of legal trouble about a will but there is a gap similar to that in Shakespeare's record thereafter. By identifying Shakespeare as 'Shakeshafte' in the household of the Hoghtons in Lancashire E. A. J. Honigmann, *Shakespeare: The 'Lost Years'* (Manchester: Manchester University Press, 1985) famously combined the possibilities of player and household employee; his account remains exceptionally speculative and wins little academic approval today.

17. John Aubrey, *Brief Lives*, ed. Oliver Lawson Dick (Harmondsworth: Penguin, 1972), 335.

This was quite possible with a grammar school background and other playwrights (notably James Shirley, who eventually took Shakespeare's place as author for the King's Men) went from this profession to the writing of plays.[18] Perhaps the strongest likelihood is that Shakespeare found work in some minor capacity connected with the law courts: the legal world was by far the biggest supplier of playwriting talent and many authors who lacked a university education (for example, Thomas Kyd and John Webster) started out in this way.[19] The list of hypotheticals, however, is potentially endless. What is certain is that in the early 1590s, with a good humanist education behind him, Shakespeare found himself on the fringes of London's theatrical scene.

Since 1576 the nation's theatre industry had rapidly expanded. Its origins, like the grammar school system, lay in the mid-Tudor period when, in William Ingram's description, 'stage playing' was 'not yet a clearly defined activity' but might have included 'dancing, tumbling, clowning, juggling, fencing, mime and minstrelsy along with (or sometimes instead of) the declaiming of lines'.[20] The Reformation gradually choked off the traditional pageant-based acting of the English mystery cycles, which had been performed by amateur players to their own community under the aegis of guilds.[21] Concurrently, court culture of the Renaissance had made dramatic secular entertainment an important business, both in elite circles and at a popular level. These twin pressures stimulated the growth of professional

---

18. See Schoenbaum, *Documentary*, 88. If Shirley's career change did mirror Shakespeare's then they shifted profession from teaching to playwriting around the same age (see Ira Clark, 'Shirley, James (*bap.* 1596, *d.* 1666)', *Oxford DNB*). Unlike Shakespeare, Shirley did have a university education, which had become a more common requirement for schoolmasters by this time.

19. Kyd was employed as a scrivener, a role that would inevitably have a legal dimension; Webster had connections with the Middle Temple. Jonathan Bate, *Soul of the Age: The Life, Mind, and World of William Shakespeare* (London: Penguin, 2008), 313–26, makes the intriguing suggestion of an early appointment at Clement's Inn for the poet. His arguments are based on the bill of Complaint in Queen's Bench, *Shakespeare v. Lambert*, in order for trial on 9 October 1589, for which see Chambers, *Facts and Problems*, ii, 35–41, which is noted above. C. C. Stopes, *Burbage and Shakespeare's Stage* (London: Alexander Moring, 1913) long ago made the case that Shakespeare came to London to press this case in person, staying with his Stratford contemporary and first printer, Richard Field. A large number of playwrights started their literary careers whilst pursuing comparable legal action.

20. William Ingram, ed., 'Part II: Players and Playing', in Wickham, Berry, and Ingram, eds., *English Professional Theatre*, 153–286 (at 153). Along with older sources such as E. K. Chambers, *The Elizabethan Stage*, 4 vols. (Oxford: Clarendon Press, 1923; repr. 2009) Wickham's source book is a mainstay of the brief historical outline that I present below.

21. See Peter Happé, ed., *English Mystery Plays* (London: Penguin, 1975), 9–34.

Figure 1. Panoramic view of London, from Georg Braun and Franz Hogenberg's *Civitatis orbis terrarum* (c.1574).

acting companies: groups of men who were technically the servants of aristocratic houses (and certainly performed there) but who also constituted a commercial enterprise.[22] While there had long been a tradition of travelling minstrels, sometimes called 'interluders', these new groups were larger and more heavily capitalized.[23] Permanent members were generally 'sharers': they had invested a set sum of money and were thus entitled to an equivalent portion of the profits. In Bentley's assessment, England's players (sharers, hired men, and boys who played the roles of women) numbered thousands over time.[24] The profession was fundamentally itinerant and the most prestigious companies had a national reach in projecting their patron's imprimatur.[25] One of the earliest great companies was Leicester's Men (attached to Robert Dudley, the Queen's favourite) and James Burbage, the builder of the Theatre, had spent much of the 1560s and '70s as the leader of this troupe.[26]

So what kind of men were the players? If we trust to the written record then their reputation in the sixteenth century was a poor one. A great deal of invective, mainly from a religious standpoint, was directed against them: they were said to be 'dissolute', 'loitering' fellows, disrespectful of authority, 'passing from country to country, from one gentleman's house to another, offering their service, which is a kind of beggary'.[27] Such testaments have only limited value, but a common theme is the players' rapid rise from travelling minstrels to gaudy and wealthy men. Stephen Gosson, in a dyspeptic but still useful analysis, contended that 'most of the players have

22. For an account of this process of professionalization, see William Ingram, 'The "Evolution" of the Elizabethan Playing Company', in John H. Astington, ed., *The Development of Shakespeare's Theater* (New York: AMS Press, 1992), 13–28.

23. David M. Bevington, *From 'Mankind' to Marlowe: Growth of Structure in the Popular Drama of Tudor England* (Cambridge, MA: Harvard University Press, 1962), 11, for example, records such a group as performing before Henry VI in 1427.

24. Gerald Eades Bentley, *The Profession of Player in Shakespeare's Time, 1590–1642* (Princeton, NJ: Princeton University Press, 1984), 5.

25. The great scholarly collaboration, Records of Early English Drama, based at the University of Toronto, continues to uncover the networks of commerce and patronage that were maintained through this way of life. On the REED project and its publications see http://www.reed.utoronto.ca/index.html.

26. On this company and its touring routes see Scott McMillin and Sally-Beth MacLean, *The Queen's Men and their Plays* (Cambridge: Cambridge University Press, 1998), 18–21.

27. William Bavande, *Touching the Ordering of a Commonweal* (1559), fol. 100[b]; John Northbrooke, *Dicing, Dancing, Vain Plays or Interludes, with Other Idle Pastimes* (1577), 71; Stephen Gardyner, Letter to Sir William Paget (PRO SP10/1 fol. 8, item 5); Anthony Munday (?), *Second and Third Blast of Retrait* (1580), 75–6, reproduced in Wickham, Berry, and Ingram, eds., *English Professional Theatre*, 157–71.

been either men of occupations, which they have forsaken to live by playing, or common minstrels, or trained up from their childhood to this abominable exercise and have now no other way to get their living'.[28] James Burbage himself, who started out in the fairly lowly trade of joiner, might be said to belong to the first class; his son Richard evidently followed directly in his father's footsteps and so belonged to the third. Another prominent early player, William Kemp, who eventually joined Richard Burbage in the Chamberlain's company, first appears in the record as 'my Lord of Leicester's jesting player' performing feats of athleticism.[29] He might therefore be typical of Gosson's second class, that of minstrels, although he was evidently far from 'common' in the abilities he displayed.

Actors seem always to have had their roots in practical professions.[30] The notion that they had 'forsaken' their occupations, however, is misleading because many actors retained their membership of guilds. John Heminges, another founding Chamberlain's man, had completed his apprenticeship in the Grocers' Company, and still described himself as a citizen and grocer in his will.[31] His own apprentices within the acting company (the boys who were trained up by playing women's parts) did so under the aegis of the Grocers' Company. Theatre thus became an institutionalized element of London's business community, which had its foundations in these medieval

---

28. Stephen Gosson, *Plays Confuted in Five Actions* (1582), G6^b.
29. Sir Philip Sidney, *Complete Works*, ed. A Feuillerat, 4 vols. (Cambridge: Cambridge University Press, 1912–26), III, 167.
30. Ingram's research into the social background of the actors, distributed across numerous articles, gives a good picture of the world of the player. His 'Arthur Savill, Stage Player', *Theatre Notebook* 37 (1983), 21–2, for example, describes the case of an actor who pursued his training in that occupation under the auspices of the Goldsmiths' Guild. Overviews are also provided in M. C. Bradbrook, *The Rise of the Common Player: A Study of Actor and Society in Shakespeare's England* (London: Chatto & Windus, 1964); Bentley, *Player*; and Siobhan Keenan, *Travelling Players in Shakespeare's England* (Houndmills: Palgrave Macmillan, 2002). Perhaps most telling of all are the conclusions of E. A. J. Honigmann and Susan Brock, *Playhouse Wills: 1558–1642: An Edition of Wills by Shakespeare and his Contemporaries in the London Theatre* (Manchester: Manchester University Press, 1993), 1–17. In the 1590s the playwrights and published poets Ben Jonson, Thomas Heywood, and William Shakespeare appeared on the London stage as actors, and the university play *The Second Part of the Return from Parnassus* (c.1601) portrays this as a common fate for impecunious young scholars. It is debatable whether such men really thought of themselves as players. Whatever its nature, however, this development appears to be an urban phenomenon of the final decades of the century, which only in very exceptional cases led to sharer status for such men.
31. Mary Edmond, 'Heminges, John (bap. 1566; d. 1630)', *Oxford DNB*. For a broader social analysis see Mary Edmond, 'Yeomen, Citizens, Gentlemen, and Players: The Burbages and their Connections', in R. B. Parker and S. P. Zitner, eds, *Elizabethan Theater: Essays in Honor of S. Schoenbaum* (Newark: University of Delaware Press, 1996), 30–49.

corporations.[32] Some of the wealthiest players descended from innkeepers: four of the capital's inns became regular venues for performance and the century's most famous tragic actor, Edward Alleyn, had a father who was an innkeeper who also held an official role as porter to the Queen.[33] There were, then, many levels to the acting profession, starting from regionally based travelling minstrels attached to local great families and going up to financial speculators in London with powerful connections at court.

It was these links with the guilds and big business that brought about the construction of playhouses. Although James Burbage's Theatre is generally credited as being the first permanent example, there had been earlier structures devoted to commercial playing. In 1567 his business partner, the grocer John Brayne, had already erected a stage and scaffolding for use by the players at a farmhouse called the Red Lion, situated about a mile from London's city walls.[34] There was also a playhouse at Newington Butts, south of the river, whose construction may even predate the work undertaken by Burbage.[35] Certainly there were soon multiple purpose-built venues, with the Curtain opening in 1577 and Henslowe's Rose joining it a decade later. The four large city inns that were available for playing overlapped in function with the outdoor playhouses and were especially attractive in the cold winter months.[36] By 1590, therefore, there were at least four substantial buildings attracting acting companies to London, with smaller venues existing besides. Playhouses proper, although partly open to the elements, could shelter thousands of spectators and were equipped with tiring houses for the purpose of costume changes and space for the storage of theatrical properties. Their occupation was

32. On the guild structure in general see, for example, Steve Rappaport, *Worlds within Worlds: Structures of Life in Sixteenth-Century London* (Cambridge: Cambridge University Press, 1989). Roslyn Lander Knutson, *Playing Companies and Commerce in Shakespeare's Time* (Cambridge: Cambridge University Press, 2001), 22–47, explores the strong connection between the guilds and theatre business. As she observes, one or two playwrights, notably Ben Jonson (22), were also members of guilds.

33. S. P. Cerasano, 'Edward Alleyn's Early Years: His Life and Family', *Notes & Queries* 34 (1987), 237–43 (at 238–40). For another case of an actor–innkeeper see William Ingram, 'Laurence Dutton, Stage Player: Missing and Presumed Lost', *Medieval and Renaissance Drama in England* 14 (2001), 122–43.

34. See William Ingram, *The Business of Playing: The Beginnings of the Adult Professional Theater in Elizabethan London* (Ithaca, NY: Cornell University Press, 1992), 105–10. For brief accounts and extracts concerning this and other early playhouses see Berry, ed., 'Playhouses, 1560–1660' in Wickham, Berry, and Ingram, eds., *English Professional Theatre*, 285–674.

35. This building was a mile south of London Bridge and is first mentioned as a venue in 1577; see Ingram, *Business*, 150–81.

36. See Berry, 'Playhouses', in Wickham, Berry, and Ingram, eds., *English Professional Theatre*, 295–305.

changeable: individual troupes would come and go depending on touring routes and the seasons. Alternative entertainment, such as fencing contests or animal baiting, was also an option for the owners when no suitable players were in town. A steady rate of playhouse construction and improvement suggests that business was good.

Acting companies and playhouses were (at least in theory) separate entities.[37] The standard arrangement was to share a day's takings, with a mutually approved 'gatherer' collecting pennies at the main door.[38] Different parts of a theatre might be assigned to specific elements in the partnership: the player Charles Massey, for example, refers in a letter to his 'gallery money' as a standard entitlement of his company share.[39] The division of responsibilities was, like the division of profits, theoretically straightforward. Shareholders like Massey would need collectively to cover performance expenses, which included payment for playtexts, apparel, and the hiring of additional men. Building and maintenance, on the other hand, were a matter for the theatre owner: itemized lists of expenses crop up regularly in the Rose and Fortune playhouse accounts.[40] In practice things could be more complicated. Several actors, Massey included, were also playhouse shareholders, known as 'housekeepers': they had bought or leased a portion of a theatre and were thus entitled to a percentage of the profits from that side of the operation as well.[41]

37. Most financial information for this period derives from the papers of Philip Henslowe and Edward Alleyn, who were the proprietors of the Rose and the Fortune. The bulk of these are now held at Dulwich College in London, although some have been dispersed to collections elsewhere. They have been printed in diverse volumes, most notably R. A. Foakes, ed., *Henslowe's Diary*, 2nd edn (Cambridge: Cambridge University Press, 2002); Carol Chillington Rutter, ed., *Documents of the Rose Playhouse*, rev. edn (Manchester: Manchester University Press, 1999); W. W. Greg, ed., *Henslowe Papers: Being Documents Supplementary to Henslowe's Diary* (London: A. H. Bullen, 1907); and W. W. Greg, *Dramatic Documents from the Elizabethan Playhouses: Stage Plots, Actors' Parts, Prompt Books*, 2 vols. (Oxford: Clarendon Press, 1969). Digital images of the Dulwich College documents, archived by Grace Ioppolo, are available at http://www.henslowe-alleyn.org.uk/index.html. I have examined all documents first hand but make reference in the first instance to printed texts where these are available. For additional material or for reference to unprinted documents I cite the Dulwich's manuscript volume numbers, which are also used online.

38. An undated letter from William Bird to Edward Alleyn refers to a dispute concerning his choice of gatherer, a certain John Russell, at the Fortune (see Greg, *Henslowe*, 85–6); a comparable role is found in other playhouses—for example, Thomas Swynnerton at the Red Bull (see Charles William Wallace, 'Three London Theatres of Shakespeare's Time', *University Studies of the University of Nebraska* 9 (1909), 287–342 (at 294)).

39. Undated letter from Charles Massey to Edward Alleyn (1613?), in Greg, *Henslowe*, 64–5.

40. See, for example, Alleyn's list of 'What the Fortune Cost me', Alleyn MSS 8, fol. 6[b], reproduced in Greg, *Henslowe*, 108.

41. Massey in the above letter refers to his 'house money' due as a sharer in the playhouse. In this case he is referring to a share of a lease rather than outright ownership. The will of Thomas

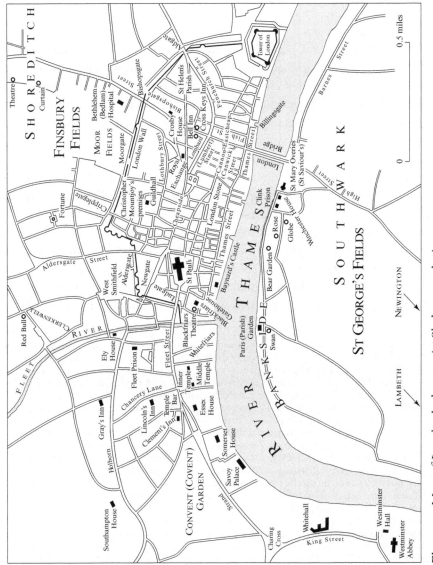

Figure 2. Map of London's theatres in Shakespeare's time.

Some owners of playhouses, conversely, invested in acting companies—buying their playtexts and apparel, lending them money, and even contracting their hired men.[42] Such investments were pursued with vigour by the proprietor of the Rose, Philip Henslowe, and the letter from Massey referring to 'gallery money' was in fact written to him requesting an additional loan. Complex mechanisms of lending and bond-holding made theatre a risky business. Fortunes were made and lost in this speculative environment and in the end only a small number of major winners emerged.

Where did the plays that were performed in these theatres come from? This is a difficult question to answer because for the first three decades of the commercial theatre, from the 1560s to the 1580s, solid information about repertories is scarce. In part, the early players were their own playwrights. The best-documented example of this practice comes from the new super-company assembled out of Leicester's ensemble in 1583, the Queen's Men, whose most famous members, Richard Tarlton and Robert Wilson, both wrote plays.[43] At least nine Queen's Men titles can be identified with confidence and these are generally characterized by what McMillin and MacLean call the 'medley' style of composition—a non-literary, visually orientated mode of drama, also termed 'literalism of the theatre'.[44] One prominent example is Wilson's moral allegory *The Three Lords and Three*

Pope, founding Chamberlain's sharer, refers separately to playhouse shares in the Curtain and the Globe (see Honigmann and Brock, *Playhouse Wills*, 68)—in the latter case, at least, he owned part of the building's structure. See also the case of Francis Grace reported in S. P. Cerasano, 'New Renaissance Players' Wills', *Modern Philology* 82 (1985), 299–304.

42. The itemizing of such loans and investments is one of the main purposes of Henslowe's *Diary*; as an example, see Foakes, ed., *Diary*, 200–1.

43. On the repertory see McMillin and MacLean, *Queen's Men*, 88–9. The Queen's Men play, *The Three Lords and Three Ladies of London* (1588) is credited to 'R. W.' on its title page and can be securely attributed to Wilson. He also wrote *The Cobbler's Prophecy* (published 1594) and the earlier *The Three Ladies of London* (1584). No work by Tarlton survives but the Plot of *The Second Part of Seven Deadly Sins*, now at Dulwich College, may relate to a lost play on the seven deadly sins written by him (see Greg, *Henslowe*, 127–32). That Plot includes entrances for 'will fool' (i.e. William Kemp), who also wrote his own material (e.g. the 'applauded merriments' in the early play *A Knack to Know a Knave*), but again no material survives. Later publications such as *Tarlton's Jests* (1638), attributed to the great comic, can give only the vaguest sense of what his original act was like.

44. McMillin and MacLean, *Queen's Men*, 85, 124, 128. The company has received a great deal of critical attention, including the recent Helen Ostovich, Holger Schott Syme, and Andrew Griffin, eds., *Locating the Queen's Men: Material Practices and the Conditions of Playing* (Farnham: Ashgate, 2009) and also Brian Walsh, *Shakespeare, the Queen's Men, and the Elizabethan Performance of History* (Cambridge: Cambridge University Press, 2009).

Ladies of London. Its rough-hewn verse and prose are far removed from the sphere of humanist rhetoric: it comes partly from the popular tradition of medieval moralities (such as *Everyman*) and suggests an extempore style of performance that fits with its actorly origins.[45] Similar in feel is the anonymous *Famous Victories of Henry V*, in which Tarlton played Dericke. Like *The Three Lords and Three Ladies* it is patriotic and moralistic in character and left considerable room for ad-libbing by the clown. From the 1560s to the 1580s the players were often accused of ransacking chronicles (as well as Bible stories and popular romances) in this manner.[46] The drama they produced had its own visual poetics in performance, but that tradition was very different from the classical one.[47]

Possibly the Queen's Men in their heyday relied exclusively on this home-grown material. At an earlier stage, however, professional 'interluders' had performed works that were written for them by authors from outside the theatrical world. In the 1530s and 1540s the evangelist John Bale staged a series of dramas (most famously *King Johan*) as a tool for Protestant propaganda. This was elite theatre put on before the monarch, but it seems also to have toured.[48] In the 1560s and 1570s various divines, notably William Wager, published small-scale interludes with messages of moral improvement. Such plays were unsuited to the big companies but, with adjustment, homiletic drama could make it to the public stage.[49] The major players performed at court, at aristocratic houses, and occasionally for the lawyers. There was thus always contact with courtiers and scholars and a hybrid drama (mixing cultured rhetoric with more colloquial theatre) is a

---

45. On the moralities as partly rooted in guild performance, see Bevington, 'Mankind', 48–9. *The Three Lords and Three Ladies* (1588) is a late example that shows Wilson adapting to the iambic pentameter whereas his earlier *Three Ladies of London* (1584) tends towards the poulter's measure associated with the mystery and morality plays.

46. On the emergence of chronicle and romance as subject matter (and reaction against this) see Bevington, 'Mankind', 170–85.

47. McMillin and MacLean, *Queen's Men*, 124–54. Bevington, 'Mankind', calls the tradition 'native' (1), and contrasts it with the more classical conventions of the academic theatre and the court. Numerous studies, Bevington's included, have examined the legacy of this medieval theatre on later Renaissance drama: especially seminal is Robert Weimann's *Shakespeare and the Popular Tradition in Theater: Studies in the Social Dimension of Dramatic Form and Function*, ed. Robert Schwartz (Baltimore, MD: Johns Hopkins University Press, 1978).

48. On the original auspices see John Bale, *King Johan*, ed. Barry B. Adams (San Marino, CA: Huntington Library, 1969), 39–47; Bevington, 'Mankind', describes a company of touring actors known almost certainly as 'my Lord Cromwell's players' as performing the play in 1537.

49. For a full survey that covers moments of likely cross-over but also stresses the division between popular and elite theatre before the late 1580s see Bevington, 'Mankind', 37–103.

likely result.[50] Martin Wiggins is no doubt right to suspect, therefore, that the known Queen's Men repertory does not adequately reflect the spectrum available in the 1580s.[51] As early as 1582 Stephen Gosson referred to 'two plays of my making [that] were brought to the stage: the one was a cast of Italian devices called *The Comedy of Captain Mario*, the other a moral, *Praise at Parting*'.[52] These plays do not survive and we do not know what company performed them. This statement from a graduate of the same grammar school as John Lyly and Christopher Marlowe, however, does confirm that human-ist-educated playwrights were now writing commercially for the public stage.

By the 1590s the Queen's company were also employing professional poets, staging *The Old Wives Tale* by Peele and *The Tragical Reign of Selimus*, which was probably the work of Robert Greene.[53] Numerous other troupes were regularly performing in the capital, including the Earl of Pembroke's, Lord Strange's, and the Admiral's Men. They provided work for a significant body of writers: Marlowe, Kyd, Lodge, Nashe, and Chettle, as well as Peele and Greene. Classics of English theatre such as *Tamburlaine* (1587–8) and *The Spanish Tragedy* (1585–9) had already been written: these plays were strongly marked by their authors' awareness of the models of Roman dramaturgy and training in rhetoric. The older, more colloquial style of drama was still being written and proved popular for decades, but it was not now a prestige product that could be brought to the court. The era of what Robert Greene half ironically termed the 'arch-playmaking poet' had arrived.[54]

---

50. The Inns of Court (where George Gascoigne's *Supposes* (1566) was performed), like the universities, had their own theatrical tradition, but they were sometimes entertained by the players. The doubtful auspices of a play such as John Lyly's *The Woman in the Moon* (on which see Leah Scragg, ed., Revels (Manchester: Manchester University Press, 2006), 3–9) are indicative of the complexities of this question.

51. Martin Wiggins, *Shakespeare and the Drama of his Time*, Oxford Shakespeare Topics (Oxford: Oxford University Press, 2000), 9.

52. Gosson, *Plays Confuted*, A7ᵃ.

53. For auspices see McMillin and MacLean, *Queen's Men*, 88; on the range of performance dates see Alfred Harbage, *Annals of English Drama: 975–1700*, 3rd edn, rev. Sylvia Stoler Wagonheim (London: Routledge, 1989), 56–8. On the attribution of *Selimus* see Robert Greene (?), *The Tragical Reign of Selimus*, ed. W. Bang (Oxford: Malone Society, 1909), v–vi. Even if not by Greene, this is certainly a product of humanist education. McMillin and MacLean, *Queen's Men*, 155–60, argue that the play was commissioned as part of an 'anti-Marlowe campaign'; but if so, it was one conducted using rhetoric very close to Marlowe's own.

54. *Greenes Groats-worth of Wit*, E1ᵇ. Wilson, like other actors of the previous generation, continued to find employment: he appears regularly in Henslowe's *Diary*—for example, receiving, payment for a co-authored play with Drayton, Dekker, and Chettle in March 1598 (Foakes, ed., *Diary*, 88). McMillin and MacLean, *Queen's Men*, argue, however, that his former company found it impossible to adapt to the demands of the rhetorical drama, and the record of court performance bears this out.

At some point between 1584 and the late summer of 1592 William Shakespeare joined this body of professional playwrights and in that period he seems certain to have met James Burbage. Whether Shakespeare introduced himself as a poet or as a player or as both is a matter for speculation. What is undeniable, however, is that the two men came from different worlds.[55] While Shakespeare studied Latin in the 1560s and 1570s James Burbage had been travelling the country at the head of Lord Leicester's players, a dangerous if rewarding pursuit. In building the Theatre in 1576 he had taken a gamble and he had needed to defend this property with cunning and even violence over the years. Burbage was an aggressive investor: he had also built tenement housing on the outskirts of the city—this too had needed physical defence against rival claimants to the land. The cut-throat conditions of playhouse management are illustrated by a confrontation between him and the widow of his business partner. In May 1592 she arrived with several men (including the alleged murderer of her husband) to demand payments, but her party was met with a beating and with the reported dismissal from Burbage of 'hang her, whore'.[56] When Margaret Brayne returned with reinforcements, he allegedly told his sons to 'provide charged pistols' and 'shoot them in the legs'. This pioneer of playhouse construction had plans for a second playhouse and was said at his death to have amassed goods and chattels 'amounting to £1000'.[57]

---

55. Shakespeare's lack of connection with the artisan groups associated with professional players and theatre managers is noted in Richard Dutton, 'Shakespearean Origins,' in Takashi Kozuka and J. R. Mulryne, eds., *Shakespeare, Marlowe, Jonson: New Directions in Biography* (Aldershot: Ashgate, 2006), 69–83 (at 79), an article that contains much revealing new information about the social world of actors in the period.

56. This account of the confrontation was narrated as eyewitness testimony by the actor John Alleyn (brother to Edward), PRO C24/228/11, C24/228/10, transcribed in Charles W. Wallace, 'The First London Theatre: Materials for a History', *University Studies of the University of Nebraska* 13 (1913), 1–297 (at 100–2, 126–7). Wallace's work on the history of the London theatre is invaluable but, because of its unusual publication history, also notoriously difficult to locate. The article was reprinted as *The First London Theatre* (New York: Benjamin Blom, 1969) but this work is also unavailable in most libraries. Herbert Berry, *Shakespeare's Playhouses* (New York: AMS Press, 1987), 19–44, checked a large sample of Wallace's transcriptions and found them accurate. He noted, however, that some PRO manuscript numbers have changed since Wallace's article and thus provided an updated list. Berry then reprinted a good proportion of Wallace's transcriptions in Wickham, Berry, and Ingram, eds., *English Professional Theatre*, 330–87. Because Berry's version is more up to date and more readily available I quote from his text rather than Wallace's where both are available. For this and the following quotation see *English Professional Theatre*, 361–2. On Miles's trial for murder see Wallace, 'First London', 14.

57. Robert Miles, April–May 1597, PRO, Req.2/241/14, in Wickham, Berry, and Ingram, eds., *English Professional Theatre*, 374. This vast sum refers only to his wife's share of his estate.

Shakespeare, in contrast, was praised in 1592 for his 'civil' demeanour, 'uprightness of dealing', 'learning', and 'facetious grace in writing'.[58] While it is risky to infer too much about his character from such statements there are many signs of a desire for rarefied cultural esteem. His first published poem, *Venus and Adonis* (1593), was produced by London's premier literary printer, responsible for George Puttenham's *The Arte of English Poesie* (1589), Sir John Harington's translation of *Orlando furioso* (1591), and the first full editions of Edmund Spenser's *The Faerie Queene* (1596) and Sir Philip Sidney's *Arcadia* (1598).[59] On its title page Shakespeare set out his ambition by means of a quotation from Ovid:

Vilia miretur vulgus: mihi flavus Apollo
Pocula Castalia plena ministret aqua

[Let the common herd be amazed by worthless things; but for me let golden Apollo provide cups full of the water of the Muses][60]

With its dedication to the Earl of Southampton, this text staked a claim to the very highest intellectual circles of Elizabethan England—a claim made good in *The Rape of Lucrece* (1594), in which the history of 'Sextus Tarquinius' was approached through Ovid, Livy, and Cicero in unprecedented depth.[61] Shakespeare was oscillating, as many did, between the two great spheres of literary employment: print and court patronage on the one hand and the stage on the other. He could, as Ben Jonson would do after a short spell of employment as a hired actor, strive primarily for independence as a writer. This was the conventional course amongst his contemporaries, albeit one pursued with mixed success. Alternatively, he might do something new

Income from the Theatre was hotly disputed and Miles was a witness with an agenda. James Burbage, however, was certainly able to pay £600 of his own money for the Blackfriars playhouse site in February 1596 and to have it fitted out in high style.

58. Henry Chettle, *Kind-Harts Dreame* (1592), A4ᵃ. This was Chettle's apology for having published *Greenes Groats-worth*. Greene died on 3 September 1592 and Chettle refers in his preface to this event as having occurred 'about three months since' (A3ᵇ).

59. On Richard Field, a Stratford connection, see David Kathman, 'Field [Feild], Richard (*bap.* 1561, *d.* 1624)', *Oxford DNB*.

60. William Shakespeare, *Venus and Adonis* (1593), A1ᵃ; translation William Shakespeare, *Complete Sonnets and Poems*, ed. Colin Burrow (Oxford: Oxford University Press, 2002), 173.

61. Shakespeare made a point of using Latin titles in the Argument prefacing this poem (*Lucrece* (1594), A4ᵇ). On this work's engagement with Latin historiography and political rhetoric, including that of Cicero, see Burrow, ed., Shakespeare, *Poems*, 42–63, and Bart van Es, 'Historiography and Biography', in Patrick Cheney and Philip Hardie, eds., *Oxford History of Classical Reception in English Literature*, vol. II: *1558–1660* (Oxford: Oxford University Press, forthcoming).

and strengthen his connection with the players. James Burbage was the kind of man who might make the latter possible: his rival Philip Henslowe certainly lent money to those wishing to buy theatrical shares.[62] In Shakespeare and James Burbage separate strands of the Elizabethan commonweal were coming together—any connection between them could have interesting results.

62. See, for example, the loan of £15 to Frances Henslowe on 8 May 1593 'to lay down for his share in the Queen's Players ... to be paid unto me at his return out of the country' (Foakes, ed., *Diary*, 7). Alternatively, some have speculated that the Earl of Southampton may have made a gift of money, which Shakespeare could have paid down for the share.

PHASE
I
Shakespeare as conventional poet-playwright (1592–1594)

I

Imitation and identity

On 3 March 1592 'harry the vj' was staged at the Rose playhouse. It is the first record we have of the performance of a play by William Shakespeare.[1] From its first speech, spoken by the Duke of Bedford, the work announces its presence in the most rhetorically ambitious tones:

> Hung be the heavens with black. Yield day to night.
> Comets, importing change of times and states,
> Brandish your crystal tresses in the sky
> And with them scourge the bad revolting stars
> That have consented unto Henry's death—
> King Henry the Fifth, too famous to live long.
> England ne'er lost a king of so much worth.
>
> (*Henry VI Part 1*, 1.1.1–7)

The delivery of these lines should mark an iconic moment in theatre history: the first instant at which we can pinpoint the reception of Shakespeare's verse. Yet, as a moment of authorial arrival, it is fraught with complications. Henslowe's 'harry the vj' is most likely the first of Shakespeare's tetralogy, but we cannot be certain. Nor can we confidently describe the language of these lines as 'Shakespearean'. In Bedford's speech and those that follow it the distinctive voice, if there is one, is that of Christopher Marlowe. The archaic imperatives, the outlandish and resplendent images, the recourse to cosmic forces in the light of an imperial superman—all these draw redolently on *Tamburlaine* and other Marlovian

---

1. R. A. Foakes, ed., *Henslowe's Diary*, 2nd edn (Cambridge: Cambridge University Press, 2002), 16. There is no absolute certainty that this *Henry VI* is Shakespeare's play, but the lack of another candidate plus match with Nashe's claims about the play's performance success make this identification a very strong likelihood (for discussion see Edward Burns's Arden3 edition, *King Henry VI, Part 1* (London: Thompson, 2000), 1–9).

works.[2] In the immediately succeeding speeches by Exeter and Winchester even the classical and biblical parallels ('Like captives bound to a triumphant car', 'The battles of the Lord of Hosts he fought') seem to be transplanted wholesale from Marlowe's plays. Shakespeare's first theatrical appearance involves a curious mixture of stridency and deference.

There are different ways of dealing with this conspicuous presence of Marlowe's language in the Henry VI trilogy and other plays. One is to posit a battle of intellect between two pre-eminent geniuses. In this version of events, Shakespeare's first years of composition are marked by an 'anxiety of influence' as he seeks to imitate and move beyond the model of his great predecessor. Marjorie Garber famously imagined this exchange as a game in which Marlowe's oeuvre is gradually counted out by Shakespeare's stronger hand. Finally, with desperation, Marlowe lays down Tamburlaine the Great Parts I and II; Shakespeare, 'with an apologetic smile', presents his cards: 'Henry IV, Part I, he says deliberately, Henry IV Part II, and Henry V.'[3] James Shapiro, too, has written about this encounter, depicting Shakespeare as nervously covering the tracks of his early borrowing from Marlowe's style.[4] From these perspectives, Shakespeare feels the influence of his fellow playwright either as challenge or oppressive weight.

While it makes for compelling reading, the narrative of Shakespeare's personal engagement with Marlowe involves some difficulties. For one thing, the opening lines of Henry VI Part 1 are, conceivably, not by Shakespeare at all.[5] Thomas Nashe (who praised the play in his pamphlet

---

2. On features of Marlowe's style see Alvin Kernan in Leeds Barroll, Alexander Leggatt, Richard Hosley, and Alvin Kernan, eds., The Revels History of Drama in English, vol. III: 1576–1613 (London: Methuen, 1975), 255–6.

3. Marjorie Garber, 'Marlovian Vision/Shakespearean Revision', Research Opportunities in Renaissance Drama 22 (1979), 3. Harold Bloom, in the second edition of The Anxiety of Influence (Oxford: Oxford University Press, 1997), pp. xxviii–xlvii, explored the presence of Marlowe in early Shakespeare at length; his perspective is discussed in my Conclusion.

4. James Shapiro, Rival Playwrights: Marlowe, Jonson, Shakespeare (New York: Columbia University Press, 1991) argues, for example, that the classical allusions in Titus Andronicus are 'a feint' designed to 'deflect our attention from the more disturbing pressure of contemporary rivals, notably Kyd and Marlowe' (118), whose influence is ubiquitous in this play. Shapiro argues convincingly that this early influence is replaced by a more knowing, parodic allusion in the later plays: for example, Henry V's oration at the gates of Harfleur.

5. The case for co-authorship is made in Gary Taylor, 'Shakespeare and Others: The Authorship of Henry the Sixth, Part One', Medieval and Renaissance Drama in England 7 (1995), 145–205. Stanley Wells's statement in Shakespeare and Co.: Christopher Marlowe, Thomas Dekker, Ben Jonson, Thomas Middleton, John Fletcher, and the Other Players in his Story (London: Allen Lane, 2006), 194, that 'the only dramatist with whom, on the basis of evidence likely to be accepted in a court of law, it can confidently be said that Shakespeare collaborated is...John Fletcher' remains accurate. Yet the case for another hand in the opening speech of Henry VI Part 1 is strong. For a fuller discussion see Chapter 14.

Pierce Penniless) is one alternative candidate as author of this scene, but George Peele, Robert Greene, and others also present themselves.[6] The opening of *Henry VI* alerts us to two features: first, the strong presence of Christopher Marlowe and, second, the shadowy operation of co-authorship. For the conspicuous borrowing in these opening lines is not the reason for doubting they are by Shakespeare. Throughout the *Henry VI* plays Shakespeare echoes Marlowe in just this way. Although the opening act may not be entirely by Shakespeare, it is, perhaps all the more, an appropriate opening point to explore the way he worked. We certainly know that the following lines from *Henry VI Part 3* are Shakespeare's, because Robert Greene in 1592 (or perhaps someone imitating him)[7] chose to parody them precisely as an instance of intellectual theft by the 'upstart crow':[8]

> Thou art as opposite to every good
> As the Antipodes are unto us,
> Or as the south to the Septentrion.
> O, tiger's heart wrapped in a woman's hide,
> How couldst thou drain the lifeblood of the child
> To bid the father wipe his eyes withal,
> And yet be seen to bear a woman's face?

> (Shakespeare, *Henry VI Part 3*, 1.4.134–40)

Both the theatre of suffering that is orchestrated by Margaret in this scene and its vocabulary of cosmic transgression take their cue from *Tamburlaine*.[9]

6. See Burns, ed., *Henry VI, Part 1*, 74–5. Hugh Craig, 'The Three Parts of *Henry VI*', in Hugh Craig and Arthur F. Kinney, eds., *Shakespeare, Computers, and the Mystery of Authorship* (Cambridge: Cambridge University Press, 2009), 40–77, even goes so far as to attribute parts of the tetralogy to Marlowe. In my view, however, the evidence put forward in his study is better understood as indicating the difficulty of defining individual authorial voices in certain classes of early modern play.
7. It is appropriate (given this wider culture in which individual style is so difficult to isolate) that Greene's authorship of *Groats-worth* has itself been disputed. Katherine Duncan-Jones, *Ungentle Shakespeare: Scenes from his Life* (London: Arden, 2001), 43–8, argues that the addition 'To those Gentlemen his Quondam acquaintance' is by Thomas Nashe and also cites scholarship that argues for an attribution to Henry Chettle. Duncan-Jones dismisses the claims for Chettle, but John Jowett, 'Johannes Factotum: Henry Chettle and *Greene's Groatsworth of Wit*', *Papers of the Bibliographical Society of America* 87 (1993), 453–86, has strongly made the case for his authorship. I continue to refer here to 'Greene' as the author. Alternative, multiple, or disputed authorship, however, make the case about Shakespeare's position with equal authority.
8. Robert Greene, addressing Marlowe and Nashe, famously taxes Shakespeare as 'an upstart Crow, beautified with our feathers, that with his *Tygers hart wrapt in a Players hyde*, supposes he is as well able to bombast out a blank verse as the best of you' (*Groats-worth*, E3[b]).
9. As is often true in Marlowe, the influence of the medieval mystery play is also strong at this point.

Greene, in his satirical portrait of Shakespeare as an aspirant 'jack of all trades', attacks exactly this kind of imitation. There is a deliberate irony in the way that the satirist's twisting of the language of *Henry VI Part 3* ('Tygers hart wrapt in a Players hyde' mocking 'tiger's heart wrapped in a woman's hide') reflects the playwright's habits of composition. Two scenes earlier in the play, in a speech always attributed to Shakespeare, Richard has roused his father's ambition with a matching Marlovian oration:

> Therefore, to arms. And, father, do but think
> How sweet a thing it is to wear a crown,
> Within whose circuit is Elysium
> And all that poets feign of bliss and joy.
>
> (*Henry VI Part 3*, 1.2.27–30)

Marlowe's Theridamas had woken ambition in Tamburlaine with just such a description:

> A god is not so glorious as a king.
> I think the pleasure they enjoy in heaven
> Cannot compare with kingly joys in earth:
> To wear a crown enchased with pearl and gold,
> Whose virtues carry with it life and death.
>
> (*Tamburlaine I*, 2.5.57–61)[10]

Here, as on other occasions, the mirroring is strikingly direct.

The old notion that Shakespeare falls under the powerful influence of Marlowe has truth in it. But that truth hides something more difficult and complex. Shakespeare is influenced by Marlowe, but so are his other contemporaries—Nashe, Greene, Peele, and others more difficult to identify. Greene, who attacked Shakespeare for his thefts, was himself equally proficient in that art. His own *Alphonsus, King of Arragon* stands out as a Marlovian imitation from beginning to end. Alphonsus claps '*Fortune* in a cage of gold,/ To make her turn her wheel as I think best' (*Alphonsus*, TLN 1481–2): a transparent reworking of Tamburlaine's 'I hold the Fates bound fast in iron chains,/ And with my hand turn Fortune's wheel about' (*Tamburlaine I*, 1.2.173–4).[11] This is exactly the same kind of borrowing

---

10. *Tamburlaine the Great*, ed. J. S. Cunningham, Revels (Manchester: Manchester University Press, 1981). Subsequent references are to this edition.
11. *Alphonsus, King of Arragon* in *The Plays & Poems of Robert Greene*, ed J. Churton Collins, 2 vols. (Freeport: Books for Libraries Press, 1905; repr. 1970). On *Alphonsus* as 'an extravagant imitation of the two parts of *Tamburlaine*' see Churton, vol. 1, 72–3. Other plays of the period

we find in *Locrine*, a tragedy in which Shakespeare is sometimes argued to have had a revising hand, where 'the Scythian Emperor/Leads fortune tied in a chain of gold' (TLN 472–73).[12] Such transference is not merely one of timbre and imagery but also one of character, relationship, and spectacle. Greene's Alphonsus enters, for example, in a Tamburlaine-like manner 'with a canopy carried over him by three Lords, having over each corner a King's head, crowned' (*Alphonsus*, TLN 1452SD) and vaunts his power over the established Moslem ruler, Amuracke, in an explicit revisiting of Tamburlaine's triumph over Bajazeth.

Marlowe's style and dramatic incidents were imitated by many of his contemporaries. Peele's *Battle of Alcazar* openly proclaims its task of bringing 'Tamburlaine into our Afric here' (1.2.35) and is likewise dominated by the language and visual icons of Marlowe's world.[13] The one-upmanship of Tamburlaine and his sons (with a proud mother looking on) corresponds directly to an exchange in Peele. In *Tamburlaine*, Celebinus boasts that if his father's chair 'were in a sea of blood' he 'would prepare a ship and sail to it' (*Tamburlaine II*, 1.3.89–90). That claim is answered still more grandly by his brother who 'would strive to swim through pools of blood,/ Or make a bridge of murdered carcasses' (1.3.92–3). In *Alcazar* we find a comparably absurd family conversation.[14] Muly Mahamet's declaration that 'through the stream and bloody channels deep,/ Our Moors shall sail in ships' is thus

share such echoes. See for example Sulla's 'fettered Fortune in the chains of power' (5.5.316), part of an extensive series of parallels including the use of a triumphant chariot in Thomas Lodge's *The Wounds of Civil War*. For a full account of this shared imagery (including links with *Alphonsus*) see *The Wounds of Civil War*, ed. Joseph W. Houppert, Regents Renaissance Drama (London: Edward Arnold, 1969), xvii.

12. Anon., *Locrine* (Oxford: Malone Society, 1908). The play was entered in the Stationers' Register 20 July 1594 and advertised on its title page as 'newly set forth, overseen, and corrected by W. S'.

13. *Alcazar* in Charles Edelman, ed., *The Stukeley Plays*, Revels (Manchester: Manchester University Press, 2005). Parallels between Peele and Marlowe are ubiquitous and influence does not necessarily always run one way. For analysis of a series of overlapping passages see Charles Tyler Prouty, ed., *The Dramatic Works of George Peele*, 3 vols. (New Haven, CT: Yale University Press, 1952–70), II, 50–3.

14. The presence of the Queen as part of this group is not indicated in the printed quarto but it is indicated in the manuscript Plot (which records the entrances of actors, etc.) surviving at Dulwich College. See Edelman, ed., *Stukeley Plays*, 72 n., and (for a wider discussion) David Bradley, *From Text to Performance in the Elizabethan Theatre: Preparing the Play for the Stage* (Cambridge: Cambridge University Press, 1992), 23–4 and *passim*. Tiffany Stern, *Documents of Performance in Early Modern England* (Cambridge: Cambridge University Press, 2009) usefully distinguishes between 'plot-scenarios', 8–35, and 'backstage-plots', 201–31, as having a different purpose; we are concerned here with the latter.

immediately answered 'and of those slaughtered bodies shall thy son/ A hugy tower erect like Nimrod's frame' (*Alcazar*, 1.2.58–9; 61–2). Again, the overlap is both visual and rhetorical—*Alcazar* literally borrows *Tamburlaine*'s chariot: items for the productions appear side by side in Henslowe's accounts.[15]

We have, then, the picture of Marlowe's dominant authorial presence reverberating through the theatrical world of the early 1590s, influencing Shakespeare and other contemporaries alike. But even that is not quite right. Marlowe's plays, just as Shakespeare's, are intercut with the work of others. A sheet of paper now at the Folger Shakespeare Library in Washington is just one piece of evidence that illustrates this reality.[16] It contains a variant version of a scene from *The Massacre at Paris* with a soldier's speech much expanded from the version in the first octavo. The speech is better and longer than that of the printed text and its *currente calamo* corrections suggest it was written out by its author, yet the hand is not that of Christopher Marlowe.[17] Most likely, this is an instance of an 'addition' made by an anonymous patcher to an existing manuscript, but the manuscript that was altered is itself irrecoverable. All that now survives of *The Massacre at Paris* through the octavo volume appears to be an actor's memorial reconstruction of Marlowe's original work. Such realities pervade the Marlowe dramatic canon. Nashe, who possibly wrote the Marlovian imitation of the opening of *Henry VI Part 1*, was listed as Marlowe's co-author in *Dido, Queen of Carthage* (1594). Yet scholarship has found no way of distinguishing Nashe's contribution from Marlowe's in this work. Similar questions

---

15. See Foakes, ed., *Diary*, 318 and 320, containing references to 'Turkes hedes' (which Foakes connects to *Alcazar*) and a 'Tamberlyne brydell'. The Plot of *Alcazar* specifically points to the use of a chariot and whips (both features of *Tamburlaine*) and confirms Alleyn in the role of Muly Mahamet. A facsimile of the Plot is printed in W. W. Greg, *Dramatic Documents from the Elizabethan Playhouses* (Oxford: Clarendon Press, 1969), vol. II. For further discussion see Bradley, *Text to Performance*, and Chapter 2 below. Clearly Henslowe's theatre continued for a long time to produce plays in this genre. *Lust's Dominion* (1599), a collaborative play of which Dekker, Haughton, and Day appear to have written parts, draws again on a scheming Moor as a Machiavellian lead villain capable of great force and 'Marlovian' rhetorical grandeur, who is eventually caught up in his own plot.

16. This is Folger MS J.b.8. For an original defence of the document's authenticity see J. Q. Adams, 'The Massacre at Paris Leaf', *The Library*, 4th series, 14 (1934), 447–69. Adams's conclusions are endorsed in J. M. Nosworthy, 'The Marlowe Manuscript,' *The Library*, 4th series, 16 (1946), 158–71, which also provides a more accurate transcript. Nosworthy argues for the text as Marlowe's, but see Maguire below.

17. For an overview of attribution see Laurie E. Maguire, *Shakespearean Suspect Texts: The 'Bad' Quartos and their Contexts* (Cambridge: Cambridge University Press, 1996), 279–81. Maguire considers the octavo a memorial reconstruction.

surround the authority of *Dr Faustus*.[18] *Tamburlaine* itself was not published under Marlowe's name until 1820.[19] Marlowe's work, like that of his contemporaries, is touched by the additions of unknown writers. In some ways, it is only through retrospective attribution that he emerges as a defined authorial voice. In all likelihood, influence did not work one way—Peele's *Alcazar* may even predate Part II of *Tamburlaine*.[20]

Shakespeare's writing of the early 1590s, like that of his contemporaries, is alive with the presence of other writers, both as co-authors and as a transformative influence. That impression is strengthened if we look purely at the printed texts of this period: *Venus and Adonis* (1593), *The Rape of Lucrece* (1594), *Titus Andronicus* (1594), and the plays set in the reign of Henry VI, *The First Part of the Contention* (1594) and *The True Tragedy of Richard Duke of York* (1595). Like most of his contemporaries, Shakespeare appears in his own name as author only in his non-dramatic poems, publications that are themselves self-consciously imitative works of art. As a playwright, Shakespeare can be difficult to isolate in these printed texts—his distinct contribution obscured both by the work of other authors and by the playing companies that owned his texts. This is, I want to suggest, not simply a matter of textual corruption. Even in early plays whose texts were printed later and in which shared authorship is not an issue (*The Comedy of Errors*, *Richard III*, *The Taming of the Shrew*) these forms of influence remain disproportionately strong. It is of course the case that the playwright would, throughout his career, pick up ideas from contemporaries and borrow wholesale the plots of earlier dramatists.[21] Yet in

18. On the possible collaborative authorship of the play, see David Bevington and Eric Rasmussen, eds., *Doctor Faustus*, Revels (Manchester: Manchester University Press, 1993), 70–7.

19. This was W. Oxberry's edition. On the history of attribution, see Cunningham, ed., *Tamburlaine*, 6–9. Richard Jones, printer of 'the two tragical discourses of the Scythian shepherd Tamburlaine', had already altered the playtext by removing 'some fond and frivolous jestures, digressing and, in my poor opinion, far unmeet for the matter' (111). These 'jestures' may or may not have been Marlowe's—either way, they illustrate the lack of unmediated authorship in *Tamburlaine*. Emma Smith, 'Author v. Character in Early Modern Dramatic Authorship: The Example of Thomas Kyd and *The Spanish Tragedy*', *Medieval and Renaissance Drama in England* 11 (1999), 129–42, observes that early modern plays, including *Tamburlaine*, were much more readily known through their lead characters than their authors. Richard Proudfoot, 'Marlowe and the Editors', in J. A. Downie and J. T. Parnell, eds., *Constructing Christopher Marlowe* (Cambridge: Cambridge University Press, 2000), 41–54, shows that 'Marlowe' as a consistent biographical and bibliographical entity was in many ways the creation of editors after his death.

20. This is also the case with the highly 'Marlovian' overreacher Sulla in Lodge's *Wounds of Civil War*. On the difficulty of determining which way influence works see Houppert, ed., *Wounds*, xviii.

21. Martin Wiggins, *Shakespeare and the Drama of his Time*, Oxford Shakespeare Topics (Oxford: Oxford University Press, 2000) provides one recent survey of such points of connection.

his middle period the dramatic logic of Shakespeare's plays remains much freer from influence. In his early works Shakespeare displays a mental habit that James Shapiro calls 'assimilative imitation': a faithful following of a path set by other poets that is distinct from either Shakespeare's later knowing parodies (such as the 'rugged Pyrrhus' speech in *Hamlet*) or the total digestion for his own purpose that we find with source texts (such as the original *Leir*).[22]

The deep, fibrous intertextuality of Shakespeare's early work is most self-consciously present in the non-dramatic poems that he produced at this time. Shakespeare, Marlowe, Lodge, Drayton, and others wrote both epyllia and historical verse that formed part of a kind of open conversation. The imperatives that drive this sort of contact are not unlike those that govern Peele's and Marlowe's scenes of filial boasting. One celebrated instance of this interconnection is the way that Marlowe's *Hero and Leander* opens with a description of its heroine's sleeve, whose 'lawn' is bordered with 'a grove/ Where Venus in her naked glory strove/To please the careless and disdainful eyes/Of proud Adonis that before her lies'.[23] That scene, of course, is the subject of Shakespeare's *Venus and Adonis*. We cannot now be sure which of these works was completed first—whether Shakespeare is lavishly expanding a detail, or Marlowe making a trinket out of a poem of over a thousand lines. Either way, there is a gamefulness in allusion here that is profoundly characteristic of the writing of the period. Certainly Shakespeare's *Venus* follows his fellow playwright Thomas Lodge's *Scylla's Metamorphosis* (1589), whose stanza it replicates and whose hero's first appeal is to Adonis 'Wiping the purple from his forced wound . . . And Venus starting at her love-mate's cry'.[24] Our perception of the connectedness of these poems is strengthened if we look at *Oenone and Paris*, published by Thomas Heywood (yet another writer moving between the stage and the printed poem) in 1594.

It may well be that the model of the 'poet-playwright', established through the example of Ovid, provided a preconceived career track for

---

22. James Shapiro, *Rival Playwrights*, 81, uses this phrase in relation to the borrowing found in *Titus Andronicus* and contrasts it with Shakespeare's later practice (126–32).
23. Christopher Marlowe, *Hero and Leander*, in *Collected Poems*, ed. Patrick Cheney and Brian J. Striar (Oxford: Oxford University Press, 2006), ll. 9–14.
24. *Scylla's Metamorphosis*, ll. 122–7, in Sandra Clark, ed., *Amorous Rites: Elizabethan Erotic Verse* (London: Everyman, 1994). See Clark's introduction for an overview of the genre of epyllion.

such professionals.[25] Heywood's epyllion perfectly adopts Lodge and
Shakespeare's stanza and replicates the mock-heroic tone that is especially
strong in *Venus and Adonis* and *Hero and Leander*. All those factors would be
there again in John Marston's *The Metamorphosis of Pygmalion's Image* of
1598. Something similar happens with *Lucrece*, which picks up the stanza and
many of the generic expectations of Samuel Daniel's earlier *Complaint of
Rosamond*. Once more, those connections are amplified by a poem published soon after. Drayton's *Matilda* (1594) again in rhyme royal, again
concerning a king's transgressive desire—opens with the pairing of Daniel's
and Shakespeare's poems and constructs its narrative through devices and
characters common to both.

The early poems, which can sometimes feel removed from the main body
of Shakespeare's dramatic output, offer strong connections with the early
plays on this front. For it is not only in the *Henry VI* plays that we find the
conspicuous presence of other shaping voices. Thomas Nashe, Greene's
closest literary associate, may conceivably have intended Shakespeare alongside the specific target of Thomas Kyd in his famous attack on those who
'leave the trade of Noverint, whereto they were born, and busy themselves
with endeavours of art'.[26] Writing the preface to Greene's *Menaphon* (1590),
Nashe certainly attacks the same undigested imitation combined with social
climbing that would be at fault with the 'upstart crow':

> English Seneca read by candlelight yields many good sentences, as 'Blood is
> a beggar,' and so forth; and if you entreat him fair in a frosty morning, he
> will afford you whole Hamlets, I should say handfuls, of tragical speeches.
> But oh grief! *Tempus edax rerum*: what's that will last always? The sea
> exhaled by drops will in continuance be dry, and Seneca, let blood line
> by line and page by page, at length must needs die to our stage; which
> makes his famished followers to imitate the kid in Aesop, who enamoured
> with the fox's newfangles, forsook all hopes of life to leap into a new
> occupation (474).

---

25. This career trajectory has been the subject of a number of studies by Patrick Cheney, notably
Marlowe's Counterfeit Profession: Ovid, Spenser, Counter-Nationhood (Toronto: University of
Toronto Press, 1997) and *Shakespeare: National Poet-Playwright* (Cambridge: Cambridge University Press, 2004)—he sees Shakespeare as offering a 'self-concealing, counter laureate
authorship' (31) through a series of allusive episodes, whereas Shakespeare's early career
track and early imitative tendencies seem to me entirely conventional.
26. J. B. Steane, ed., Thomas Nashe, *The Unfortunate Traveller and Other Works* (Harmondsworth:
Penguin, 1972), 474.

Nashe's attack comes too early to be targeting any surviving plays by Shakespeare.[27] Yet the patterns of composition here, as with Greene, do touch upon the early plays. If we accept the attribution of Act 1 of the first part of the *Henry VI* trilogy to Nashe then this accusation again comes with undercutting ironies. Nashe was as likely as any to work by imitation. In drama for the public stage humanist poetics fused easily with a more mercantile instinct for formulas and sequels. The bombastic rhetoric we now associate with Marlowe, just as much as Seneca, was quickly accommodated to the common stock. The same patterns exist in comedy. Plays such as Peele's *Old Wives Tale* and the anonymous *Fair Em* borrowed freely from established successes like Greene's *James IV* and *Friar Bacon*.[28] Nashe condemns those who 'bodge up a blank verse with ifs and ands' by compounding Seneca with popular sources (475). Greene castigates the 'ape' who 'beautified with our feathers... supposes he is as well able to bombast out a blank verse as the best of you'. In reality, this is common theatrical practice, which the two are determined to restrict to their coterie.

We have only limited textual survival from this period, but works such as Peele's *Alcazar* or Greene's *Alphonsus* alert us to the commonplace and at times spectacularly inventive deployment of imitation in 1590s drama. Working together on *Titus Andronicus* (a play now widely considered to have involved an element of co-authorship), Shakespeare and Peele found this shared palette of classical imitation, rhetoric, and character a subtle and flexible medium. A key nodal point for these lines of connection comes at the beginning of Act 4, where the Andronici read Ovid's *Metamorphoses* and Titus quotes lines from a Senecan tragedy. It is a scene that Brian Vickers ascribes to Peele, but Shakespeare is just as ready in his portions of the script to make the play's imitative patterning evident.[29] The scene that

27. Supposing Shakespeare was the 'W. S.' who has 'newly set forth, overseen, and corrected' *Locrine* then that play's ubiquitous Senecan tags, well-worn mythological allusions, and ghostly speeches of revenge would certainly be vulnerable to this criticism. Though registered in 1594, even in its revised state it is quite likely to be an earlier work.

28. *John of Bordeaux, or The Second Part of Friar Bacon* (Oxford: Malone Society, 1936), viii–xii, provides an account of the overlap of plot and rhetoric across a number of comedies, also including *A Knack to Know an Honest Man*. That play, *John of Bordeaux*, and *Fair Em* all follow *Friar Bacon* to give the story of true love threatened by royal power. On Greene's complaints about *Fair Em*'s plagiarism and justification for this charge, see *Fair Em: A Critical Edition*, ed. Standish Henning (New York: Garland, 1980), 28, 65–9. On Peele's wider borrowing from Greene see George Peele, *The Old Wives Tale* (Oxford: Malone Society, 1908), vi.

29. Marcus's speech at 2.3.41–3 concerning 'a craftier Tereus' and a Lavinia 'that could have better sewed than Philomel' is one example of Shakespeare's employment of this myth in the same play. On the division of labour in *Titus* see Brian Vickers, *Shakespeare, Co-Author:*

literally brings Ovid onto the stage thus functions as a signpost for a well-established literary matrix: pointing to the 'tragic tale of Philomel', Lavinia explains her fate as 'patterned by that the poet here describes' (*Titus* 4.1.47, 57)—both the initial crime and the revenge for it being knowing expansions of famous myths.

There is much of that 'patterned' quality in all of the play's narrative. Titus himself follows closely the feigned madness of the wronged father in Kyd's *Spanish Tragedy*.[30] The theatrical production of Titus' revenge is a reworking of Hieronimo's murderous 'stately-written' court drama (4.1.159), with Kyd's hero, who enters the stage alone with a book of Seneca's tragedies (3.13), having likewise taken the resolution for revenge through classical precedent. Ovidian motifs—above all the Philomela narrative—must have seemed almost unavoidable. The legend (which Shakespeare used, probably simultaneously, for *The Rape of Lucrece*) stood alongside the Icarus story as a commonplace, featured even in the plot of *The Seven Deadly Sins*.[31] Progne's macabre feast had been recalled at Tamburlaine's great banquet (*Tamburlaine I*, 4.4.23–5) and would go on to provide the conclusion of Marston's *Antonio's Revenge*. It was also already there in Seneca's *Thyestes* (an important influence on *Titus* and the classical mainstay of *The Spanish Tragedy*, mocked in the Preface by Nashe). In *Thyestes*, Atreus' action is explicitly constructed as an overgoing of Progne's: 'animum Daulis inspira parens/ sororque; causa est similis' [Breathe your spirit into me, you Daulian mother and sister: our case is comparable].[32] That same invocation is made by Titus as he declares his plan of revenge:

A Historical Study of Five Collaborative Plays (Oxford: Oxford University Press, 2002), 449. Attribution in Shakespeare's early work is an area of particular contention (continued uncertainty here supports a key part of my argument). Vickers's conclusions on Peele's part in the play are investigated at the close of MacDonald P. Jackson, *Defining Shakespeare: Pericles as Test Case* (Oxford: Oxford University Press, 2003), 195–203. Jackson endorses Vickers's conclusions in the sample examined but has not assessed the whole of the play. Jackson, 195 n., also provides an overview of opinions on the *Titus* attribution question. Brian Boyd, 'Kind and Unkindness: Aaron in *Titus Andronicus*', in Brian Boyd, ed., *Words that Count: Essays on Early Modern Authorship in Honor of MacDonald P. Jackson* (Newark: University of Delaware Press, 2004), 51–77 (at 73–4 n.) adds further scholarship on the same theme.

30. On the wider influence of Kyd's play see Lukas Erne, *Beyond The Spanish Tragedy: A Study of the Works of Thomas Kyd* (Manchester: Manchester University Press, 2001), 5 and *passim*. Erne sees 'tightly dramatised causality' (4) as the most important of Kyd's innovations to influence Shakespeare.

31. *Lucrece*, ll. 1128–9; W. W. Greg, ed., *Henslowe Papers* (London: A. H. Bullen, 1907), 132.

32. Lucius Annaeus Seneca, *Thyestes* in *Tragedies*, ed. John G. Fitch, Loeb, 2 vols. (Harvard, MA: Harvard University Press, 2002–4), II, ll. 275–6. Unless otherwise stated subsequent references to Seneca's tragedies are to this edition and appear in the text.

> Far worse than Philomel you used my daughter,
> And worse than Progne I will be revenged.

> > *(Titus Andronicus*, 5.2.194–5)

What is true of narrative structures is equally so of character and scene. If Titus follows Kyd's Hieronimo in his character, speeches, and actions, the other distinctive figure of the play, Aaron, most obviously bears the imprint of Marlowe's stage Machiavels. Here, as with the easy adoption of *The Spanish Tragedy*'s plot devices, we find a characteristic moment of synergy between doctrines of imitation and theatrical sense. As author of *The Battle of Alcazar*, Peele had already created a black African villain capable of fiendish betrayal and high 'Marlovian' rhetoric. Aaron's opening soliloquy of plotting, which Vickers attributes to Peele, is thus replete with what we might call the 'Marlovian' cadences of Peele's Mahamet:

> Now climeth Tamora Olympus' top,
> Safe out of fortune's shot, and sits aloft,
> Secure of thunder's crack or lightning flash,
> Advanced above pale envy's threatening reach.
> As when the golden sun salutes the morn
> And, having gilt the ocean with his beams,
> Gallops the zodiac in his glistering coach
> And overlooks the highest-peering hills,
> So Tamora.
> Upon her wit doth earthly honour wait,
> And virtue stoops and trembles at her frown.
> Then, Aaron, arm thy heart and fit thy thoughts
> To mount aloft with thy imperial mistress,
> And mount her pitch whom thou in triumph long
> Hast prisoner held, fettered in amorous chains
> And faster bound to Aaron's charming eyes
> Than is Prometheus tied to Caucasus.

> > *(Titus Andronicus*, 1.1.500–16)

It is unlikely that this is a case of intentional allusion, but in situation and language it is extraordinarily close to the corresponding first soliloquy of Marlowe's Duke of Guise, who likewise aims to rise through the power of a female monarch. The Duke begins by invoking 'those deep-engend'red thoughts/ To burst abroad those never-dying flames/ Which cannot be extinguish'd but by blood'.[33] His speech's influence on Aaron's lines has been carefully explored, first by Muriel Bradbrook and then by James Shapiro. Aaron's speech is 'a compendium of Marlovian rhetorical and metrical devices'.[34] The image of the 'glistering coach' gestures at the figure of Phaeton, who stands alongside Icarus as Marlowe's favourite type of the aspiring overreacher.[35] The same might be said of the contrasting instance of Prometheus' captivity. Alongside these classically driven pressures of upward and downward movement, there is also the luxuriant language of riches—'golden', 'glistening', 'shine in pearl and gold'—and of masochistic entrapment—'virtue stoops and trembles', 'prisoner held, fettered in amorous chains', 'bound', 'tied', 'slavish weeds'.[36] Strikingly close to Guise's Catherine who 'works wonders for my sake,/ And in my love entombs the hope of France' (2.77–8) is Aaron's sense of Tamora as 'this siren that will charm Rome's Saturnine/ And see his shipwreck and his commonweal's' (1.1.523–4). Perhaps most 'Marlovian' of all is the speech's tendency to drive the pentameter beat through exotic polysyllabic words: 'Prometheus', 'Caucasus', 'Semiramis'. Bradbrook and Shapiro explore

33. Christopher Marlowe, *The Massacre at Paris*, in *Works*, ed. E. D. Pendry (London: Everyman, 1976), 2.34–7.
34. Shapiro, *Rival Playwrights*, 119, gives a reading of this speech comparable to (and proving a strong influence on) my own. This and the other instance below were explored earlier in M. C. Bradbrook, *English Dramatic Form: A History of its Development* (London: Chatto & Windus, 1965), Chapter 3, and in Bradbrook, 'Shakespeare's Recollections of Marlowe', in Philip Edwards, Inga-Stina Ewbank, and G. K. Hunter, eds., *Shakespeare's Styles* (Cambridge: Cambridge University Press, 1980), 191–3. The same register is picked up by Greene in *Alphonsus*, where the prologue to Act 2 announces 'thus from the pit of pilgrims' poverty/ *Alphonsus* 'gins by step and step to climb/ Unto the top of friendly Fortune's wheel' (TLN 352–4).
35. The flight of Daedalus and Icarus appears in *Alphonsus* (4.3). Phaeton is invoked by the aspiring Scythian King's son in *Locrine* when he compares himself to 'Lucifer mounted upon his steed', who 'brings in the chariot of the golden sun' (539–40). These authors, like Marlowe, draw repeatedly from a shallow pool of widely known classical myths.
36. Once more, all of this is there in Greene's *Alphonsus*—for example, in Carinus' vision of the hero's triumph:

> Me thought I saw *Alphonsus*, my dear son,
> Plast in a throne all glittering clear with gold,
> Bedecked with diamonds, pearls and precious stones,
> Which shined so clear, and glittered all so bright,
> *Hyperion's* coach that well be termed it might.
> Above his head a canopy was set,
> Not decked with plumes, as other Princes use,
> But all beset with heads of conquered kings.
>
> (*Alphonsus*, TLN 1245–52)

such correspondences in establishing Shakespeare's early obsession with Marlowe. If we attribute the speech to Peele, however, the correspondences tell a somewhat different story. They show, once again, that the 'Marlovian' mode was much more widely distributed. Even an essentially comic play such as Greene's *Orlando furioso* has recourse to this same register—Orlando's closing speech on the riches of the fleet (TLN 1435–42) could be transferred with little difficulty into the mouths of most of Marlowe's tragic characters.

Shakespeare, in *Titus Andronicus,* is as consistently imitative as his contemporaries. This is true of the exploitation of motifs from Seneca, Ovid, and Thomas Kyd and equally so of Marlowe. Just like Peele, we find him searching for scenic correspondences: exploiting and innovating in relation to an established rhetorical mode. Aaron's burlesque catalogue of evil-doing (again cited by Bradbrook and Shapiro) is a good example:

> AARON: Even now I curse the day – and yet I think
>   Few come within the compass of my curse –
>   Wherin I did not some notorious ill,
>   As kill a man or else devise his death,
>   Ravish a maid or plot the way to do it . . .
>
> *(Titus Andronicus,* 5.1.125–8)

As James Shapiro points out, there is a knowing gesture of connection at the close of this oration. Marlowe's Barabas (in the speech beginning 'I walk abroad o' nights/ And kill sick people groaning under walls') had closed upon his suicidal victim's body: 'pinning upon his breast a long great scroll/ How I with interest tormented him'.[37] In Shakespeare's version the Machiavel overgoes his predecessor: Aaron has 'on their skins, as on the bark of trees . . . carved in Roman letters,/ "Let not your sorrow die though I am dead"' (5.1.138–40). There is an element of specific allusion. Yet the connections in this scene also extend more widely. Aaron's boasts of having orchestrated the play's carnage, for example, relate equally to Muly Mahamet's speech in *Alcazar* beginning 'Now have I set these Portugals awork/ To hew a way for me unto the crown' (*Alcazar,* 4.2.70–1). Aaron's presentation as a diabolic black-skinned outsider also matches closely with Peele's villain, as does the play's final exemplary punishment:

---

37. Christopher Marlowe, *The Jew of Malta,* ed. N. W. Bawcutt, Revels (Manchester: Manchester University Press, 1978), 2.3.176–7; 199–200.

> Set him breast-deep in earth and famish him;
> There let him stand and rave and cry for food.
> If anyone relieves or pities him,
> For the offence he dies.
>
> (*Titus Andronicus*, 5.3.178–81)

This victor's speech, by Shakespeare, relates back to that of the conquering hero at the same point in Peele's earlier play. In *Alcazar* Muly Mahamet's corpse becomes a macabre public admonition:

> That all the world may learn by him to avoid
> To hale on princes in injurious war,
> His skin we will be parted from his flesh,
> And being stiffened out and stuffed with straw [...]
> So to deter and fear the lookers on
> From any such fool fact or bad attempt.
>
> (*Battle of Alcazar*, 5.1.249–54)

The fate of Marlowe's Jew of Malta also bears a resemblance to this grotesque act of public punishment, although Peele's is likely to be the earlier work.[38] On both fronts, Aaron's depiction leans heavily on earlier drama. It makes more sense to explore his 'character' in the light of Barabas and Muly Mahamet than it does to 'understand' him through the action of the play itself.

Titus Andronicus is continually driven by the inventiveness fostered by such intertextual engagements, whether with Marlowe, Kyd, Seneca, or some more amorphous dramatic tradition. Shakespeare's style, as Brian Vickers contends, is often distinguishable from Peele's through the subtlety of its tropes and figures.[39] Yet the forces that direct the deployment of his rhetoric have what we might call an 'architectural' rather than a 'psychological' quality. John Kerrigan has pointed to the consummately mechanical nature of the plot, in which action triggers action with impeccable logic just as rhymes and gestures echo one another across the play.[40] Beneath the violence there is a scarcely concealed pantomime absurdity that leaves its mark in the inevitable tick-tock of its rhymes:

---

38. Harbage, *Annals of English Drama: 975–1700*, 3rd edn, rev. Sylvia Stoler Wagonheim (London: Routledge, 1989), 54, dates *Alcazar* to 1588–9 and *The Jew of Malta* to *c.*1589–90.
39. See Vickers, *Shakespeare, Co-Author*, 239, on the differences in quality and quantity that he considers separate Shakespeare and Peele as authors.
40. John Kerrigan, *Revenge Tragedy* (Oxford: Clarendon Press, 1996), 194–203.

SATURNINUS: What, was she ravished? Tell who did the deed.
TITUS: Will't please you eat? Will't please your highness feed?
TAMORA: Why hast thou slain thine only daughter thus?
TITUS: Not I, 'twas Chiron and Demetrius.

(*Titus Andronicus*, 5.3.52-5)

As Shakespeare follows the automatized exchanges of Senecan stichomythia we find a fusion of sources for both plot and structure. The play is filled with such macabre echoes. The conclusion of *Titus Andronicus* artfully combines, amongst other works, *The Spanish Tragedy*, *The Jew of Malta*, and *Thyestes*. Even as he kills his daughter, Titus calls up yet another instance from Roman literature (this time the story of Virginius from Livy's *History*) to provide 'a pattern, precedent, and lively warrant' (5.3.43) for his action. In a conclusion that continually evokes literary analogues and sources, Tamora also elects to play the figure of Revenge, who had performed the final punishments of *The Spanish Tragedy*. The conclusions of works like Marston's *Antonio's Revenge* and Middleton's *Revenger's Tragedy* would continue to develop these motifs. Thus, in a scene not included in the Quarto, Titus harps with grating bathos on a topos already painfully present to the audience: 'O handle not the theme, to talk of hands' (3.2.29). Shakespeare's early drama is often spectacularly imitative and as a result his personal voice is much less distinct.

2

The working conditions
of the playwright

I n Chapter 1 I set out to show that Shakespeare's rhetoric in his early plays
and poems is closely comparable to that of his contemporaries—so much
so that the voices of men such as Marlowe, Greene, Kyd, and Peele merge,
almost imperceptibly, with his own style. Rather than evidence of a personal
infatuation with Marlowe, I argued, this closeness should be understood as
normative imitation. For all its brilliance, Shakespeare's writing in the first
few years of the 1590s follows the compositional habits of its time.

There is inevitably a connection between the literary features of a work
and the material conditions of its creation. Of course, lines of poetry are
crafted by individuals, but they are also moulded by surrounding social
contexts and tailored to specific practical demands. What, then, were the
pressures that shaped literary writing for the stage in this period? In this
chapter I will present a general picture of the aesthetic assumptions and
working conditions of playwrights in the early 1590s. Thereafter, I will
make an assessment of Shakespeare's likely employment circumstances at
this time. If Shakespeare's art in some ways matches that of his contemporaries in this period, then it would be significant if this was also true of his life.

Addressing the conditions of dramatic authorship in the years 1590 to
1594 it is useful to return to Greene's *Groats-worth*, the pamphlet whose
concluding epistle so famously insults Shakespeare as an 'upstart crow'. For
all its evident bias, this text does provide a starting point for exploring the
conditions under which playwrights in this period were working. *Groats-
worth* is presented as thinly disguised biography—the young Roberto's life,
Greene (or his ghost author) tells us, is 'in most parts agreeing with mine'
(E1[a]). The main narrative describes a young scholar's exclusion from his
father's will and his failed attempt at a confidence trick upon his brother.

Only at this point of utter penury is Greene's alter ego recruited by the players. His story of the career of a playwright is a unique piece of testimony that gives evidence both on Shakespeare as a person and on the culture that he would have encountered when he came to London at some point prior to September 1592.

As a commercial writer of plays Roberto is by no means poorly rewarded or regarded: 'his purse like the sea sometime swelled, anon like the same sea fell to a low ebb; yet seldom he wanted, his labours were so well esteemed' (D4^a). The pamphlet describes how he is housed and employed by a particular company of actors, who have a high regard for his rhetorical skills. Yet even when lodged 'at the town's end in a house of retaile' at the players' expense and 'famozed for an arch-playmaking-poet' he remains hostile to his employers (D3^b–D4^a). Above all, he makes clear that the players can have no control over his output, keeping the rule that 'what ever he fingered afore hand, was the certain means to unbind a bargain' (D4^a). Even pre-paid arrangements are not honoured. Roberto has no investment in his texts as dramatic entities—indeed he boasts of having worked doggedly to maintain their non-dramatic genesis.

Of course, Greene's pose is not entirely to be trusted. *Groats-worth* is an all too carefully crafted narrative of conversion. As well as the Christian motif of the justified sinner, Greene's expression of contempt for the players is part of a narrative that promotes an Augustan removal from the material motiv-ation for his work. Elsewhere he deployed the Roman precedent of Publius Servilius, who told a player to 'be not so brag of thy silken robes, for I saw them but yesterday make a great show in a broker's shop'.[1] Even so, Greene's narrative—crammed both with the idealized social fabrications of his class and with the authentic detritus of day-to-day living—is not to be dismissed. For the lines of demarcation between player-sharers and authors in the 1590s were probably stronger than they had been at any time. By 1592

---

1. Robert Greene, *Never Too Late* (1590) 2C1^a (the book *Francesco's Fortunes, or The Second Part of Greenes Never Too Late* was bound up with this text as a single volume). The return of the broker's shop here is especially galling because the subject of the story, Francesco, is himself forced to pawn his apparel before being employed by the players. The idea of the shallowly beautified player also appears in Greene's *Quip for an Upstart Courtier* of 1592—the social climbing both in performance itself and in players' accumulation of wealth is thus doubly dependent on the decline of the scholar. The number of players who had this kind of wealth was, in reality, limited. Bentley, *The Profession of Player in Shakespeare's Time, 1590–1642* (Princeton, NJ: Princeton University Press, 1984), 5, thinks such descriptions might have applied to some twenty out of a total thousand dramatic performers in the period.

the verse of a play like *The Pedlar's Prophecy*, which was probably written by the actor Robert Wilson, would look comically outdated. Its 'medley' style ('this heavy pack,/ It is so heavy, it hath almost broke my back/ Time it is to set it down,/ Would to God I were near some good town') was quite different from the now fashionable blank verse and the humanist-educated author of *Greenes Groats-worth* makes easy capital out of this gap.[2] The player who hires Roberto is himself a 'country author' who has 'penned the *Moral of Man's Wit*, *The Dialogue of Dives*, and for seven years space was absolute interpreter to the puppets' (E1[a]). Greene's mocking quotation from the player's extempore composition 'The people make no estimation,/ Of morals teaching education' (E1[a]) is clearly a jibe at this older practice. The coming of a new generation of writers established stronger boundaries between literary men and such 'puppets', and the production of numerous anti-theatrical pamphlets by playwrights is testament to that fact.

The world of *Groats-worth of Wit* (including its famous epistle with its insult to Shakespeare) is a fictional creation filled from beginning to end with caricatures. These include the materialistic and ignorant player, a dissolute young Machiavel, a cynical satirist, the 'upstart' new writer, and—most artificial of all—the penitent Roberto himself. Yet this creation (in which Greene, Chettle, and quite possibly other writers played a part) does speak to a divide between the literary world and the world of play performance in the 1590s. This divide was based on class, aesthetics, and economics. It was voiced most commonly in a university graduate context (where like-minded young men bound together through social fraternity could mock the players and complain of their lot). But non-university playwrights such as Dekker and Jonson could be equally vociferous in their resentment of the playhouse and acting establishment, which con- tinued to set the artistic agenda and held control of the flow of funds.

Class was often the issue closest to the surface, although given the parentage of most professional playwrights it did not always run as deep as they might profess.[3] The cultivated anti-theatricality of Robert Greene's publication is thus also to be found in the writings of Stephen Gosson and Anthony Munday. The latter confessed that 'ere this I have been a great

---

2. *The Pedlar's Prophecy* (Oxford: Malone Society, 1914), ll. 120–3.
3. David Mann, *The Elizabethan Player: Contemporary Stage Representation* (London: Routledge, 1991), 93–100, tends to endorse a picture of relative hostility between authors and players, again suggesting a gradual change with the turn of the century.

affector of that vain art of playmaking' but claimed to be disgusted that 'unseemly sentences passing out of the mouth of a ruffenly player doth more content the hungry humours of the rude multitude and carrieth better relish in their mouths than the bread of the word, which is the food of the soul'.[4] Gosson, in *Plays Confuted*, feels the same awkward complicity. In an earlier pamphlet by Greene, *Never Too Late* (1590), the author tells another tale of gentlemanly decline to employment by players. This combination of dependence and resentment is also there in the student drama of the *Parnassus* trilogy (a set of vacation interludes performed by undergraduates at St John's College, Cambridge) where employment by actors is the low point of the downward career of two Cambridge graduates. University audiences at the beginning of the seventeenth century could still be rallied to this flag of separatism.

These testimonies are significant not only as expressions of class resentment, but also as glimpses into the aesthetic assumptions of this intellectual group. *Never Too Late* by 'Rob. Greene *in artibus Magister*' (A1[a]) is thus partly a tale of frustrated social elevation, yet within this narrative the author also enfolds a disquisition on literary values, offering a cultural history of Rome in which the achievements of Plautus and Terence are laid waste by the emergence of a profiteering theatrical class. As the Palmer who tells this tale is asked by his host to 'show me your judgement of plays, playmakers and players', the overlap with Greene's biography is again impossible to resist.[5] In *Plays Confuted* Gosson's mention of high-status 'Italian Devices' is likewise significant.[6] Still more so are the attitudes in the *Parnassus* plays, where it is the high mode of Furor and Seneca that is prized. The alienation that the young students feel from the fellows of the acting companies is aesthetic as well as social. In the famous scene where Studioso and Philomusus meet the Chamberlain's Men we hear William Kemp complain that 'Few of the university [men] pen plays well, they smell too much of that writer *Ovid*, and that writer *Metamorphoses*, and talk too much of *Proserpina & Jupiter*'.[7]

---

4. 'A Third Blast' in *A Second and Third Blast of Retrait from Plaies and Theatres* (1580), 49, 60. The text is anonymous and in part a translation but the editor of the collection confirms the author's credentials as a playwright who has worked recently in London.
5. Greene, *Greenes Never Too Late*, 2B4[a]–2C1[a].
6. *Plays Confuted*, A7[a–b]. Gosson's explanation for the continued staging of his plays, which he claims were written two years previously, is (tellingly) that he has no control over their dramatic production.
7. J. B. Leishman, ed., *The Three Parnassus Plays* (London: Nicholson & Watson, 1949); *Second Part of the Return*, 4.3 TLN 1761–3. Subsequent references are to this edition and appear in the text.

Modern aesthetic sympathy may well lie with Kemp and Burbage, who attempt to coach the students away from academic patterns of speech and gesture. The comedy, however, is intended to work at the expense of Kemp, a man supposed ignorant enough to think *Metamorphoses* a writer. The simple-minded pursuit of naturalism is a mark of the ill-educated: the players transparently lack 'art'.[8] Kemp's dismissal of the types, figures, and patterns of the poetic playwright ('I was once at a comedy in Cambridge, and there I saw a parasite make faces and mouths of all sorts on this fashion' (4.3 TLN 1761–3)) mark him out as another version of the ignorant, exploitative player who offered employment to 'Roberto' Greene. In the words of J. B. Leishman, the *Parnassus* plays give us 'perhaps the ablest of all the academic dramatists ... revealed in this brief illuminating flash, sundered by an impassable gulf of class-prejudice and divergent ideals of art'.[9]

Class and education were important, but ultimately the most powerful dividing force was financial. Cultural documents of the period repeatedly throw up the image of the player as a monopolistic exploiter of the talents of better men. In the anonymous seventeenth-century work *Ratseis Ghost* the would-be sharer is advised 'when thou feelest thy purse well lined, buy thee some place or Lordship in the Country, that growing weary of playing, thy money may there bring thee to dignity and reputation'.[10] This is simply one of many versions of Greene's player who by his 'outward habit' is assumed 'a gentleman of great living' and who boasts his 'share in playing apparel will not be sold for two hundred pounds' (*Groats-worth* D4[b]). While this wealth was restricted to a very few London-based sharers and theatre owners, its purchase on the collective imagination was based on the fundamental norms for the possession of intellectual property.

For the playwright (whether contracted to an acting company or working freelance) there was no continued income from dramatic success. There is evidence throughout this period of a convention of one-off performance payments. Henslowe's *Diary* (the Memorandum Book of his transactions), for example, records a sum 'received of Mr Henslowe

8. 'Naturalism', it should be noted, is a relative concept. Tiffany Stern, *Rehearsal from Shakespeare to Sheridan* (Oxford: Clarendon Press, 2000), 58, sees this rehearsal in terms of formal comic and tragic lines of descent. Clearly, however, Kemp is criticized here for a lack of classical pedigree and the idea of a more natural movement (rather than stationary declamation) is important to him.

9. Leishman, ed., *Parnassus Plays*, 40.

10. Reproduced in Chambers, *William Shakespeare: A Study of Facts and Problems*, 2 vols. (Oxford: Clarendon Press, 1930; repr. 1988), II, 215.

for Mr Munday and the rest of the poets at the playing of *Sir John Oldcastle* the first time'.[11] The measly nature of such gratuities, however, was often remarked upon. Indeed, our knowledge about them is frequently sourced in complaints.[12] It is thus, for example, that Thomas Dekker pictured the prospect of a 'benefit' payment for a third day's performance:

> It is not Praise is sought for (now) but *pence*,
> Though dropped from greasy-apron *audience*.
> Clapped may he be with *thunder*, that plucks *bays*,
> With such *foul hands*, and with *squint eyes* does gaze
> On *Pallas' Shield*, not caring so he *gains*,
> A grand *third day*, what *filth* drops from his brains.[13]

Benefit payments are here set as an opposite to artistic achievement. This prologue to a printed play is full of resentment about what the Preface calls the 'hard housekeeping' at the Fortune Theatre, although Dekker is more positive about his treatment by the Queen's Men.[14] Beyond such one-off payments no document in all the volumes of Alleyn's papers refers to ongoing interest by an author in the performance of his plays. This is quite different from the position Shakespeare was eventually to enjoy, where court performances of his Elizabethan plays were still bringing him

11. Philip Henslowe, *Diary*, ed. R. A. Foakes, 2nd edition (Cambridge: Cambridge University Press, 2002), 126. On the term 'Memorandum Book' as a better definition of the Folio account book known as the *Diary* see S. P. Cerasano, 'Henslowe's "Curious" Diary', *Medieval and Renaissance Drama in England* 17 (2005), 72–85 (at 73). Cerasano provides a comprehensive overview of the volume's content and context. On the *Diary* as evidence for such working practices see Neil Carson, *A Companion to Henslowe's Diary* (Cambridge: Cambridge University Press, 1988), 54–66. The note in this case is written in the hand of Samuel Rowley, a sharer in the acting company. Brome's contract for the Salisbury Court is the first firm evidence of a share of receipts from a single performance as a standard arrangement. It is quite likely, however, that such arrangements would also have been made for attached professionals such as Fletcher working for the King's Men. For details of Brome's contract and reasons for thinking it reveals earlier practice, see Bentley, *The Profession of Dramatist in Shakespeare's Time, 1590–1642* (Princeton, NJ: Princeton University Press, 1971), 128–30.

12. In a letter to Henslowe on 23 August 1613, for example, Robert Daborne referred to 'the overplus of the second day' as received payment, but did so as part of a complaint about his poor financial conditions (see W. W. Greg, *Henslowe Papers* (London: A. H. Bullen, 1907), 75). A recent careful review of the practice is found in Tiffany Stern, 'A Small-Beer Health to his Second Day': Playwrights, Prologues, and First Performance in the Early Modern Theater', *Studies in Philology* 101 (2004), 172–99 (at 195–6).

13. Thomas Dekker, *If it Be not Good, the Devil is In It* (1612), A4ᵃ. The preface and prologue are characteristic of Dekker's invective against money-men in the theatre, most famously that of *The Gull's Hornbook* (1609) against 'the covetousness of sharers' (C2ᵇ).

14. The Queen's Men in question are the Jacobean company, not the sixteenth-century troupe. Dekker was apparently outraged at his treatment by Henslowe and Alleyn (the preface is full of dark hints about them) and was soon to begin a spell of seven years' imprisonment for debt.

income during the reign of King James. For other writers, once a playwright submitted a manuscript, control over that copy ceased.[15] The one exception to this rule was performance by the boys' companies, whose conventions were much more closely tied to the dramatic tradition of the grammar schools.[16] There had, however, been no commercial children's company in London since 1590, when apparent scandal involving the Martin Marprelate controversy had ended with St Paul's Boys being dissolved. Such companies would not re-emerge in the capital until 1599.

Of course, it is impossible that a decade of efficient dramatic production (involving the creation of hundreds of plays) could have been built on constantly seething levels of resentment.[17] By the middle of the 1590s, and probably for many years before, regular patterns of employment did exist.[18] The dramatic documents at Dulwich College show that, even in the 1590s, relations between acting companies and teams of writers could be businesslike and cordial. Writers worked with the expectation and some-times the contractual commitment of a buyer.[19] We know from Henslowe's correspondence that companies might offer a monetary advance to collab-orative teams of authors on the basis of an initial pitch for a composition. Later writers might also come on board to complete 'plots' set in train by others, as was the case with Ben Jonson's outline for a new tragedy.[20] It was seemingly customary for authors to present their work to a company by

15. On this legal situation (and the exception of boys' companies) see Andrew Gurr, *The Shakespearean Stage, 1574–1642*, 3rd edition (Cambridge: Cambridge University Press, 1992), 19, and Bentley, *Dramatist*, 62.
16. See E. K. Chambers, *The Elizabethan Stage* (Oxford: Clarendon Press, 1923; repr. 2009), II, 18–19. Marlowe, Nashe, and Peele had all, it seems, been attracted initially by the boys' theatre. The great precedent for successful dramatic control by a humanist-educated play-wright had been John Lyly, who had held the lease of the theatre where the boys performed. Comparable circumstances would return at the turn of the century, the consequences of which are discussed in Chapter 10 below.
17. On the numbers of plays, see Leeds Barroll et al., eds., *The Revels History of Drama in English*, vol. III: *1576–1613* (London: Methuen, 1975), 242.
18. A summary is provided by Gurr, *Shakespearean Stage*, 18–22.
19. On contractual ties and the basic direction of plays to their expected performers see Tiffany Stern, *Making Shakespeare: From Stage to Page* (London: Routledge, 2004), esp. 60–72; Andrew Gurr, *The Shakespeare Company: 1594–1642* (Cambridge: Cambridge University Press, 2004), esp. 15–22; and Bentley, *Profession of Player*, 206 (though see also incidences of broken agreements, transfer of plays, etc. in Bentley, 206–10).
20. On 3 December 1597 Henslowe reported payment to Jonson 'upon a book which he showed the plot unto the company which he promised to dd unto the company' (Foakes, ed., *Diary*, 85); that play seems not to have been delivered and on 23 October 1598 Henslowe forwards £3 intended for Chapman for 'his play book and three acts of a tragedy of Benjamin's plot' (Foakes, ed., *Diary*, 100). For the most extensive account of plotting see Stern, *Documents of Performance in Early Modern England* (Cambridge: Cambridge University Press, 2009), 8–35.

means of a reading of the play.[21] Such a system provided a solid baseline. Yet the distance between this and sustained theatrical control and ownership is pronounced. Examining Henslowe's manuscripts, the picture is still of writing quickly for standard fees, of composition separate from the company, not of careful honing to create a dramatic whole. Page after page of Henslowe's *Diary* records part payments to writing teams working rapidly to complete transactions. Surviving letters attest to time pressure, financial need, and an emphasis on basic copy. At a social level there is a contrast between players who rub shoulders daily and the somewhat removed playwriting fraternity.[22] Daborne, for whom the record is best, sees the players only occasionally and is unwilling to read to the company until the entire play is done.[23] Almost invariably, his letters beg for monetary advances. It is a fact too easily overlooked that the Henslowe playwrights— Daborne, Dekker, Lodge, and others—continually faced the threat and the reality of arrest for debt.

In recent years a number of scholars have worked to modify orthodox assumptions about the functioning of the theatrical market in early modern England.[24] That orthodoxy, it should be noted, was by no means the

21. Stern, *Rehearsal*, 59–60, nuancing Bentley's observations here, describes this as a two-stage process. The first 'was low key, private, and often given before one, or a small group, of actor-sharers; this was the reading in which the play itself was "auditioned" for suitability' and 'the playwright did no more than offer the substance of his play for approval'. The second took place when the playwright read in front of the full company. In her assessment it was these occasions that 'introduced the story of the play to the players, and also gave the playwright a chance to speak the text in the manner which he wished to hear it performed—the nearest, perhaps, he might get to having any "directorial" influence over the production'.

22. On this contact and on the residences of company members see Gurr, *Shakespeare Company*, 18–21. S. P. Cerasano, 'The Geography of Henslowe's Diary', *Shakespeare Quarterly* 56 (2005), 328–53, provides a great deal of evidence for Henslowe's active (though sometimes geographically distant) control over his companies (e.g. Henslowe's control of, and presence at, court performances).

23. See Carson, *A Companion to Henslowe's Diary*, 55, and Daborne correspondence printed in Greg, *Henslowe Papers*, 65–84. In addition to evidence from the Henslowe letters, a good deal is known about Daborne's financial dealings (including a shareholding in the Children of the Queen's Revels at an earlier stage, on which see Lucy Munro, *Children of the Queen's Revels: A Jacobean Theatre Repertory* (Cambridge: Cambridge University Press, 2005), 28). Additional complicating factors include Daborne's legal wrangling with his relatives about his paternal inheritance (see Donald S. Lawless, 'Robert Daborne, Senior' *Notes & Queries* 222 (1977), 514–16) and a later legal battle about his and his wife's occupation of a house in Shoreditch (see Donald S. Lawless, 'Some New Light on Robert Daborne', *Notes & Queries* 26 (1979), 142–3). For an overview of the life, see Fredson Bowers, ed., *Jacobean and Caroline Dramatists* (Detroit, MI: Gale, 1987), 50–9.

24. Key pronouncements on the conventions of theatrical employment are found in Andrew Gurr's *Shakespearean Stage*, esp. 18–22; *The Shakespearian Playing Companies* (Oxford:

caricature of exploitative accumulation that certain revisionists have made it seem. G. E. Bentley's original 1971 monograph discussed in detail the correspondence drawn upon in more recent critiques of his work.[25] Bentley was clear on the comparatively high income and the implicit writing contracts enjoyed by established playwrights. He too acknowledged the instances of textual revision brought to the fore in recent work. There was the practice of long-term employment amongst what Bentley called 'Attached or Regular Professionals'.[26] By the mid-1590s a team like Chettle's was in the regular employ of the Admiral's Men: Henslowe's *Diary* records part payments to them over sustained periods, both at points of part completion and for the 'mending' of company theatrical stock.[27] From this evidence (as indeed from the 'well esteemed' (E1[b]) labours of Greene's Roberto) it seems theatrical production could be efficient and swift.

A renewed insistence on the circulation of playhouse manuscripts and multiplicity of stakeholders is useful. Over the last two decades theatre scholarship has made significant advances in tracing networks of association between theatre owners and other parties involved in the production of dramatic work.[28] A more focused approach to the history of acting

Clarendon Press, 1996), 59–61 and 102; and *Shakespeare Company*, 151–61. Bentley's *Profession of Dramatist* remains the established authority in this field.

25. Grace Ioppolo, *Dramatists and their Manuscripts in the Age of Shakespeare, Jonson, Middleton and Heywood: Authorship, Authority, and the Playhouse* (London: Routledge, 2006), 11, argues that Bentley drew 'sometimes selectively' on archival records to depict 'as normal an antagonistic working environment in which dramatists lacked "respect" from their employers and "control" over their texts'. She also feels that 'such an argument is implicit in Andrew Gurr's generalisation in *The Shakespearean Company, 1594–1642* (Cambridge: Cambridge University Press, 2004), p. 2, that "the company bought the play from the author and did with it whatever they pleased"', although she contends 'his argument is less extreme than those of theatre historians E. K. Chambers and G. E. Bentley that a dramatist worked under the tyranny of an acting company which dismissed him as soon as his foul papers of a contracted play were "surrendered"' (*Dramatists*, 1n.).

26. On this group and those playwrights who might fall into this category see Bentley, *Profession of Dramatist*, 30–6.

27. Foakes, ed., *Diary*, 84–138, records a string of these payments by Henslowe (gradually adding to the debt of the Admiral's company). See 101 for payment made for 'mending'.

28. Ingram, in *The Business of Playing: The Beginnings of the Adult Professional Theater in Elizabethan London* (Ithaca, NY: Cornell University Press, 1992) and numerous individual articles, has looked carefully at the financing of the first permanent playhouses (the Theatre, the Curtain, and the playhouse at Newington Butts) and has set out the complex joint ventures of players, land owners, and guild members (as well as the interference of various authorities) that made their construction possible. Much detailed work by S. P. Cerasano (e.g. 'Anthony Jeffes, Player and Brewer', *Notes & Queries* 31 (1984), 221–5) has also extended knowledge of the financing of theatrical business during Shakespeare's lifetime. Knutson, *Playing Companies and Commerce in Shakespeare's Time* (Cambridge: Cambridge University Press, 2001), likewise

companies, for example, has identified shared patronage between authors, investors, and printers associated with the Children of the Queen's Revels, during the years 1600 to 1613.[29] It is important, however, not to move from this to an assumption of 'guild-like' cooperation or to ignore the realities of practical ownership. Both the financial records and the tenor of social contact between the groups run counter to that idea. Misreadings of the tone of author–sharer relations have been compounded by an effort to minimize the power and influence of Philip Henslowe. This figure becomes simply a banker and landlord or even a 'theatrical angel' in the revisionist account.[30] The details of the Henslowe-Alleyn papers show something different: together, father and son-in-law made decisions about the acceptance of texts, took directly for themselves a half-share of performance revenue, had hired actors under contract, took effective possession of theatrical stock (meaning both apparel and playbooks), and even made decisions on the physical movement of companies.[31] This proprietorial control over

looking at guild membership and stressing the importance of episodes of unified playing amongst acting companies, has worked to counter assumptions about fierce competition between parties. Yet all of this evidence, complex though it is, still suggests that at least until the early seventeenth century the 'business of playing' was the concern of players and theatre owners, not authors. The nature of shareholding will be discussed in detail in Chapter 5 below, as will the (largely financially unsuccessful) attempts by the playwrights Daborne, Marston, and Drayton to invest in playing companies in the first part of the new century.

29. See Munro, *Children of the Queen's Revels*, esp. 27–30. The fortunes of this enterprise were erratic, but playwrights Robert Daborne and John Marston were sharers for a spell. Munro (28) considers Marston's two- to four-year period as a shareholder in the Blackfriars operation and Daborne's position as a shareholder in the years 1610–13 at Whitefriars. Daborne's shareholding may date back to the earlier spell at Blackfriars because in 1608 he was found to owe £50 to the principal investor, Robert Keysar. No work by Daborne, however, can be linked to the company. On Keysar as an investor, see William Ingram, 'Robert Keysar, Playhouse Speculator', *Shakespeare Quarterly* 37 (1986), 476–85. A more substantial comparison with Shakespeare's position in the Chamberlain's/King's Men is pursued in Chapter 7 below.

30. Carol Rutter's introduction to the revised Revels edition of *Documents of the Rose Playhouse* (Manchester: Manchester University Press, 1999) makes this revisionist case most strongly, referring to Fleay's 'spectacular error' in asserting 'that Henslowe kept "his actors" perpetually in debt' (3). She considers Henslowe's standing as guarantor for an author's debts only as 'blundering ineptitude' (6) because she understands him as a landlord who 'did not employ any player or playwright' (9). Grace Ioppolo lauded Henslowe as a 'theatrical angel' in her paper 'Philip Henslowe, Edward Alleyn, and the Invention of Theatre' at the Shakespeare Association of America Conference in Boston, 2012.

31. There are five statements here: (i) For instances in which it is Alleyn and Henslowe jointly who decide upon commissions see, for example, 'Robert Daborne to Philip Henslowe (8 May 1613)', where the playwright asks Henslowe to 'appoint any hour to read to Mr Alleyn'. In a second letter (16 May 1613) Daborne makes an arrangement to 'meet you and Mr Alleyn' to read part of the play but declares himself 'unwilling to read to the general company till all be finished' (see Greg, *Henslowe Papers*, 69–70). (ii) For performance income, as is well known, a central function of Henslowe's *Diary* is to record his share of gallery receipts; until finally

other companies makes Shakespeare's eventual position as a sharer in the Lord Chamberlain's Men still more radically different from the norm.

Examining just one letter from the playwright Robert Daborne, for whom the record is strongest, gives us an impression of this backdrop. Grace Ioppolo has claimed that Daborne, along with all other writers, exerted 'the same kind of artistic control' as Shakespeare.[32] Yet in late October 1613 he wrote to Philip Henslowe as follows:

> Sir I have been twice to speak with you both for the sheet I told you of as also to know your determination for the company whether you purpose they shall have the play or no. They rail upon me, I hear, because the King's Men have given out they shall have it. If you please I will make you full amends for their wrong to you in my last play before they get this. For I know it is this play must do them good if you purpose any to them. I have sent you two sheets more so that you have ten sheets and I desire you to send me 30 shillings more which is just eight pound besides my rent which I will fully satisfy you either by them or the King's Men as you please. Good sir let me know your mind for I desire to make you part of amends for your great friendship to me. Wishing my labour or service could deserve you so trusting one your gentleness which cannot long be without satisfaction now I rest
> ever at you[r] command
> Rob: Daborne[33]

offering the former Admiral's (now Palsgrave's) Men a long-term lease on the Fortune this was also a steady source of income for Alleyn. (iii) On contracts, the *Diary* contains copies of performance contracts in which Henslowe specifically binds hired men 'to serve me and not to depart from my company'. These entries, made with the book reversed (233^a–229^b), are commonly witnessed by Edward Alleyn (see Foakes, ed., *Diary*, 239–43). (iv) On ownership of plays and apparel, Alleyn MSS 1, Article 2, is a Deed of Sale by Richard Jones to Edward Alleyn for 'all and singular such share part and portion of playing apparel, play books, instruments, and other commodities' that were previously held 'jointly with the same Edward Alleyn' and others (see Greg, *Henslowe Papers*, 31). Alleyn continued to purchase playtexts and apparel (see, for example Alleyn MSS 1, Article 30, which is an inventory of theatrical apparel in his hand (see Greg, *Henslowe Papers*, 52–5)). The properties that Henslowe listed in the *Diary* were owned by the companies. However, Alleyn MSS 1, Article 106, the 'Articles of Grievance and of Oppression against Philip Henslowe' of 1615, contains the claim by the fellows of the Lady Elizabeth's Men that Henslowe kept hold of and then sold their stock valued at £400. The document also contains other claims about Henslowe's control of playbooks and apparel (see Greg, *Henslowe Papers*, 86–90). (v) For evidence on Henslowe's power over the physical movement of the company see, for example, 'Robert Daborne to Philip Henslowe (5 June 1613)' where the former has heard from the company that he (i.e. Henslowe, reading it) was expected yesterday 'to conclude about their coming over or going to Oxford' (see Greg., *Henslowe Papers*, 72).

32. Grace Ioppolo, Letters, *TLS*, 4 May 2007, p. 15.
33. 'Robert Daborne to Philip Henslowe', printed in Greg, *Henslowe Papers*, 76–7. Daborne's letter itself is not dated, but endorsement for payment was made on 29 October 1613.

The document survives because it was taken by Henslowe as a bill recording a further loan of 20 shillings (Daborne having requested 30). Its solicitous tone is revealing. Over anxious, Daborne repetitively stresses the respectful 'you': 'I will make you full amends', 'good sir let me know your mind for I desire to make you part of amends'.[34] He has come twice to see Henslowe without success; it is Henslowe who will make the decision about his play for the company. The point at issue is also telling—the possibility that a rival company will take his current offering. Contrary to the way in which this episode is reported by Ioppolo, this was not a case where Daborne 'exploited the idea of competition' and 'demands' to know Henslowe's decision; nor is he 'coney-catching' by selling a play elsewhere.[35] It is Henslowe who is unwilling to commit and Daborne who claims (whether truthfully or not) that he can also sell to another company.[36] Henslowe, who will be owner of the play, will get the payment in either case.[37] A short time later Daborne writes 'Sir if you do not like this play when it is read you shall have the other which shall be finished with all expedition'.[38] The need for money and the constant haste are also

34. That tone is characteristic of the correspondence, not just in the case of Daborne and Henslowe—the same year the Admiral's Men sharer Charles Massey is profusely apologetic to Alleyn for having 'presumed to write unto you thus, not daring to trouble you any longer I commit you to God to whom I will ever pray to bless you' ('Charles Massey to Edward Alleyn (1613?)', printed in Greg, *Henslowe Papers*, 64–5). The letter, as usual, is a request for money. Although rather poorly preserved the manuscript gives a great deal of detail on company structure.

35. For this reading see, for example, Ioppolo, *Dramatists*, 26. The anonymous *Defence of Conny Catching* (1592) famously demands of Greene to 'ask the Queen's Players if you sold them not *Orlando furioso* for twenty Nobles, and when they were in the country, sold the same play to the Lord Admirals men for as much more' (C3^{a-b}). There are other instances of such practice. On Lady Day in 1602 Henry Chettle signed a bond to write for the Admiral's Men, but he nevertheless wrote or contributed to several plays for the Earl of Worcester's company in the following thirteen or fourteen months (see Bentley, *Profession of Dramatist*, 36). Possibly Chettle's move came with Henslowe's approval (on his allocation of plays at this stage see Gurr, *Playing Companies*, 320)—Worcester's Men were also of his stable and Henslowe would have had more hold on Chettle than the Admiral's did. Either way, these instances all testify to a lack of connection between playwright and playing company.

36. A slightly different, but comparable, situation is found where Nathan Field writes to Henslowe, probably in 1613, asking for credit to secure a play. Field writes that 'Mr Daborne may have his request of another company' ('Nathan Field to Philip Henslowe (undated)', printed in Greg, *Henslowe Papers*, 84). At this point Daborne is free and (Field claims) able to sell the play elsewhere.

37. Carson, *Companion to Henslowe's Diary*, 55, notes that during the correspondence of the years 1613–14 Daborne's dealings seem to have been with Henslowe rather than the players.

38. 'Robert Daborne to Philip Henslowe (11 March 1614)', printed in Greg, *Henslowe Papers*, 82.

representative. Elsewhere Daborne informs Henslowe he 'sat up last night till past twelve to write out this sheet'.[39] On that occasion the players already had the third act in parts, suggesting imminent production. But it was always possible for work to be rejected—in another case Richard Hathaway had his papers returned and needed to refund his advance.[40]

What the Henslowe correspondence illustrates is a fairly distant, practically minded exchange between authors and the buyers of their texts. In financial terms the realities are stark. Henslowe's and Alleyn's wealth stands in awe-inspiring contrast to their associates'. The full run of the Alleyn papers give us a solid sense of the range and extent of their assets. Volume eight of the bound manuscripts records how in 1605 Alleyn 'bought the Lordship of Dulwich of Sir Francis Calton, knight, this 20th of October for £5000 whereof £2000 is paid in hand the other—£3000 at the end of six years'.[41] Over the course of the volume, in document after document, Alleyn continues to extend credit to Calton, whose letters (like those of Daborne) become increasingly solicitous, angry, and desperate.[42] In the final years of his life Alleyn, who had merged his business with Henslowe's, was spending over £1000 per annum where ordinary playwrights would do well to earn £30.[43]

39. 'Robert Daborne to Philip Henslowe (18 June 1613)', printed in Greg, *Henslowe Papers*, 73.
40. 'Samuel Rowley to Philip Henslowe (April 1601?)', printed in Greg, *Henslowe Papers*, 56. Ioppolo, *Dramatists* (13–14 and *passim*) claims Daborne and Brome as instances of close actor-author collaboration. Traffic between the players and these dramatists certainly existed, but can more easily be read as evidence the other way. Both men broke arrangements for play transferral and in each case relations with the actors concluded acrimoniously. Ioppolo's limited information about the circulation of manuscripts is generally taken from correspondence whose principal concern is financial distress. The orthodoxy of a conflictual relationship between authors and their employers that Ioppolo posits never really existed (see Bentley's treatment of the Rowley correspondence in *Profession of Dramatist*, 63–7). Any new orthodoxy that Shakespeare 'exerted the same kind of artistic control which was available to most other dramatists, including Robert Daborne, from the early 1590s to at least the late 1630s' (Ioppolo, Letters, *TLS*, 4 May 2007) carries far greater risks.
41. Alleyn MSS 8 (Memorandum Book of Edward Alleyn), fol. 8^b.
42. See, for example, Alleyn MSS 3, Items 16 and 46 (Sir Francis Calton to Edward Alleyn).
43. See Alleyn MSS 9 (Diary and Account Book, 1617–22), fol. 62f^a; on the final page Alleyn records that 'the general disbursed for these 5 years is £8504 04s 8½d'. The financial record is printed in William Young's *History of Dulwich College*, 2 vols. (London: T. B. Bumpus, 1889), II, 254. On the income of dramatists see Bentley, *Profession of Dramatist*, 89–110). For a study of Henslowe and Alleyn's connections and power, see S. P. Cerasano's 'The Patronage Network of Philip Henslowe and Edward Alleyn', *Medieval and Renaissance Drama in England* 13 (2000), 82–92. An indication of the scope and strength of the Henslowe–Alleyn business empire is also evident in their loans to the crown, on which see S. P. Cerasano, 'Cheerful Givers: Henslowe, Alleyn, and the 1612 Loan Book to the Crown', *Shakespeare Studies* 28 (2000), 215–19.

Pretty much all of those writing for the companies for which Henslowe acted as banker were under extreme pressure of debt. By early modern standards professional playwrights were not badly paid, but they were not asset holders (as the sharers or theatre owners were) and thus could not move beyond the short-term horizons that are typical of waged labour at this time. For Henslowe and Alleyn, in contrast, playtexts became a fixed asset. The degree of personal connection to playtexts was inevitably affected. Original authors could be called upon by playing companies to modify their scripts.[44] But other authors could just as easily be employed for that same task—the choice was Henslowe's, Alleyn's, and the company's.[45] The professional playwright of the 1590s could have no prospect of sustained income from or artistic influence on the production of his text.[46] Even if Greene's *Groats-worth* is an artfully constructed polemic, it does speak to some fundamental realities of the London theatrical world.

So was Shakespeare's position as a playwright in the early 1590s any different from that of his contemporaries? There is only limited information through which to answer this question. Yet in practice his circumstances as an author are unlikely to have differed from those experienced by authors like Greene and Peele. At the time that *Groats-worth of Wit* was composed, Shakespeare's role may to some extent have blurred the division between

44. Ioppolo (*Dramatists*, 16) points to an instance of this on 15 May 1602, when Chettle and Porter were paid for 'mending' *Cardinal Wolsey*, a play originally produced by these dramatists. She also argues (although the evidence here is more debatable) that the theatrical manuscripts of Heywood's *Captives*, Shakespeare's scenes in *Sir Thomas More*, and Massinger's *Believe as You List* show authors working in consultation with the company bookkeeper (see Ioppolo, *Dramatists*, 94, 104–8, 138). I discuss *Believe as You List* (Egerton 2828) in Chapter 4, and *The Captives* (MS Egerton 1994, fols 52–73) and *Sir Thomas More* (Harleian MS 7368) in Chapter 14 below, noting that in all cases it is the bookkeeper alone who controls the physical specificity of casting.

45. Famous incidents include Jonson's payment for changes to Kyd's *Spanish Tragedy* and Bird and Rowley's additions to Marlowe's *Faustus* (for details see Thomas Kyd, *The Spanish Tragedy*, ed. J. R. Mulryne, New Mermaids, 2nd edn (London: A. & C. Black, 1989), xxxiii–xxxiv; and Christopher Marlowe, *Doctor Faustus: A- and B-Texts*, ed. David Bevington and Eric Rasmussen, Revels (Manchester: Manchester University Press, 1993), 62–77). For complaints from Nashe and acceptance from Heywood about players' ability to change their lines see Ioppolo, *Dramatists*, 128. Numerous authors (famously including Ben Jonson in his preface to *Sejanus*) complain about changes in their texts made at performance (see also Bentley, *Profession of Dramatist*, 236–67).

46. The first record we have of authorial payment for performance appears in Henslowe's *Diary* in the 1610s, but even this is a discretionary single payment, not an entitlement to sustained income. Stern, *Rehearsal*, claims 'many authors were encouraged not to attend group rehearsal and, when they did so, frequently found important decisions had already been made by manager and prompter: the theatre and the playwright were often in opposition to one another' (12).

playwright and player. That pamphlet's famous sentence about 'Shake-scene' being 'beautified with our feathers' and 'wrapped in a player's hide' seems to tar him with an actor's feathers. We should not conclude, however, that this shows him to have been a professional player. Given Shakespeare's social and educational background it is extremely unlikely that his first calling would have been to a life on the stage.

Whoever wrote the concluding epistle to *Groats-worth of Wit* (whether it be Greene, Nashe, Chettle, or another) intended to wound Shakespeare. A phrase that implied he might be an actor was the easiest way to do this, but unfounded suggestions that poets were really players were not uncommon at this time. Ben Jonson would later be mocked by his rivals as 'a poor journeyman player' and at an earlier date Anthony Munday had likewise been attacked as 'a stage player'.[47] Such insults were to be expected when grammar-school-educated writers displayed ambition, but they are not evidence of a professional commitment to a life on the stage. Probably Shakespeare had (like the playwright Thomas Heywood thereafter) found employment as a hired man at the theatre, a supplement to the work of composition that was not uncommon at this time. Yet no other evidence from the early 1590s suggests he was an actor. The author who presents himself in the dedications to *Venus and Adonis* and *The Rape of Lucrece* shows no hint of actorly associations. The evidence of co-authorship in the early drama (in the *Henry VI* plays, *Titus Andronicus*, and probably *Edward III*) shows him working closely with other humanist-educated playwrights. Everything in Shakespeare's early biography (even the insult about acting) is typical of the life of a young professional poet setting out on a literary career.

Whatever Shakespeare's position in the early 1590s, it was emphatically not that of a sharer in a stable acting company.[48] From what we can reconstruct, he shifted between employers as was common practice amongst

47. Thomas Dekker, *Satiromastix* in *Works*, ed. Fredson Bowers, 4 vols. (Cambridge: Cambridge University Press, 1953), 4.1.128; Thomas Alfield (?), *A True Report of the Death and Martyrdom of M. Campion* (1582), D4ᵇ. I examine these and other quotations more extensively in van Es, '*Johannes fac Totum?*: Shakespeare's First Contact with the Acting Companies', *Shakespeare Quarterly* 61 (2010), 551–77, which presents the argument of this paragraph at greater length.
48. On this non-appearance in theatrical documents see Gurr, *Playing Companies*, 270 and Chambers, *Facts and Problems*, 1, 60. Chambers, *Facts and Problems*, 1, 38–55, gives a documentary overview of the rapid changes in acting companies from the beginning of the 1590s to 1594, including (52) the probable distribution of plays between companies. Before 1594 it is often difficult to speak of fixed companies, but after that date Chambers charts the shared

writers at this time.[49] There is a chance that he began by writing piecemeal for the Queen's Men.[50] Yet Shakespeare plays were also owned by the Earl of Pembroke's players: *The True Tragedy of Richard Duke of York* is first published in quarto as played by that company; and the Folio text names actors (including Gabriel Spenser) who would later be part of the Admiral's Men and seem certain to have come from Pembroke's.[51] Plays by Shakespeare, including *Henry VI Part 1*, were performed by Lord Strange's Men at Henslowe's Rose. It is likely he had some connection with this company, a significant number of whose sharers would form part of the foundation of the Chamberlain's Men. Yet, no direct evidence connects the dramatist with Strange's. He is not mentioned in Edward Alleyn's correspondence while the actor was travelling with the troupe. His name does not appear on the warrant of 6 May 1593 listing members of the company, nor is it on the plot of the Strange's play *The Second Part of the Seven Deadly Sins* (a document that identifies minor roles as well as leads).[52]

Even supposing Shakespeare was already a shareholder in an acting company in the early 1590s (a proposition against which all the evidence

---

'supremacy of the London stage' (1, 47) enjoyed by the Admiral's and Chamberlain's Men from 1594 until at least the beginning of the seventeenth century.

49. As Chambers, *Facts and Problems* (1, 61), notes, it is possible that Shakespeare was writing for three companies in the period 1592–4. On this period of Shakespeare's career see also Gurr, *Playing Companies*, 263 and 271. Gurr thinks it evident from Greene's gibe that Shakespeare was 'serving as a player' in the summer of 1592, though not in what capacity. On the status of hired men see Bentley, 'Hired Men', in *Profession of Player*.

50. For speculation about the Queen's Men connection see Scott McMillin and Sally-Beth MacLean, *The Queen's Men and their Plays* (Cambridge: Cambridge University Press, 1998), 160–5, and Schoenbaum, *Documentary*, 125.

51. See Scott McMillin, 'Casting for Pembroke's Men: The *Henry VI* Quartos and *The Taming of A Shrew*', *Shakespeare Quarterly* 23 (1972), 141–59. McMillin explores some of the difficulties of casting the play's thirteen distinct male roles. A second set of Pembroke players joined the Admiral's Men in 1597 after the failure of their enterprise at the Swan. If a portion of *Edward III* can be attributed to Shakespeare then this would be a further case of his producing work for this company (see MacDonald P. Jackson, '*Edward III*, Shakespeare, and Pembroke's Men,' *Notes & Queries* 210 (1965), 329–31).

52. The Plot itself is kept at Dulwich College, Alleyn MS 19, and is reproduced in facsimile by W. W. Greg, *Dramatic Documents from the Elizabethan Playhouses: Stage Plots, Actors' Parts, Prompt Books,* 2 vols. (Oxford: Clarendon Press, 1969) and Greg, *Henslowe Papers,* 129–32. David Kathman, 'Reconsidering *The Seven Deadly Sins*', *Early Theatre* 7 (2004), 13–44, argues that the play might date not 1590–1 but 1598, when it would have been prepared for the Chamberlain's Men. This claim for redating is dubious on numerous grounds: the Plot's provenance, the apparent non-sharer status of Burbage, the absence of Shakespeare and other sharers, the unlikelihood of Chamberlain's performing this morality in 1598, etc. For a careful account of the difficulties with Kathman's claim see Andrew Gurr, 'The Work of Elizabethan Plotters, and *2 The Seven Deadly Sins*', *Early Theatre* 10 (2007), 67–87.

is stacked), then the playwright would still not have been writing for a stable entity. The companies themselves were rapidly separating and merging. McMillin and MacLean call the period a 'watershed' that proved devastating for at least one major company, the Queen's Men.[53] Henslowe's *Diary* records that Pembroke's Men (for whom Shakespeare had written) also collapsed at this time. The early 1590s saw a series of regroupings as a result of shifts in patronage that may in part relate to changes in literary fashion. There were also severe plagues in the years 1593–4 and many companies found it difficult to survive this period unchanged. We know, for example, that in May 1593 Edward Alleyn (an Admiral's Man who until 1589 had been a member of Worcester's company) was travelling with Lord Strange's Men.[54] Companies, it appears, saw no problem with temporary cooperation. This seems to have occurred, for example, in Shrewsbury in late 1593, where payment was made 'to my Lord Strange and my Lord Admiral's players' as a single entity.[55] It was under this kind of joint venture (with Strange's now travelling as the Earl of Derby's Men) that *Titus Andronicus* was performed a very short time later. This, the first Shakespearean play to be printed, was published as 'Played by the Right Honourable the Earl of Derby, Earl of Pembroke, and Earl of Sussex their Servants'.[56] The detail of this title page, like so much other evidence, shows that the

53. McMillin and MacLean, *Queen's Men*, 6. An accessible account is provided in Gurr, *Shakespearean Stage* comparing 'The Early Adult Companies', 33–41, and 'The Strong Companies', 41–9.
54. On Alleyn's shift from Worcester's to the Lord Admiral's, see Gurr, *Shakespearean Stage*, 36–8, 90–1, and also John Tucker Murray, *English Dramatic Companies, 1558–1642*, 2 vols. (London: Constable & Co., 1910), I, 47. Alleyn still appeared as an Admiral's Man in the procession list of 1603 (see Murray, I, 207). On the composition of the Lord Chamberlain's Men and its development out of a core of players from Lord Strange/Earl of Derby's Men see Murray, *English Dramatic Companies*, I, 73–91.
55. Bailiff's Accounts SRO 3365/535 bifolium 2 f [1]* (*After 24 July*) printed in J. Alan B. Somerset, ed., *Shropshire*, REED, 2 vols. (Toronto: Toronto University Press, 1994), I, 277. This payment records the same sum of 40 shillings as was paid in the previous entry to 'my lord president's players'; the preceding entry on the Admiral's at Shrewsbury shows them at that stage to be travelling alone. See also, for example, Henslowe's accounts in his diary 'beginning at Easter 1593 the Queen's Men and my Lord of Sussex together' (Foakes, ed., *Diary*, 21). Andrew Gurr, 'The Chimera of Amalgamation', *Theatre Research International* 18 (1993), 85–93, expresses doubts about how often such arrangements were genuine fusions, although he does note the fact of Alleyn's playing with Strange's.
56. Title page, *Titus Andronicus* [Q] (1594). The Earl of Derby's company was also Lord Strange's and would go on to make up the bulk of the Chamberlain's Men; Pembroke's was a separate body which 'broke' soon after and contributed some members to the Admiral's Men; Sussex's was another company again—they are recorded as playing at the Rose (e.g. Foakes, ed., *Diary*, 21) and had ownership, amongst other plays, of *George-a-Greene, The Pinner of Wakefield* (see Gurr, *Playing Companies*, 182 and also Murray, *English Dramatic Companies*, I, 302–3).

production of Shakespeare's early work was a changeful and unpredictable affair.

The mixture of companies listed on the title page of the *Titus Andronicus* Quarto is highly unlikely to have been envisaged by its author or authors at the point that work began on the play. The level of variables was striking. Yet such company collaborations and textual handovers were not uncommon. A large proportion of the plays dateable to the early 1590s moved from company to company or were performed by temporarily amalgamated troupes. *Fair Em* (one of many imitations of Greene's *Friar Bacon*) went from Sussex's to Strange's; *Bacon* itself may have moved from the Queen's to Strange's, back to the Queen's and finally to the Admiral's Men.[57] Its sequel, *John of Bordeaux*, was acted by the Queen's Men, then Strange's, and then once more by Queen's and Sussex's Men together.[58] Playwrights, Shakespeare included, were thus working with little knowledge of the acting ensemble that would perform their work in the long term.

The distribution of Shakespeare's pre-1594 plays is broadly comparable to those of his contemporaries. Although Greene's phrase, 'Tyger's hart wrapt in a Players hyde' suggests a wish to depict him primarily as an actor, there is no evidence that backs this insinuation: the apology for the offence caused by it was swift and self-abasing in the extreme.[59] Shakespeare was like many grammar school men who came into the theatrical profession. Such writers could have little control over the dramatic fortunes of their output; they had no ownership or ongoing income for plays handed over to the companies' control. Whether as actors or as writers, these men were the employees of the acting companies. By writing their most polished work in carefully printed, non-dramatic poems addressed to patrons, such writers were, at the very least, keeping their options open. In some cases, they seem actively to have sought an escape. The distance between Shakespeare, Munday, and Kyd and university-educated playwrights such as

---

57. See *Fair Em*, ed. Henning, 28. On Greene's, not unfamiliar, accusations of plagiarism see Henning, 65–9. On the movement of *Bacon*, see W. L. Renwick, ed., *John of Bordeaux, or the Second Part of Friar Bacon* (Oxford: Malone Society, 1936). This interpretation is disputed in Scot McMillin, 'The Ownership of *The Jew of Malta*, *Friar Bacon*, and *The Ranger's Comedy*', *English Language Notes* 9 (1972), 249–52, and McMillin and MacLean, *Queen's Men*, 90.

58. *John of Bordeaux, or the Second Part of Friar Bacon* (Oxford: Malone Society, 1936), viii. The editor notes 'this is not the only possible explanation, but it would account for the known facts' (pp. viii–ix).

59. See Henry Chettle, *Kind-Harts Dreame* (1592), A3ᵃ–A4ᵇ, analysed in van Es, '*Johannes fac Totum?*', 564–6.

Greene, Nashe, Marlowe, Peele, and Heywood was not great. Indeed, it was the disappearance of this distinction that *Groats-worth of Wit* was designed, desperately, to resist. Shakespeare's working conditions in the early 1590s were very similar, and in many cases identical, to those of his fellow dramatists.

3

Shakespeare as literary dramatist

It is often said that had Shakespeare died in 1593 along with Christopher Marlowe, it is Marlowe and not Shakespeare who would have gone down as the greater talent.[1] The view is revealing, not so much as an absolute judgement of merit, but as a reflection on literary style. In the first years of the 1590s the conditions under which Shakespeare worked were broadly similar to those of his contemporaries. Through my opening chapter's comparison with Marlowe, I have also begun to suggest that this similarity carried over into style. Authors like Peele, Marlowe, Nashe, and Greene had recourse to the same modes of rhetoric. They explored common poetic forms, myths, and set pieces, imitated freely, and thought relatively little about the interaction of distinctive characters. Paradoxically, changefulness in the conditions of dramatic production enforced generic stability. In their various forms, the handovers between collaborators and acting companies made sustained and complex character development a difficult thing to achieve. Partly as a result, it is often hard to distinguish between individual playwrights in this period. A kind of house style predominates. While this can be brilliant in its set pieces, it is also relatively anonymous when it comes to the shape of plays as a whole.

Above all, sustained and gradual individualization of characters is not found in this drama. This is true of Marlowe's protagonists, where a shift in behaviour, if it occurs (as in the case of Barabas and perhaps Faustus), tends to be sudden and inconsistent. It is still more true of Marlowe's contemporaries. If we look at any work by Greene we find an extraordinary flatness beyond the central character. *Orlando furioso*'s rival courtiers, for example, speak with one voice, and even Orlando himself does not change the way

---

1. The observation is made, for example, by Stanley Wells in *Shakespeare & Co.* (London: Allen Lane, 2006), 78.

he speaks until he switches instantly to madness. During these years, even Shakespeare is limited when it comes to the development of individuality. In comparison with Greene, he stands out as an exceptional genius, but in works like the *Henry VI* plays or *Titus Andronicus* it can still be difficult to identify his distinctive voice.

What is true of possibly co-authored plays such as *Titus Andronicus* is, I suggest, also apparent in other Shakespearean work of the early 1590s—the years when he was working as a freelance and not as a company man. It would be crude to claim 1594 as the moment at which everything changes. The range of 1590s theatrical production is too broad, its survival too piecemeal, to make unequivocal claims about Shakespeare's divergence from the mainstream after this date. Dating Shakespeare's plays is also not straightforward. While most works can be placed either side of the 'company membership' line with confidence, for *The Two Gentlemen of Verona* and *King John* the complexities of possible revision entail a more jagged narrative. There are differences of genre and subject matter to contend with. The later period saw wider developments in literary fashion in which Shakespeare himself inevitably took part.[2] Even so, a corner is turned in 1594 that is worth examining. In order to do this we need, first, to establish a direction of travel in the preceding years.

In the time leading up to the formation of the Lord Chamberlain's Men in 1594, Shakespeare was establishing himself as a literary author. Through *Titus*, most likely written in late 1593, he had probably developed connections with George Peele, a university dramatist. The polished non-dramatic poems of 1593 and 1594 offered comparison with Samuel Daniel and Thomas Lodge. Not unlike Jonson's some years later, Shakespeare's new drama fused classical and Italian influence in a way likely to appeal to elevated tastes. *The Comedy of Errors*, as an almost scene-for-scene transposition of the *Menaechmi*, is the most striking instance of this pattern. Bruce Smith has placed it squarely in the humanist tradition of *commedia erudita*.[3] It is not simply characters and structural elements that are transposed here,

2. Roslyn Lander Knutson, *The Repertory of Shakespeare's Company, 1594–1613* (Fayetteville: University of Arkansas Press, 1991), esp. 168–9, argues that Shakespeare's production followed commercial fashion. James P. Bednarz, *Shakespeare and the Poets' War* (New York: Columbia University Press, 2001) also presents a picture of Shakespeare responding acutely to the work of rival playwrights at the time of the emergence of 'humours' comedy.
3. Bruce R. Smith, *Ancient Scripts and Modern Experience on the English Stage, 1500–1700* (Princeton, NJ: Princeton University Press, 1988), 161.

but a larger classical decorum governing relations between masters and servants and between male and female characters. The play was almost certainly new in 1594. Performed as part of the Gray's Inn Christmas celebrations that year (recorded in *Gesta Grayorum*), it would have rewarded academically minded scrutiny even though proceedings that night were notoriously riotous.[4] Connections with university drama are certainly multiform.[5] The printed text's neat five-act division, and stage directions to the three 'houses', the strict unity of time and place, the absence of music cues all connect it closely to that milieu. Throughout *The Comedy of Errors* Shakespeare artfully expands motifs already present in the minds of his audience. He doubles Plautus' twins, for example—adding two servants to the two masters of the Roman original—drawing explicitly on a secondary source in the Plautine *Amphitryon*. The poetics of such exchanges are characteristically humanist. Through them, Shakespeare set the standard for the neo-classical comedy that Ben Jonson would eventually perfect.

What is so transparently true of *The Comedy of Errors* also applies, in more qualified ways, to Shakespeare's earlier composition *The Taming of the Shrew*. Of all Shakespeare's plays, *Shrew* draws most directly on the Italian drama produced in the mid-century by Ariosto and his contemporaries. Such plays combined the *commedia erudita*, which worked directly from the classics, with the improvised *commedia dell'arte*, with its repertoire of 'masks'. Taking motifs found in Plautus and Terence, these authors increased romantic content by replacing antagonistic wives and courtesans with more spirited citizen heroines.[6] The owner–slave dynamic of the Roman stage was changed into that of master and servant. The characters on which this comedy depended were thus adapted and expanded classical archetypes: the *senex* or old man; *pantalone*, miserly and jealous; *il dottore*, corpulent, pompous, pedantic; *zanni*, the unpredictable and inventive servant; *il capitano*, the braggart soldier; and the *innamorati*, the infatuated couple at

---

4. See *Gesta Grayorum*, ed. W. W. Greg (Oxford: Malone Society, 1914). D. S. Bland, 'The "Night of Errors" at Gray's Inn, 1594', *Notes & Queries* 13 (1966), 127–8, presents reasons for thinking that the night had not been planned as an occasion of disorder.
5. See Frederick S. Boas, *University Drama in the Tudor Age* (Oxford: Clarendon Press, 1914)—the anonymous academic play *Hymenaeus*, surviving in manuscript at St John's Cambridge, is one revealing point of comparison.
6. On the widespread tendency in the Renaissance to heighten the love interest in Plautus and Terence see Robert S. Miola, *Shakespeare and Classical Comedy: The Influence of Plautus and Terence* (Oxford: Clarendon Press, 1994), 7 and *passim*.

the centre of the plot.[7] Such plays were driven by generational conflict, by the action of 'blocking' characters who tried to prevent the happy union, and by the confusion generated through substitution and mistaken identity.

The comedies of Plautus and Terence, modified by the Italian influence above all of Ariosto, were dominant at English universities by the mid-Tudor period. After Gascoigne's *Supposes*, the Italian vogue became strong on the capital's stage. Gosson in *Plays Confuted* (1582) writes of how 'bawdy comedies, in Latin, French, Italian, and Spanish have been thoroughly ransacked to furnish the playhouses in London'. He himself confesses to have penned 'a cast of Italian devises, called *The Comedy of Captain Mario*'.[8] Perhaps included in Gosson's condemnation was *The Buggbears*, of unknown authorship and uncertain date—an adaptation of Grazzini's *La spiritata* (1561), with episodes from *Gl'ingannati* and the *Andria* of Terence.[9] Peele's *Hunting of Cupid* and the anonymous *Dead Man's Fortune*, of which only traces survive, also look to operate in this mode.[10] Survival of such plays in the vernacular is patchy, but there can be no doubt that the same motifs were played over and over again.[11] Indeed, the pleasure of this drama comes in significant part from the reworking of episodes already known by an audience. *The Comedy of Errors*, by interspersing the *Menaechmi* with other (largely classical) models, responds directly to this mode.

Shakespeare's plays often contain traces of the *commedia erudita*. *Twelfth Night*, for instance, with its twin brother and sister, also borrows loosely from the *Menaechmi*.[12] A character such as Dogberry in *Much Ado About Nothing*, equally, might be related back to the type of the *Tartaglia* from the

---

7. For this description see John Lennard and Mary Luckhurst, *The Drama Handbook: A Guide to Reading Plays* (Oxford: Oxford University Press, 2002), 77–9, and John Rudlin, *Commedia dell'arte: An Actor's Handbook* (London: Routledge, 1994).

8. Gosson, *Plays Confuted*, A7[a–b].

9. Boas, *University Drama*, 134.

10. Few firm conclusions can be made about Peele's play. Annotations in Drummond's commonplace book, plus the quotations in *England's Parnassus*, however, suggest Ariosto's play was an important influence upon it. See *The Hunting of Cupid*, a lost play by George Peele, *Collections IV & V* (Oxford: Malone Society, 1911), 307–15. Only the Plot of *Dead Man's Fortune* survives, but this play (probably performed by the Admiral's Men at the Theatre around 1590) clearly had its sub-plot modelled on Italian impromptu farce with the Pantaloon as a stock character (see W. W. Greg, *Dramatic Documents from the Elizabethan Playhouses* (Oxford: Clarendon Press, 1969), I, 94).

11. Miola, *Shakespeare and Classical Comedy*, 8–11, gives a brief overview.

12. For examination of *Twelfth Night* in these terms, see Miola, *Shakespeare and Classical Comedy*, 38–61. Miola goes on to discuss other Shakespearean plays with a Plautine influence, including *Much Ado* and *Merry Wives*.

commedia dell'arte. These, however, are more partial examples. *The Taming of the Shrew* (like *The Comedy of Errors*) comes much closer to absorbing an established world. Gascoigne's *Supposes* (translating Ariosto's *I suppositi*) provided Shakespeare with a much larger architecture of characters, relationships, and scenes: the stratagem of changed places with servant Tranio, rivalry with a rich suitor, and the later ruse of replacing a distant father with a traveller who is afraid of arrest. Behind Ariosto stood a series of classical models, notably *The Eunuch* by Terence. Almost all the constituent parts of *The Taming of the Shrew* thus relate to existing Roman and Italian works.

The Taming of the Shrew does not involve the kind of artful following we find in the later *Comedy of Errors*. Even so, we do find the wholesale borrowing of scenes. One striking instance is that of Vincentio's arrival at his son's house at the opening of Act 5. Here, knocking at a door where he expects a courteous welcome, the father is barred in the most brazen fashion by a man who has stolen his identity. The origins of this situation are there in Plautus' *Amphitryon*, in which the gods Jupiter and Mercury take the form of slave and master and deny the titular hero entry to his house. The master's blustering complaints—'You scoundrel! Still asking me who I am, you death-on-rods, you? By gad, I'll warm you up with a whip today for this insolence!'—set against an impudent doorkeeper placed safely aloft provide the essentials of this comic motif.[13] The situation is transposed directly to Ariosto's plot: in *Supposes* the Siennese traveller who pretends to be Philogano also appears on high to be subjected to impotent raging: 'I wonder at thy impudiencie, . . . ribauld villain, and lying wretch that thou art.'[14] Shakespeare knew the scene in both versions. In *The Comedy of Errors* he would add *Amphitryon* to his material from the *Menaechmi* to replay exactly this motif. Here again we have frantic knocking and expressions of outrage from the substituted party: 'O villain, thou hast stol'n both mine office and my name'; 'You'll cry for this, minion, if I beat the door down.'[15]

In Act 5 of *The Taming of the Shrew*, Shakespeare is thus exploring a situation already familiar to an audience in multiple versions: the substitution

---

13. See *Amphitryon*, trans. Paul Nixon in *Plautus*, Loeb Classical Library, 5 vols. (Cambridge, MA: Harvard University Press, 1961), I, ll. 1029–30.

14. Gascoigne, *Supposes*, 4.5.32–4, in Geoffrey Bullough, ed., *Narrative and Dramatic Sources of Shakespeare*, 8 vols. (London: Routledge and Kegan Paul, 1961), I.

15. *The Comedy of Errors*, Arden2, ed. R. A. Foakes (London: Methuen, 1962); these lines are spoken by Dromio of Ephesus (3.1.44) and Antipholus of Ephesus (3.1.59) respectively. In contrast to the *Suppositi*, *Amphitryon* also involves a double substitution, with Mercury assuming the shape of the slave Sosia and Jupiter taking that of Amphitryon himself.

of *Amphitryon*; the twin masters of the *Menaechmi*; and their combination in
the *Supposes* plot. He follows Ariosto's scenic arrangement very closely, both
in the physical position of the speakers (with the impostor appearing at a
window) and in the building expressions of outrage from the father who is
imposed upon. As in *Supposes*, the confrontation with the impostor, aloft, is
followed by a second with the supposed son upon the main stage. There are
differences. In Shakespeare's version Tranio boldly challenges Vincentio
('Sir, what are you that offer to beat my servant?') rather than simply being
caught on the run.[16] Essentially, however, Shakespeare is willing to transfer
an established situation *en bloc*.

What is true of Act 5's scenic layout is still more apparent on the level of
character throughout the play. Near enough all of *The Shrew*'s protagonists
have an explicitly archetypal quality, drawing very openly on European
tradition. In the 1623 Folio, Grumio is a 'Pantelowne' and the gentleman of
Mantua a 'Pedant'.[17] Other characters also retain the markers of their pre-
existence. Grumio calls Lucentio 'an amorous', paralleling the *commedia*
term 'amoroso'. Hortensio's name was also commonly used for characters
of this type.[18] The wily servants such as Tranio and Grumio, abused by their
masters, are the stock-in-trade of Roman comedy. Baptista and Vincentio,
the stern fathers, are familiar 'blocking' characters. Katerina, as shrew,
combines the abusive wife of classical tradition with domestic stereotype.[19]
As with *The Comedy of Errors*, these characters, relatively fixed in identity,
also move in space defined by the 'houses' of classical comedy. Again, there
is an insistence here on time pressure and penetrable disguise. In consequence, what Manfred Pfister terms the 'qualitative correspondences' of the
protagonists tend to be stable: servants are exposed for their presumption;
superior wit triumphs; excessive personal affectations (notably Kate's) are

---

16. William Shakespeare, *The Taming of the Shrew*, ed. Brian Morris, Arden2 (London: Methuen,
    1981), 5.1.56.
17. *Shrew*, TLN 348 and TLN 2200 and *passim*.
18. Shakespeare, *Shrew*, 1.2.142; on *innamorati* and other types see Rudlin, *Commedia dell'arte*, 106.
19. On the characters' and story's widespread vernacular distribution before Shakespeare's time
    see Jan Harold Brunvand, 'The Folktale Origin of *The Taming of the Shrew*', *Shakespeare
    Quarterly* 17 (1966), 345–9. Such a fusion of influence is not uncommon: Lyly's *Mother Bombie*,
    for example, combines the motifs of Roman New Comedy with vernacular types; the same is
    true of Nicholas Udall's *Ralph Roister Doister*, a possible source for Shakespeare's play. Udall's
    Henrican play, printed in 1566, adopts elements from *Eunuchus* by Terence and *Miles gloriosus*
    by Plautus. On Ralph as a model for Petruchio see Susan E. James, 'A New Source for
    Shakespeare's *The Taming of the Shrew*', *Bulletin of the John Rylands University Library* 81 (1999),
    49–62.

purged.[20] In these ways *The Taming of the Shrew* has deep affinities with classical and Italian comedy. It is perhaps not surprising that John Fletcher, who drew strongly on Italian drama, should have provided a continuation in *The Tamer Tamed*—the only contemporary instance of this happening with a Shakespeare play.

In their scenic arrangement, characterization, and power relationships, *The Comedy of Errors* and *The Taming of the Shrew* show the deep-rooted influence of academic drama. Though written before Jonson's arrival, it would be fair to call them the most Jonsonian of Shakespeare's plays. As such, they provide a useful base from which to explore developments in Shakespeare's later writing. Pfister's terminology is helpful in setting out what is (without pejorative connotation) the wider conventionality of these plays. Related to 'correspondences' (based on class, gender, and wit), Pfister's structural analysis also explores the 'configurations' through which characters exist. In Pfister's formulation 'the identity of a dramatic figure takes shape and evolves in the series of configurations in which it participates, and the contrasts and correspondences that develop between one particular figure and the others become clear when they are meaningfully juxtaposed on stage'.[21] Broadly speaking, *Errors* and *The Shrew* deploy simple or archetypal configurations. The case is clearest with the former, where neat master–servant relations are the driver of the plot. Yet Petruchio, too, is involved in a series of one-to-one exchanges with Grumio and Katerina in which, after conflict, 'qualitative correspondence' is enforced. In larger group configurations (such as the meeting in Act 1 Scene 1 with Baptista and his family) the power balance is stable. Speeches are largely referential in function or expressive in fairly basic terms (displaying Katerina's shrewishness or Tranio's cheek). What Pfister terms 'appellative' and 'phatic' function (involving influence and the establishment of bonds between participants in dialogue) are limited.[22] When Baptista announces his intention 'not to bestow my youngest daughter/ Before I have a husband for the elder' (1.1.50–1) it makes little sense to use this as a key to his character

---

20. See Manfred Pfister, *The Theory and Analysis of Drama*, trans. John Halliday (Cambridge: Cambridge University Press, 1988), 166–70. Pfister's analysis of correspondences in Restoration comedy provides a useful point of comparison for *The Taming of the Shrew*; see Chapter 6 of this study for the less stable correspondences in later Shakespearean drama.
21. Pfister, *Drama*, 172.
22. On the terms 'referential', 'expressive', 'appellative', and 'phatic' see Pfister, *Drama*, 105–13.

or to explore the way he intends to affect individual listeners on the stage. In this respect Shakespeare's later comedy would show notable development.

In its range of characters and in its staging, *The Taming of the Shrew* often advertises convention. Of course, the artifice of the work is central to its conception: the play is announced as a performance from first to last. Yet the act of 'framing' itself is also more widely characteristic of Shakespeare's early literary production, perhaps increasingly so as he grew in status and experience. *The Comedy of Errors* is the Shakespeare play that most emphatically recalls a prestigious earlier work, not in any ironic appropriation but as a model to overgo. If we follow Wells and Taylor's dating, then in the years immediately before he became a sharer in the Chamberlain's Men, Shakespeare produced, in probable succession, *Titus Andronicus*, *Richard III*, *Venus and Adonis*, *The Rape of Lucrece*, and *The Comedy of Errors*.[23] Read in the context of the culture of the 1590s this suggests, if anything, a gradual move towards more erudite and 'artificial' work. It certainly does not appear as a coherent movement towards the Shakespearean qualities of interiority, complex on-stage interaction, and distinctiveness of character. The notion that Shakespeare followed a progressive arc towards that achievement is problematic; it makes little sense to label a work like *The Comedy of Errors* of 1594 as 'immature'. Self-evidently, the early works display extraordinary virtuosity, yet they do contain their achievement within a somewhat different set of parameters. In the period before his attachment to the Lord Chamberlain's Men, Shakespeare did less to distinguish his characters from one another. In individual scenes, the balance of power between speakers is generally predictable. Though always an exceptional writer, Shakespeare, nevertheless, much more consistently, had recourse to standard rhetorical modes and scenic arrangements.

In making such a contrast it is difficult not to give the impression that one is merely being evaluative. A degree of qualitative assessment is perhaps inevitable. But *Richard III*, the most celebrated of the pre-1594 works, can

---

23. Stanley Wells and Gary Taylor, *William Shakespeare: A Textual Companion* (Oxford: Clarendon Press, 1987)—this remains the most exhaustive and authoritative chronology of Shakespeare's work. Chronological ordering in the pre-1594 work is always contentious, but the vast consensus of scholarly opinion is clear about the dating that separates work up to and beyond 1594. Alfred Harbage, *Annals of English Drama*, 3rd edition (London: Routledge, 1989) confirms this division except on *King John*. Harbage dates *Two Gentlemen* later than Wells and Taylor (1593 rather than 1590–1). For both *Two Gentlemen* and *King John*, where the greatest discrepancies exist, there are strong reasons to posit substantial revision of earlier texts. For discussion of this see Appendix.

open the way for a less coloured form of comparison. This work enjoyed continued theatrical success with Shakespeare's move to the Chamberlain's Men, with Richard Burbage coming to be personally associated with its protagonist.[24] Yet at first performance King Richard is at least as likely to have been played by Edward Alleyn. The play's early history, which is shadowy, offers possible ownership by Strange's, Pembroke's, or Admiral's and possible performance by the mixed company of which Alleyn was a part.[25] The play, therefore, is the product of the same material conditions as *Titus Andronicus* or *The Taming of the Shrew* and shares some important structural features with those works. Indeed, given its fifty-two speaking parts, the play in many ways exemplifies Shakespeare's relative early detachment from an individual playing company as a focus for creativity.

Like other pre-1594 plays, *Richard III* shows a marked willingness on the part of its author to draw wholesale on the rhetoric and scenic resources of existing drama. From Richard's opening soliloquy declaring his ill intentions to the catalogue of ghosts who taunt him on the eve of the battle of Bosworth Field, *Richard III* reveals the conspicuous influence of earlier writing: the plays of Seneca, Marlowe, Kyd; the Tudor moralities and the Elizabethan *Mirror for Magistrates*. It trades on those influences persistently in a way that is not found in the works produced in what I will call the 'company period'. It is dominated by its hero-villain protagonist just as Marlowe's plays are centred on Tamburlaine, Faustus, or Barabas. It is also structured quite brilliantly around a series of dramatic and rhetorical set pieces in the way also found in Shakespeare's other early tragedy, *Titus Andronicus*. These features tie the work to a contemporary body of drama, notably the writing of 'arch playwriting poets' such as Kyd, Greene, Peele, and Marlowe. The relative absence of certain features of characterization, I shall go on to argue in the following chapter, also separates this play from the kind of drama that Shakespeare would go on to produce with the Lord Chamberlain's Men. Returning to the structuralist analysis of Pfister, I will suggest that appellative and phatic function, combined with complex configuration, increase markedly between *Richard III* and the post-1594 drama.

24. For Manningham's anecdote about Burbage as Richard versus 'William the Conqueror' see Samuel Schoenbaum, *William Shakespeare: A Documentary Life* (Oxford: Clarendon Press, 1975), 152.
25. See William Shakespeare, *Richard III*, ed. James R. Siemon, Arden3 (London: Methuen, 2009), 44–51, and also the earlier *Richard III*, ed. Antony Hammond, Arden2 (London: Methuen, 1981), 61–8, on early performance history.

What Beckerman calls 'dimension' in dramatic character is expanded as a result.[26]

In exploring the Senecan influence on *Richard III* it is well to bear in mind G. K. Hunter's carefully judged expressions of caution about the impact of Latin tragedy on early modern plays.[27] The roots through which elements such as stichomythia, ghosts, or a devotion to horror made their way to the Renaissance stage were a complex tangle of medieval, early Renaissance, and other classical traditions. Even a work as Senecan as *The Spanish Tragedy* draws as heavily on Ovid as on Roman dramatic precedent.[28] In all kinds of ways, the practicalities and traditions of Elizabethan popular theatre also differed from the rarefied, largely action-free, dramatic context of works such as *Hercules furens*—the distance here is markedly greater than that between classical and Renaissance comedy. *Richard III* is not like *Hercules furens* any more than it is like *The Mirror for Magistrates*. What any specific parallel with Seneca illustrates is not the dominance of a single model, but rather a wider pattern of adaptation and borrowing, a pattern that would change once Shakespeare came to work more closely with an acting company. Crucial to this process is the habitual attraction to established verbal patterning. This is also what distinguishes the Senecanism of *Richard III* from that of *Hamlet*. In the later play Shakespeare's hero recognizes the tropes of the Senecan revenger or the Marlovian hero as clichés: they are precisely the means through which he distances himself from artifice. In the lost original *Hamlet* (as in *Titus Andronicus*, *The Spanish Tragedy*, or in a later play such as Marston's *Antonio's Revenge*) we may take it that Seneca was a much less oppositional element.

Senecan drama, as John Fitch says, 'is a drama of the word'.[29] Fitch's description, which prefaces the new Loeb translation of the tragedies, is worth drawing on at length. As he observes, Seneca is a master of pace and diction (contrasting long, flowing sentences with brief, pithy ones, and

---

26. On this concept see Bernard Beckerman, *Dynamics of Drama: Theory and Method of Analysis* (New York: Knopf, 1970), 214–17.

27. G. K. Hunter, *Dramatic Identities and Cultural Tradition: Studies in Shakespeare and his Contemporaries* (Liverpool: Liverpool University Press, 1978), 'Seneca and the Elizabethans: A Case-Study of "Influence"' (59–73) and 'Seneca and English Tragedy' (174–213).

28. The observation is equally relevant to *Titus Andronicus*. Jonathan Bate, *Shakespeare and Ovid* (Oxford: Clarendon Press, 1993), 196–7 and 215–16, makes a revealing contrast between the place of this influence in *Titus* and the early non-dramatic poetry and the later plays.

29. John G. Fitch, ed. and trans., Seneca, *Tragedies*, 2 vols. (Cambridge, MA: Harvard University Press, 2002–4), 1. The following paragraph closely follows Fitch's analysis.

varying high-flown poetic language with simple direct speech). That pattern, crucially for theatre history, 'invites comparison immediately with the verve of blank verse in the hands of Marlowe or Shakespeare' (1). The flow of Seneca's rhetoric carries easily to the catalogue, which becomes an important source of *inventio*. Standing against this expansiveness is the development of pointed, epigrammatic statements, closely allied to the dramatist's famous *sententiae*. Inner thoughts, as Fitch shows, are revealed through dramatic techniques rarely found in the drama of ancient Greece, but developed thereafter: the aside, the soliloquy, and the entrance monologue in which an entering character voices his thoughts before interacting with others. These rhetorical tendencies match closely with Senecan characterization, which 'makes a virtue of excess, in the sense that its excesses match excesses of emotion and attitude in the *dramatis personae*' (1). Lead protagonists tend to be defined by monomaniac passions: revenge, desire, the will to power. Together with this increased introspection comes an increased isolation of the individual. Not only is the amount of dialogue reduced, but 'the pointed quality of the dialogue in Seneca lessens the sense of real interaction between the characters' (6). The building blocks of Seneca's drama—the five-act structure; the defining entrance monologue; stichomythia; an emphasis on the individual speech or scene and at the expense of gradual characterization (Fitch, 16–21)—are a defining influence on Kyd and Marlowe and also on *Titus Andronicus* and *Richard III*. Rather like the conventions of Plautus and Terence in comedy, they tend to put a limit on dimension in dramatic character.

Richard of Gloucester's entrance in Act 1 Scene 1 ('Now is the winter of our discontent...') is characteristically Senecan in a multitude of ways. It sets a unified mood of foreboding by offering an extended monologue rather than an opening exchange. The tyrant's character, motivation, and intended action are made evident from the first. The whole premise of surface reconciliation hiding deep and disproportionate resentment is also Senecan: Kyd had found that keynote in *Thyestes* and used it for the opening of *The Spanish Tragedy*. As is the case with classical comedy, it is misleading to distinguish between vernacular and direct Latin influence in cases such as this. The devices that are so prominent at the opening of *Richard III* had been rendered in English compositions such as Heywood's translations, in neo-Latin university plays, and in commercial productions on the public stage. In a way that is strikingly similar to *Titus Andronicus*, *Richard III* melds elements derived from Seneca with those mediated by the work of Kyd.

What is important is the underlying matrix that comes to fashion scenic form.

Following *Richard III*'s signature opening, Act 1 Scene 2 again offers a characteristic conjunction of this kind. Here Lady Anne, accompanying the hearse of King Henry VI, is accosted by Richard, who proceeds (outrageously) to persuade her to marriage. The Senecan scene that stands most directly behind this encounter is the wooing of Megara by Lycus in *Hercules furens*—another case of an apparently defenceless widow subjected to a proposal from her husband's enemy.[30] Seneca's Lycus, as a usurper subjected to extensive cursing, has parallels to Richard. His proposal strikes 'exsangues tremor' (a 'cold shudder') in Megara's body, and the scene proceeds through an extensive passage of stichomythia:

LYCUS: Animosne mersus inferis facit?
MEGARA: Inferna tetigit, posset ut supera assequi.
LYCUS: Telluris illum pondus immensae premit.
MEGARA: Nullo premetur onere, qui caelum tulit.
[LYCUS: You take courage from a husband sunk in the underworld?
MEGARA: He visited the underworld to gain the upper world.
LYCUS: He is crushed by the weight of the vast earth.
MEGARA: No burden will crush the one who carried the heavens.]

(Seneca, *Hercules furens*, ll. 422–5)

The exchange, which continues over sixteen lines, clearly lends itself to the historical circumstances of Richard's marriage. Thomas Legge's *Ricardus Tertius*, a neo-Latin tragedy produced at Cambridge around 1580, had already made this exact transposition. Shakespeare probably knew the play. He would certainly follow its practice: the wooing scene comes more directly from Seneca than it does from any chronicle source.[31] As so often, however, there are parallel routes of transmission. *The Spanish Tragedy* has an analogous early encounter where the abandoned Bel-imperia is the subject of equally unwelcome advances from Don Balthazar. True to his Senecan model, Kyd orchestrated this episode through the use of stichomythia:

LORENZO: But here the prince is come to visit you.
BEL-IMPERIA: That argues that he lives in liberty.

---

30. Parallel instances of Senecan stichomythic exchanges involving a comparable context include the exchange between Cassandra and Agamemnon (*Agamemnon*, ll.792–8).
31. Boas, *University Drama*, 126, shows the extensive parallels between the two plays and Legge's exploitation of them.

BALTHAZAR: No madam, but in pleasing servitude.
BEL-IMPERIA: Your prison then belike is your conceit.
BALTHAZAR: Ay, by conceit my freedom is enthrall'd.
BEL-IMPERIA: Then with conceit enlarge yourself again.
BALTHAZAR: What if conceit have laid my heart to gage?
BEL-IMPERIA: Pay that you borrow'd and recover it.
BALTHAZAR: I die if it return from when it is.
BEL-IMPERIA: A heartless man and live? A miracle!
BALTHAZAR: Ay lady, love can work such miracles.

(*Spanish Tragedy*, 1.4.79–89)[32]

In a characteristic alloy, Kyd combines classical drama with the traditions of Renaissance love poetry. The conjunction is a common one. The unknown author of the historical romance *Fair Em* had followed exactly this form for the furtive dialogue between the lovers Mariana and Lubeck; we find it again for Moorton and Sidanen in *John a Kent*; the King and Scythian Queen in *Locrine*; or with the unwelcome attention fixed on Dorothea in *The Scottish History of James the Fourth*.[33] What survives from Seneca, as well as the basic structure of line-by-line exchange, is a concern with elaborate symmetries and dissonances of language. Kyd delights in the building complexity of his stichomythic encounters (later having the exchange between Bel-imperia and her true lover, Horatio, interrupted by the chiming mutters of the onlooking conspirators). Just as with the counter-point between 'earth' and 'heaven' in *Hercules furens*, patterns of chiasmus, paronomasia, and echo are fundamental to the exchanges involving Bel-imperia. In the instance cited, 'prison'/'freedom', 'borrow'/'return', 'death'/'life' are bounced across the lines between the speakers. Elsewhere we have matching stichomythia and three-line structures (2.2.18–31), stichomythia and rhyming couplets (2.4.38–49), and patterns of three-way shared lines (3.11.95–8).

These patterns are also the building blocks of Scene 2 of *Richard III*, in which there are three stichomythic exchanges driven by exactly this Senecan logic of

32. Thomas Kyd, *The Spanish Tragedy*, ed. Philip Edwards, Revels (London: Methuen, 1959); subsequent references are to this edition.
33. See *Fair Em*, ed. Henning, viii.58–67; Anthony Munday, *John a Kent & John a Cumber* (Oxford: Malone Society, 1923), TLN 174–79; Anon., *Locrine* (Oxford: Malone Society, 1908), tln 1508–11, 1520–24; Robert Greene, *The Scottish History of James the Fourth*, ed. Norman Sanders, Revels (London: Methuen, 1970), 4.4.19–24, 5.1.94–99 (with Dorothea in disguise). These situations all have parallels with those in Kyd and Shakespeare—each centring on the overbearing claims of a powerful figure on a loyal woman's love.

reversal and echo. The first sets Anne's previous husband in heaven against her husband-to-be in hell:

RICHARD: For he was fitter for that place than earth.
ANNE: And thou unfit for any place but hell.
RICHARD: Yes, one place else, if you will hear me name it.
ANNE: Some dungeon.
RICHARD: Your bedchamber.
ANNE: Ill rest betide the chamber where thou liest.
RICHARD: So will it, madam, till I lie with you.

(Richard III, 1.2.110–16)

The framework of ideas appears to grow loosely from that same contrast in the exchange between Lycus and Megara:

LYCUS: Cogere.
MEGARA: Cogi qui potest nescit mori.
LYCUS: Effare thalamis quod novis potius parem
   regale munus.
MEGARA: Aut tuam mortem aut meam.
LYCUS: Moriere demens.
MEGARA: Coniugi occurram meo.
[LYCUS: You will be forced.
MEGARA: One who can be forced does not know how to die.
LYCUS: Say what kingly gift should I prepare instead for our new marriage.
MEGARA: Either your death or mine.
LYCUS: You will die, madwoman.
MEGARA: Then I shall find my husband.]

(Seneca, Hercules furens, ll. 426–9)

We need not necessarily think of allusion, but there is a comparable kinship between shared line exchanges in The Spanish Tragedy:

BALTHAZAR: 'Tis I that love.
BEL-IMPERIA: Whom?
BALTHAZAR: Bel-imperia.
BEL-IMPERIA: But I that fear.
BALTHAZAR: Whom?
BEL-IMPERIA: Bel-imperia.

(Spanish Tragedy, 3.10.96–7)

and those that appear later in Shakespeare's scene:

ANNE: Name him.
RICHARD: Plantagenet.
ANNE: Why that was he.
RICHARD: That selfsame name, but one of better nature.
ANNE: Where is he?
RICHARD: Here.   [*She spits at him*
             Why dost thou spit at me?

                   (*Richard III*, 1.2.145–7)

The pattern here—with its rhyming shared lines split by a single pentameter—both concerns and harnesses systems of contrast and parallel. Richard and the deceased Edward are both opposite and 'selfsame', and the verse is all about exploring that paradox. Both lines contain questions, yet Shakespeare wittily employs antanaclasis in pitching 'why' as demonstrative in the first usage with 'why' as interrogative in the second. The contrasting yet echoing 'he' and 'me' of the ending work to the same effect. Seneca's rhetoric, too, is commonly driven by such subtle patterns of opposition. In the long line-by-line exchange between Lycus and Megara that haunts the exchanges between Richard and Anne there is continual play on the contradiction of Hercules' position as slave and god—a paradox with rich potential for Christian analogy of a kind that comes to the surface in Shakespeare's play. In Seneca, as the heat of their exchange builds, Lycus and Megara answer one another successively with rhetorical questions. Lycus asks if a servant ('famulus') is more powerful than his kingship or sceptre ('sceptro'); Megara, repeating the word 'famulus', asks how many kings this 'servant' has delivered to death. Disputing the nature of the key term 'valour', the two use the word in successive lines in descending cases as Megara insists that valour comes in subduing what others fear, even if that fear should be of subjection itself.

It is this architectural quality to the verse, familiar from Seneca and from him through Kyd, that stands at the fore as Shakespeare's Richard parries Lady Anne's expressions of doubt:

ANNE: I would I knew thy heart.
RICHARD: 'Tis figured in my tongue.
ANNE: I fear me both are false.
RICHARD: Then never man was true.
ANNE: Well, well, put up your sword.
RICHARD: Say then my peace is made.
ANNE: That shall thou know hereafter.

RICHARD: But shall I live in hope?
ANNE: All men, I hope, live so.
RICHARD: Vouchsafe to wear this ring.
ANNE: To take is not to give.

(*Richard III*, 1.2.195–205)

The process of give and take in this exchange is consummately choreographed. The trimeter dialogue is the most direct instance of Seneca's verse
in the play. On a gestural level, too, the 'putting up' of Richard's sword is
allusive. The scene of his kneeling (inviting death) in the context of wooing
matches a turning point in Seneca's *Phaedra*. The humanist poetics of such a
speech go beyond imitation. In this sequence 'hear' is set against 'tongue' as
'false' is set against 'true'; 'live' and 'hope' complement 'hope' and 'live' to
form a chiastic matrix; Anne's questioning of Richard's heart is succeeded by
his questioning of hers. Such compositional arrangement is, of course, the
lifeblood of sixteenth-century rhetoric. It is with the same governing
aesthetic (and the same conjunction of eroticism and violence) that Kyd
has Balthazar undercut the protestations of Don Horatio:

HORATIO: On dangers past, and pleasures to ensue.
BALTHAZAR: On pleasures past, and dangers to ensue.

(*Spanish Tragedy*, 2.2.27–8)

Ultimately, it is this rhetorical and scenic premise that connects *Richard III*
with contemporary writing. Throughout this play speakers fall into patterns:
those established by lines preceding theirs and those set by literary precedent. Another dazzling instance comes in Act 4, Scene 4. Here we find a
series of echoing speeches of Senecan cursing succeeded by a second
instance of forced courtship that knowingly evokes the first:

KING RICHARD: Sweetly in force, unto her fair life's end.
ELIZABETH: But how long fairly shall her sweet life last?
KING RICHARD: As long as heaven and nature lengthens it.
ELIZABETH: As long as hell and Richard likes of it.
KING RICHARD: Say I, her sovereign, am her subject low.
ELIZABETH: But she, your subject, loathes such sovereignty.

(*Richard III*, 4.4.351–6)

Stichomythia here extends, almost unbroken, over twenty-six lines. As Richard attempts, perversely, to stake his claim on Lady Elizabeth, Shakespeare

exploits a vast constellation of echoes, both within his own composition and between it and earlier works.

Such concentration on harmonic effect at times brings *Richard III* closer to traditions of non-dramatic poetry. This is true of the play's numerous scenes of cursing, one notable instance being that of Act 5, Scene 3. The catalogue of ghosts that confronts King Richard here also has Senecan parallels.[34] Yet it is the appeals of *The Mirror for Magistrates* that provide the dominant paradigm.[35] The ghosts of young Edward, King Henry, Clarence, and Lady Anne, amongst others, deliver their complaints in a manner that instantly recalls this popular form:

GHOST OF PRINCE EDWARD: Think how thou stab'st me in my prime of youth
  At Tewkesbury. Despair therefore, and die.
GHOST OF HENRY VI: Think on the Tower and me. Despair and die;
  Harry the Sixth bids thee despair and die.
GHOST OF CLARENCE: Tomorrow in the battle think on me,
  And fall thy edgeless sword. Despair and die.
GHOST OF ANNE: Tomorrow in the battle think on me,
  And fall thy edgeless sword. Despair and die.[36]

These pronouncements are part of a wider set of incantations repeated eight times. That insistent concatenation is typical of the *Mirror* tradition. Similar patterns of anaphora are found in *The Rape of Lucrece*, where Shakespeare again reflects on this prototype. What is important at such points is not characterization, but contact with recognized forms.

The plays, like the poems, of the period 1590–4 bristle with imitative overlap and the conspicuous artistry of arranged patterns. In this respect, to say that Shakespeare's constructions in *Richard III* are like those of his contemporaries involves no judgement on merit. Just as the early poems manipulate set structures to unprecedented effect, so these plays commonly make use of existing building blocks to produce extraordinary drama. Yet

34. Agrippina in the pseudo-Senecan *Octavia* is the strongest presence here. Her ghost invokes the presence of other victims of her son, the dictator Nero, as she curses his fortunes (ll. 593–645). Though most now accept the play is not by Seneca, the work is entirely within the tradition of his drama. Comparable revenging ghosts are found in Kyd's *Spanish Tragedy* and the ghosts of Albanact and Corineus in *Locrine*.
35. On the way in which this scene takes the moral (providential) imperatives of the *Mirror* tradition rather than the Senecan emphasis on fate, see Hunter, *Dramatic Identities*, 188–99. Hunter's analysis again stresses the complex fusion of Senecan, Ovidian, and Christian literary influences.
36. Shakespeare, *Richard III*, 5.3.119–20; 126–7; 134–5; 162–3.

they are not, characteristically, plays about the interaction of individuals. This is so in part because the imperatives of their compositional mode tend to push against sustained differentiation. Even Richard (who has a highly developed 'character' with its origins both in the Vice of medieval drama and the 'overreacher' of Marlowe's plays) cannot always be distinguished. At key points, the logic governing his expression is fundamentally inter-twined with that of his interlocutor. Richard's '"Tis figured in my tongue' follows inevitably from Lady Anne's 'I would I knew thy heart.'

A work like *Richard III* is 'literary' in the sense that it derives its impact from an expansive network of high-status classical and vernacular drama. For this reason, it provides an exemplary instance of the way that Shake-speare functioned as a 'literary dramatist' in his early years. The phrase 'literary dramatist' is now closely associated with Lukas Erne, who has set out to counter the orthodoxy that the playwright was indifferent to the printing of his plays. Erne's emphasis on Shakespeare's ambition has cer-tainly been helpful to a renewed understanding of the poet's elite reputa-tion, as has his well-researched contention that a longer 'reading' copy might exist alongside the performance version of a Shakespeare play.[37] It is quite possible that the dramatist circulated a work like *Richard III* in manuscript to potential patrons: its choreographed rhetoric would reward the close scrutiny of such readers. He may likewise have produced a text that was intentionally too long for performance and may thus have envis-aged readers as well as listeners as he composed. This does not mean that Shakespeare sought print for plays with any concerted ambition. The Quarto of *Richard III* that was published and frequently reprinted in the author's lifetime was based on an unreliable memorial reconstruction; Shakespeare did nothing to provide his publishers with a better version, which would not emerge until the Folio of 1623.[38] This is consistent with a general pattern. Ambitious playwrights of the early 1590s such as Shake-speare, Kyd, and Marlowe cannot be shown to have taken active care over the printing of their playtexts. From what we can tell, a work's primary 'literary' reception took place in performance and perhaps also in manu-script circulation; only sporadically would such manuscripts find their way

37. See Lukas Erne, *Shakespeare as Literary Dramatist* (Cambridge: Cambridge University Press, 2003), 23.
38. The precise origin of Q1 is amongst the most difficult questions in textual scholarship, but for this consensus judgement see Wells and Taylor, *A Textual Companion*, 228–32.

to the press. Erne is surely right, however, that Shakespeare should not be categorized from the outset as 'a man of the theatre' and it is possible that he took some satisfaction in seeing his plays in print. His first influences look more 'literary' than 'theatrical' and these qualities of length, virtuosity, and allusiveness made him highly attractive to readers. For this reason the title of 'literary dramatist' suits him well.

Yet in the course of 1594 we see the beginnings of a change in Shakespeare's compositional method, and that shift can be related to an alteration in the conditions under which the playwright produced his work. By 1594 Shakespeare was already established as a very significant poet. As he appears in the dedications of *Venus and Adonis* and *The Rape of Lucrece* he is a would-be 'servant' to his patron the Earl of Southampton—clearly not a sharer (and thus a servant to the Lord Admiral or other company patron, as Alleyn would style himself) but a man who looks to make connections on his own account. These publications establish affinities with Marlowe (whose *Hero and Leander* would come to be dedicated to Walsingham) and Daniel (whose *Rosamond* was offered to the Countess of Pembroke). In producing both a neoteric and an historical poem he was in good company.[39] Shakespeare might easily have taken Munday's or Jonson's trajectory, abandoning piecemeal employment as a player and devoting himself entirely to writing as a professional career. The anxiety about the 'dyer's hand' in Shakespeare's Sonnet 111 shows the possibility of a retained distaste for the 'public means' of the stage. Yet, quite exceptionally, Shakespeare was to cement himself in an acting company: a company that would prove uniquely independent and successful over the ensuing decades.

Had Shakespeare died in 1593 along with Christopher Marlowe the two men would have looked much more alike as writers—their output split between dramatic writing, verse history, and epyllion; their compositional habits structurally in line with those of other professional dramatists such as Peele, Greene, and Munday. Co-authorship was common to both: each had apparently worked with Thomas Nashe.[40] Their output was owned by a diverse group of acting companies: both, in all likelihood, wrote plays with

39. On the wider currency of this pairing see Bart van Es, 'Michael Drayton, Literary History and Historians in Verse', *Review of English Studies* 58 (2007), 255–69.
40. *Dido, Queene of Carthage* was published in 1594 as 'Written by Christopher Marlowe and Thomas Nash. Gent'. Nashe's work is suspected in several other Marlowe plays. As noted in Chapter 1 above, Nashe is one of several suspected collaborators on the *Henry VI* plays (for an overview see Burns, ed., Shakespeare, *King Henry VI, Part 1* (London: Arden, 2000), 73–84).

the lead actor Edward Alleyn in mind.[41] Each had produced an outstanding tragedy with the figure of an overreaching, supremely eloquent anti-hero at the centre. Neither appeared by name in any theatrical document.

Marlowe did not live to see 1594, but for Shakespeare this year would prove pivotal. Of his plays written after this date none would have affinities with its own age in quite the same way. When Shakespeare wrote the dedication to *Lucrece*, entered in the Stationers' Register on 9 May 1594, he was still able to declare 'What I have done is yours, what I have to do is yours, being part in all I have, devoted yours.' By the middle of that year the author was 'part' of another body: the shared entity of the Lord Chamberlain's Men. Thereafter he would be the 'devoted servant' of his fellow sharers and behind them of Baron Hunsdon, Lord Chamberlain. He would not present himself to the world in the conventional form of the dedications of *Venus* and *Lucrece* again. After 1594 Shakespeare's source of income would be quite different (and, it would soon prove, more reliable) than fees for playtexts and the gifts of dedicatees. With that income would come a change in social position, and a change in day-to-day habits of work. Becoming a sharer in the Lord Chamberlain's Men would coincide with a remarkable alteration in the art of Shakespeare's plays.

41. Harbage, *Annals*, has Marlowe producing work for the following performers: *Dido, Queen of Carthage*, 'Chapel'; *1 and 2 Tamburlaine* and *Faustus*, Admiral's; *Jew of Malta* and *The Massacre at Paris*, Strange's; *Edward II*, Pembroke's. Even this picture may suggest too high a level of fixity. The Admiral's Men, for example, appear to have changed considerably in early 1589 by the addition of a group of players from Worcester's Men (see Gurr, *The Shakespearian Playing Companies* (Oxford: Clarendon Press, 1996), 238–9, and also Murray, *English Dramatic Companies 1558–1642* (London: Constable & Co., 1910), I, 114). An account of the likely movement of the plays in this period is provided by Andrew Gurr in 'The Great Divide of 1594', in Brian Boyd, ed., *Words that Count: Essays on Early Modern Authorship in Honor of MacDonald P. Jackson* (Newark: University of Delaware Press, 2004), 29–48. On Alleyn as a star actor for whom playwrights produced specific roles and around whom a company was structured see S. P. Cerasano, 'Edward Alleyn, the New Model Actor, and the Rise of Celebrity in the 1590s', *Medieval and Renaissance Drama in England* 18 (2005), 47–58. The distribution of Shakespeare's plays before 1594 is discussed in Chapter 2 above.

PHASE
II
Shakespeare as company man (1594–1599)

4

Control over casting

It is a striking thing that amongst the first four plays that Shakespeare produced as a sharer in the Lord Chamberlain's Men two should present the process of casting actors for a performance. Dating Shakespeare's plays is not an easy business, but on the dividing line of 1594 there is little dispute.[1] *Love's Labour's Lost* was the first new play that Shakespeare wrote for his company and over the course of the next eighteen months there followed *Richard II, Romeo and Juliet*, and *A Midsummer Night's Dream*. The sub-plot of *A Midsummer Night's Dream*, of course, concerns the preparations of the 'rude mechanicals' for a production of 'Pyramus and Thisbe' for Theseus and his new bride. Though the depiction of rehearsal was not itself unprecedented in English plays, there are signs that the taking on of roles had become a new interest for Shakespeare in the preceding months. *Love's Labour's Lost*, begun during the course of 1594 while the Chamberlain's Men were coming into being, also features amateur acting. It is therefore intriguing that, in his first full year in the fellowship, Shakespeare should twice have concluded a play with a performance that depends on the matching and mismatching of parts.

There are practical reasons why the assignment of roles (so rich with comic potential) should not earlier have been exploited. There was, of course, always a degree of workaday contact between authors of plays and performers. A high proportion of plays were prepared with a specific company in mind: in these cases writers often took a role in the casting of principal parts, with the matching to a player's 'disposition' being counted as a significant skill.[2]

---

1. Wells and Taylor, *William Shakespeare: A Textual Companion* (Oxford: Clarendon Press, 1987); Harbage, *Annals of English Drama: 975–1700*, 3rd edn (London: Routledge, 1989) plus relevant recent editions all give a compositional date range for these plays that makes them early Chamberlain's.
2. Bentley, *The Profession of Player in Shakespeare's Time, 1590–1642* (Princeton, NJ: Princeton University Press, 1984), 206. Stern, *Rehearsal from Shakespeare to Sheridan* (Oxford: Clarendon

Yet while the distance between playwrights and actors should not be exaggerated, it is also easy to overestimate the degree of authorial control, especially in the 1590s. The phenomenon of the attached poetic playwright (writing for only one company) was initiated by Shakespeare: it did not extend elsewhere until the seventeenth century and even then was a more modest and occasional affair.[3] Writers other than Shakespeare may indeed have suggested lead characters to particular sharers, but theirs was a suggestion only and their influence could not have extended to minor parts.

For a writer not in on the process of casting, the character span of *A Midsummer Night's Dream* would have been all but impossible to construct. Stern's study of early modern rehearsal suggests that performance preparation was often a fairly minimal, last-minute affair. Once the physical 'parts' were distributed (in the form of scrolls containing a player's speeches and his cues) the majority of effort appears to have gone into the private 'study' of lines.[4] Evidence from Henslowe's theatre shows that at times 'parts' could be learned even while the play was not yet completed.[5] It is generally clear that contact between an author and rehearsing actors was minimal or non-existent. True, authors could use playbooks to give notes to the actors: William Percy, for example, provided copious suggestions on matters such as tone of voice in the manuscripts he submitted to the master of the child actors at St Paul's.[6] Such instructions, however, suggest distance from, as

Press, 2000), states that 'almost all playwrights with any say in production at all were concerned with the casting of major characters' (84). For instances of this process see Stern *Rehearsal*, 82–7, and Simon Palfrey and Tiffany Stern, *Shakespeare in Parts* (Oxford: Oxford University Press, 2007), 42.

3. The case of Massinger's *Believe as You List* is revealing. The author followed Fletcher as an attached playwright on the Shakespearean model (although not as a sharer) and worked closely with the company. Yet even in his holograph playtext (British Library MS Egerton 2828), where he revised the play following censorship, Massinger did not specify performers. The playhouse scribe added production details later, not only assigning parts to the actors but also amalgamating minor characters when the need for this arose.

4. See Stern, *Rehearsal*, 55–6. The introduction to her study (1–5) gives an overview of other scholars' positions on the likely nature of rehearsal. The 1614 actor's contract for Robert Dawes (Greg, *Henslowe Papers* (London: A. H. Bullen, 1907), 123) details attendance at rehearsal as an established commitment for the players.

5. The evidence here is Daborne's letter to Henslowe dated 25 June 1613 (see Greg, *Henslowe Papers*, 73).

6. Percy was, at the least, an eccentric playwright. The margins of his scripts for *The Wasp* (Alnwick Castle, MS Percy 507), *The Faerie Pastoral* (Alnwick MSS 508 and 509), and *The Cuck-Queanes* and *Mahomet and his Heaven* (Alnwick Castle, MS Percy 509) are crowded with annotations that offer suggestions for production. They are not to be taken as an indication of common practice, but they do reveal something of the process through which a script might be adapted for performance.

much as closeness to, production. The manuscript for Percy's *Mahomet and his Heaven* is prefaced by a letter that hopes for acceptance, but we do not know if the play ever made it to the stage.[7]

It appears likely that by 1592 Shakespeare had already been hired to serve as a performer in some capacity, an arrangement that was not unprecedented amongst playwrights at this time. But he was not a sharer and (given the dispersal of his plays amongst various companies) there was no prospect of sustained control over the performance of his work. By 1595, when he wrote *A Midsummer Night's Dream*, Shakespeare was an established co-owner in the Chamberlain's Men. He knew his company intimately and was clearly central to its business dealings, appearing in the records as receiving payment for their attendance at court. Although the congruence has not been remarked upon previously, it is logical that there should be some connection between this new institutional position and well-attested developments in the playwright's style at this time.

In *A Midsummer Night's Dream* Shakespeare demonstrates, for the first time, a genuinely technical interest in the process of dramatic performance. There can be no doubting that technical facility. Indeed, the rehearsal scenes in this play, along with the exchanges with the players in *Hamlet*, are today a principal source for scholars who wish to reconstruct Renaissance productions.[8] In what is explicitly termed a 'rehearsal', Peter Quince's performers make all the errors of first-time performers. They read their cue lines as part of their scripts and fail to pick up on the cues in the speeches of their fellows (3.1.93–5). They misread their lines (3.1.78), worry themselves over props and staging (3.1.15–20, 48–67), and continually demand alterations to the text (3.1.15–25, 33–45). Both the awareness of such problems and the ability to present this difficult business on the stage must spring from a close connectedness to the performance. Even though Shakespeare must previously have had some experience of acting, his position in a fellowship inevitably drew him closer to the mechanics of a play's transfer to the stage.

Knowledge of the rehearsal process (whatever form that took) is one thing. Authority over casting, however, is more fundamental. Professional

---

7. For the letter to the master of St Paul's see William Percy, *Mahomet and his Heaven*, ed. Matthew Dimmock (Aldershot: Ashgate, 2006), 55–6 and *passim*. In the Alnwick manuscripts of *Pastoral* and *Mahomet* Percy offers alternative staging possibilities for St Paul's and 'for Actors' (meaning adults), so he evidently had no certainty about the performance venue.

8. See, for example, Stern, *Rehearsal*, 22–45, and also Palfrey and Stern, *Shakespeare in Parts*, 66.

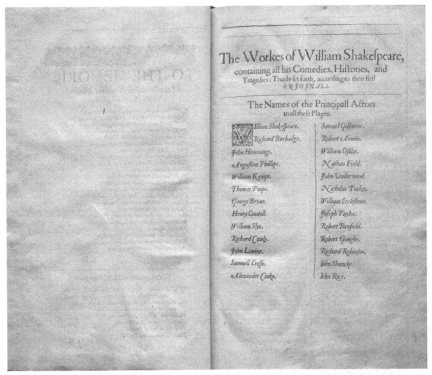

Figure 3. Principal actors listed in William Shakespeare's *Works* (1623), A8^b.

playwrights submitting their manuscripts to a company either produced a
blank list of *dramatis personae* or left the entire business of constructing one to
the in-house bookkeeper.[9] Authority over casting was a company matter
and the process of assigning parts appears to have occurred at a full meeting

9. Blank descriptive lists of characters are found, for example, in the manuscripts of Arthur
   Wilson's *The Inconstant Lady* (*c*.1630) (Folger MS J.b.1) and Walter Mountfort's *The Launching
   of the Mary* (1632) (British Library, MS Egerton 1994, fols. 317–49). The former is a fair copy
   annotated by the author and the latter appears to be an authorial holograph. These became
   working playhouse documents (as opposed to presentation copies) and were thus adapted for
   production by a playhouse scribe. In other comparable instances, such as Anon., *Faithful Friends*
   (Victoria and Albert Museum, MS Dyce 25.F.10), we find a text that is at least partly in the
   author's hand but lacks a list of characters (in the case of *Faithful Friends* one was supplied by the
   playhouse adaptor on a separate sheet). David Bradley, *From Text to Performance in the Elizabethan Theatre* (Cambridge: Cambridge University Press, 1992), 84, notes that a cast list must
   have existed in the hand of the playhouse scribe and this is indeed the case with the unique
   manuscript of Massinger's *Believe as You List* (British Library, MS Egerton 2828). This manuscript features the names of the actors Taylor, Lowin, Benfield, and others in the hand of the
   stage adaptor and is discussed in further detail below.

of the fellowship.[10] This does not mean that authors were necessarily excluded from the decision-making process (the second reading of a play, when
it had been completed, appears to have been an opportunity for poets to make
recommendations for the choice of lead roles). Yet it does indicate a fundamental principle about the ownership of texts. As Stern says, authors were
discouraged from attending group rehearsal and, if they did attend, found the
decisions already taken by the manager and prompter; in this way the power
of the playwright and the theatre were always potentially opposed.[11] While
actors' names do occasionally appear in early theatrical prompt books, or in
printed texts that derive from them, such directions are invariably non-
authorial.[12] As Greg observed, in 'every instance in which an actor's name
appears in a manuscript play it is written in a different hand from the text, or at
any rate in a different ink and style, showing it to be a later addition and not
part of the original composition.'[13] Yet Shakespeare, as a sharer, would at the
very least have been a senior partner in the process of casting his compositions. Indeed he occasionally slipped into the use of performers' names as he
worked. Writing the Dogberry scenes in *Much Ado About Nothing*, he supplied lines for the players Kemp and Cowley rather than using the names of
the characters that they took on.[14] The same is true where Shakespeare writes
'Enter Will Kemp' in the working papers that are the source of the Second
Quarto of *Romeo and Juliet*.[15] The appearance of performers' names in
authorial foul papers is truly exceptional to Shakespeare and it is a process
that we can only identify securely in the years after 1594.[16]

---

10. On the playhouse plot as a likely tool in this process, with a very clear description of the role of
    plotter in casting, see Bradley, *Text to Performance*, 78–85.
11. Stern, *Rehearsal*, 12.
12. For a survey of actors' names' appearances in prompt books, see Charles H. Shattuck, *The
    Shakespeare Promptbooks: A Descriptive Catalogue* (Urbana: University of Illinois Press, 1965)
    plus 'The Shakespeare Promptbooks: First Supplement', *Theatre Notebook* 24 (1969), 5–17.
13. W. W. Greg, *Dramatic Documents from the Elizabethan Playhouses* (Oxford: Clarendon Press,
    1969), II, 216.
14. The first printed text of the play (Q) was set from authorial foul papers untouched by a
    playhouse scribe (see William Shakespeare, *Much Ado About Nothing*, ed. Claire McEachern,
    Arden3 (London: Methuen, 2007), 128–33). In this text, *Much Ado About Nothing* (1600),
    Dogberry and Verges repeatedly appear as 'Kemp' and 'Cowley' (G3^b–G4^b).
15. The second printed text of this play (Q2) was set, at least in large part, from authorial foul
    papers. In this text, *Romeo and Juliet* (1599), we find the entry of Peter marked '*Enter Will
    Kemp*' (K3^b). For details see William Shakespeare, *Romeo and Juliet*, ed. Brian Gibbons,
    Arden2 (London: Methuen, 1980), 13–23.
16. A particularly thorny issue here is the status of the actor's names (the name 'Sinklo' and probably
    that of two others) in the Folio *Henry VI Part 3*. The origin of this specification (whether authorial
    or coming from the bookkeeper) is the subject of extensive discussion in *King Henry VI, Part 3,*

Figure 4. Quarto text of William Shakespeare's *Much Ado About Nothing* (1600), G3^b–G4^a.

The appearance of casting scenes in *Love's Labour's Lost* and *A Midsummer Night's Dream*, then, is unlikely to be coincidental. For in these plays Shakespeare was experimenting with a new kind of comedy, one that exploited acting with and against physical type. It would seem that the playwright relished this new technical capacity, which was subtly different from what we find in corresponding scenes by Shakespeare's contemporaries. In Anthony Munday's *John a Kent*, for example, we also find a rehearsal by a group of rustic characters. Here Turop, in the main clown role, orchestrates a performance by his 'fellow mates'. Yet Munday, in contrast to Shakespeare, can make nothing of distinctions between more minor performers.[17]

ed. John D. Cox and Eric Rasmussen, Arden3 (London: Thompson, 2001), 148–76, but the editors decide against making conclusions. I suggest that it is much more likely that the specification of Sincler is a later addition. There is certainly nothing physically distinctive about the keeper as a character that would have made the playwright think of the emaciated Sinklo/Sincler, whose later significance in Shakespeare's drama is discussed below.

17. See Anthony Munday, *John a Kent & John a Cumber* (Oxford: Malone Society, 1923), TLN 334–404.

What is different about *A Midsummer Night's Dream* is the exploitation of specificity, and at the centre of the matrix that Shakespeare was able to use in the play stood William Kemp. We know a good deal about him, especially since the pioneering work of David Wiles.[18] He was a generation older than Richard Burbage and Shakespeare, having been in Lord Leicester's service as a performer during the Earl's campaigns in the Low Countries in the mid-1580s. At one point he is recorded delivering letters on the Earl's behalf to Sir Philip Sidney. Kemp had also been part of the troupe of English actors that, at the end of that decade, visited the King of Denmark at the palace of Elsinore. He was a man of enormous fame and significant connections and would therefore have been the Lord Chamberlain's Men's pre-eminent star.[19]

As such, Kemp arrived with an existing on-stage persona. His 'Applauded Merriments' advertised with the play *A Knack to Know a Knave* are testament to this reputation, which centred in part on his exceptional skill as a dancer of jigs. Throughout the life of the early theatre Kemp continued to live on in the national imagination, being lauded in Heywood's *Apology* as the successor to Tarlton and appearing in Rome in a scene of *The Travels of the Three English Brothers* even after his death.[20] When, at a late stage in the actor's career, Henslowe paid 30 shillings 'to bye A sewte for wm kempe' he seemed already to acknowledge this super-fictive quality. The *Diary*'s usual practice is to link costumes to assumed characters, but the actor seems himself to have become such a 'character' in the course of his life.[21]

18. David Wiles, *Shakespeare's Clown: Actor and Text in the Elizabethan Playhouse* (Cambridge: Cambridge University Press, 1987). Much of my treatment of Kemp is in some way indebted to this study.

19. Edwin Nungezer, *A Dictionary of Actors* (Ithaca, NY: Cornell University Press, 1929), records the fact of Kemp's London reputation by 1590, Nashe giving a clear sense of him as principal comedian.

20. Heywood, *An Apology for Actors* (1612), reports that Kemp succeeded Tarlton both 'in the people's general applause' and 'in the favour of her Majesty' (E2[b]). On the encounter in Rome (John Day and others, *Three English Brothers* (1607), E4[a]–F1[a]) and the way it defines Kemp see David Mann, *The Elizabethan Player* (London: Routledge, 1991), 68–71. Katherine Duncan-Jones, 'Shakespeare's Dancing Fool', *TLS*, 13 August 2010, argues that the description 'Kemp, a man' in the register of burials at St Saviour's, Southwark, on 2 November 1603, is so vague that it could not refer to the death of the famous actor. In her assessment, therefore, Kemp would still have been alive when *Three English Brothers* was performed. Against this, Alan H. Nelson, in his presentation 'Henslowe and Alleyn in Southwark' at the Shakespeare Association of America annual meeting of April 2012, noted that the record of burial is more specific than is reported by Duncan-Jones, in fact specifying the name William. According to Nelson, 'a man' is used for all adult males in the register, irrespective of fame or occupation, simply as a designation of gender. It would not, therefore, be ill suited to someone of Will Kemp's fame.

21. Foakes, ed., *Diary* (Cambridge: Cambridge University Press, 2002), 215.

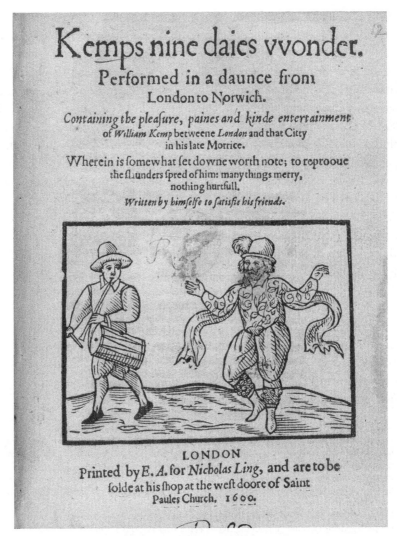

Figure 5. Title page of William Kemp's *Nine Days Wonder* (1600).

Above all, it is Kemp's physical capacity, his strength and energy, that comes through from the record. His *Nine Days Wonder*, written in 1599, famously records the morris dance that he performed in day-stages from London to Norwich. Throughout, Kemp's prodigious stamina is a principal point of interest. Arriving in Norwich, he performs a leap that is recorded for posterity, the buskins in which he performed it being left as memento on the wall of the city's guildhall.[22] What is also clear from the way Kemp writes and presents himself is his role as a plain speaker and deflator of pretension. That role is one taken from a position of knowledge. Leaving London and refusing the offer of a drink, for example, Kemp remarks that drinking 'stands not with the congruity of my health', and then catches himself, as it were, in a moment of pomposity with the following correction:

> Congruity said I? How came that strange language in my mouth? I think scarcely that it is any Christen word, and yet it may be a good word for ought I know, though I never made it, nor do very well understand it; yet I am sure I have bought it at the word-mongers, at as dear a rate, as I could have had a whole 100 of Bavines at the wood-mongers.[23]

In *Nine Days Wonder* Kemp presents himself as the spokesperson and embodiment of a plain, pleasure-loving Englishness. In the undergraduate *Parnassus* plays, as I have noted, Kemp is mocked for his lack of learning, but there is perhaps also an awareness on the part of the dramatist that this ignorance is part of an act:

> KEMP: Few of the university [men] pen plays well, they smell too much of that writer *Ovid*, and that writer *Metamorphoses* . . . our fellow *Shakespeare* puts them all down.[24]

The actor is certainly presented here as one of the principal artistic forces in the company: a trainer of fellow performers and commissioner of plays. His working relationship with 'our fellow Shakespeare' is understood as a close one. It is also a partnership that specifically facilitates a move away from an academic and artificial dramatic style.

We can be near enough certain that the part of Bottom was written for this actor. An awkward stumbling over technical words is one of his comic mainstays: Dogberry (designated as a Kemp role in the manuscript from which the printers set the *Much Ado* Quarto) is the most elaborate expression of that particular line. The contrast with Robert Armin (who went on to replace him) is significant. Parts written for Armin (such as Touchstone, Feste, and the Fool in *Lear*) are marked by a particular linguistic fluency and, in the latter two cases, by an ability to sing.[25] Bottom's malapropisms ('I will move storms, I will condole in some measure' (1.2.22–3), 'we may rehearse most

22. William Kemp, *Nine Days Wonder* (1600), D1[a].
23. Kemp, *Wonder*, A3[b]–A4[a].
24. Anon, *Second Part of the Return*, in *The Three Parnassus Plays*, ed. J. B. Leishman (London: Nicholson & Watson, 1949), 4.3, TLN 1766–9.
25. On Armin's roles see Chapter 9 below.

obscenely and courageously' (1.2.100–1)) are typical of the kind of humour that Shakespeare crafted for Kemp.[26] Typical, too, is the dogged optimism of this character. Kemp's passion for taking on wagers and physical challenges drives the narratives of *Nine Days Wonder*.[27] There is a version of this in Bottom's boundless enthusiasm for taking on all of the parts in 'the most lamentable comedy and most cruel death of Pyramus and Thisbe' (1.2.11–12): he wishes not only to act Pyramus the lover, but also a great tyrant, the god Hercules, the lady Thisbe, and—finally—the lion as well.

Kemp's physicality is a part of what places him comically out of context. The bellowing of the weaver has to differ as starkly as possible from the song that the enchanted Titania thinks she hears:

TITANIA: I pray thee, gentle mortal, sing again:
   Mine ear is much enamour'd of thy note;
   So is mine eye enthralled to thy shape.

        (*Midsummer Night's Dream*, 3.1.132–4)

This exchange depends on a mismatch between what the audience and an on-stage character is hearing and seeing. The same thing happens when Quince sets out Bottom's suitability to play the lover's role:

QUINCE: You can play no part but Pyramus: for Pyramus
   is a sweet-faced man; a proper man as one shall see
   in a summer's day; a most lovely, gentleman-like
   man: therefore you must needs play Pyramus.

        (*Midsummer Night's Dream*, 1.2.79–82)

This description evidently functions as foil to Kemp's visual performance. The lack of beauty and eloquence (combined with physical vigour) are again an established part of Kemp's crafted persona. In *Nine Days Wonder* the player writes that one 'looks as soon to see beauty in a blackamoor, or hear smooth speech from a stammerer, as to find any thing but blunt mirth in a morris dancer, especially such a one as *Will Kemp*' (A3[b]). As Quince and

---

26. William Shakespeare, *A Midsummer Night's Dream*, ed. Harold F. Brooks, Arden2 (London: Routledge, 1979)—subsequent references are to this edition, checked against the more recent Oxford text.

27. See, for example, Kemp, *Wonder*, B3[a–b], where the author triumphs first over 'a lusty tall fellow, a butcher by his profession, that would in a Morrice keep me company' and then does the same against 'a lusty country lass': 'for indeed my pace in dancing is not ordinary'.

Titania elaborate on these conspicuously absent virtues, Kemp no doubt roared and gurned to outrageous effect. The indecorousness of Kemp's presence links to a more profound aspect of his characterization. As Patrice Pavis writes in *Analyzing Performance*, 'the actor's body is not simply a trans-mitter of signs, a semaphore tuned to throw out signals in the direction of specators', it is 'already impregnated by the surrounding culture' and thus 'implicated in the process of signification'.[28] This physicality and connection with audience is something that Shakespeare could exploit much more exten-sively as a company playwright. Across all of Kemp's major roles—Lance, Bottom, Gobbo, and Dogberry—there is an element of pathos as well as comedy that stems from a discrepancy between character and circumstance. Because the part is an absurd one it is easy to underestimate it as an artistic achievement, but Lytton Strachey had a serious point when he described Bottom as 'the first of Shakespeare's master-pieces in characterisation'.[29]

A Midsummer Night's Dream shows the potential released by Shakespeare's writing for a known actor. The specific adaptation to Kemp, however, is not the transformative element of the play's dramaturgy. Before setting out what *is* new about Shakespeare's control over casting as a sharer it is worth surveying common practice amongst contemporary playwrights, both before and after the year 1594.

Plays throughout the early modern period could be constructed to accommodate the talents of leading players. This was evident even in the early part of the decade, when Edward Alleyn, on the basis of his perform-ance in *Tamburlaine*, stimulated the composition of an entire generation of cosmic overreachers.[30] Shakespeare, like other authors, probably catered to this market: his *Titus Andronicus* was first performed by an ensemble in which Alleyn featured and its transgressive villain Aaron looks very much as if it was written with Alleyn in mind.[31] Famous actors were easy to typecast

28. Patrice Pavis, *Analyzing Performance: Theater, Dance, and Film*, trans. David Williams (Ann Arbor: University of Michigan Press, 2003), 66. An analysis like Pavis's classic account of the Louis de Funès in *L'Avare* (*Analyzing Performance*, 69–86) could hypothetically have been applied to Kemp, but the historical resources are limited. For a revealing comparative account based mainly on Peter Brook's 1970 Royal Shakespeare Company production of the play see Robert Hapgood, *Shakespeare the Theatre-Poet* (Oxford: Clarendon Press, 1988), 25–32, and also Peter Brook's account of the process of casting and rehearsal of several Shakespeare plays in *The Empty Space* (New York: Macmillan, 1968), 103–30.

29. G. L. Strachey, 'Shakespeare's Final Period', *The Independent Review* (August 1904), 401–18 (at 417).

30. For details see S. P. Cerasano, 'Edward Alleyn, the New Model Actor, and the Rise of Celebrity in the 1590s', *Medieval and Renaissance Drama in England* 18 (2005), 47–58.

31. As noted in Chapter 1 above, Aaron's characterization is closely based on a number of Marlowe's stage Machiavels and also parallels the black-skinned Muly Mahamet in Peele's *The Battle of Alcazar* (a part that Alleyn certainly played, as is evident from the surviving Plot).

and comic performers, too, could set models for composition. Tarlton and Kemp improvised and wrote their own material—it was thus inevitable that writers from outside their companies would supply characters and plotlines for them to exploit. There is substantial evidence for this kind of tailored composition. Various writers in the seventeenth century, for example, wrote roles to suit Robert Armin, who replaced Kemp in the Chamberlain's Men. The jester Passarello in Marston's *The Malcontent* (adapted in 1604) provides one instance of a character specifically written for this actor, and something similar seems to have happened with the creation of Abel Drugger in Jonson's *The Alchemist*.[32] Even prior to 1594 it is likely that Shakespeare had written specifically for Kemp's talents. Lance in *The Two Gentlemen of Verona* looks to be an instance of Kemp's brand of physical humour and it is probable that the routine of his exchanges with the dog Crab (2.3.1–30) was adapted from an existing act.

The modelling of parts to players, then, was an established practice. Yet for an ordinary playwright (with no stake in a company) the personal characteristics of performers were as much a constriction as an artistic resource. Adaptation to individual actors often occurred *after* a play was submitted to a company. This may in fact have happened with *The Two Gentlemen of Verona*, because the scenes involving Lance are only minimally integrated with the main body of the play.[33] It was certainly the case with Shakespeare's scenes for the co-authored manuscript of *Sir Thomas More* (which was probably produced in the early 1590s): in these a clown's part was added after he had completed his work.[34] The example of *The Malcontent*'s adaptation for the King's Men in 1604 confirms the fact that player-specific tailoring could be the responsibility of someone other than the original author. At least some of

In mid-1593, when *Titus* was most likely under construction, Alleyn was travelling with members of Strange's/Derby's Men (see Letter from Edward Alleyn to Joan Alleyn, 2 May 1593, in W. W. Greg, ed., *Henslowe Papers* (London: A. H. Bullen, 1907), 34). These were among the original cast of the play.

32. For details on Passarello see John Marston, *The Malcontent*, ed. George K. Hunter, Revels (Manchester: Manchester University Press, 1975), xlvi–liii, and Jane Belfield, 'Robert Armin as Abel Drugger', *Notes & Queries* 28 (1981), 146. For further discussion see Chapter 9, 'Robert Armin', below.

33. For the evidence behind this thesis, which was originally forwarded by Clifford Leech, see William Shakespeare, *The Two Gentlemen of Verona*, ed. William C. Carroll, Arden3 (London: Thompson, 2004), 80–4; 123–30. It is also supported by Wiles, *Clown*, 73–4. Stern, *Rehearsal*, 14, shows that revision in playtexts of the period is often concentrated on individual parts.

34. On the date of this manuscript, which is notoriously difficult to establish, and for a wider discussion of what it shows about Shakespeare's involvement with co-authorship, see Chapter 14 below.

this work's additions were produced by John Webster and not John Marston, who had lost control of the text. This alienation of manuscripts from their creator was evidently common practice amongst companies and it is frequently recorded in Henslowe's *Diary*.

Even when authors were still involved when their play went into production their impact on the company's choices was advisory at best. The late instance of Philip Massinger's *Believe as You List* is a particularly well-documented example, because the playhouse manuscript survives. By the time this play was written Massinger was contracted as a regular playwright for the King's Men. He must have worked with some awareness of the actors: his main comic role, the fat Berecinthius, for example, was probably always intended for the actor John Lowin, who had played Epicure Mammon in Jonson's *The Alchemist*.[35] Yet, even so, Massinger did not feel confident enough to mark Lowin's name in his manuscript; it was the playhouse adaptor who recorded the casting decisions and made the final adjustments to the playwright's text. Elsewhere, that same adaptor had no qualms about removing physical specificity when this detail did not suit the company's plans. In the key recognition scene featuring the hero, Antiochus, almost all of Massinger's language about his features was deleted, presumably because it did not match with the appearance of Joseph Taylor, to whom the actors had assigned this role.[36] Another revealing instance is the list of *dramatis personae* on the opening page of the manuscript of William Percy's *Mahomet and his Heaven*. Here Percy's notes repeatedly offer suggestions but also uncertainty about the physical characteristics of his performers. Thus the Queen of the Desert may be 'low of stature' or 'taller' depending on whether the company can get 'so convenient an actor' to play the part.[37]

As a sharer-playwright Shakespeare would have suffered none of this uncertainty. What is special about *A Midsummer Night's Dream*, therefore, is the depth and above all the *breadth* of adaptation to company. Given Shakespeare's position within a stable fellowship, it became possible for him not just to construct physically distinct characters, but to develop

35. On this earlier casting see James A. Riddell, 'Some Actors in Ben Jonson's Plays', *Shakespeare Studies* 5 (1969), 284–98 (at 285).
36. British Library, MS Egerton 2828, fol. 8ᵃ; fol. 29ᵇ. This play was first submitted to the Master of the Revels for censorship in January of 1631 [New Style] and rejected; the surviving manuscript is the revised version passed by Sir Henry Herbert in May of that year. For details see Philip Massinger, *Believe as You List*, ed. Charles J. Sisson (Oxford: Malone Society, 1927).
37. Alnwick Castle, MS Percy 507, *Mahomet*, fol.1ᵃ [foliation mine].

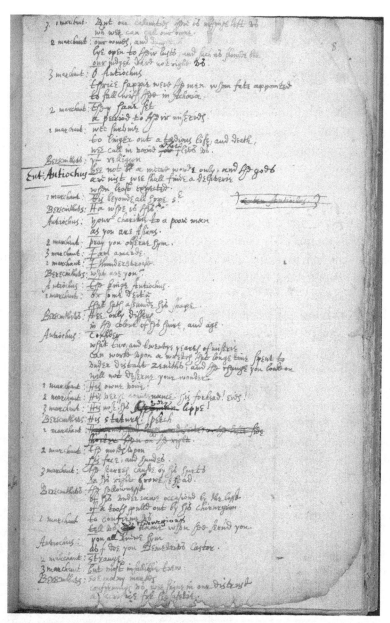

Figure 6. Authorial holograph of Philip Massinger's *Believe as You List*, British Library, MS Egerton 2828, fol. 8[a].

exchanges *between* characters where physical distinction was part of the dramatic effect. That fact, simple as it might seem, constitutes a formative element in the creation of psychological complexity. In cases such as Lance, Passerello, and Berecinthius we see adaptation of single characters to single dominant traits. In common with Marlowe's anti-heroes, such figures have a stand-alone quality: they are extractable as independent entities, little damaged by the removal of their interlocutors. This is not the case with the characters that Shakespeare introduced in his position as a sharer from 1594 onwards: these figures emerge through their interaction with other speakers on the stage.

As Manfred Pfister makes clear, the development of 'depth' in on-stage characterization is significantly dependent on the balance between 'telling' and 'showing': characterization is partly 'explicit' (i.e. what characters tell us about themselves and what other characters tell us about them). But it is also 'implicit':

> Implicit-figural characterization techniques are only partially verbal because a dramatic figure is presented implicitly not only through what it says and how it says it, but also through its appearance, its behaviour and the context within which it operates (clothing, properties, interiors, etc.).... The decision to favour the predominance of implicit techniques is thus tantamount to emphasising the 'showing' of specific things and encouraging the audience to think for itself, rather than the more abstract 'telling' that does not require much audience involvement. In rhetorical terms, the justification for such a decision is the greater degree of 'evidence' and sensuous immediacy, and thus the greater persuasive powers wielded by techniques that are concrete and implicit.[38]

A conflict between 'explicit' and 'implicit' characterization is particularly conducive to dramatic complexity. The case of Peter Quince's attempt to persuade Bottom is a straightforward instance. As Quince elaborates Pyramus' qualities ('a proper man as one shall see in a summer's day...') he develops what Beckerman terms 'length' and 'depth' both in his own and in Bottom's dramatic character.[39] It is easy to over-elaborate, but the exchanges here also illustrate the 'polyfunctionality' that Pfister pinpoints

38. Manfred Pfister, *The Theory and Analysis of Drama*, trans. John Halliday (Cambridge: Cambridge University Press, 1988), 190. Pfister prefers the term 'dramatic figure' to 'character' because this makes clear that we are talking about a theatrical effect rather than a psychological reality.
39. Bernard Beckerman, *Dynamics of Drama: Theory and Method of Analysis* (New York: Knopf, 1970), 214–17, cited in Pfister, *Drama*, 176–7.

as necessary for long and deep characterization. Quince's praise is appella-tive (if ironically so) in its attempt to depict Bottom. It is simultaneously expressive (reflecting the speaker's cajoling manner), phatic (working to effect connection), and metalingual (encoding Quince's character through his repetitive vocabulary).[40] These functions ensure that Bottom's status amongst his fellows subtly develops over the course of the scene. Such dynamic correspondences contrast with the more stable qualitative relationships in earlier drama, both by Shakespeare and by his contempor-aries.[41]

This interest in the shifting status of dramatic figures is, I suggest, intim-ately connected to the physical specificity of the characters in *A Midsummer Night's Dream*. It is not just in the case of Nick Bottom that Shakespeare is working with and against a set of known bodily characteristics. In the scene where Peter Quince assigns the parts of the play, we thus also encounter Francis Flute, who must play Thisbe but pleads 'Nay, faith, let not me play a woman: I have a beard coming' (1.2.43-4). The actor performing the part of Flute must appear physically girlish, even as he asserts his masculinity. Clearly the comedy of this interaction is dependent on a mismatch between a dramatic figure's 'self estimation' and the 'reality' of an external character's opposing estimate. It is precisely this conflict between explicit and implicit characterization that is essential for the creation of Beckerman's concepts of 'length' and 'depth'.

With Flute it appears that Quince has done the job of casting rather well. Conversely, among the other 'rude mechanicals', the comic energy derives from Quince's failure. Robin Starveling is set down to be Thisbe's mother; Snug the joiner must take the lion's part. These two performers (as is clear from their characters' names) are comically undernourished: the matronly older woman and the man-eating lion, in contrast, are demonstrably cap-acious parts.

Very likely the role of Starveling was taken by John Sincler, a hired man of the Chamberlain's company, who was famously emaciated.[42] As such,

---

40. For illustrations of these terms see Pfister, *Drama*, 105-17.
41. On the concept of qualitative correspondences see Pfister, *Drama*, 166-70. Inevitably, such a comparative evaluation may appear impressionistic. See, however, my discussion of corres-pondences in *The Taming of the Shrew* and *The Comedy of Errors* in Chapter 3 above.
42. On Sincler (also named Sinclo or Sinklo) see Palfrey and Stern, *Shakespeare in Parts*, 44. Stern and Palfrey speculate that Shakespeare developed characters by expanding standard roles (such as the 'braggart' role that sometimes appears in working documents) with individual actors in

this performer provides a telling instance of the way in which physical specificity could become a resource for Shakespeare as sharer-playwright. In two of the plays composed before 1594 we also find actors' names that made their way by accident into the playtext, and both of these feature Sincler. The source of these directions cannot be determined with certainty, but they are likely to be the bookkeeper's jottings, perhaps made in preparation for a later performance of these plays.[43] It is revealing that in these pre-1594 appearances Shakespeare does nothing to exploit Sincler's physical characteristics. In the Folio text of *Henry VI Part 3* one of the keepers who appear with crossbows is recorded as 'Sinklo' (3.1.0SD).[44] Yet neither of the men in this scene has a distinctive appearance. 'Sincklo' also appears in the Folio *Shrew* in a speech heading for the Second Player.[45] It is conceivable that this role does have an element of performer specificity (the Lord remembers him as having 'play'd a farmer's eldest son' who 'woo'd the gentlewoman so well' (IND. 1. 82)), but if this is an in-joke on one of Sincler's earlier appearances it is one that the dramatist failed (or, more likely, was unable) to utilize for dramatic effect. From what we know of John Sincler, the role of successful lover would be comically ill suited; it would have been rather neat to set the memory of this past performance as a suitor against his current part in the play that is to be put on for Christopher Sly. In spite of this, the Second Player's reply ('I think 'twas Soto that your honour means' (IND. 1. 86)) closes down such possibilities: there is no further development in this role.

Sincler is a minor actor on whom we happen to have quite a lot of detail. The way that his roles change from the early 1590s to the Chamberlain's Men period is an indicator of the new conditions governing Shakespeare's author-

---

mind. Sincler, they suggest, may have played Aguecheek, Cassius, Slender, and Starveling, characters that all appear to be intended as physically thin.

43. In both cases these are texts in the 1623 Folio. They were taken either from newly transcribed manuscripts originating in foul papers or from papers that had been in the company's possession for more than three decades. For analysis see *King Henry VI, Part 3*, ed. Cox and Rasmussen, 148–76, and *The Taming of the Shrew*, ed. Brian Morris, Arden2 (London: Methuen, 1981), 2–12. The playbook of Massinger's *Believe as You List* again provides a useful point of comparison. Here the bookkeeper inserts actors' names into the author's manuscript when he is tidying up the play for performance and amalgamating some parts (for discussion see Massinger, *Believe as You List*, ed. Sisson, xxii).

44. See *Henry VI Part 3* in *The First Folio of Shakespeare*, Norton Facsimile, prepared by Charlton Hinman, 2nd edn (New York: Norton, 1996), TLN 1396–1499. The name is used nine times in the scene. All subsequent references to the 1623 Folio *Works* are to the Norton Facsimile.

45. *The Taming of the Shrew* in *First Folio*, TLN 99.

ship. From what we can reconstruct, Sincler moved from Strange's Men in the early 1590s to Pembroke's and then finally to the Chamberlain's, where he long remained a hired man.[46] As we have seen, in plays written before 1594 the parts that he took were not written to exploit his distinctive thinness. Yet in *Henry IV Part 2* (written around 1597 for a now well-established Chamberlain's company) the case is quite different. This is the third of the four times that the player's name appears in a printed playtext.[47] Unlike the two previous instances, this is a definitive case of an authorial working manuscript and it is clear that, as he composed, Shakespeare thought with intensity about the physical characteristics of the performer for whom he wrote the part. In just one short scene the First Beadle is described as a stick-like 'nut-hook', 'tripe-visaged rascal', 'paper-faced villain', 'thin man in a censer', 'filthy famished correctioner', 'starved bloodhound', 'goodman death, goodman bones', 'atomy', and 'thin thing'.[48] The visual narrative of this exchange is compelling: a heavily pregnant Doll Tearsheet (bulked out, according to the Beadle, by a cushion) stands in contrast to the skin-and-bones Sincler. It is a scene that could only have been composed by an author who had a specific company in mind.

This same sense of a matrix of well-known actors is essential to the composition of *A Midsummer Night's Dream*. It is there in the rehearsal scenes and also in the confrontations between Hermia and Helena. Boy actors playing women and children were, like many hired men, committed to a company for years.[49] As with the later case of Doll Tearsheet haranguing Sincler in the role of Beadle, the standoff between Hermia and Helena is premised on the opposition of actors whom the playwright has in mind as he constructs his scene. Where the former is dark and diminutive

46. Sincler first appears alongside Burbage (and many other future Chamberlain's Men) in *The Second Part of the Seven Deadly Sins* plot (see Greg, *Henslowe Papers*, 129–32). On Sincler's likely movements and his appearance in these texts see Andrew Gurr, 'The Work of Elizabethan Plotters, and *2 Seven Deadly Sins*', *Early Theatre* 10 (2007), 67–87 (at 81–2).

47. The final appearance is the Induction to Marston's *The Malcontent*, an addition specifically tailored to the company by John Webster, which therefore made much of Sincler's thinness (Marston, *Malcontent*, Induction ll. 17–137).

48. William Shakespeare, *King Henry IV, Part 2*, ed. A. R. Humphreys, Arden2 (London: Methuen, 1981), 5.4.8–9, 11, 19, 21, 27–30.

49. There is a good deal of evidence for long-term connections between boy apprentices and their masters. Boy players were attached to an established sharer rather than the company as a whole. These ties could be affectionate and familiar. Nicholas Tooley, for example, left £29 13s. to Sarah Burbage, daughter of his 'late master'. The *Alcazar* plot (Greg, *Henslowe Papers*, 138–9) refers to boy actors through their masters (e.g. 'mᵣ Allens boy, mr Townes boy'). For details of the apprentice system, see David Kathman, 'Grocers, Goldsmiths, and Drapers: Freemen and Apprentices in Elizabethan Theater', *Shakespeare Quarterly* 55 (2004), 1–49 (at 8).

(an 'Ethiope' (3.2.257), 'tawny Tartar' (3.2.263), 'puppet' (3.2.288), 'dwarf' (3.2.328), and 'minimus' (3.2.329)) the latter is notably paler and taller (a 'princess of pure white' (3.2.144), 'tall personage' (3.2.292), and 'painted maypole' (3.2.296)). The interplay between these characters again exploits the possibility of running against apparent type. Thus Hermia 'though she be but little ... is fierce' (3.2.325) and Helena, while physically bigger, is 'a right maid for ... cowardice' (3.2.302). It is precisely such contrasts that Beckerman saw as conducive to 'depth' in characterization, where external behaviour and inner life do not stand in predictable correspondence. The shifting power balance between the two female characters is also another exemplary instance of what Pfister calls 'polyfunctionality' in a dramatic exchange. The pleas and insults that the pair exchange continually complicate their respective statuses. This is notably different from earlier scenes of cursing such as those in *Richard III* or *The Taming of the Shrew*.

The plays that Shakespeare wrote in or shortly after the watershed year of 1594 show a new concern with the process of casting individual performers. Most obviously, this is demonstrated in the amateur theatricals of *Love's Labour's Lost* and *A Midsummer Night's Dream*, where we see the playwright responding directly to the bodily features of his cast. But the evidence and consequences of writer–performer connection might also run deeper. Starting with physical distinctiveness, a writer who has a secure knowledge of the company that will perform his plays has other advantages. In the performance of the pageant of the nine worthies in *Love's Labour's Lost*, just as in the rehearsals of Peter Quince, we find Shakespeare creating pathos out of the imbalance between aspiration and true capacity. The 'foolish mild' Nathaniel ('a very good bowler') is 'a little o'erparted' in taking on Alexander the Great.[50] Moth is too small to be Hercules, so must play him 'in minority' (5.2.586) and, conversely, Armado is too bulky to be Hector ('Hector was not so clean-timbered'; 'his leg is too big for Hector's'; 'more calf, certain' (5.2.633–5)). There is more to this than appearance-specific casting. Holofernes, presumably another Sincler role, is viciously attacked for his drawn face as he attempts to play Judas Maccabaeus: 'thou hast no face'; 'a cittern-head'; 'the head of a bodkin'; 'a death's face in a ring'; 'the face of an old Roman coin, scarce seen'; 'the carved-bone face on a flask'; 'Saint George's half-cheek in a brooch' (5.2.602–11). Yet his

---

50. William Shakespeare, *Love's Labour's Lost*, ed. H. R. Woudhuysen, Arden3 (London: Cengage, 1998), 5.2.575–9. Subsequent references appear in the text.

measured anger in response ('this is not generous, not gentle, not humble' (5.2.623)), like Armado's later defence of Hector, lends a depth and dignity to the characterization of Holofernes that is a more profound marker of Shakespeare's distinctiveness as a writer.

My argument in this chapter has been that the development of Shakespeare's techniques of characterization in the mid- to late 1590s is a consequence of his new position as owner and controller of the dramatic life of his plays. Shakespeare could now plan an entire play by thinking about the capacities of his actors—making the contrasts between them a building-block in the construction of scenes. The neologism 'o'erparted' is a revealing product of this period: it shows the playwright exploiting the gap between a character's imagined and physical selves. Equally important, it shows another speaker responding to this mismatch. Belief in the depth and plasticity of Shakespeare's creations is stimulated by such three-way interactions. The rehearsal scenes that the playwright wrote at this turning point in his development are thus significant above all because they are dynamic, with physical stability in the performer facilitating the illusion of an internal change. After 1594, as Shakespeare composed, he occasionally used actors' names instead of the names of characters and such slips reveal a new kind of creative process quite different from the humanist models that he had imbibed at school. Control over casting enabled the creation of psychological depth.

5
The events of 1594

I have argued that there is a connection between compositional style and material situation. So what had changed for Shakespeare by the middle of 1594? On 5 June that year Philip Henslowe made the first surviving record of a performance by the Lord Chamberlain's Men—Shakespeare's acting company.[1] Four months later the existence of the company is confirmed in a note from the Lord Chamberlain himself requesting that his 'now company of players' be permitted to play at the Cross Keys Inn, a place where it seems they are already working.[2] From these uncertain beginnings—flitting between temporary residences—would grow early modern England's dominant theatre company: a group that would eventually control two theatres and hold the King himself as patron. That Christmas the Lord Chamberlain's Men are recorded as performing at court, and Shakespeare, alongside Kemp, is listed in the accounts as receiving payment.[3] It is the first time that his name appears in any performance-related document.

1. R. A. Foakes, ed., *Henslowe's Diary*, 2nd edn (Cambridge: Cambridge University Press, 2002), 21. It is convenient to call the company the Chamberlain's Men until their 1603 assumption of the King's patronage but in reality between 23 July 1596 and 17 March 1597 they bore the title of Lord Hunsdon's Men. This window covers the time between the death of Henry Carey, Lord Chamberlain, and the assumption of that office by his son, the company's new patron, George Carey.
2. E. K. Chambers, *The Elizabethan Stage* (Oxford: Clarendon Press, 1923; repr. 2009), II, 193. The company's stay at this small courtyard venue is likely to have been short. Although we have no absolute proof that the Chamberlain's Men worked at the Theatre until Lodge's *Wit's Misery* (dated 5 May 1596) a move long before that is by far the most likely. By late 1597 the company had been forced to abandon the Theatre and were apparently making use of the Curtain (for the compound evidence for these moves, see Chambers, *Elizabethan Stage*, II, 192–203, and Andrew Gurr, *The Shakespeare Company: 1594–1642* (Cambridge: Cambridge University Press, 2004), 1–10).
3. Chambers, *Elizabethan Stage*, II, 194. The payment is recorded on 15 March 1595; Chambers notes that reference to a performance on 28 December is probably an error, because the company were almost certainly performing *Errors* at Gray's Inn that night.

So what changed in 1594 for the theatre industry? The radical nature of the shake-up that year has been most forcefully championed by Andrew Gurr, according to whose interpretation of the evidence the Lord Chamberlain was himself instrumental in the establishment of a 'duopoly'.[4] Two dominant new companies, he argues, were established by government edict: the Lord Chamberlain's own and the Lord Admiral's. These ensembles were given a Privy-Council-endorsed monopoly on London playing and were the only two companies thereafter permitted to play at court.[5] As a result, the Chamberlain's and Admiral's Men became the nation's only 'strong' acting ensembles, entities which, in Gurr's words, 'came to bestride the London scene like the monopolistic colossi they were'.[6] The earlier system whereby many touring companies circulated at London's playhouses was replaced by a new one: from this point on the strong companies had a semi-permanent residence at a single venue; their touring reduced, and the radical instability of the earlier period (in which companies repeatedly split and amalgamated) was succeeded by a more tranquil mode of existence.[7] While patrons changed and while individual actors retired and were replaced over the decades, the two strong companies established in 1594 would continue as stable entities all the way up to the closure of the theatres at the outbreak of the Civil War in 1642.

Gurr's account of a clean break in 1594 is one version of the history, but the radical effect of the Lord Chamberlain's intervention that year is not accepted by all scholars. In spite of government action, it could be argued, many of the old companies continued to function.[8] The fact that a new theatre, the Swan, was constructed to high specifications in 1595 proves that the 'duopoly' was not thought of by all as a permanent settlement. Players

4. The case is most recently stated in Andrew Gurr's *Shakespeare's Opposites: the Admiral's Company 1594–1625* (Cambridge: Cambridge University Press, 2009), 1–5, 15–18; see also Gurr, *Shakespeare Company*, xiii and *passim*.
5. Gurr, *The Shakespearean Stage, 1574–1642*, 3rd edn (Cambridge: Cambridge University Press, 1992), 42.
6. Gurr, *Shakespearean Stage*, 41.
7. Gurr, *Shakespearean Stage*, states that after the brief spell sharing the Rose between 5 and 15 June 1594 Admiral's and Chamberlain's 'settled in their separate homes for good' (41).
8. This is the central argument of Holger Schott Syme's 'The Meaning of Success: Stories of 1594 and its Aftermath', *Shakespeare Quarterly* 61 (2010), 490–525, which points to the continued presence of multiple theatres and other playing spaces in spite of the Privy Council order restricting London playing companies to two. Given the survival of these venues, it is indeed possible that companies such as the Queen's Men remained an occasional London presence. There is, however, no evidence of their commissioning new plays.

made use of the Swan from that year onwards and in February 1597 the Earl of Pembroke's Men signed contracts with its owner, Francis Langley, to remain in residence for a year.[9] As it turned out, the Pembrokes' stay proved disastrous: their licence was revoked, the company split in two, and the playhouse was eventually abandoned, all probably as a result of the performance of a libellous play, *The Isle of Dogs*.[10] Evidently, however, the duopoly was not watertight: theatre speculation continued and it is clear from the records that Lord Derby's Men had appeared in London before the decade was out. As is always the case with early theatre history, the evidence for any narrative is limited: it is thus possible that other companies made use of the remaining playhouses, which Gurr assumes were left derelict. On the ground, it may be that 1594 would not immediately have felt so special after all.

To some extent, Gurr's famous account of the establishment of a duopoly is a strong theory rather than a hard fact of history. Yet, whatever the underlying mechanism, taking the long view, 1594 would unquestionably prove pivotal. From that point on, a duopoly of some sort was for many years the official position. On 19 February 1598, the Privy Council sent a letter to the Master of the Revels and the Justices of the Peace for Middlesex and Surrey confirming that the Admiral's and the Chamberlain's were the only authorized performers in London and that all other companies were to be suppressed.[11] These two official companies were also linked to two official theatres. On 22 June 1600 the Privy Council sent orders to the Lord Mayor and the Justices that all but the two licensed playhouses should be closed. At this stage these were the Globe (for the Lord Chamberlain's Men) and the Fortune ('now in hand to be built' by Edward Alleyn.).[12] While such orders were not wholly successful they did set a baseline that accorded privilege to London's pre-eminent companies.

---

9. See Herbert Berry, 'Playhouses', in G. Wickham, H. Berry, and W. Ingram, eds., *English Professional Theatre, 1530–1660* (Cambridge: Cambridge University Press, 2000), 437–40.
10. *The Isle of Dogs* does not survive and the narrative of the Swan's closure remains shadowy. Although the combination of the duopoly and the libellous production forms part of the orthodox narrative there are other elements to the story. William Ingram, 'The Closing of the Theatres in 1597: A Dissenting View', *Modern Philology* 69 (1971), 105–15, for example, cites Langley's involvement with diamond theft as a contributory and perhaps more important aspect of the case. William Ingram, '"Neere the Playe Howse": The Swan Theater and Community Blight', *Renaissance Drama* 4 (1971), 53–68, adds his neglect of the local amenities as a further element in the mix.
11. Chambers, *Elizabethan Stage*, IV, 325.
12. Chambers, *Elizabethan Stage*, IV, 329–32 (330).

Numerous pieces of evidence confirm this change in the marketplace. For one thing, 1594 saw the virtual invention of the printed play.[13] Suddenly, a large body of dramatic manuscripts came into the possession of publishers. While companies' attitudes to the publication of their playtexts were more variable than theatre historians used to assume, it is highly likely that manuscripts were sold because troupes of players were under pressure and beginning to leave London. Henslowe writes in late 1593 of the parlous state of Pembroke's Men and their resultant attempt to pawn their apparel.[14] In September, Pembroke's were on the point of departure, and even if they and the Queen's Men returned thereafter to visit the capital they cannot have done so in a prosperous state. The companies left without a court commission appear to have purchased few plays after the creation of the duopoly: in the *Annals of English Drama* there are no new works listed for outfits other than the Admiral's and Chamberlain's for several years. With the exception of Pembroke's short-lived venture at the Swan, this dominance of the market remains in place until the re-emergence of the boy players.[15] The pattern of play distribution across companies is thus very different after 1594 from that which existed earlier. At court the dominance of the two companies was likewise total, so in major ways the year did involve a reshaping of the theatrical map.[16]

Above all for Shakespeare, the change was dramatic.[17] From 1594 onwards he writes only for one company and his involvement with co-authorship (common before this time) drops away until the very late stages of his career.

13. See Edward Arber, ed., *A Transcript of the Registers of the Company of Stationers of London, 1554–1640 AD* (London: privately published, 1875–94) II, 1576–95, for the spike in play publication.
14. W. W. Greg, *Henslowe Papers* (London: A. H. Bullen, 1907), 40.
15. Alfred Harbage, *Annals of English Drama: 975–1700*, 3rd edn, rev. Sylvia Stoler Wagonheim (London: Routledge, 1989), 62–74. The 'addenda' listed in Harbage, 74–8, are revivals commissioned either by Admiral's or by other companies before this time. The count does not include public entertainments, closet, or university performances. The one possible exception is the lost Queen's Men play *Valentine and Orson* (entered in the Stationers' Register in 1595), but this is almost certainly an earlier play.
16. In 1599 there was a slight inroad into this duopoly, with Robert Browne (a Derby's Man) being paid for a performance on 18 December. This was, however, an unusual situation (with no company being named) and the formal position of two companies was still in place. For details of this performance see Richard Rowland, ed., Thomas Heywood, *The First and Second Parts of King Edward IV*, Revels (Manchester: Manchester University Press, 2005), 5. Before the 'duopoly' the court hosted performances from many more companies, as is evident from the tables printed in Charles William Wallace, *The Evolution of the English Drama up to Shakespeare with a History of the First Blackfriars Theatre* (Berlin: Georg Reimer, 1912), 197–225.
17. Roslyn Lander Knutson, 'What's so Special about 1594?', *Shakespeare Quarterly* 61 (2010), 449–67 (467), agrees that from a Shakespeare-centric perspective the date is significant, although she suggests that the playwright's commitment to the company may for a while have been a provisional one.

This alteration in work pattern is not found in any other early modern writer, so evidently a major change occurred. On this front the financial evidence is also compelling, because it is after 1594 that the poet begins to accumulate substantial wealth. Shakespeare's money-lending, property purchases, theatrical investments, and acquisition of a coat of arms over the remainder of the decade set him substantially apart from the condition of dependency suffered by other playwrights.[18] These investments were, in the main, ways to lay up capital rather than speculative ventures: they show that Shakespeare had a surfeit of ready money and was (in an age before private banking) looking for secure ways to tie it up. Combined with a change in the style of his composition, these are externally verifiable markers of the impact of Shakespeare's position as a sharer in the Chamberlain's Men.

What, then, did it mean to be a sharer? At the most basic level, sharers were those entitled to a portion of the day's takings after a performance. Gate receipts were collected in a box and (after the deduction of overheads) divided into equal amounts upon the sharers' table.[19] Sharers were different from hired men: these were also actors and they might have a long association with a group of players, but they lacked a stake in the company's assets and were entrusted only with minor roles. Hired men were contract workers; sharers were fellow participants in an artistic and commercial enterprise.

Becoming a sharer involved a substantial investment of capital.[20] Henslowe's diary records a loan of £15 for a half share in the Queen's Men in 1593 and two decades later Charles Massey valued his full share in the Admiral's at 'three score and ten pounds'.[21] Massey's letter, which is a

18. For an overview contrast Samuel Schoenbaum, *William Shakespeare: A Documentary Life* (Oxford: Clarendon Press, 1975), 155–94, with Gerald Eades Bentley, *The Profession of Dramatist in Shakespeare's Time, 1590–1642* (Princeton, NJ: Princeton University Press, 1971), 89–110, and also discussion below.
19. On the sharing of takings, including Brome's reference to the 'sharing board' see Bentley, *The Profession of Player in Shakespeare's Time, 1590–1642* (Princeton, NJ: Princeton University Press, 1984), 57–8.
20. For an overview of the evidence about these cash investments, see Bentley, *Profession of Player*, 29–37, and also S. P. Cerasano, 'The "Business" of Shareholding, the Fortune Playhouses, and Francis Grace's Will', *Medieval and Renaissance Drama in England* 2 (1985), 231–51, who provides much new information and cautions against too standardized a model.
21. On the purchase of the half share see Foakes, ed., *Diary*, 7–9. The record, which is scored through (acknowledging payment) appears at the bottom of a page listing 'what I have laid out about my playhouse'. The value of a Queen's Men share at this point is likely to have been lowered, given the company's troubles at this time. On the next sheet, dated 1 June 1595, Henslowe notes that his cousin's loan of £9 'for his half share with the company which he doth play with' is 'all to be paid unto me when he doth receive his money which he lent to my Lord Burt' (fol. 3ᵛ). For Massey's letter see Greg, *Henslowe Papers*, 64–5.

long and formal appeal to secure a loan, is particularly expansive about the ongoing redeemable value of the share that he is able to offer as security:

> Never would I desire you should hazard the loss of one penny by me, for, sir, I know you understand that there is the compositions between our company that if any one give over with consent of his fellows, he is to receive three score and ten pounds (Antony Jeffes hath had so much) if any one die his widow or friends whom he appoints it to receive fifty pounds (Mistress Pavie, and Mistress Toune hath had the like).[22]

At a later point, acting company shares (which were inherited by widows or offered as security by impecunious players) came close to being a tradable commodity.[23] The fellowship of sharers, however, was intended to be a lasting fraternity and (especially for the strong companies) membership conventionally lasted until retirement. Sharers' claims were equal. Henslowe and Alleyn write repeatedly of meeting 'the sharers' as a collective body and playwrights also refer to companies in this way.[24] Although occasionally provisions were made for the holding of a half share, the dominant picture was of partners holding collective responsibility.

Trust was essential amongst sharers because they held both assets and liabilities in common. In principle, they had collective ownership of two very valuable stocks of material: their apparel and their playbooks. In *Groatsworth of Wit* the player boasts that his 'very share in playing apparel will not

---

22. 'Charles Massey to Edward Alleyn (1613?)', printed in Greg, *Henslowe Papers*, 64. Cerasano, 'The "Business" of Shareholding', 241, discusses the nature of Massey's claims. She also notes Alleyn's sale of his share in the Admiral's Men for £50 in 1597 and gives several other instances of such payments.

23. Cerasano, 'The "Business" of Shareholding', 243, identifies the first instance of an inherited acting share in 1624. For further detail on sharer contracts and trading see Bentley, *Profession of Player*, 25–9.

24. In the late 1610s and early 1620s Edward Alleyn was divesting himself of his theatrical property as he built up the endowment for his Dulwich College foundation. At this time he met frequently with the company now resident at the Fortune Playhouse (the former Admiral's/Prince Henry's Men, which had now come under the patronage of the Elector Palatine or Palgrave). MSS 9, Alleyn's Diary and Account-Book, records a series of dinner meetings with the fellowship, a group of men whom Alleyn evidently regards as a collective body, both in financial terms in making a final settlement of their debts, and in personal terms as they are invited to social gatherings as a unit. MSS 9, fol. 24b, for example, records expenses after dinner to celebrate the signing of a lease recorded on 31 October 1618. This sense of the company as a collective legal and social body matches with the references we find earlier in Henslowe's correspondence. Daborne, for example, is also consistent in referring to collective decisions by an acting fellowship in his letters of 29 October and 13 November 1613 (Greg, *Henslowe Papers*, 76–8). For details of the negotiations between Alleyn and Palsgrave's Men see Bentley, *The Jacobean and Caroline Stage*, 7 vols. (Oxford: Clarendon Press, 1941–68), I, 137–50.

be sold for two hundred pounds' (D4^b). In the same work Roberto also sells his plays to the company rather than any individual, an instance of the general practice of collective sharer ownership of dramatic texts. It was always the case that sharers took collective responsibility when it came to adding a play to their repertory. Only where a company broke were plays redistributed wholesale, with sharers attempting to recover their original financial stake. Without doubt, membership of a company brought with it status and privilege. Sharers were marked out in documents with the appellation 'Mr'.[25] They took the major roles, had an equal portion of the profits, and had a secure place in what was intended to be a lasting settlement.[26]

There were both strong and weak companies. In the popular imagination of the 1590s the joint asset structure of the playing companies was associated with exploitative riches and sharers were commonly depicted as wealthy and powerful men. Gosson writes of artisans 'suffered to forsake their calling because they desire to walk gentleman-like in satin and velvet with a buckler at their heels', warning, as Greene had done, that little was to be made by working for such men.[27] John Field in his *Godly Exhortation* of 1583 stresses how 'pounds and hundreds can be well enough afforded, in following these least pleasures' and how 'every door hath a payment and every gallery maketh a yearly stipend'.[28] Thomas Dekker's *Gull's Hornbook* of 1609 constantly blames the 'covetousness of sharers' for various theatrical ills, such as the seating of audience members upon the stage.[29] The wealth of sharers was almost proverbial. Even so, not all company shares were equal and in many cases the reality of membership did not live up to the theory. Most asset-holders survived on a tight margin and some became so indebted that they became, in practice, their creditor's employees.[30]

25. On 'Mr' as indicative of sharer status see Greg, *Dramatic Documents from the Elizabethan Playhouses: Stage Plots, Actors' Parts, Prompt Books* (Oxford: Clarendon Press, 1969), I, 37–8.
26. On the casting of sharers in major roles see Bentley, *Profession of Player*, 215, and T. J. King, *Casting Shakespeare's Plays: London Actors and their Roles, 1590–1642* (Cambridge: Cambridge University Press, 1992), 10–11. By examining surviving plots and manuscripts King makes a fairly solid distinction between the roles taken by hired men and sharers. For documentary evidence on the Chamberlain's sharer contract see Chambers, *William Shakespeare: A Study of Facts and Problems* (Oxford: Clarendon Press, 1930), I, 78–80, and II, 71–87; and, on sharing in general, Chambers, *Elizabethan Stage*, I, 348–88.
27. Stephen Gosson, *Plays Confuted* (1582), G7^a.
28. John Field, *Godly Exhortation* (1583), B6^a. These and numerous other tracts repeating such assertions are surveyed alongside defences of the theatre in Chambers, *Elizabethan Stage*, IV, 195–259.
29. Thomas Dekker, *The Gull's Hornbook* (1609), C2^b.
30. On the general financial condition of players see Bentley, *Profession of Player*, 5–10.

The corollary of collective ownership was the dangerous fact of joint liability. It is under conditions of stress (such as Langley's venture at the Swan) that we see this principle coming into play as a potential burden for the members of a fellowship. Pembroke's Men had promised to perform for Langley exclusively. When the Swan deal went sour and a lack of employment forced some of the players to work for Henslowe they found themselves pursued by Langley, who had secured a hold on them by means of £100 bonds.[31] For the former Pembroke's sharers, moreover, the flight to the Rose may have taken them from frying pan to fire. Henslowe lent them money so that they could release themselves from their obligations to Langley, but debt to Henslowe was itself often a means of gaining control. His companies (and he was explicit about this proprietorial naming) developed extraordinary collective debts to their landlord. At the turn of the century, for example, the sharers in the Admiral's Men all signed their names to acknowledge a joint obligation to pay £300 to their landlord and banker.[32] Even where players had cleared their individual debts to Henslowe, they were still liable for their company's arrears. Thus, on 12 March 1602, when the player William Bird paid off just over £18, he was reminded not just of his remaining personal obligations but also of the 'debts and such stock and covenants as I may claim and challenge of him by reason of his conjunction with the company'.[33]

There was a pattern to such indebtedness that made the Admiral's Men and the new companies that joined the Alleyn–Henslowe stable at the turn of the century relatively 'weak' fellowships. The day-to-day income of the performers may have been reasonable, but the financial trapdoor upon which their company sat meant they had little power to affect the long-term artistic and financial direction of their enterprise. From the accounts of Henslowe and his business partner Edward Alleyn it is clear that assets conventionally thought of as sharer property (such as playbooks, costumes, and contracts with hired men) were in fact controlled by these impresarios. Henslowe's *Diary* records charges to his companies for all kinds of assets, including at one point 'for my boy James Bristow'.[34] Such underlying obligations could cause financial problems to spiral: the most spectacular

---

31. See Gurr, *Shakespearean Stage*, 42–4.
32. Foakes, ed., *Diary*, 136.
33. Foakes, ed., *Diary*, 174.
34. Foakes, ed., *Diary*, 167. The boy is recorded as being 'bought' by Henslowe from a player on 18 December 1597 for £8 (*Diary*, 241).

case being that of the Lady Elizabeth's Men, whose sharers put together a bill of complaint against Henslowe, detailing the financial mechanisms that had eaten away at their company from the inside.[35]

It is clear, then, that there were weak companies. There was also a company that was exceptionally strong. From the long view of history the Lord Chamberlain's Men proved a remarkably robust outfit: two decades on, the core of the fellowship would still be intact and prosperous to an outstanding degree. In 1614 Shakespeare, Condell, Heminges, and Richard Burbage would still be sharers and by that point they would all also have a stake in two highly prestigious playhouses: the Globe and Blackfriars. Even in the 1590s the company was evidently prosperous—no other group of actors proved wealthy or independent enough to construct its own playhouse, as the Chamberlain's did only five years after their formation. In terms of financial security and royal patronage the Chamberlain's/King's Men would soon pull ahead of the Admiral's. There are also indications of artistic pre-eminence: while evidence here is more uncertain, it seems that major actors and writers alike felt the pull of what, in 1603, would come to be singled out as the monarch's favourite performance troupe.[36] Shakespeare, after 1594, was thus writing not just as a sharer, but as a sharer in an exceptionally strong company.

At least three things changed for the playwright at this juncture. First, the dispersed corpus of his plays was gathered into a unit. Either immediately or gradually, works such as *The Taming of the Shrew* (initially linked to Pembroke's) and *Titus Andronicus* (first listed as Sussex's) were taken up by the Chamberlain's Men, whose surviving members would eventually print them after the playwright's death.[37] Second, the theatrical marketplace

35. The 'Articles of Grievance and of Oppression against Philip Henslowe' survive at Dulwich College. For a transcription see Greg, *Henslowe Papers*, 86–90. On this case see Bentley, *Profession of Dramatist*, 72–3.

36. Chamberlain's/King's were able to attract established talents such as Nathan Field, John Lowin, and Robert Armin, all of whom had been members of other groups. William Kemp is the only example of transfer in the opposite direction and his can hardly be seen as an upward move. Freelance playwrights wrote for all companies, but a high proportion of canonical work was performed by Chamberlain's/King's. It is notable too that John Fletcher, Philip Massinger, and James Shirley (successors in turn to Shakespeare as the company's principal playwright) should all have remained loyal to the King's Men.

37. Initial company ownership of neither play is certain. The printing of *Taming of a Shrew* as Pembroke's in 1594, with some other evidence, is generally seen as the best indication of *The Shrew's* origins (see *The Taming of the Shrew*, ed. Brian Morris (London: Methuen, 1981), 50–65, and Stanley Wells and Gary Taylor, *William Shakespeare: A Textual Companion* (Oxford: Clarendon Press, 1987), 109–11). *Titus* first appears as performed by Sussex's in Henslowe's

became more stable. Whatever the nature of the 'duopoly', the two newly formed fellowships now resided long-term at specific venues and became exclusive providers of dramatic entertainment at court: the rapid turnover, amalgamation, and breaking of companies that had characterized the first half of the 1590s came to an end.[38] Third, Shakespeare personally committed himself to the role of player. We know little of his daily activity before the middle of this decade, but his absence from performance-related documents such as travelling warrants, Privy Council minutes, stage plots, personal letters, and legal papers before this date is conspicuous.[39] Prior to 1594 no evidence ties him to a company and just one sentence in *Greenes Groats-worth of Wit* connects him with acting of any kind. After 1594 his name appears regularly, not just in the court records for payment but in the Herald's Office as a 'player' and in the printed list of performers of Ben Jonson's plays.[40] The events of this year, therefore, were pivotal: they transformed, in an instant, his day-to-day working practice. In retrospect, the commitments into which he entered some time that summer must be counted as the most decisive of his professional career.

Diary (Foakes, ed., 21) and was then printed as performed by Derby's, Pembroke's, and Sussex's (see *Titus Andronicus*, ed. Jonathan Bate (London: Routledge, 1995), 69–79, and Wells and Taylor, *Textual Companion*, 113–15). A similar gathering of works from different companies occurred when Thomas Heywood became a sharer in Worcester's but, following the failure of his company, that playwright suffered a new dispersal of his texts.

38. As discussed above, this was not a straightforward transition, but see Greg, *Henslowe Papers*, 33–45; Foakes, ed., *Diary*, 16–31; Neil Carson, *A Companion to Henslowe's Diary* (Cambridge: Cambridge University Press, 1988), 85–100; and Carol Chillington Rutter, ed., *Documents of the Rose Playhouse*, rev. edn (Manchester: Manchester University Press, 1999), 49–83, for basic documentary evidence that illustrates the change in circumstance for these two pre-eminent fellowships.

39. It is notable that all the other confirmed founding members of the company (Richard Burbage, William Kemp, Thomas Pope, George Bryan, Augustine Phillips, William Sly, and John Heminges) along with hired men do appear in such papers, with all but Heminges (who appears in the travelling warrant of 1593) being listed in the *2 Seven Deadly Sins* plot (see Greg, *Henslowe Papers*, 130–2; Chambers, *Elizabethan Stage*, II, 123).

40. See Schoenbaum, *Documentary*, 136, 172, 150.

6

Relational drama

The event of Shakespeare's becoming a sharer coincides with some decisive changes in his activity as a writer. Most obviously, Shakespeare ceased to take a primary interest in print. *Venus and Adonis* (1593) and *The Rape of Lucrece* (1594) had been produced to the highest standards as authorial publications complete with a personal letter of dedication. After joining the Chamberlain's Men, however, Shakespeare would never again show such open commitment to printed poetry and quite possibly he ceased to play any part in the publication of his work.[1] This was a pattern of career development quite different from that of his contemporaries. Poets such as Jonson, Drayton, and Chapman continued to publish verse even as they worked as playwrights, but for Shakespeare the common features of the life

---

1. The issue of Shakespeare as writer for print is too complicated to be addressed in full at this juncture. Katherine Duncan-Jones, 'Was the 1609 *SHAKE-SPEARES SONNETS* Really Unauthorized?', *Review of English Studies* 34 (1983), 151–71, has made the case that the *Sonnets* were in some way a legitimate publication. Yet the degree of authorial oversight of the printed copy was undeniably much lower than for *Venus and Adonis* or *Lucrece* (see Shakespeare, *Complete Sonnets and Poems*, ed. Colin Burrow (Oxford: Oxford University Press, 2002), 91–103): there is no clear dedication, and the material artefact of the *Sonnets* does not indicate an author with a significant investment in print. Since Lukas Erne's *Shakespeare as Literary Dramatist* (Cambridge: Cambridge University Press, 2003) the playwright's lack of interest in printed plays is no longer axiomatic. The plays published in his lifetime, however, are unlike those of his laureate rivals because they lack authorial dedications and show few other signs of the poet's commitment to them as texts. As the King's Men grew in power, moreover, the publication of plays by Shakespeare diminished, with his company intervening more and more successfully to suppress their appearance in print (see E. K. Chambers, *William Shakespeare: A Study of Facts and Problems*, 2 vols. (Oxford: Clarendon Press, 1930), I, 145–50). It is possible that the company did acquiesce in the release of certain playtexts, especially once poor quality pirated copies had been printed. All such instances, however, differ markedly from the production of *Venus* and *Lucrece*. Richard Dutton, 'The Birth of an Author,' in Cedric C. Brown and Arthur F. Marotti, eds., *Texts and Cultural Change in Early Modern England* (New York: St. Martin's Press, 1997), 153–78 (at 153), makes a clear case for the special impact of Shakespeare's company attachment. For a wider historical exploration of the dramatist's relationship to print see David Kastan, *Shakespeare and the Book* (Cambridge: Cambridge University Press, 2001).

of the poet-playwright that he had hitherto shared (including print publication, the search for literary patronage, co-authorship, and composition for
multiple companies) dropped away.[2]

As a sharer Shakespeare had taken long-term dramatic ownership of his
drama. Not only did he now play a determining role in first performance,
his plays would take a permanent and central place in the company's
repertory and would remain alive to him over the decades. In court
performances in the early seventeenth century, for example, Shakespeare's
1590s comedies were still favourites, with *The Merry Wives of Windsor*, *The
Comedy of Errors*, and *Love's Labour's Lost* all being revived for King James.[3]
No other playwright had this sustained financial and artistic investment,
because while it was common practice for dramatic companies to refresh old
plays in new versions it was also common practice for this re-tailoring to be
done by outside agents. Such plays—as we can see from Henslowe's
accounts for the 'additions' to *The Spanish Tragedy*, *Dr Faustus*, and other
works—were altered without the authority of their original authors, and
without those original authors being paid.[4] For Shakespeare, after 1594, the
case was different. The examples we have of Shakespearean textual revision
(most spectacularly in *Hamlet* and *Lear*) tend to suggest careful and purposive
action, either solely by the author or by him in consultation with the
company.[5] More radical alterations (notably to *Macbeth*) appear to have

2. For none of the plays that Wells and Taylor date between 1594 and 1605 is there a serious claim
   for co-authorship. According to some scholars Shakespeare wrote three additions to *Sir Thomas
   More* towards the end of this period (Stanley Wells and Gary Taylor, *William Shakespeare:
   A Textual Companion* (Oxford: Clarendon Press, 1987), 124–35), but this revision of an earlier
   text cannot be counted as collaboration. Middleton's possible modest revisions to *Measure for
   Measure* date from after Shakespeare's death, so again are not a case of co-authorship (see
   Thomas Middleton, *Collected Works*, ed. Gary Taylor and John Lavagnino (Oxford: Clarendon
   Press, 2007), 1542–6). The complex case of *Timon of Athens*, if it is an instance of collaboration,
   must be dated over a decade after the formation of the Chamberlain's Men (Wells and Taylor,
   Textual Companion, 127–8). Laurie Maguire and Emma Smith, 'Many Hands: A New Shake-
   speare Collaboration?', *TLS*, 19 April 2012, 13–15, propose that *All's Well that Ends Well* is
   another case of a Shakespeare–Middleton collaboration, but they also endorse a redating of this
   play to '1606–07 (or later)'. Brian Vickers and Marcus Dahl, 'What is Infirm... *All's Well that
   Ends Well*: An Attribution Rejected', *TLS*, 9 April 2012, 14, provide a counter-argument to
   Maguire and Smith's case. For further discussion see Chapters 1 and 14.
3. For the Revels Accounts for Christmas 1604–5 see Chambers, *Facts and Problems*, II, 331–2.
4. There are many tens of instances of such payments. See, for example, Henslowe, *Diary*, ed.
   R. A. Foakes, 2nd edn (Cambridge: Cambridge University Press, 2002), 182, for Ben Jonson
   for alterations to 'geronymo' (*The Spanish Tragedy*) or *Diary*, 206, for William Bird and Samuel
   Rowley's additions to 'docter fostes' (*Faustus*).
5. On Shakespeare as a creative reworker of his plays, see for example 'Shakespeare as Reviser' in
   John Kerrigan, *On Shakespeare and Early Modern Literature: Essays* (Oxford: Oxford University

been made only after Shakespeare's departure.[6] While Shakespeare lived, he seems to have been responsible for minor adjustments to his compositions and, as the company developed, he evidently wrote new works that responded to the capacities of the fellowship.[7] The company—its sharers, its hired men, and its apprenticed boy players taking women's and children's parts—were the matrix through which he could structure his thinking. Having a literary playwright at the centre of commissioning, casting, rehearsing, and performing plays was transformative. The formation of the Chamberlain's Men thus inaugurated a mode of production that was unprecedented and would rarely if ever be repeated on the English stage.

The original fellowship had eight sharers. In 1596 these men were Richard Burbage, William Shakespeare, William Kemp, Thomas Pope, George Bryan, Augustine Phillips, William Sly, and John Heminges; Henry Condell had replaced George Bryan by the following year.[8] Of these original members it is only for Burbage and Kemp that we have substantial detail on performance, but it is also possible to recover a good deal about Robert Armin, Kemp's replacement in the new century. On Condell, Pope, and Shakespeare as actors we have only scraps of information. The same is true of hired men, such as Richard Cowley and John Sincler, or of the boy players in the company. Thus (although it is clear that

Press, 2001), 3–22, or John Jones, *Shakespeare at Work* (Oxford: Clarendon Press, 1995). Wells and Taylor, *Textual Companion*, 17–31, put forward more of a company model for the process of these revisions.

6. Gary Taylor and John Jowett, *Shakespeare Reshaped: 1606–1623* (Oxford: Clarendon Press, 1993) argue that there were some significant changes made to the playwright's work after his departure from the company (most notably they posit changes made by Middleton to *Measure for Measure* and *Macbeth*).
7. Likely minor adjustments include the expansion of the role of Edgar in *Lear*'s Folio version (see William Shakespeare, *King Lear: A Parallel Text Edition*, ed. René Weis (Harlow: Longman, 1993), 7–12) and the move away from a singing Desdemona in the 1622 Quarto of *Othello* (see Tiffany Stern, *Rehearsal from Shakespeare to Sheridan* (Oxford: Clarendon Press, 2000), 15). On such changes more generally see, for example, Tiffany Stern, *Making Shakespeare: From Stage to Page* (London: Routledge, 2004), 30–72. The most obvious major adaptation is to the skills of Robert Armin, whose impact on the fellowship is discussed in Chapter 9 below.
8. See Andrew Gurr, *The Shakespearean Stage, 1574–1642*, 3rd edn (Cambridge: Cambridge University Press, 1992), 44, and *The Shakespeare Company: 1594–1642* (Cambridge: Cambridge University Press, 2004), 13. Of William Sly's original membership we cannot be certain, but he was one of the 'principal comedians' by the time of Jonson's *Every Man in his Humour* of 1598 and was undoubtedly a sharer by the time of the patent of 1603. Henry Condell is also listed in both of these documents. On Sly and Condell as sharers see Chambers, *Facts and Problems*, 1, 80.

performers were recognized for particular specialisms) it is impossible to reconstruct anything like a complete list of acting lines.[9]

The important concept, however, is company organization and not the identification of individual parts, for the stability of the Chamberlain's Men must have had creative as well as economic consequences. Its sharers, hired men, and boy actors remained conspicuously loyal over the decades, thus producing an acting fraternity whose stable make-up contrasted not only with the situation pre-1594, but also with the ongoing vicissitudes of other ensembles, including the Admiral's Men.[10] We know from anecdotal evidence that players were eager for major roles and that authors did adapt plays to companies.[11] Once assigned, a role became a player's lifetime possession, so that when a new sharer bought into a company, he conventionally took over a number of parts from the actor whom he replaced.[12]

Shakespeare, then, was able to compose his plays with a concrete sense of a body of actors who already had an established on-stage character and repertoire. While players were not restricted to any particular genre some broad patterns across Shakespeare's compositions do suggest a degree of

9. This was the great project of T. W. Baldwin's *The Organization and Personnel of the Shakespearean Company* (Princeton, NJ: Princeton University Press, 1927), a work that effectively destroyed the intellectual respectability of any enquiry into early modern actors' performance. Baldwin's reconstruction of the casts of Shakespeare's plays was absurdly speculative (for an early refutation see S. L. Bethell, 'Shakespeare's Actors', *Review of English Studies* 1 (1950), 193–205). Yet elements of his research (for example, his working back from the Beaumont and Fletcher Folio to reconstruct the collection of parts taken by individual players) do provide useful background on the nature of early modern performance traditions. For a comprehensive, if not indisputable, account of what can be reconstructed of the casting of plays in this period, see T. J. King, *Casting Shakespeare's Plays: London Actors and their Roles, 1590–1642* (Cambridge: Cambridge University Press, 1992).

10. On hired men, Andrew Gurr, 'The Work of Elizabethan Plotters, and *2 Seven Deadly Sins*', *Early Theatre* 10 (2007), 67–87 (at 81) points to the way John Holland and John Sincler (who had previously been mobile) apparently found a permanent role in this capacity with the Chamberlain's. This also applies to Richard Cowley, who progressed to being a sharer in the company. Admiral's during this period lost its principal performer, Edward Alleyn, and was also changed by the incorporation of several sharers from the Pembroke company that failed at the Swan. The relative financial dependence of rival companies, which stands in contrast to the Chamberlain's, is discussed in Chapters 4 and 7.

11. Simon Palfrey and Tiffany Stern, *Shakespeare in Parts* (Oxford: Oxford University Press, 2007), 40–50, describe a significant number of cases. They also note Shakespeare's unique situation in having long-term certainty in the assignment of parts.

12. The practice of passing on of roles is described in a prologue attached to the 1641 quarto of George Chapman's *Bussy D'Ambois* (A2$^{a–b}$), and the 1623 quarto of John Webster's *Duchess of Malfi* (A2^{b}) lists, in succession, the actors who have taken the major parts. On this process see also G. E. Bentley, *The Profession of Player in Shakespeare's Time, 1590–1642* (Princeton, NJ: Princeton University Press, 1984), 210; King, *Casting*, 18; Stern, *Rehearsal*, 15; and Palfrey and Stern, *Shakespeare in Parts*, 8, 32 and *passim*.

tailoring to his performers. His *dramatis personae*, for example, tend to age with his company and Hamlet's reference to the set tasks of the theatrical profession ('he that plays the King', 'the Adventurous Knight', 'the Lover', 'the Humorous Man', and 'the Clown'), joins with others to confirm at least the assumption of consistency in set major roles.[13]

In this context, the set relationships between specialists were undoubtedly important. When Shakespeare composed the lines of Dogberry in *Much Ado About Nothing* he specified the hired man (Cowley) who should work alongside Will Kemp in his role as company clown.[14] Kemp is also very likely to have had a working comic partnership with Pope, as the two had travelled to Elsinore together in the 1580s and would leave the company at around the same time.[15] Pope would be remembered alongside Kemp as a comedian.[16] The sustained interaction between comic characters in the rehearsal scenes of *A Midsummer Night's Dream* and *Love's Labour's Lost* would seem to draw strength from the established networks of performers in a specific mode.

Alongside clowning, swordsmanship was also a distinctive skill that is likely to have promoted a pairing or clustering of performers.[17] Across Shakespeare's oeuvre there is often a charismatic 'counter figure' to his hero (Bolingbroke against Richard II; Hotspur versus Hal; Laertes versus Hamlet; and MacDuff in opposition to Macbeth). This rival ages at the same rate as the tragic lead taken by Burbage, so that in the last of Shakespeare's

---

13. William Shakespeare, *Hamlet*, ed. Ann Thompson and Neil Taylor, Arden 3 (London: Thompson, 2006), 2.2.285–8. 'The Clown' is not listed in Q2 but is present in Q1 and F. For further discussion of type casting see Stern, *Rehearsal*, 70–2.

14. As noted in the previous chapter, Cowley's name repeatedly appears alongside Kemp's in 4.2 as printed in Q1 *Much Ado About Nothing* (1600), G3^b–G4^b.

15. See E. K. Chambers, *The Elizabethan Stage*, 4 vols. (Oxford: Clarendon Press, 1923; repr. 2009), II, 334.

16. Samuel Rowlands in his *Letting of Humours Blood* (1600), D8^a, asks 'are Ploughmen simple fellows now days?/ Not so, my Masters: What means *Singer* then?/ And *Pope* the Clown, to speak so Boorish, when/ They counterfeit the Clowns upon the Stage?'. In context these lines appear to refer to a performance of Jonson's *Every Man in his Humour*. Kemp and Pope are paired as part of a list of famous comedians in John Taylor, *Works* (1630), 2F^b, and Thomas Heywood, *An Apology for Actors* (1612), mentions Pope in the sentence following his praise of Kemp, apparently as a performer of the same type. The Elsinore payroll records that Pope was in the Danish service from 17 June to 18 September 1586 and also testifies to the presence of Kemp and another future Chamberlain's man, George Bryan (see Chambers, *Elizabethan Stage*, II, 272).

17. James L. Jackson, 'The Fencing Actor-lines in Shakespeare's Plays', *Modern Language Notes* 57 (1942), 615–21, gives a convincing overview of swordsmanship in Shakespeare's plays, although he rather over-confidently assigns the 'counter' role to William Sly.

martial plays Coriolanus faces Aufidius. The likeliest candidate for this 'counter' role is Henry Condell, who appears, in the same way as Pope with Kemp, to have had a long working partnership with the company star. Condell first appears in the theatrical record at exactly the same time as Burbage, as a young non-sharer in the *2 Seven Deadly Sins* plot.[18] He also left the stage in the same year as the lead actor, performing in no more plays after Burbage's death in 1619.[19] The two were certainly widely famous as conjoined names, because in the 'Induction' to *The Malcontent*, their fellow sharer Will Sly appears as a playgoer desperate to see 'Harry Condell, Dick Burbage, and Will Sly' (ll. 11–12) in this tragicomedy. The one case of a surviving cast list also confirms this pairing: in *The Duchess of Malfi* Burbage and Condell respectively took the principal male roles of Ferdinand and his brother the Cardinal.[20] There is likewise strong evidence that the two were paired as Volpone and Mosca in Jonson's comedy for the King's Men, because a contemporary playgoer marked the names of these actors in a printed copy of the play.[21] Only on one occasion do we have direct evidence that Shakespeare, too, thought of them alongside each other. In his will, the playwright left money for rings of mourning 'to my fellows John Heming, Richard Burbage, and Henry Condell'.[22] This is hardly a basis for creating a cast list, but it is further evidence that the fellowship was to prove amongst the strongest bonds of his life. By the time that Shakespeare composed his last testament these were the only surviving members of the original company. In 1623 it would be the last two founding fellows (Condell and Heminges) who arranged the publication of Shakespeare's plays.

The bonds between members of the fellowship are likely to have been important in the creation of *Richard II*, a play that was almost certainly written in 1595. Sir Edward Hoby probably referred to an early perform-

---

18. It is conventionally conjectured that Condell is the 'harry' who appears twice in the plot (see W. W. Greg, ed., *Henslowe Papers* (London: A. H. Bullen, 1907), 130, 132, 152, and Edwin Nungezer, *A Dictionary of Actors* (Ithaca, NY: Cornell University Press, 1929), 98).

19. Condell lived until 1627, but Nungezer, *Actors*, 100, concludes that he must have retired around 1619 (when he appeared in John Fletcher's *The Humorous Lieutenant*) because he ceases to appear in the actor lists after this date. Burbage died on 13 March 1619 and had (like Condell) appeared very regularly as an actor up to this date.

20. Webster, *Duchess* (1623), A2^b.

21. James A. Riddell, 'Some Actors in Ben Jonson's Plays', *Shakespeare Studies* 5 (1969), 284–98, describes a copy of Jonson's 1616 Folio in which the names of the actors are marked out 'almost certainly in a seventeenth century hand' (285). In the text of *The Alchemist* Burbage is marked down for Subtle, Condell for Surley.

22. Chambers, *Facts and Problems*, II, 172.

ance of Shakespeare's play in December 1595, when he invited Robert Cecil to attend his house in Westminster to see 'K. Richard present himself to your view'.[23] That identification is not a certainty, but if correct it falls around eighteen months into the life of the Lord Chamberlain's Company. A date of composition significantly earlier is, for various reasons, next to impossible, so this must be an early example of Shakespeare's work as a company man.[24] There is no solid evidence on the play's original casting, but it is almost inevitable that, as he wrote the following lines for King Richard on his deposition, Shakespeare imagined them being spoken by his lead tragedian, the young Richard Burbage:

> Here, cousin, seize the crown. Here cousin,
> On this side my hand, and on that side thine.
> Now is this golden crown like a deep well
> That owes two buckets, filling one another,
> The emptier ever dancing in the air,
> The other down, unseen and full of water.
>
> (*Richard II*, 4.1.182–7)

In general terms King Richard matches with the kind of parts for which Burbage was remembered: in manuscript elegies he is memorialized as 'a sad lover... meant to dye' who has played 'young Hamlet, old Hieronimo,/ Kinge Lear, the grieved Moore, and more beside'.[25] The biographical connection to Burbage, however, is much less important to this passage than the emotional connection between the two actors on the stage as this speech is delivered. For the tipping transition of power from King Richard to Bolingbroke as each holds a hand to the crown is emblematic of the complex interdependence of characters in this scene and in the play as a whole.

As with the speeches and scenes of *Henry VI*, *Titus Andronicus*, and *Richard III* analysed in Phase I of this book, the deposition scene in *Richard II* recalls other drama of Shakespeare's contemporaries, most obviously that of Christopher Marlowe, who had died in May 1593. Like Marlowe's weak king,

---

23. Chambers, *Facts and Problems*, II, 320–1.
24. Shakespeare, *King Richard II*, ed. Charles R. Forker, Arden3 (London: Thompson, 2002), 111–20, amasses various sorts of evidence in favour of autumn 1595 as the date of first performance, including style tests and the influence of contemporary drama. Strongest of all is Shakespeare's use as a source of Daniel's *First Four Books of the Civil Wars* (1595), printed early that year. For this date see also Wells and Taylor, *Textual Companion*, 117–18. My quotations are from the Arden3 text.
25. Anon., British Library, MS Stowe 962, fol. 62[b]. On other versions of this elegy and on Burbage's acting style more generally see Chapter 11.

Edward II, Richard toys with the object of the crown as he contemplates abdication; like Marlowe's necromancer, Faustus, the King waxes elegiac as he faces the inevitable loss of his powers. There is even direct verbal allusion as Shakespeare repeatedly echoes one of the most famous phrases of *Dr Faustus* in his soliloquy: 'was this the face/ That like the sun did make beholders wink?/ Is this the face which faced so many follies?'[26] Marlowe's characters, however, function as what Emily Bartels astutely terms 'the source and site of spectacle': they perform their character in an outward, projecting sense.[27] Shakespeare's King Richard, in contrast, exists within a tense, relational web of power.[28]

Seen from this point of view the difference between *Richard II* and Shakespeare's earlier drama is considerable. The pre-1594 plays tended still to fall back on the established imagery and scenic patterning of contemporary playwrights—Shakespeare's tragic heroes were insulated within a cocoon of self-defining rhetoric. It is my contention that the relationship of Shakespeare with his performers facilitated the creation of a new kind of drama—a kind of drama that was itself concerned with relationships. The change, though not absolute, is already evident in the comparison of the two historical plays that Shakespeare wrote on either side of the 1594 line of division: *Richard III* and *Richard II*. As with the development in Shakespeare's comedy that allowed the use of conscious miscasting, there is a degree of individuation in *Richard II* that sets it apart from Shakespeare's previous plays. A prevailing feature of Shakespeare's earlier work had, I have argued, been the interaction of writers: through co-authorship, borrowing, and conspicuous allusion to their work. The prevailing feature of *Richard II*, however, is the balance of power between men. Distribution of roles here is radically different from Shakespeare's earlier historical tragedy. Both are plays about the transfer of the crown, but in the later work it is the *interaction* of rival claimants that is key. The point is partly to be made through

---

26. Compare Shakespeare, *Richard II*, 4.1.283–5 with Marlowe's deposition scene in *Edward II*, 5.1, and also Marlowe's *Faustus*, 5.1.91 (A Text) or 5.1.94 (B Text). All Marlowe references are to the Revels editions.

27. See Emily C. Bartels, *Spectacles of Strangeness: Imperialism, Alienation, and Marlowe* (Philadelphia: University of Pennsylvania Press, 1993) and also her essay 'Christopher Marlowe' in Arthur F. Kinney, ed., *A Companion to Renaissance Drama* (Oxford: Blackwell, 2002), 446–63 (at 453).

28. The notion that Shakespeare's characters exist in relation to a social network is, of course, a commonplace of criticism. The distinctiveness of this quality is explored, for example, in Robert Weimann, 'Society and the Individual in Shakespeare's Conception of Character', *Shakespeare Survey* 34 (1981), 23–31.

numbers. In *Richard III* the lead speaks 1,116 lines to his challenger's 139; in *Richard II* the King has 749 to Bolingbroke's 399 and York's 280.[29] That division reflects the way that characters in *Richard II* are substantial and distinctive, each given a mode of speaking that remains consistent across the whole. Two pivotal scenes are worth contrasting in this light.

At the crucial moment of *Richard III* where things begin to tilt against the King, Shakespeare deployed a full armoury of rhetorical and dramatic constructions. He created a scene of exceptional balance and artistry, but not one in which individuation was a primary concern. Act 4, Scene 4 of *Richard III* uses dazzling stichomythia and rhythmic cursing as the generations of royal women line up to catalogue their losses and express their grief: it is the repetitive, almost choric, quality of these speeches that gives them their power. The turning point of *Richard II* (the famous deposition scene) is very different. It is structured much less by literary convention and much more by the exigencies of power. Because this play is all about the conflicted loyalties and ambitions of men such as York, Aumerle, and Northumberland as they are pulled between the orbits of Richard and Bolingbroke it makes sense to talk about the emotional pressure acting on such non-lead characters in a way that is much less true of the equivalent figures in *Richard III*, *Titus Andronicus*, *Edward II*, *Faustus*, or other earlier drama. The deposition scene (which is but one exemplary instance of this pattern) is driven by a series of claims for dramatic and personal authority. Most spectacularly these are the appeals of the Duke of Aumerle (facing accusations of treason) and Richard (facing the loss of his crown). In each case Shakespeare gives careful attention to status. Aumerle and his accuser Bagot (like Richard and Bolingbroke) are thus made intensely aware of a perverse mismatch in their rank. Aumerle is by far the higher-ranking aristocrat and as (in the opening stages of 4.1) he faces accusations of murder from the base-born Bagot he finds it almost impossible to lower himself to the level of a response:

> Shall I so much dishonour my fair stars
> On equal terms to give him chastisement?

29. For line counts see tables in King, *Casting*. It should be acknowledged that there is no remarkable turnaround on this point. As King says, 'Shakespeare's earliest tragedy (1594) and a late romance (1611) have the same basic plan for casting' and 'this plan for casting Shakespeare's plays is derived from common theatrical practice at London playhouses of this period' (19).

> Either I must, or have mine honour soiled
> With the attainder of his sland'rous lips.
>
> (*Richard II*, 4.1.22–5)

As with the later action of the two hands upon the crown, there is explicit awareness here from a character that authority involves interdependence. This scene repeatedly involves three- or four-way personal interactions (generally with Bolingbroke intervening to resolve a stand-off between complicatedly mismatched adversaries). Dramatic authority shifts with extraordinary subtlety. Carlisle, for example, begins by declaring his incapacity ('worst in this royal presence may I speak' (4.1.116)). Yet, like Bagot, he rises in influence as he delivers his message. Adopting the tone of indignant prophecy earlier deployed by a similarly powerless John of Gaunt ('if you crown him, let me prophesy . . .' (4.1.137)), Carlisle dominates the listeners' attention, only to be cut down at last by the icy minimalism of the Earl of Northumberland.

The handover of power from Richard to Bolingbroke in Act 4 Scene 1 is notable for the comprehensiveness of its colouring in speech and emotional attitude. As speakers and as operators not only Richard and Bolingbroke, but Carlisle, Aumerle, and Northumberland are distinct: Richard is histrionically self-pitying; Bolingbroke suavely powerful; Carlisle filled with apocalyptic religiosity; Aumerle bombastically heraldic; Northumberland grindingly Machiavellian. One would not easily mistake, for example, the fastidious disdain of Aumerle's phrase 'being all too base/ To stain the temper of my knightly sword' (4.1.29–30) for the biblically charged grandeur that we find in Carlisle's 'field of Golgotha and dead men's skulls' (4.1.145).

It is not just that these characters speak in a distinctive way, they also show acute awareness of the way in which others have spoken. King Richard, for example, is particularly attuned to the possibility of slights from his former inferiors:

NORTHUMBERLAND: My lord—
RICHARD: No lord of thine, thou haught insulting man. (4.1.253–4)
BOLINGBROKE: The shadow of your sorrow hath destroyed
  The shadow of your face.
RICHARD: Say that again!
  The shadow of my sorrow? Hah, let's see. (4.1.292–4)

BOLINGBROKE: Name it, fair cousin,
RICHARD: 'Fair cousin'? I am greater than a king;
  For when I was a king, my flatterers
  Were then but subjects. Being now a subject,
  I have a king here to my flatterer.

              (*Richard II*, 4.1.304–8)

This sensitivity in Richard to the power dynamic implicit in the words addressed to him is symptomatic of a wider tendency in the play, in which speakers are repeatedly seen to infer complex motivation from the words and deeds of others.

From *Richard II* onwards the distinctive feature of Shakespeare's dramaturgy is the relationship within and between clusters of characters. What I mean by this is something different from the discovery of 'inwardness' or 'debatable' character in the course of the 1590s.[30] Celebrated dramatic figures such as Hieronimo, Faustus, Edward II, or Richard III have this quality and can express it through soliloquies. Yet they do not have complex developing relationships with other dramatic figures. Nor do the plays they inhabit explore such inwardness across a range of distinctive characters. Shakespeare's mid- to late 1590s drama is conspicuously 'relational'. This is powerfully the case if we examine the rival 'courts' of Richard and Bolingbroke on which Shakespeare focuses across the second and third acts. In the two scenes that bridge Bolingbroke's landing in England (2.2; 2.3), for example, the audience is presented in turn with the beleaguered royal party and the radiantly optimistic rebel forces, who are moving at speed. There are in these scenes at least four highly differentiated speakers. On one side we have the Queen, whose language is characterized by fatalistic images of childbirth, and York, who has the broken expression of a powerless old man. On the other, Bolingbroke speaks with the simplicity of confidence and Northumberland offers vacuous, oily praise. These character traits are not scene-specific and, what is more, they are conveyed in the course of personal interaction rather than through self-descriptive speech. York, for instance, responds to news of the invasion with ineffectual orders to those around him. As his main oration runs on, his verse becomes ragged (strikingly so in a play that stands out in its metrical regularity):

---

30. That development is the subject of Katharine Eisaman Maus's celebrated *Inwardness and Theater in the English Renaissance* (Chicago: University of Chicago Press, 1995). See also Ruth Lunney, 'Rewriting the Narrative of Dramatic Character, or, Not "Shakespearean" but "Debatable"', *Medieval and Renaissance Drama in England* 14 (2001), 66–85.

Well, somewhat we must do. [*to Queen*] Come, cousin, I'll
Dispose of you.—
Gentlemen, go muster up your men,
And meet me presently at Berkeley Castle.
I should to Pleshy too,
But time will not permit. All is uneven,
And everything is left at six and seven.

(*Richard II*, 2.2.116–22)[31]

The collective mood of the loyalists, which gradually sours, is impressed on the audience by means of such speech acts. The fact that Bushy, Bagot, and Green fail to follow York's orders after his exit makes this relational production of meaning all the stronger.

Even though there is no information on the specific original casting of *Richard II*, it is a fair supposition that this play's remarkable span of character interaction stems from the closeness of its dramatist to the performers. Shakespeare knew the players for whom he was writing and he must have been instrumental in the way the drama was rehearsed. Most importantly, he could have confidence in the long-term connection between himself, company, and playtext: the play would still be revived more than half a decade after it was first performed.[32]

In the first phase of Shakespeare's career, before he was a sharer, plays such as *The Comedy of Errors*, *The Taming of the Shrew*, and *Richard III* were relatively simple in their character configuration. What drives the responses of speakers in these earlier plays is more often a 'poetic' logic, by which echoes, reversals, and allusions are central to a literary enjoyment of the exchange. In *Richard II*, in contrast, exchanges are commonly grounded in (to return to Pfister's terminology) appellative, phatic, and metalingual

31. The *mis-en-page* here, like the text, is that of Forker's Arden3 edition. In neither Q1 nor F is York's irregular verse indicated through the page layout, but for a justification of this as authorially intended see *Richard II*, ed. Forker, 166; 283–4n; 286–7n.

32. This was the performance linked to the Essex rebellion. Blair Worden, 'Shakespeare in Life and Art: Biography and *Richard II*', in Takashi Kozuka and J. R. Mulryne, eds., *Shakespeare, Marlowe, Jonson: New Directions in Biography* (Aldershot: Ashgate, 2006), 23–42, has argued that this is unlikely to have been Shakespeare's play, proposing instead that it was a dramatization of John Hayward's *History*. No reference to such a play based on Hayward's *First Part of the Life and Reign* exists, however, and it seems unlikely that the Chamberlain's Men would have purchased a second play covering the exact same events as a play by Shakespeare that they already owned. For a full refutation, see Paul E. J. Hammer, 'Shakespeare's *Richard II*, the Play of 7 February 1601, and the Essex Rising,' *Shakespeare Quarterly* 59 (2008), 1–35.

function: speakers try to influence each other, to maintain emotional contact, and to pick up on the verbal habits of their interlocutors.[33] Pfister notes that it is unusual for pre-modern drama to use phatic and metalingual communication.[34] In *Richard II* and subsequent drama, however, Shakespeare uses these techniques extensively. For example, when Bolingbroke orders the imprisonment of Richard with the words 'Go, some of you, convey him to the Tower', he is characteristically combining command with euphemism and Richard's response 'O, good—"Convey"!' picks up precisely on those qualities (4.1.316–17). The shifting alliances of this play (such as Aumerle's growing intimacy and then break with Richard, or York's clinging to his nephew's cause and his ultimate act of betrayal) are marked by Shakespeare's attuned use of such language of persuasion and affinity. In this play it is possible to chart, almost by the second, the relative strength of the bonds between protagonists. If we compare *Richard II* to the thematically comparable *Edward II* the divergence on this point is conspicuous. In Marlowe's play neither Edward nor Mortimer can be said to have developing relationships (even with the respective objects of their passion, Gaveston and Isabella): their attachments are instant and absolute.[35] King Edward's abdication in Act 5 is a grand personal spectacle, but it is in no way a piece of relational drama since none of the characters present have previously appeared on the stage.[36]

Shakespeare's ability to focus on the distinct character trajectories of a small core of principal roles taken by known sharers connects in some ways with the experience of modern writers and directors. Keith Johnstone, for example, famously put the 'see-saw principle' at the centre of his 'status change' experiments at the Royal Court Theatre in the 1960s—an approach that proved influential on contemporary playwright Patrick Marber,

33. See Manfred Pfister, *The Theory and Analysis of Drama*, trans. John Halliday (Cambridge: Cambridge University Press, 1988), 111–17.
34. Pfister, *Drama*, 113, 116.
35. See Christopher Marlowe, *Edward II*, ed. Charles R. Forker, Revels (Manchester: Manchester University Press, 1994). The King is already fully infatuated with Gaveston in 1.1; Mortimer junior, conversely, expresses no desire for Isabella until the end of the play at 5.2, where his wooing meets instant acceptance.
36. Marlowe, *Edward II*, 5.1. The Earl of Leicester does appear briefly in the preceding scene when he arrests the King, but for the rest none of Trussel, Berkeley, or the Bishop of Winchester has had a previous entry. As a result Edward's declaration to Leicester that 'kind and loving hast thou always been' (5.1.7) can carry little force with the audience and there is indeed no sign of such affection in the Earl.

working directly with an acting company as he composed his work.[37] While it would be reductive to transpose such experiences unaltered into the sixteenth century it is also highly unlikely that Shakespeare's establishment within the nation's most stable and successful ensemble of players would occur without artistic effects. The playwright was now writing for men whose equal status alongside him as sharers was important. Under such circumstances it was undoubtedly easier for him to envisage dramatic relationships within a group.

From the mid-1590s onwards, Shakespeare takes exceptional interest in the evolving power-dynamics that occur amongst clusters of characters. We see this in generational conflict as much as in aristocratic status battles. In *Richard II* the young Richard is berated by old Gaunt (2.1); young Hotspur is chided by his father Northumberland (2.3); Bolingbroke is reproved by old York (2.3). In each case there is explicit characterization based on age, and, in a late spectacular scene (5.3), we find an entire family (in York, Aumerle, and the Duchess) pleading against one another on these grounds. The moment at which York discovers his son's conspiracy against the King is particularly telling because questions and commands (which in playscripts are conventionally a cue for speech or action) are now instead used as a device through which a lack of power is exposed:

YORK: Boy, let me see the writing.
AUMERLE: I do beseech you, pardon me. I may not show it.
YORK: I will be satisfied. Let me see it, I say.
　　　　　　　　He plucks it out of his bosom and reads it.
　　Treason, foul treason! Villain, traitor, slave!
DUCHESS OF YORK: What is the matter, my lord?
YORK [*Calls offstage.*]
　　Ho! Who's within there?
　　　　　　　　[*Enter* Servingman.]
　　　　　　　　Saddle my horse.
　　God for His mercy, what treachery is here!
DUCHESS OF YORK: Why, what is't my lord?

37. For a description of these experiments, see Keith Johnstone, *Impro: Improvisation and Theatre* (London: Faber & Faber, 1979; repr. Methuen, 1989), 33–74. Patrick Marber wrote and directed his first play, *Dealer's Choice*, on the basis of workshops with the Royal National Theatre (Cottesloe), starting with status experiments with actors who would eventually become the performing cast. I am grateful for conversations on this process with the author during his time as Cameron Mackintosh Professor of Contemporary Theatre at St Catherine's College, Oxford, from 2004 to 2005.

YORK: Give me my boots, I say. Saddle my horse.

> [*Exit Servingman.*]

  Now, by mine honour, by my life, by my troth,
  I will appeach the villain!

DUCHESS OF YORK: What is the matter?

YORK: Peace, foolish woman!

DUCHESS OF YORK: I will not peace. What is the matter, Aumerle?

AUMERLE: Good mother, be content. It is no more
  Than my poor life must answer.

DUCHESS OF YORK: Thy life answer?

YORK [*to Servingman offstage*]
  Bring me my boots! I will unto the King.

> *His* Servingman *enters with his boots.*

DUCHESS OF YORK: Strike him, Aumerle! Poor boy, thou art amazed.
  [*to Servingman*]
  Hence, villain! Never more come in my sight!

YORK: Give me my boots, I say.

> [*Servingman helps York put on his boots, then exit.*]

DUCHESS OF YORK: Why, York, what wilt thou do?

> (*Richard II*, 5.2.69–88)

The stage directions in square brackets in the above quotation are those of the Arden3 edition. There are no equivalent instructions in the Quarto (which is closest to Shakespeare's working papers); indeed, no early modern manuscript provides the kind of detailed directions that would be necessary for the staging of this scene.[38] It is worth reflecting, in this light, on how difficult it would be to orchestrate such an exchange as an author without direct contact with the performers. For actors dependent only on their individual 'parts' with cue lines, or on a 'reading' before the company, the movements of individual performers would quickly become confused. Action is here dependent not only on character but on a perceived set of character relations. Shakespeare develops such connections across the full length of *Richard II* and thus creates what is unfashionably but rightly called 'believable' interdependence between clusters of characters.

---

38. Compare Q1, William Shakespeare, *Richard II* (1597), H4^b–11^a; the Folio version, which is more strongly marked up for production, is no more explicit about the objects of speeches in this scene (see Shakespeare, *Richard II*, in *First Folio*, TLN 2440–62). On the authority of these texts see *Richard II*, ed. Forker, 506–41. On the paucity of information, especially the limited nature of cues in actors' parts, see Palfrey and Stern, *Shakespeare in Parts*, 97–111. The authors argue that the immediacy of Shakespeare's theatre is partly effected by the playwright's strategic use of surprise in providing limited information to his actors in cases such as this.

By 'relational drama' I mean something more limited than the onto-logical transformation that Harold Bloom proposed in *Shakespeare: The Invention of the Human* and something more technical than the 'unguarded truism' of the life-like, which is set out by A. D. Nuttall in *A New Mimesis*.[39] Specifically I refer to dispersed and sustained character individuation (which need not necessarily be naturalistic), combined with speech that is both phatic and metalingual. Such relational drama is closely associated with the tight-knit social groupings that are a recurrent feature of Shakespeare's mid-to late 1590s drama. We may think, for example, of *Romeo and Juliet*'s Capulets and Montagues; of the jurisdictions of Messina and Aragon in *Much Ado About Nothing*; and above all of the extended generational tensions of the *Henry IV* plays. In all of these we have at least two clusters of characters with their own distinctive locale and ethos.[40] This kind of writing follows logically from the condition of an author who is himself bound up in a sustained relationship with the actors for whom he writes.

39. Harold Bloom, *Shakespeare: The Invention of the Human* (New York: Riverhead Books, 1998); A. D. Nuttall, *A New Mimesis: Shakespeare and the Representation of Reality* (London: Methuen, 1983), 181.
40. Alan C. Dessen, *Elizabethan Stage Conventions and Modern Interpreters* (Cambridge: Cambridge University Press, 1984), 96–8, suggests that the audience perception of locale in early modern theatre related closely to the presence of groups of representative figures. His distinction between this experience and that of stage realism (*Stage Conventions*, 162–3) is pertinent here.

7
Shakespeare's singularity

I t is one thing to claim that becoming a sharer in an acting company was a transformative event for Shakespeare. It is another to describe that event as unique. Having made the argument that the events of 1594 resulted in a significant change in Shakespeare's dramaturgy, I want now also to propose that his resulting position as a sharer, performer, and dramatist was without parallel amongst his contemporaries. This is partly an assessment of the facts of theatrical history, but it also involves judgement on the artistic logic of plays in this period. While sketching a picture of the theatrical marketplace after 1594 I thus also set out to illustrate that the development of 'relational drama' from the mid-1590s was a phenomenon exclusive to Shakespeare. In terms of working practice, literary style, and financial success, his career diverged radically from that of other dramatists after this date.

Uniqueness admits no degree. Yet the extent of Shakespeare's outlier status must obviously be addressed in comparison to others. The best-known names of early modern English drama—Kyd, Greene, Chapman, Peele, Marlowe, Jonson, Dekker, Middleton, Ford, Webster, Beaumont, Fletcher, Shirley, Massinger—were certainly not sharers. Some others—John Marston, John Lyly, Robert Daborne, and Michael Drayton—did attempt theatrical investments in the children's companies, but these fell short of the status of sharer–playwright and none was sustained for more than a couple of years.[1] The only literary playwright to become a fellow in

---

1. John Marston, according to the testimony of Robert Keysar, obtained a stake in the Blackfriars children's syndicate (see Charles William Wallace, 'Shakespeare and his London Associates as Revealed in Recently Discovered Documents', *University Studies of the University of Nebraska* 10 (1910), 261–360 (at 337–9); Michael Shapiro, *Children of the Revels: The Boy Companies of Shakespeare's Time and their Plays* (New York: Columbia University Press, 1977), 23, 25; and Lucy Munro, *Children of the Queen's Revels: A Jacobean Theatre Repertory* (Cambridge: Cambridge University Press, 2005), 25). That position, for which no other evidence exists, could have lasted for no more than four years and was obviously not that of an actor–sharer. Even so,

an acting company was Thomas Heywood; his, therefore, is a potentially comparable situation that will require sustained comparison below.

Of course, it could be objected that Shakespeare was not a writer turned player but a player turned writer. I think this highly improbable but, supposing it were true, it is again important to see if there might be a parallel case. There were clearly always performers who contributed dramatic material and in the early days of the commercial theatre legendary clowns (such as Skoggins, Tarlton, and later Kemp himself) are known to have been responsible for at least partial playtexts. As has been mentioned, travelling players in the 1580s seem also routinely to have written moralities and histories, the Queen's Men's player Robert Wilson being a notable figure of this time. In the seventeenth century we find the actors Nathan Field, Samuel Rowley, William Rowley, and Robert Armin revising and supplementing plays by full-time professionals and, to a more limited extent, writing single-author works. In their education and style of composition these men do look more like literary playwrights than did the travelling performers of the 1580s. Still, none were published poets and none produced a corpus of independently authored plays.[2]

In summary, although some writers had a degree of investment in property and although a number of principal actors also took a role in the creation of playtexts, the professions of 'player' and 'playwright' remained

as I argue in Chapter 10, the playwright's commitment to the indoor stage did have an impact on his writing. John Lyly's sporadic success in various earlier boy company ventures provides an interesting point of comparison, but again these investments were nebulous and did not last for much more than a year (see Charles William Wallace, *The Evolution of the English Drama up to Shakespeare with a History of the First Blackfriars Theatre* (Berlin: Georg Reimer, 1912), 169–72; John Lyly, *Campaspe* and *Sappho and Phao*, ed G. K. Hunter, Revels (Manchester: Manchester University Press, 1991), 33–9, and *Endymion*, ed. David Bevington, Revels (Manchester: Manchester University Press, 1996), 49–60). On Daborne's disastrous attempt at an investment in a theatre, the aborted Porter's Hall, see S. P. Cerasano, 'Competition for the King's Men?: Alleyn's Blackfriars Venture', *Medieval and Renaissance Drama in England* 4 (1989), 173–86, and Munro, *Children of the Queen's Revels*, 28. Both accounts stress Daborne's indebtedness and Munro notes that no plays written by Daborne for the Children (if they existed) survive. Drayton was part of an attempt to establish the Children of the King's Revels at Whitefriars, but this venture likewise did not succeed (see E. K. Chambers, *The Elizabethan Stage* (Oxford: Clarendon Press, 1923; repr. 2009), II, 64–8; 515–17).

2. The case of Shakespeare's fellow King's Man Robert Armin is discussed in detail in Chapter 9. Armin did publish his verses and his translation of a short Italian verse romance as well as a single securely identifiable play. Such poetry, however, is in the tradition of comic doggerel and does not attempt to emulate the non-dramatic compositions of poet-playwrights. I discuss William Rowley's compositions alongside Armin's. On the careers of Field and Samuel Rowley see *Oxford DNB*.

separate ones. Thus Shakespeare's full involvement in both composition and performance stands (pending an examination of Heywood) as an unparalleled case.

The developments of 1594 may also have brought changes for writers besides Shakespeare, but these are not likely to have been substantial. The authorities' implementation of the 'duopoly' was patchy and a number of the old proscribed companies continued playing after the formation of the new Chamberlain's and Admiral's Men. By 1597 the new outfit of Pembroke's at the Swan was in operation and although this was not successful, another outlet for new writing would come with the revival of the boys' companies and the arrival of Derby's. The theatrical marketplace of the late 1590s was therefore, like that of the first half of the decade, a world of unforeseeable dramatic prospects for all but the asset-holders in theatres or companies. True, the Admiral's Men would have been a fairly stable company to write for. Men such as Chettle, Porter, Dekker, Drayton, and the young Jonson at the Rose would have had a good idea of the actors for whom they were writing, and Grace Ioppolo has argued forcefully for a practice of adaptation to company amongst such professionals.[3] Henslowe's *Diary*, however, shows that the pattern of shared authorship continued and for much of the work of Shakespeare's contemporaries in this period it remains difficult to define a distinct authorial voice. The archive of Henslowe's and Alleyn's papers is also compelling evidence of the financial difficulties of most and probably all of these writers.[4] Henry Porter is known now only through the bawdy and very basic verse of *The Two Angry Women of Abingdon*, printed as played by the Admiral's Men in the final year of the decade.[5] In its prologue (although it reads more like a preface to a printed edition) we hear the author described as a 'poor scholar' who needs 'a mite of your favours' to 'pay for his lodging among the muses'.

We get a detailed picture of the continued running of the company from Henslowe's correspondence. We see, for example, that Daborne (under pressure to get *The Arraignment of London* finished) is happy to hand over the

---

3. Grace Ioppolo, *Dramatists and their Manuscripts in the Age of Shakespeare, Jonson, Middleton and Heywood* (London: Routledge, 2006), 30–1 and *passim*.
4. Extensive correspondence and other documentation relating to debt is to be found for numerous writers for the Henslowe–Alleyn business, including Lodge, Dekker, and Daborne.
5. See Henry Porter, *The Two Angry Women of Abington* (Oxford: Malone Society, 1913). This play is sometimes known as *Part I, Two Angry* although no second part survives. Admiral's at this point was also known as Nottingham's. The quotation below is from this edition.

writing of one act of this commission to Cyril Tourneur.[6] For Henslowe's companies there developed a triangular process of decision making, where playwrights pitched ideas or offered playtexts to the company and where a company member then appealed to Henslowe for finance. A note from Robert Shaa to Philip Henslowe on 8 November 1599 gives a good sense of this process. On a small strip of paper (previously used to plan out stage entrances) Shaa writes:

> We have heard their book and like it; their price is eight pounds, which I pray pay now to Mr Wilson, according to our promise. I would have come myself, but that I am troubled with a scytation.[7]

At times, such notes refer to a play that is in the first stages of construction. Thus, Samuel Rowley appeals to Henslowe early in the new century as follows concerning a new co-authored play:

> Mr Henslowe, I have heard five sheets of a play of the Conquest of the Indies and I do not doubt but it will be a very good play; therefore, I pray you, deliver them forty shillings in earnest of it and take the papers into your [own] hands and on Easter Eve they promise to make an end of all the rest.[8]

The example is revealing because while, on the one hand, it shows an efficient transaction it also makes clear that the playwrights, in order to secure an advance, must hand over their physical copy of the playscript. Clearly authorial control would be minimal in such a case. On some occasions, there was a more protracted process of consultation. At a date around 1613, for example, Nathan Field writes to Henslowe that Daborne and he 'have spent a great deal of time in conference about this plot, which will make as beneficial a play as hath come these seven years'.[9] Even so,

6. 'Robert Daborne to Philip Henslowe (5 June 1613)' printed in W. W. Greg, *Henslowe Papers* (London: A. H. Bullen, 1907), 71–2. Daborne here differentiates between the co-authored *Arraignment* and 'my own play'.
7. 'Robert Shaa to Philip Henslowe (8 November 1599)' printed in Greg, *Henslowe Papers*, 49; Henslowe's *Diary*, ed. R. A. Foakes, 2nd edn (Cambridge: Cambridge University Press, 2002), Appendix I, corrects Greg's transcription from 'seytation' to 'scytation' (the word refers to an attack of sciatica). It is often said that the scene division (rather than the note to Henslowe) is a jotting on scrap paper. However, the generously spaced italic script of the scene plan (plus the note's presence amongst Henslowe's papers) makes this seem the more likely first use of the sheet. Alleyn MSS 1, fol. 45 is a similar note, again referring to a co-authored composition.
8. 'Samuel Rowley to Philip Henslowe' printed in Greg, *Henslowe Papers*, 56. The note has no date but an addition in Henslowe's hand below states 'Lent of the 4 April 1601.' Such documents were evidently kept by Henslowe as receipts recording payment.
9. 'Nathan Field to Philip Henslowe (undated)' printed in Greg, *Henslowe papers*, 84.

assignment of this scenario remained uncertain. Later in the note Field observes that if Henslowe does not advance £10 'Mr Daborne may have his request of another company'. It always remained evident that Henslowe would make the decision and that, if payment was made, the play's ownership would effectively be his.

It is difficult to say how far the convention of co-authorship, so common in the Henslowe–Alleyn playhouses, carried over into Shakespeare's company, but it is evident that author–actor relations here were likewise more often businesslike than intimately attuned. One play that provides particularly strong manuscript evidence is Arthur Wilson's *Inconstant Lady*, which the playwright produced before 1630 while studying at Oxford.[10] When he came to London, Wilson presented a fair copy to the King's Men, who accepted it with relatively minor revisions. In Wilson's authorial manuscript we see him reworking the details of various speeches in a different ink, mainly removing possible causes of offence. Act 3, Scene 3 of the original text caused problems and after some initial attempts at interlineal revision it was scrapped and rewritten. As a result of this replotting, alterations also needed to be made to the final scene. Here Wilson produced a number of short speeches on separate scraps of paper, placing marks in the manuscript where these should be inserted as was conventional with other companies. The whole text was then resubmitted and worked over by the King's Men's prompter, who inserted various details necessary for staging and made a series of minor cuts. Overall, the work was little altered (and certainly not adapted in its individual parts). Characters in the list of *dramatis personae* remain impersonal outlines (such as 'A Bawd' or 'A Lover'). The final performed version of the work (for which we have a separate documentary record) thus did not differ significantly from the play that Wilson wrote while alone in Oxford, where he could have had little thought as to the performing company.

In the case of *The Inconstant Lady* the play's original single author was responsible for its revision and there is good evidence that this was the preferred practice of Shakespeare's company, something that may suggest a stronger emphasis on artistic unity amongst the Chamberlain's Men. Theatrical manuscripts from the later years of the company—notably those connected with the attached playwrights Fletcher and Massinger—suggest

---

10. This is Folger MS J.b.1. For a reconstruction of the play's history, see R. C. Bald, 'Arthur Wilson's *The Inconstant Lady*', *The Library*, 4th series, 18 (1937), 287–313.

easygoing collaboration. Yet what we see of adaptation comes more from censorship than from actor-specific demands. For the Chamberlain's Men as much as for Henslowe's companies, then, changes for performance were a company matter, something accepted by all concerned. Even the proprietorial Ben Jonson acquiesced in this arrangement, so that in the prefatory epistle to *Sejanus* he observed without rancour that his original manuscript 'was not the same with that which was acted on the public stage, wherein a second hand had a good share'.[11] The author states that his original verses were 'no doubt less pleasing' than those produced by the revising author's 'genius' but he insists on the former to maintain the integrity of his work.

So if working practices changed little, what about literary fashions? The mid- to late 1590s certainly saw a continuation of older popular genres: domestic tragedy (such as *A Warning for Fair Women* performed by the Chamberlain's Men), pseudo-historical romance (such as Oxford's *The Weakest Goeth to the Wall*), and old-style Marlovian horror (like the Admiral's Men's *Lust's Dominion*) or documentary history (for example the Chamberlain's Men's *Larum for London*).[12] These plays are now anonymous and many are likely to have been co-authored.[13] Some productions were revivals, such as *The Battle of Alcazar* (for which the Admiral's produced a new theatrical plot). Others were major adaptations, clearly written with a sound sense of a company's traditions and preferences. Dekker's *Old Fortunatus*, for example, appears to be a fusion of two older plays on the same subject in the Admiral's repertory.[14] Right from its opening, the author demonstrates an arch awareness of the company's other productions, with its preliminary tableaux showing Bajazeth (Tamburlaine's victim) as Fortune's fool bound in chains. Throughout, the play is also comically

11. Ben Jonson, *Sejanus* (1605), 2[b]. Part of the author's concern here, it should be noted, may have been to avoid connection with the play's apparent political subtext.

12. For texts and commentary on these plays see Anon., *A Warning for Fair Women*, ed. Charles Dale Cannon (The Hague: Mouton, 1975); Anon., *The Weakest Goeth to the Wall* (Oxford: Malone Society, 1912); and Anon., *Lust's Dominion*, ed. J. Le Gay Brereton, Materials for the Study of Old English Drama (Louvain: Librairie universitaire, Uystpruyst, 1931) and also Alfred Harbage, *Annals of English Drama: 975–1700*, 3rd edn, rev. Sylvia Stoler Wagonheim (London: Routledge, 1989), on dating.

13. If *Lust's Dominion* was also known as *The Spanish Moor's Tragedy* then it was probably the work of Haughton, Dekker, and Day.

14. See Thomas Dekker, *Dramatic Works*, ed. Fredson Bowers, 4 vols. (Cambridge: Cambridge University Press, 1953–61), I, 107. Kathleen E. McLuskie, *Dekker and Heywood: Professional Dramatists* (London: Macmillan, 1994), 13, on the basis of the £2 payment, thinks Dekker's role restricted to the court adaptation of the opening and close of the play.

reminiscent of *Faustus* (it borrows that work's 'morality play' apparatus and adapts its formula of outlandish locations and magical stunts).

Clearly Dekker was attuned to the Admiral's Men's requirements (down to the level of once more recycling *Tamburlaine*'s bridles, kingly footstools, and chains). Yet the nature of his commission (a payment of £6 for 'the whole history of Fortunatus') could give little room for adaptation to the personal capacities of that company. Examining the full run of surviving Admiral's plays from the middle to the end of the decade it is impossible to make the case that these works explore the relationship between distinctive characters. Dramas such as Dekker's *Old Fortunatus* or Chapman's *The Blind Beggar of Alexandria* are fast-moving and inventive comedies. Their authors delight in a surfeit of disguises, locations, twists, and turns. Sustained characterization (even comic characterization), however, is not their objective. Indeed, both plays make a virtue of the improbable changefulness of their protagonists.

The major innovation that attracted the labour of literary playwrights in this period was humoural comedy.[15] It might be called the equivalent of the 'Marlovian' drama of the first part of the decade, in the sense that it was in this genre that ambitious playwrights most consistently displayed inventiveness in relation to a known set of high-status norms. Though the mode might now be called 'Jonsonian' it was, in reality, much more widely distributed. As Jonson observes in *The Case is Altered* (played around 1598 under unknown auspices) it 'pleases the gentlemen' to 'have every day new tricks, and write you nothing/ but humours' even if the 'common sort' care nothing for the new comedy and bemoan the loss of the clown.[16] In some ways Chapman's *Blind Beggar of Alexandria*, put on by the Admiral's Men in 1596, already anticipated this form of drama. Its hero switches identity between radically different aliases: a usurer, two different noblemen, and the blind beggar of the title. It is Chapman's *An Humorous Day's Mirth* of 1597, however, that is generally credited with introducing humours comedy—a mode that continued to be vastly influential until at least the close of the next century.

It is a cliché to suggest that writers such as Chapman (and Jonson, who came to perfect the form) somehow produced plasterboard caricatures. In

15. For an overview of this innovation, see Martin Wiggins, *Shakespeare and the Drama of his Time*, Oxford Shakespeare Topics (Oxford: Oxford University Press, 2000), 64–78.
16. *The Case is Altered* in *Works*, ed. C. H. Herford and Percy Simpson (Oxford: Clarendon Press, 1927), III, 1.2.61–3.

fact, *An Humorous Day's Mirth*, like Jonson's *Every Man in his Humour* (performed with much success by the Chamberlain's) is immensely inventive in its creation of characters. Besides Labervele, the jealous *senex* husband, and Blanuel, the imitating courtier, it introduces some very up-to-date character types in the hypocritical puritan Florila and the melancholic Dowsecer. The differentiation of these figures melded easily with the sophisticated Italian *commedia* tradition. In the wake of Chapman's humours play a wave of literary playwrights contended to produce fresh characters—generally monomanic creations based on modern fads ranging from verbal tics to ruling passions. Juniper in Jonson's *The Case is Altered* ceaselessly comes out with outlandish neologisms. He is joined by the painfully circumlocutory lover Paulo, the irascible Count Ferneze, the miser Jaques, and the indiscriminate consumer of popular culture, Onion. The joy of such characters lies in their mental isolation: they cannot genuinely interact with others because they are trapped in a comically reductive way of viewing the world.

The identification of a humour bore an aspect of clinical diagnosis. This humoural thought about character anticipated the vast enthusiasm for Theophrastan types (such as the characters of Thomas Overbury or Joseph Hall) in the seventeenth century, but the moral ideal (in both tragedy and comedy) was a kind of stoical non-character. As the god Mercury says of Crites, the perfect balanced man in Jonson's *Cynthia's Revels* (performed by the Children of Blackfriars in 1600), he is 'a creature of a most perfect and divine temper' and 'one in whom the humours and elements are peaceably met, without emulation of precedencie'.[17] This ideal, a figure of a classical temperament undistorted either by modern fads or medical ailments, is a character common to Jonsonian dramaturgy: Cordatus in *Every Man out of his Humour*, Horace in *Poetaster*, Cordus and Sabinus in *Sejanus* are all men of this mettle. Paradoxically, the supreme achievement of characterization in these plays is the evisceration of individuality. Comedies such as *The Case is Altered* highlight this purgation narrative in their very titles: it is a standard feature of humours plays by Jonson and others that they conclude with the sudden disappearance of the ruling passions of their protagonists.

The trend towards fixity and purgation is the very opposite of the trajectory in Shakespeare's drama in this period, where individual performers negotiate developmental arcs of increasing complexity. This is one quality that separates Shakespeare's *Merchant of Venice* from a contemporary

17. Jonson, *Cynthia's Revels*, in *Works*, ed. Herford and Simpson, IV, 2.3.123–5.

comedy on a comparable theme such as Haughton's *Englishmen for My Money*. In both plays a set of lovers are kept apart by a usurious, foreign, blocking figure (Haughton's Pisaro has more than a little of Shakespeare's Shylock). Yet in Shakespeare's drama the enmity between Antonio and Shylock is explicable and deep-rooted. The drawn-out trial scene of Act 4 Scene 1 (not unlike the deposition scene at 4.1 in *Richard II*) is all about the drama of persuasion: it plays upon antipathies and loyalties that have evolved over the course of the play. In Shakespeare it is important that Antonio has a history of slighting Shylock, that Bassanio has long been indebted to Antonio, and that Bassanio has pledged his troth to Portia. All those relationships are put under stress by the dramatist in the fourth act. In *Englishmen for My Money*, in contrast, behaviour is governed by the mechanical logic of farce. It is therefore much easier for Pisaro in *Englishmen* to conclude by embracing the young gentlemen who have outdone him. In *The Merchant of Venice* the laws of comedy cannot just sweep Shylock along in their wake.

Relational drama continues to differentiate Shakespeare's work from that of his contemporaries in the mid- to late 1590s. *The Merry Wives of Windsor* has been cited as part of the fashion for humoural citizen comedy, although if it was performed for the Garter Feast on 23 April 1597 then it predates Chapman's *An Humorous Day's Mirth*, the play now credited with starting the fashion.[18] Certainly Shakespeare's play initiates or follows characteristics that became commonplace: a focus on cuckoldry, comic attention to specific English locations, the idea of a jealous humour, plus a farcical plot in which a reformed gallant (here the lightly drawn Master Fenton) succeeds in getting the girl. Yet, in spite of the surface connections with city comedy, the play's cast of characters functions differently. Indeed, *The Merry Wives of Windsor* is based on an act of characterization entirely unheard of in earlier English drama: the transplantation wholesale of a network of characters from one genre into an entirely different one. Falstaff, Mistress Quickly,

---

18. Roslyn Lander Knutson, *The Repertory of Shakespeare's Company, 1594–1613* (Fayetteville: University of Arkansas Press, 1991), 43, arguing for Shakespeare's position in the mainstream of fashion, classes these plays alongside one another. *An Humorous Day's Mirth* is first mentioned by Henslowe on 11 May 1597 (see Foakes, ed., *Diary*, 58). The long-standing claim that Shakespeare's play was written specifically for the Garter Feast is supported by T. W. Craik, *The Merry Wives of Windsor* (Oxford: Oxford University Press, 1990), 1–13, and by Stanley Wells and Gary Taylor, *William Shakespeare: A Textual Companion* (Oxford: Clarendon Press, 1987), 120, but it is emphatically rejected in Giorgio Melchiori's Arden3 edition (London: Methuen, 2000), 18–30, where a date of 1599 is preferred. My quotations are from the latter and sources appear in the text.

Pistol, and Bardolf are lifted from the London tavern of *Henry IV Part 1* into the countryside of Windsor. And if, as is likely, *Henry IV Part 2* had also been written by that time, then Justice Shallow was transported from his native Gloucestershire to be rooted in this new location as well.[19] Relational characterization had become a habit of Shakespeare's, so much so that Fenton is briefly coloured in as a character through a harmless rakish background as a companion to Prince Hal of the *Henry IV* plays.[20] The characters still retain from their past lives their distinctive speech and physical characteristics: Falstaff his bulk and mock-heroic grandeur; Pistol his bluster; Shallow his age, nostalgia, and repetitive phrasing; Bardolf his red face; Mistress Quickly her inconsequential garrulousness. More than this, they retain a kind of memory of their past experience, so that Pistol labels Mistress Quickly (now a housekeeper) as a prostitute or 'punk' in spite of her change of circumstance (*Wives*, 2.2.127). The reality that such transfers are somewhat imperfectly effected is in fact testimony to the player-centredness of Shakespeare's thinking. For the dramatist was not attempting any logical continuation of an historical person's story. Rather, he wanted quickly to assemble an occasion-specific comedy and this trusted matrix of characters was something that he and the company had readily to hand.[21]

The interrelated network of Falstaff's acquaintance that spans *Henry IV Part 1* and *Part 2*, *The Merry Wives of Windsor*, and even *Henry V* is intimately connected to the practicalities of work as a company dramatist. Just as in *Richard II*, but now not just across a single play but across years of composition, we find sustained attention to the language and power relations between individuals. In Pistol we find that Marlovian rhetoric (which Shakespeare had earlier imitated freely) becomes a feature of characterization. Of course, the braggart's words (most famously his 'pamper'd jades of Asia' speech (*2 Henry IV*, 2.4.160–6)) echo Marlowe's, but this is borrowing of which his fellow speakers are well aware. Falstaff in *Henry IV Part 2* scoffs that Pistol can 'do nothing but speak nothing' (2.4.189) and he still seizes on

19. Craik, ed., *Wives*, 11, maintains the possibility that the play was written midway between the two *Henry IV* histories; if this is right then Shallow took a journey in the opposite direction, north-westward, instead.

20. Master Page, affirming Fenton's unsuitability as a match for his daughter Anne, asserts that Fenton 'kept company with the wild Prince and Poins' (*Wives*, 3.2.65–6), something that must have occurred in the timeframe of *1 Henry IV* and/or *2 Henry IV*.

21. As noted, the nature of this occasion remains contentious. Craik, ed., *Wives*, 1–13, is confident about the date and first performance location at Windsor; Melchiori, ed., *Wives*, 18, is more sceptical but still calls this a 'garter play'.

these same qualities in *The Merry Wives of Windsor* when he complains of 'red-lattice phrases' and 'bold beating oaths' as the 'shelter' of Pistol's honour (2.2.26–8). Whether *Henry IV Part 2* was written after, alongside, or before *The Merry Wives of Windsor* this remains an extraordinarily sustained example of character relatedness.

Shakespeare's distinctive form of drama was immensely popular in the mid- to late 1590s, so inevitably there were attempts to imitate his success. The *Henry IV* plays, especially, can be shown to have inspired contemporary responses. Yet, in terms of characterization, these plays have little in common with Shakespeare's original. *Sir John Oldcastle*, like *Henry IV*, was a work in two parts that dealt with the fall of Henry V's former companion. In this version of the story, Oldcastle (Shakespeare's original name for Falstaff) is rehabilitated as a martyr who falls victim to a clerical plot.[22] This is not, however, a drama about relationships. Oldcastle, like the other protagonists, effectively exists alone and drifts in picaresque fashion through a series of trials. While Part 1 opens with the treatment of high-church politics, it concludes with a rapid series of costume changes and mistaken identities. In this it has much in common with the trilogy of Robin Hood plays performed around the same time by the Admiral's Men, which move easily from farce to tragedy and are happy to bend their characters in shape to the generic requirements of the situation to hand.[23] *Oldcastle*'s Sir John Wrotham, who is the play's equivalent of Falstaff, has no group of associates: like Oldcastle he operates as a single entity as he pursues the alehouse quarrels, comic robberies, and lecherous assignations that imitate Shakespeare's lead. The play has sixty-nine parts and thus requires exceptional doubling for a company of around fourteen performers.[24] All of these features militate against the creation of Beckerman's concepts of breadth, length, and depth.

The failure to achieve relational characterization in *Sir John Oldcastle* can be traced to the conditions of its composition. The original authors, who were

22. Part 2 of *Sir John Oldcastle* is lost, but this was undoubtedly the play's conclusion. On *Oldcastle*'s commissioning, performance, and publication history see Michael Drayton, *Works*, ed. William Hebel, 5 vols. (Oxford: Basil Blackwell, 1961), v, 44–8.

23. These are *Look About You* (featuring the young Robin and set in the turbulent reign of Henry II), *The Downfall of Robert, Earl of Huntingdon* (featuring the outlaw Robin and set in the turbulent reign of King Richard I) and *The Death of Robert, Earl of Huntington* (featuring the slowly dying Robin and set in the turbulent reign of King John). These plays are probably all Chettle/Munday collaborations of the late 1590s. They might charitably be described as uneven in quality.

24. For a full reconstruction see Anthony Munday et al., *The Life of Sir John Oldcastle* (Oxford: Malone Society, 1908).

paid by Philip Henslowe, were Anthony Munday, Michael Drayton, Robert Wilson, and Richard Hathaway.[25] Their play was first performed by the Admiral's, but within three years it was passed on to another Henslowe ensemble, Worcester's Men. On 17 August 1602 that company is recorded in the *Diary* as having borrowed 40 shillings 'to pay unto Thomas Dekker for new additions in *Oldcastle*' and additional payment for changes is recorded the following month.[26] This was evidently a significant reshaping of the work, done without reference to the original four authors. One reason for that reshaping is likely to have been the arrival of Will Kemp, who at the time of the work's original composition would still have been a member of the Chamberlain's company. On 22 August Henslowe laid out 5 shillings for Kemp 'to buy buckram to make a pair of giant hose'.[27] As the following entry is for the purchase of Oldcastle's suit it is probable that this cloth was used for the costume of another of the play's characters. Possibly Kemp played the decadent Sir John Wrotham, using the 'giant hose' to pad out his frame. Such a late alteration would have adapted Wrotham to Kemp's performance characteristics, but if this happened there is no trace of it in the playtext as we now have it, which has its origins in the quarto published two years before.[28] *Oldcastle*, both as a dramatic work and an instance of theatrical history, shows how difficult it was for playwrights to maintain contact with their works as performed entities. Shakespeare, by contrast, could adapt in the rare cases where there were changes.[29] If Kemp had played Sir John Falstaff then the playwright was able to respond to his departure because in *Henry V*, where the other characters in his entourage make their appearance, the knight has a theatrically convenient offstage death.

The case of *Sir John Oldcastle* is typical of attempts to emulate or rival Shakespeare's success in the mid- to late 1590s. The *Edward IV* plays provide another example. Written largely by Thomas Heywood, they are a transparent

---

25. On 16 October 1599, Henslowe records payment of £10s to Munday, Drayton, Hathaway, and Wilson 'for the first part of the life of Sir John Oldcastle and in earnest of the second part'. A further 10s was laid out as a gift 'for Mr Munday and the rest of the poets at the playing of Sir John Oldcastle the first time' (Foakes, ed., *Diary*, 125–6). On the wider culture of play alteration, see Tiffany Stern, 'Re-Patching the Play', in Peter Holland and Stephen Orgel, eds., *Redefining British Theatre History* (Houndmills: Palgrave Macmillan, 2004), 151–68.

26. Foakes, ed., *Diary*, 213. Payment for apparel and additional changes is recorded at 214–16; this entry is again paired with a charge for 'making of William Kemp's suit' (215).

27. Foakes, ed., *Diary*, 214.

28. See Munday et al., *Sir John Oldcastle*, v–vii.

29. Kemp was the only sharer to depart from the Chamberlain's/King's Men in Shakespeare's life for a reason other than death or retirement.

attempt to recreate the serio-comic world of Shakespeare's trilogy on the life of Henry V. Their central character is closely based on Shakespeare's: an aristocrat who plays truant from court and spends his time with distinctive 'low-life' figures such as the plain-speaking John Hobbs, the tanner of Tamworth. Many individual scenes could be said to have a reciprocal, social quality to their exchanges. What is striking, however, is that no set of relationships stretches or develops across the play as a whole. Hobbs, for instance, meets the King only halfway through *Part 1* and then needs, somewhat awkwardly, to travel to London in order to meet him again at the play's close. There are practical reasons for this lack of focus on relational development, because, like so many dramas of this period, the play shifted unpredictably between authors as well as companies.[30] In the late 1590s Heywood was still operating like other playwrights, writing sometimes collaboratively and sometimes singly on projects like *The Famous History of the Life and Death of Captain Thomas Stukeley* and putting his laureate ambitions into carefully printed non-dramatic poems. He was already well established as a poet and playwright, but experience in itself did not bring theatrical control.

The developments in Heywood's career from the mid-1590s into the new century provide a potential parallel to Shakespeare's. Having abandoned his university studies in 1593 for financial reasons, Heywood had travelled to London, where he published his Ovidian neoteric poem *Oenone and Paris* in 1594. Like many others, he found regular employment writing for the theatres and in 1598 he was also hired as 'covenant servant' to perform minor roles at the Rose.[31] In 1601 a remarkable opportunity arose, very like the one that Shakespeare grasped seven years earlier. A new company, Worcester's Men, was effectively added to the 'duopoly' of licensed adult performers. Heywood almost certainly joined as a founding sharer and this event had a major effect on his work.[32] His change of status in 1601 confirms the significant implications of company membership on authorial identity.

The most remarkable testament here is his *Apology for Actors* of 1612. This treatise stands alone in early modern England as a sustained defence of the

30. For details see Thomas Heywood, *The First and Second Parts of King Edward IV*, ed. Richard Rowland, Revels (Manchester: Manchester University Press, 2005), 1–9.

31. For the contract in Henslowe's *Diary* see Foakes, ed., 241.

32. Ioppolo, *Dramatists*, 13, claims Heywood was a sharer in four companies: Worcester's, Queen Anne's, King's, and Queen Henrietta's Men. Queen Anne's was the later name of Worcester's. There is no sign that Heywood was ever a sharer in King's or Queen Henrietta's, though he certainly wrote for them after the breaking of Worcester's/Queen Anne's.

acting profession (Heywood's use of the word 'actor' as opposed to 'player' is itself significant). The fact that the sole example of such a work should come from the sole parallel instance of an author–sharer is telling. More telling still is the manner in which the *Apology* exudes a profound sense of collective ownership and endeavour. Once he is a sharer, all of Heywood's new compositions are written for his own company.[33] It is also clear that (as with Shakespeare) Heywood was able to bring with him to the ensemble a number of his plays that had earlier been held by a range of other companies, a step that indicates a sense of dramatic ownership quite different from non-attached playwrights such as Jonson and Middleton.[34]

Scraps of detail on the production of Heywood's dramas tend also to point to a closeness of playwright to performance. David Wiles notes that Heywood is the most consistent of all early modern dramatists in his use of 'the clown' in stage directions, with, unsurprisingly, Shakespeare following close behind.[35] The dramatist had a strong relationship with the principal comic actor of his company (Thomas Greene, who apparently replaced Kemp) and wrote parts specifically with him in mind.[36] Following Greene's death, Heywood wrote in praise of 'my entirely beloved Fellow, the actor', stating that 'there was not an actor of his nature in his time of better ability in performance of what he undertook'.[37] This is a level of closeness in public address to actors that we do not find in any other early modern playwright. Again, as with Shakespeare, there was not only a gathering of earlier

33. See Harbage, *Annals*. After 1600 all the works attributed to Heywood go to Worcester's/Queen Anne's. Conceivably Heywood may have assisted Chettle on the lost comedy *The First Part of the London Florentine*, but we have no text or secure attribution. Another lost play of the period is also sometimes associated with Heywood. That play belonged to Derby's, with whom he had been working in the late 1590s, and is likely to date from that period. These very doubtful instances aside, the record is consistent. Intriguingly William B. Long, 'Dulwich MS. XX, *The Telltale*: Clues to Provenance', *Medieval and Renaissance Drama in England* 17 (2005), 180–204, suggests that an author's position within a company shows up in the nature of his playtexts, with Shakespeare and Heywood needing fewer advisory directions in their scripts because of their daily contact with the actors (202).

34. McLuskie, *Dekker and Heywood*, 60, discusses the case of *Four Prentices*. This was probably Heywood's first play (perhaps written as early as 1592–4) but it was newly adapted for a Worcester's revival in 1602. That pattern holds true for other plays for Admiral's and Derby's in which Heywood had the main hand.

35. David Wiles, *Shakespeare's Clown: Actor and Text in the Elizabethan Playhouse* (Cambridge: Cambridge University Press, 1987), 67.

36. On Heywood's specific use of the clown Thomas Greene and the gallant Richard Perkins in *The Wise-Woman of Hogsdon* and *The Fair Maid of the West, Part 1* (which were also written during his period as sharer) see Paul Merchant, ed., *Thomas Heywood: Three Marriage Plays*, Revels (Manchester: Manchester University Press, 1996), 12–13.

37. Thomas Heywood, 'To the Reader', in John Cooke, *Greenes Tu quoque* (1614), A2ᵃ.

playtexts but also a change in production involvement. As was seemingly true of Shakespeare, Heywood had worked as a hired man before becoming a sharer—a role that might involve play-patching as well as acting in minor roles.[38] Neither playwright became a notable actor and possibly both retained the antipathy to public performance that was ingrained amongst educated men. This, however, did not prevent close involvement with production, a fact that is demonstrated by the appearance of Heywood's name in Henslowe's *Diary*, for example on 5 February 1602 making an expensive purchase for the heroine of his new play.[39] The black dress bought by the playwright for the production of his *A Woman Killed with Kindness* is evidence of a new kind of participation, which contrasts with earlier entries in the *Diary* that concern only payment for plays.[40]

There are some signs too that adoption into Worcester's Men had an artistic impact on Heywood. *A Woman Killed with Kindness*, the first surviving play that he wrote for the company, is more complex in its characterization than any of the playwright's earlier compositions.[41] Four characters are caught up in an evolving marital crisis: an insecure husband, Frankford; his young wife from a rich, impetuous family, Anne; the suave gentleman, Wendoll; and a plain-speaking servant who has served Frankford from his infancy, Nick. Throughout the play these individuals have distinct ways of operating and speaking and are connected with each other through crossed lines of obligation. Frankford, for example, is emotionally dependent on Wendoll ('He cannot eat without me,/ Nor laugh without me. I am to his body/ As necessary as his digestion,/ And equally do make him whole or sick').[42] Yet Wendoll survives on Frankford's generosity and expresses his feelings of guilt even as he makes advances on his wife. The domestic card game that is the tipping point of the drama is remarkable for involving all four of the protagonists in tense, developing power relations and it was envisaged by Heywood with a specificity that is very unusual in dramatic

38. Heywood's contract as a hired man is dated 25 March 1598 (Foakes, ed., *Diary*, 241).
39. Foakes, ed., *Diary*, 223.
40. On Heywood's activities as recorded by Henslowe see Foakes, ed., *Diary*, 50, 102, 104, 107–8, 213, 215–24, 226, 241, and 243, and also Neil Carson, *A Companion to Henslowe's Diary* (Cambridge: Cambridge University Press, 1988), 64–5.
41. For a detailed survey of the play's rise in critical appreciation and success in performance since the middle of the twentieth century see Richard Rowland, *Thomas Heywood's Theatre, 1599–1639: Locations, Transactions, and Conflict* (Farnham: Ashgate, 2010), 97–154.
42. Thomas Heywood, *A Woman Killed with Kindness*, ed. R. W. van Fossen, Revels (London: Methuen, 1961), 6.40–3. Subsequent references, unless otherwise stated, are to this edition.

documents (specifying, for example, that Frankford should enter 'as it were brushing the crumbs from his clothes with a napkin, and newly risen from supper').[43]

The exchanges are compelling above all because of their tendency to complicate status: Frankford should be master of the house, yet Wendoll's interventions (for example, his taking over the deck of cards) subvert that position; Nick should be a servant to Anne, yet his asides continually run against this. Frankford's concluding abandonment of the game on account of illness is thus characteristically double-edged. It marks the low point of the infirmity that Wendoll has exploited, but is also the move that helps establish a return to authority as he decides now to trust the accusations of his servant, Nick. The combined menace and delicacy of such exchanges is notable—they are an exemplary instance of the 'natural and affecting' qualities that made Charles Lamb describe Heywood as 'a sort of prose Shakespeare'.[44]

Both material and artistic evidence shows the impact of Heywood's decision to become a sharer and, as for Shakespeare, its consequences would prove sustained. All the same, it would be too much to claim his as a parallel instance. For one thing, the textual evidence is piecemeal: the dramatist's reluctance to publish his plays (perhaps itself a consequence of his sharer status) means we are often dependent on memorial reconstructions or on versions that were radically restructured after his company's collapse. That collapse also separates Worcester's/Queen Anne's from the Chamberlain's/King's Men. Whereas for Shakespeare there survived a company whose leading men could publish the posthumous Folio, for Heywood in his final years there was no equivalent organization to take care of his legacy. By the end of his life Heywood observed that most of his plays had been 'negligently lost' by the 'shifting and change of companies' and that, even where he wished to publish, his works were 'still retained in the hands of some actors' who thought it 'against their peculiar profit to have them come in print'.[45] Returning to write for the stage in the 1620s, Heywood found

43. Heywood, *Woman Killed*, 8.23 SD. As is noted by Brian Scobie in his New Mermaid edition of the play, these directions must be original to the author's manuscript because at times they are insufficiently precise to transfer directly to production. See Thomas Heywood, *A Woman Killed with Kindness*, ed. Brian Scobie (London: A. & C. Black, 1985), 39n.
44. Charles Lamb, *Specimens of English Dramatic Poets* (Philadelphia, PA: Willis P. Hazard, 1857), 106n.
45. Thomas Heywood, 'To the Reader', *The English Traveller* (1633), A3ᵃ.

himself back in the common position of a hired playwright. Though he knew Beeston (by whom he was employed), his manuscripts (such as that of *The Captives*) show that textual control now lay with the company and not the playwright.[46] In the case of a late play such as *Calisto*, we see Heywood working rapidly to condense his earlier company work for a revival by Beeston, a situation that the playwright, not without an edge of resentment, was forced to accept.[47]

At the start of the century, when Heywood joined Worcester's, his situation may well have looked similar to Shakespeare's around seven years earlier. The company was patented as a third licensed London ensemble and in their early years they appeared regularly at court. Yet for various reasons its fortunes would prove unsteady. Early on they built up debts to Philip Henslowe and though the *Diary* does not continue long enough to track how these obligations developed it is possible that, like other companies, they were undermined by their financial planning from the start. The real problems, however, came with the death in 1612 of Thomas Greene, their lead comic player, for not only did this entail a loss of talent, leadership, and finance, it also started a legal battle that dragged on for years.[48] The damaged company was finally broken through internal conflict involving Christopher Beeston, who, according to other sharers, fraudulently saddled them with a debt of £400.[49] Heywood's will does not survive, but the indications are that following these disasters he (like his contemporaries) generally worked in response to immediate financial need.

46. British Museum, MS Egerton 1994 shows the bookkeeper adding performer names and cutting the text (for details see *The Captives*, ed. Arthur Brown (Oxford: Malone Society, 1953), xi). For the final scene of the manuscript (ll. 2827–3240) the reviser actually cut two parts, reassigning their lines where necessary. Ioppolo, *Dramatists*, 94–9, discusses the play as a case of the circulation of manuscripts between author and playing company. Though she may be right that the relationship was cooperative, the realities of control were by this time different from those for Shakespeare's plays.

47. *Calisto* or *The Escapes of Jupiter* condenses and revises Heywood's earlier *The Golden Age* and *The Silver Age* so as to create one play. It is also in the author's hand and follows *The Captives* in MS Egerton 1994. The company's identity is uncertain, but it is likely to have been Beeston's at the Cockpit. The tone of the preface to the reader in *The English Traveller* is notably different from Heywood's earlier embrace of the acting profession. It would seem from the evidence on the legal dispute of 1619 (on which see Chambers, *Elizabethan Stage*, II, 239) that Beeston was blamed by Heywood for the company's collapse.

48. Greene was an actor–financier whose influence in the company can reasonably be compared to that of Richard Burbage in the Chamberlain's/King's Men. He managed the company and was the primary housekeeper in their playhouse. For details on this and the conflicts that followed his death see Herbert Berry, 'Greene, Thomas (*bap.* 1573, *d.* 1612)', *Oxford DNB*, and Chambers, *Elizabethan Stage*, II, 236–8.

49. Chambers, *Elizabethan Stage*, II, 239.

In the dedication of his *Nine Books of Various History Concerning Women* (1624) he writes to the former patron of his now collapsed acting company as a 'poor yet faithful servant' (A3[b]). That dedication alludes to financial difficulties and the *Nine Books* were hurriedly prepared for the press, almost certainly under pressure for ready money. Heywood's vast output of mass-market material, plus his oft-quoted claim to have had 'an entire hand, or at least a main finger' in 220 plays (*English Traveller*, A3[a]), all indicate a weakened position. Although, as David Kathman suggests, Heywood's early days as a author–sharer probably provided a steady income, this was not a situation that was set to last.[50]

For Shakespeare the case was different, both financially and artistically. Before 1594 we find no trace of any investments by him. Once he is established as a sharer in the Lord Chamberlain's, however, a stream of documents testifies to his growing wealth. By October 1596 he was rated as a householder in London and that same month he began the expensive business of applying for a coat of arms.[51] In May 1597 Shakespeare bought the New Place Manor House in Stratford, being recorded as paying £60 in silver. Even this large sum may be a legal fiction: Schoenbaum concludes that 'the figure may well seem absurdly low' for such a great house (173). The following year—in possession of the manor house and its substantial lands—Shakespeare was in a position to hoard malt. Holding on to his stockpiles and waiting for the market to rise further, he was evidently under no pressure to sell. Neighbours knew that Shakespeare had further money for investments: early in 1598 news circulated 'that our countryman Mr Shakespeare is willing to disburse some money upon some old yard land' and that 'he thinketh it a very fit pattern for him to deal in the matter of our tithes' (179). Over this period Shakespeare was also offering substantial sums to personal borrowers (180–8) but, even so, in 1599, he and the majority of his fellow sharers still had cash to spare for the construction of the Globe.

This kind of wealth separated Shakespeare from contemporary poet-professionals.[52] It appears, for example, that Heywood regarded him with

50. Kathman, 'Heywood, Thomas (*c.*1573–1641)', *Oxford DNB*. A bequest from Heywood's uncle, Edmund Heywood (who is mentioned in the dedication to *English Traveller*) on 18 January 1633 may have helped to ease the situation.
51. Samuel Schoenbaum, *William Shakespeare: A Documentary Life* (Oxford: Clarendon Press, 1975), 161, 167. References in the remainder of this paragraph are to this work and appear in the text.
52. Andrew Gurr's lengthy calculation leads to the conclusion that Shakespeare would have made as much as £60 per annum from his proportion of the profits as sharer. Like Heywood, he is highly likely to have been paid for his plays out of company accounts on top of that sum. This

a respect that did not stem purely from literary achievement. In the con-cluding epistle appended to his *Apology for Actors* Heywood expresses regret that his work has been published under Shakespeare's name in *The Passionate Pilgrim* and says of the poet–shareholder 'I must acknowledge my lines not worthy of his patronage, under whom [the printer William Jaggard] hath published them'.[53] The testaments to Shakespeare's personal qualities that survive suggest a sense of distance as well as of 'gentleness'.[54] His position as a sharer put him in some ways in a comparable position of power to that of Henslowe and Alleyn: like them he diversified his financial interests, was able to lend money, and developed a growing stake in the physical infra-structure of the theatre world.[55] In the case of the Chamberlain's/King's Men, as opposed to the Admiral's, influence was more evenly distributed across the members of a company. The wills of the sharers who died in the early seventeenth century show both wealth and loyalty across the fellow-ship, and Shakespeare (whose name appears repeatedly in their business dealings) was evidently a leading figure in the conduct of affairs.[56]

The Burbage–Shakespeare partnership has substantial affinities with that centred on the Rose, Fortune, and Bear Garden enterprise. Alleyn and Henslowe's business (for which, unlike the Chamberlain's/King's Men, we have coherent records) gives an insight into the source of the wealth

---

compares with Thomas Dekker's optimum income from writing for Henslowe of about £20 a year. As Gurr notes dryly, 'unlike Shakespeare, Dekker spent several years in a debtor's prison' (*The Shakespeare Company: 1594–1642* (Cambridge: Cambridge University Press, 2004), 97).

53. Heywood, *Apology*, G4[a–b].

54. 'Gentle' is the word used by Ben Jonson on the first sheet of the 1623 *Works*; John Aubrey, apparently using William Beeston as his authority, wrote that Shakespeare 'was not a company keeper' (see E. K. Chambers, *William Shakespeare: A Study of Facts and Problems*, (Oxford: Clarendon Press, 1930, II, 252 and the Conclusion of this book).

55. Shakespeare's investments in the Globe and Blackfriars playhouses are discussed in Chapters 8 and 12 respectively; his money lending, investment in land, cereals, and other goods is documented in Schoenbaum, *Documentary*, especially 178–92. Alleyn MSS 3, amongst other volumes in the Dulwich collection, is a vast gathering of documentation on these assets held by Henslowe and Alleyn. In MSS 3, Article 9, for example, is a letter from John Langworth to Alleyn, dated 6 February 1599, informing him that the land, about which he had enquired, was worth £80 a year, 'if corn bear any good price', and asking whether he would 'be willing to take a yearly annuity of me for the money I have of yours or not'. The payment of tithes becomes a matter of dispute that takes up many documents in MSS 3.

56. The legacies of Pope, Phillips, and Sly were all substantial. Pope, like Shakespeare, had investments in land and property in addition to his theatre shares. Longer-lived sharers such as Shakespeare, Burbage, Heminges, and Condell would all die wealthy. In most cases mention is made of other sharers in their wills. See E. A. J. Honigmann and Susan Brock, *Playhouse Wills: 1558–1642* (Manchester: Manchester University Press, 1993).

that Shakespeare was investing in Stratford, or that which men such as
Burbage, Phillips, and Condell would leave at their deaths.[57] Henslowe's
start-up capital for the building of the Rose came from a loan from a wealthy
London grocer. In exchange for a share of the receipts plus the exclusive
right to an adjacent tenement 'to keep victualing in, or to put to any other
use', the investor put up over £816.[58] In spite of these obligations, Henslowe made rapid financial progress, becoming, together with Alleyn, the
leading entertainment financier of the age. Alleyn's residence was purchased
for £5000, two-fifths of it in paid in cash.[59] That sum would have been
sufficient to build the Rose, the Globe, the Fortune, and Blackfriars together, and Henslowe probably left a comparable sum at his death.[60] These
are major fortunes to have accumulated. Although Alleyn and Henslowe,
like Shakespeare, had other sources of income (such as the Bear Garden and
the loan book) their principal investment was in playhouses, playing apparel,
and playtexts. It was the profits from London's theatres that made both
Alleyn and Henslowe immensely rich.[61] Their wealth (like Alleyn's house)
dwarfs Shakespeare's, but only in proportion to their relative stakes in their
companies.

57. According to contemporary gossip, Burbage left 'better than £300 land' to his heirs (Edwin
Nungezer, *A Dictionary of Actors* (Ithaca, NY: Cornell University Press, 1929), 70). By his death
Heminges, having taken up portions from other members, owned three-sixteenths of the
Globe and held two-eighths of the Blackfriars lease (Nungezer, *Actors*, 181).
58. The contract is the separately bound Muniment 16 in the Alleyn papers at Dulwich, a deed of
partnership between Philip Hinshley (that is, Henslowe) of London, dyer, and John Cholm-
ley, of London, grocer, for eight years and three months. The deed of partnership, dated 10
January 1586/7, is reproduced in Greg, *Henslowe Papers*, 2–4.
59. For details on the purchase of Dulwich Manor from Sir Francis Calton on 20 October 1605
see Alleyn MSS 8 (Memorandum Book), fol. 8[b]; Alleyn recorded payment of the remittance
in a different ink in 1613.
60. Neil Carson, *Companion*, 4, suggests Henslowe's estate may have been worth eight times the
official valuation of £1700. 12s. 8d. Carson's introduction is a useful guide to the sources of
this wealth.
61. Alleyn's and Henslowe's empires have been the subject of numerous articles by Susan
Cerasano. As she notes in 'Edward Alleyn's Early Years: His Life and Family', *Notes & Queries*
34 (1987), 237–43, Alleyn's inheritance from his father was substantial but not lavish and grew
rapidly as a result of theatre investments. Henslowe's start in life (on which see S. P. Cerasano,
'Revising Philip Henslowe's Biography', *Notes & Queries* 32 (1985), 66–72, and Cerasano,
'Revising Philip Henslowe's Biography: A Correction', *Notes & Queries* 32 (1985), 506–7) was
likewise no more than moderately prosperous. On the bear garden and on Alleyn's income
generally see also Cerasano's 'The Master of the Bears in Art and Enterprise', *Medieval and
Renaissance Drama in England* 5 (1991), 195–209. It is revealing to contrast Alleyn and
Henslowe's successes with failure elsewhere (see, for example, William Ingram, 'Robert
Keysar, Playhouse Speculator', *Shakespeare Quarterly* 37 (1986), 476–85).

Shakespeare stands out because of the sustained successful nature of his partnership, marked by a closeness between writer and acting company that was artistic as well as financial. As Jeffrey Knapp has recently argued, the uniqueness of this situation was evident to contemporary observers and was at times a topic for introspection on the part of the playwright himself.[62] Not simply at a technical level in the development of characterization, but possibly also in his self-presentation as author, Shakespeare's drama is shaped by the special conditions brought about by his position as a sharer. The availability of Shakespeare as in-house dramatist provided the company with an ambitious, literary mainstay of drama that was especially important for royal and aristocratic patronage.[63] To a degree the Chamberlain's (now King's) Men tried to maintain this successful integration once Shakespeare retired. Fletcher, Massinger, and Shirley in turn took on the attractive role of contracted dramatist and we can see from their manuscripts that these poets worked easily with the performers.[64] But, of course, these men were not sharers. Moreover, by this point in the financial history of theatres the centre of gravity had moved away from sharing and towards housekeeping—a still more exclusive category, which Shakespeare joined in 1599.[65]

What could be seen as distinctive to the years 1594 to 1599, as opposed to Shakespeare's career in the seventeenth century, is the particularly balanced nature of the fellowship. During those years the company had only limited control of their performance venue. The Theatre playhouse was partially

---

62. See Jeffrey Knapp, *Shakespeare Only* (Chicago: University of Chicago Press, 2009). In his opening chapter Knapp convincingly critiques the belief of some materialist critics that the concept of authorship is anachronistic in the period.

63. For a series of useful articles on the special circumstances of these networks see Paul Whitfield White and Suzanne R. Westfall, eds., *Shakespeare and Theatrical Patronage in Early Modern England* (Cambridge: Cambridge University Press, 2002).

64. Ioppolo, *Dramatist*, 134–9, examines manuscripts of *Honest Man's Fortune* and *Believe as You List*, emphasizing cooperation between the covenanted writers Fletcher and Massinger and the King's Men. Her argument about Fletcher is speculative (based as it is on the supposition that the blank spaces in the performance manuscript were left for adaptation by the author, who died before he was able to work on the text). The evidence from Massinger certainly shows cooperation, although it should be noted that this is a case of adaptation following censorship rather than evident tailoring to the performance characteristics of a company.

65. This shift in power is evident in the legal wrangles between mere sharers and housekeepers at the Globe in the 1630s. By that time the Admiral's (now Palgrave's) Men had also (in a more limited way) become housekeepers by leasing their theatre from Alleyn. In the run-up to the Civil War control by single managers over acting companies became increasingly evident and it was on that model that the theatre would return with the Restoration. Richard Heton and Christopher Beeston are examples of these managers. On Heton's legal control over his actors, see N. W. Bawcutt, 'Documents of the Salisbury Court Theatre in the British Library', *Medieval and Renaissance Drama in England* 9 (1997), 179–91 (at 186).

run by the Burbages, but the lease for its land was running to an end. The young Richard Burbage, consequently, would hold less financial sway than he did later and Will Kemp must logically have been an opposing influence. Shakespeare's early company style can be traced to those material conditions. Its mix of the comic and the serious reflects the balance of abilities amongst its lead actors, for although Burbage played in comedies, it was for non-comic roles that he would be remembered. Burbage and Kemp were the leading lights of a company that was, in financial input, also evenly balanced. Without the divisive element of housekeepers versus mere sharers, and with a company made up almost entirely of its founding membership, the on-paper status of the sharers would be similar. That balance in the membership is reflected in the balance of Shakespeare's compositions during this period. In each the size of roles across the principal parts is remarkably even: the largest exceeding the second largest by no more than fifty per cent.[66] The 'mixed' and 'even' quality of Shakespeare's works dateable between 1594 and 1599 is noteworthy—they contrast appreciably with those that fall before and after this span. During these early years of the fellowship Shakespeare was singular as a playwright within a company of relative equals, but with the construction of the Globe the nature of this singularity would change.

66. For these counts see T. J. King, *Casting Shakespeare's Plays: London Actors and their Roles, 1590–1642* (Cambridge: Cambridge University Press, 1992). On the tendency amongst actors to relate length of part to status see Simon Palfrey and Tiffany Stern, *Shakespeare in Parts* (Oxford: Oxford University Press, 2007), 32.

PHASE III

Shakespeare as playhouse investor (1599–1608)

8

The Globe partnership

By the end of 1598 Shakespeare had, for more than four and a half years, been in a unique position as author–sharer in the Lord Chamberlain's Men. No other English literary playwright had ever held such a position, and over the previous half-decade it had made him wealthy and had given him unprecedented control over the performance of his work. There was one writer who would soon follow him in becoming a sharer: in 1601 Thomas Heywood would join Worcester's Men. Heywood was artistically an admirer of Shakespeare and he was likewise following him in this course. Yet Worcester's never approached the Chamberlain's in wealth and independence.[1] By the time that Heywood became a sharer, moreover, Shakespeare had gone one decisive step further. This was a move that no literary artist in England would successfully imitate: in 1599 he became part owner of the most impressive performance venue in London. No other playwright would come to own part of a playhouse, or at least not one that was in operation for more than a couple of months.[2] Financially, this move would

---

1. On the gradual collapse of the company after the death of its leading actor, Thomas Greene, in 1612 see Charles William Wallace, 'Three London Theatres of Shakespeare's time', *University Studies of the University of Nebraska* 9 (1909), 287–342. When Worcester's/Queen Anne's Men moved to the new Red Bull playhouse around 1603 at least one of its players, Thomas Swynnerton, did become a housekeeper, but he soon sold his interest. It was not unprecedented for players to become part owners of playhouses: the Chamberlain's sharer Thomas Pope still held a financial stake in the Curtain when he died in 1603 (see E. A. J. Honigmann and Susan Brock, *Playhouse Wills: 1558–1642: An Edition of Wills by Shakespeare and his Contemporaries in the London Theatre* (Manchester: Manchester University Press, 1993), 68) and various playhouse ventures involved tenancies in common (see Charles William Wallace, 'Shakespeare's Money Interest in the Globe Theater', *The Century* 80 (1910), 500–12 (at 510)). Instead, as I discuss below, it was the protracted majority ownership of the Globe by men who were also company sharers that was exceptional.
2. It is conceivable, although unproven, that Heywood for a time held shares in the Red Bull, which was (as is noted in footnote 1 above) occupied by his company. Marston was for a few years a sharer in the syndicate that ran the boys' company at Blackfriars, however they did not

elevate Shakespeare still more impressively above his literary contemporaries. Equally important, it cemented him still more firmly within a small elite body of actors. If 1594 had made Shakespeare institutionally exceptional, 1599 placed him in a category entirely of his own.

It is worth going back for a moment to the performance spaces where Shakespeare's company had worked before coming to the Globe playhouse. These were, first, Newington Butts; then the Cross Keys Inn in Gracious Street; soon after, London's oldest playhouse, the Theatre; and finally its near neighbour, the Curtain. In addition to these there were, of course, performances at court, at noblemen's houses, at city institutions, and on numerous temporary stages when the company decided to tour. The striking thing about this list of home venues is its length, which contrasts markedly with the other court-licensed company, the Admiral's, who remained throughout this period at Henslowe's Rose. Four London establishments in as many years looks decidedly unstable when compared to four decades at the Globe. Blackfriars in 1608 would be an addition and not a replacement: after the vicissitudes of early theatre history the Globe brought stability that (in spite of the 1613 fire) would take nothing less than the Civil War, with its ban on public performance, to disturb.

The stability of the Globe was based on its underlying financial structure. Conversely, the transience of the company's earlier residence at the Theatre can be traced to its horribly twisted contractual roots. Again, it is worth examining what preceded the Globe before setting out the innovative arrangement that guaranteed its success. Following a brief spell at Newington (well south of the metropolis) and the Cross Keys (right in the heart of it), the Chamberlain's might be thought to have found a secure home at the Theatre. That playhouse was in the 'liberties' to the north of the old city wall and thus close enough to attract custom and yet sufficiently far away to

---

own the theatre (see Charles William Wallace, 'Shakespeare and his London Associates as Revealed in Recently Discovered Documents', *University Studies of the University of Nebraska* 10 (1910), 261–360 (at 339–41)). Michael Drayton is listed as an initial investor in the private Whitefriars playhouse, but the King's Revels who were to occupy it survived only briefly and there is no further indication of his interest (see Charles William Wallace, 'Shakespeare and the Blackfriars', *The Century* 80 (1910), 742–52 (at 750), and E. K. Chambers, *The Elizabethan Stage*, 4 vols. (Oxford: Clarendon Press, 1923), II, 64–8, 515–17). Robert Daborne, still more unluckily, was part of the venture to establish Porter's Hall as a playhouse, but this theatre was demolished by government order before a single play was performed (see Chambers, *Elizabethan Stage*, II, 472–4). Across these four cases there is no instance of a play performed at a venue in which its author held a stake.

evade the sporadic attempts at suppression by the capital's civic authorities. All the same, as a base for the new company, it was anything but secure.

Everything about the Theatre was compromised—a fact borne out by the wealth of material generated in the legal disputes between its constructors, investors, landlords, and creditors. It is often said that the Theatre was owned and built by James Burbage (father of Richard, the leading actor in the Chamberlain's Men). The story then goes that Giles Allen, who owned the land on which the playhouse was built, refused to extend the twenty-one-year lease (which expired in 1597) and that as a result the Burbages tore down the building and used its timbers to construct the Globe across the river on the south bank. While it is useful in outline, this account radically obscures the foundational precariousness of the building's history, in which there is such a farcical degree of pursuit and reversal that it almost defies belief.

All of the elements in the standard potted history are misleading. First, the land on which the Theatre was built did not securely belong to Giles Allen. No land in this period could properly be said to 'belong' to those who held it because, according to the principles of a residual feudalism, it was only the right to its *use* that devolved from the monarch.[3] This right of use was then fed through the great lords of the kingdom down to the yeoman class. Inevitably this made things complicated, but that legal problem aside, the right to use the land on which the Theatre was built was also more directly contested. It had passed through several hands since being sold around 1555 by Sir George Peckham; but Peckham's son, Edmund, having come of age, now disputed his father's right to have made the sale in the first place and thus pursued Allen in the Court of Wards.[4] Edmund Peckham also physic-

3. For details of how 'bastard feudalism' continued to operate in Elizabethan and Jacobean land law see J. H. Baker, *An Introduction to English Legal History*, 4th edn (London: Reed Elsevier, 2002), 223–313.
4. See Peckam *v.* Alleyn [i.e. Allen], Court of Wards 1589, in C. C. Stopes, *Burbage and Shakespeare's Stage* (London: Alexander Moring, 1913), 166–70. Stopes's work has been criticized for inaccuracy, most notably by her rival theatre historian Charles William Wallace. Herbert Berry, *Shakespeare's Playhouses* (New York: AMS Press, 1987), has made a representative check of her work on these documents and does indeed find frequent minor errors of transcription, although never to the point of distorting the facts. Where the more reliable Wallace has transcribed the same documents I cite his version in preference, but (in line with Berry's recommendation) I also use Stopes where hers is the only version available. Berry's Handlist in *Shakespeare's Playhouses* gives references to the manuscript numbers of the documents used by Wallace and Berry in cases where these have changed since the early twentieth century. Berry, 'Playhouses, 1560–1660', in G. Wickham, H. Berry, and W. Ingram, eds., *English Professional Theatre, 1530–1660* (Cambridge: Cambridge University Press, 2000), also

ally harassed Allen's tenant, Burbage, requiring a round-the-clock guard on the Theatre itself.[5]

Second, James Burbage did not securely hold the lease for the land on which the Theatre was built. Not only had he agreed to share it with his business partner, he had also mortgaged the lease (to a certain John Hyde) in order to obtain further finance to construct the playhouse.[6] Burbage then failed to keep up payments and following various legal wrangles he was eventually forced to deliver the lease into the hands of Hyde.[7] It was Hyde who then allowed Burbage to remain as a kind of tenant, receiving some payments (though, he claimed, inadequate ones) from the profits of the enterprise. It was thus to Hyde as well as to Giles Allen that James Burbage was beholden when it came to his rights to the land.

Third, James Burbage did not straightforwardly build or own the structure of the playhouse. To finance the construction he had (in addition to the mortgage from Hyde) offered 50 per cent equity to his brother-in-law, John Brayne, who had (along with his wife) worked manually, free of charge, to assist in putting the building up. Burbage and Brayne soon fell out over the nature of their agreement, which appears never to have been written out. The two fought violently over control of the property (at one point coming to blows in the very office of the scrivener who was to draw up a document of agreement).[8] Brayne also had separate financial troubles and ended up giving away his assets to friends as a means of protection from his creditors.[9] These friends and creditors thus joined Allen and Hyde in pursuing Burbage for money. Matters were hardly simplified by Brayne's death in 1586, which left not just his widow but also her new friend Robert Miles making extravagant financial demands on Burbage. Miles was not likely to be restrained in his methods given that he had a track record of assault including the very

prints selective extracts from the documents under discussion—these are cited in the footnotes where relevant.

5. On these 'sinister means' see Allen's answer on 20 October 1589 in Stopes, *Burbage*, 168.
6. In 1635 Cuthbert Burbage, fighting a case against the actor Robert Benfield, provided an account of the borrowing that financed the construction of both the Theatre and the Globe playhouse (see E. K. Chambers, *William Shakespeare: A Study of Facts and Problems* (Oxford: Clarendon Press, 1930), II, 65–6).
7. Charles W. Wallace, 'The First London Theatre: Materials for a History' in *University Studies of the University of Nebraska* 13 (1913), 1–297 (at 9).
8. PRO, C24/26/11 [pt 1]. The notary William Nicholl's account of the fistfight is to found in Wallace, 'First London Theatre', 7, 150–3. See also Berry, 'Playhouses', in Wickham, Berry, and Ingram, eds., *English Professional Theatre*, 337–8.
9. Wallace, 'First London Theatre', 8–9, 14.

beating that had hastened Brayne's death.[10] When Brayne's widow herself died six years later she, somewhat suspiciously, left everything she owned to Miles, a man whom she had first accused of her husband's murder.[11] With at least one unexplained death on his record, Miles pursued the Burbages for all they were worth.

Neither the land, nor the lease, nor the physical structure of the Theatre was uncontested in its ownership. There were over half a dozen separate litigants laying claim to the property, most of whom were prepared to use violence as well as legal action to pursue their ends. James Burbage was only giving as good as he got when he shouted to one group of claimants who turned up at the playhouse that the next time they did so he would get his sons, Richard and Cuthbert, to fetch pistols.[12] Nor was Richard, when he threatened to pay Robert Miles with stick beatings instead of money, the first to make a proposition of this kind.[13] Yet, in spite of these problems, the Theatre was clearly making money. We may not entirely credit Allen's assertion that Burbage was sitting on a £2,000 profit, but it is evident that he was desperate to renew the lease on the property, even at nearly double the rent.[14] The essential success of the venture must also underlie James Burbage's search for an alternative. It could only have been on the basis of profits that he made the purchase of the great hall of Blackfriars, inside the walls of the city, for which on 4 February 1596 he paid the extraordinary

10. Wallace, 'First London Theatre', 14, reports that Brayne accused Robert Miles of giving the 'stripes' that would lead to his death.

11. It was at Margaret Brayne's suit that Miles had been tried for murder (Wallace, 'First London Theatre', 14), but in her will (Wallace, 'First London Theatre', 153–4) she is bizarrely effusive about him as a man for whom 'all the goods I have in the whole world' would not be reward enough (154). She makes him her executor, the sole inheritor of her goods and property rights, and even hands over the care of her husband's daughter.

12. PRO C24/228/11, C24/228/10 in Wallace, 'First London Theatre', 18. See also Berry, 'Playhouses', in Wickham, Berry, and Ingram, eds., English Professional Theatre, 361–2.

13. Mary Edmond, 'Yeomen, Citizens, Gentlemen, and Players: The Burbages and their Connections', in R. B. Parker and S. P. Zitner, eds., Elizabethan Theater: Essays in Honor of S. Schoenbaum (Newark: University of Delaware Press, 1996), 30–49 (at 34), casts doubt on the testimony that is the basis for this famous story about Shakespeare's lead actor. There must always be an element of doubt surrounding witness statements from those in Miles's circle, but the deponent, John Alleyn (brother of the actor Edward Alleyn), is a reasonably neutral witness and there are other sources that testify that James Burbage, at least, was capable of violent acts.

14. In PRO. Req.2/87/74 (4 February 1600) Giles Allen claims profit on the theatre 'doth amount to the sum of £2,000 at the least'. Cuthbert's reply details the numerous inducements that he offered for a renewal, including £10 increase in rent. See Wallace, 'First London Theatre', 191–8, 203–4, and also Berry, 'Playhouses', in Wickham et al., eds., English Professional Theatre, 379–82 (382).

sum of £600.[15] At further 'great charge and trouble' Burbage converted the premises to an indoor playhouse, bringing the dream of an independent and secure venue (comparable to Henslowe's Rose) tantalizingly close to hand.[16] When, following a petition of November 1596, the residents then succeeded in blocking performances he is likely to have been shocked profoundly.[17] Dying only a month or so later, James Burbage was a thwarted man.

The Theatre, unlike the Rose on the south bank, was the subject of furious and intractable conflict. But none of this significantly affected Shakespeare or his company. The Chamberlain's Men were merely tenants at the playhouse, which had previously been used by other companies and had, for example, hosted Tarlton's celebrated mocking of Richard Harvey's prophecies.[18] Though the scuffles may have disturbed the odd performance, these conflicts were, at the end of the day, nothing to do with them. When the expiry of the lease brought a halt to playing at the Theatre, the Chamberlain's simply moved their custom to Lanman's Curtain, in which their fellow Thomas Pope was a sharer, only a stone's throw away.[19] It is often said, because of the subsequent move to the Globe, that this must have been an inadequate venue. But there is no evidence to back this assumption, which is really based on a muddying of the distinction between playhouse proprietor and acting company. In the wake of the 'duopoly' (however inadequate its enforcement) the licensed ensemble were in a strong position as buyers. There were other performance spaces available that were currently underused, picking up custom either from travelling companies like

15. Folger MS L.b.348. For the Deed of Feoffment or contract for this purchase, see J. O. Halliwell-Phillipps, *Outlines of the Life of Shakespeare*, 6th edn, 2 vols. (London: Longmans, Green, & Co., 1886), I, 273–8, which details the exact nature of the property and confirms receipt of payment and James Burbage's inheritable rights on the property. On this arrangement and on the expensive building work that Burbage carried out on his acquisition see Charles William Wallace, *The Evolution of the English Drama up to Shakespeare with a History of the First Blackfriars Theatre* (Berlin: Georg Reimer, 1912), 195. The document is also reproduced in Berry, 'Playhouses', in Wickham et al., eds., *English Professional Theatre*, 504–7.
16. The description of this 'great charge and trouble' comes from Cuthbert Burbage's much later plea against Eyllaerdt Swanston and associates, which is recorded in Stopes, *Burbage*, 132, and in abbreviated form in Berry, 'Playhouses', in Wickham et al., eds., *English Professional Theatre*, 526.
17. PRO, SP12/260, fol.176. For a transcript of a copy of this petition, which is found in the State Papers, see Halliwell-Phillipps, *Outlines*, I, 278 and Berry, 'Playhouses', in Wickham et al., eds., *English Professional Theatre*, 507–8.
18. On Tarlton's attacks see Chambers, *Elizabethan Stage*, II, 394.
19. In his will dated 22 July 1603 Thomas Pope bequeathed rights in the Curtain as well as the Globe playhouse (see Honigmann and Brock, *Playhouse Wills*, 68).

Pembroke's and Queen's (who made their way to the capital in spite of the government ban) or from one-off entertainments such as fencing matches, poetic contests, or stand-up entertainment by clowns. Chamberlain's could have had its pick of these venues.[20] If the Curtain was not adequate, the company could easily have moved again and performed at the Swan.[21]

Acting companies were traditionally mobile units. They had their origins in the old travelling outfits, and even in the late 1590s, with the London base of the Chamberlain's and Admiral's solidly established, it was still the assumption that players could move from space to space. Most likely there was, on the whole, an agreement that they would commit for a stretch of time to a particular playhouse. This was the plan when Pembroke's took up residence at Langley's Swan in 1597, although that case also illustrates that when the situation changed the performers were always liable to jump ship. The basic arrangement was that players and theatre owners each took an agreed share of the day's takings. This meant that there could be either conflict or happy collaboration, but playing companies and theatres were in principle separate entities.[22]

The remarkable thing about the Globe venture of 1599 is that it broke this convention.[23] Probably this was an accident resulting from desperation after the disappointments at the Theatre and Blackfriars, but if so it was an accident that worked in favour of the Chamberlain's Men.[24] Although technically company and playhouse remained separate entities, the deal of

20. Such occasional entertainments are recorded at the Swan, for example; see Chambers, *Elizabethan Stage*, II, 411.
21. The Swan was the newest of the playhouses and was commended by the Dutch visitor John de Wit as its smartest (see Chambers, *Elizabethan Stage*, II, 361).
22. This division is evident, for example, in Robert Miles's accusation that James Burbage stole from the actors at the Theatre by having a false key made for their cash box (see Wallace, 'First London Theatre', 7).
23. One might argue that this convention was also being broken at Henslowe's Rose and later at the other Henslowe–Alleyn playhouses. But in these cases the break went the other way: by making their tenants dependent on their credit, by tying hired men directly to playhouses, and by taking ownership of company stock in the form of apparel and playbooks Alleyn and Henslowe were also blurring the dividing line between company and playhouse. Here it was the players who came to be 'owned' by the playhouse, rather than the other way round.
24. A comparable accident may be said to have occurred with the Fortune in 1621 following a fire, with Alleyn (who now wished to commit his capital to his great charitable and perhaps dynastic ventures) offering Palgrave's Men shares in the rebuilt house. A significant difference, however, lay in the rights over the leasehold, which (characteristically) still gave Alleyn the upper hand. For details of the transfer to Palgrave's Men in 1618 and the syndicate of 1621 see Chambers, *Elizabethan Stage*, II, 442, and Berry, 'Playhouses', in Wickham et al., eds., *English Professional Theatre*, 544–5, 640–1.

1599 in effect locked the lead performers and the theatre impresario into one unit by means of a set of durable and mutually beneficial bonds. Never before had a playhouse been constructed for the exclusive use of one company; in its more than forty-year history no other performers would ever come to use the Globe.[25] Although the ensemble would continue on occasion to travel, this playhouse, eventually joined by Blackfriars, would become their permanent London home.[26]

The key agent in the 1599 deal was not Richard but Cuthbert Burbage. It was the elder brother who had, even before his father's death, repurchased the Theatre lease from John Hyde, to whom it had been mortgaged.[27] The enforcement of this deal was a close-run thing (which Cuthbert only managed by calling in favours from friends in high places), but once completed it placed him in the driving seat. After Cuthbert Burbage took over the lease he worsted the Brayne faction as rival claimants: in the wake of this intervention, widow Brayne, her helpmate Robert Miles, and the deceased Brayne's friends and creditors failed utterly to make any headway in court. All that Cuthbert now needed was an extension on the lease from Giles Allen (who, thanks to the aid of the Burbages, had by now won out in his battle with the Peckham family over control of the land).[28] Cuthbert was evidently determined to achieve the promised extension: he offered to all but double the rental payments, offered to pay arrears (even though he denied knowledge of them), and eventually even promised that if Allen liked he would pull down the playhouse and replace it with another building after five years of use.[29] Allen, however, played for time and refused to commit. He prevaricated long enough for the lease to expire and in this way (as he later confessed) intended to gain control of the playhouse buildings and also of a set of tenements that James Burbage had fitted to a

25. See Chambers, *Elizabethan Stage*, II, 416.
26. For records of travel by the Chamberlain's/King's Men, which was sporadic but not infrequent, see Chambers, *Facts and Problems*, II, 321–33, and relevant volumes of REED.
27. See Wallace, 'First London Theatre', 16.
28. Cuthbert Burbage *v.* Roger Ames and others (Coram Rege Rolls, Hil. Term. 41 Eliz, f. 320) shows Burbage legally pursuing agents of the Peckham family for trespass. Subsequent depositions show Allen reporting how his tenant Burbage has resisted attempts at trespass by agents of this family, who are now headed by Roger, Earl of Rutland. Following witness depositions, the case is not thereafter pursued (for the records of these proceedings see Stopes, *Burbage*, 184–94).
29. These details appear in the replication of Cuthbert Burbage made in April 1600, transcribed in Wallace, 'First London Theatre', 200–5. They are in large part confirmed by subsequent witnesses.

barn on the site.[30] Giles Allen believed his position to be a strong one; it was the resulting intransigence that pushed Cuthbert to develop his remarkable innovation—building a new playhouse on secure ground in partnership with the acting company in which his brother was the leading man.

Everything about the financial set-up of the Globe suggests that Cuthbert had learnt from the fraught history of his father's experience with the Theatre. In Nicholas Brend he secured a reliable landlord: one who had an uncontested hold on the patch of land over the river near the existing Rose playhouse and who was willing to offer a twenty-one-year lease, soon extended by a further ten. Brend was a member of the Inner Temple and so would have seen the Chamberlain's Men perform there soon after their formation: clearly he had no objection to their business and he may even have been an enthusiast for their art.

The Brend family proved entirely reliable landlords. Much more innovative, however, was the nature of the joint enterprise amongst the leaseholders and the builders of the Globe playhouse itself. It was unprecedented to bring the core of an acting company into a playhouse venture. In the past some players had, it seems, acquired shares in performance venues (the Chamberlain's sharer Thomas Pope would leave a share in the Curtain in his will and, at a later date, Charles Massey would refer to 'that little moiety I have in the play houses' in his letter requesting a loan).[31] In the Globe deal, however, an initial six out of eight sharers in the acting company also became sharers of the new playhouse—they did so, moreover, as a collective entity. This was a deliberate policy to integrate the lead actors with their theatre building. At least for the early years, there was a drive to include new sharers within the housekeeper fraternity if at all possible, so that Sly and Condell, who were not signatories in the initial venture, soon became part of the Globe's ownership as well.[32]

Not only were the core of the company—Richard Burbage (who had a larger portion as a result of his inheritance), William Shakespeare, Augustine Phillips, Thomas Pope, John Heminges, William Kemp, and soon after-

30. Details of the tenements constructed by James Burbage are given in the witness statements found in Exchequer Depositions, 44–5 Eliz. No. 18. Ironically this was a case where the Burbages were helping Allen retain control of the land (see Stopes, *Burbage*, 189–93).

31. Honigmann and Brock, *Playhouse Wills*, 68; and W. W. Greg, ed., *Henslowe Papers* (London: A. H. Bullen, 1907), 64.

32. For clear tables showing the Globe's changing ownership see Joseph Quincy Adams, 'The Housekeepers of the Globe', *Modern Philology* 17 (1919), 1–8. See also Chambers, *Elizabethan Stage*, II, 418.

wards Henry Condell and William Sly—invited to invest in the building; an ingenious financial device also ensured that their ownership would continue to be held in common. Thanks to a legal case that occurred nearly two decades later, we know a good deal about the precise mechanisms of the 1599 deal and its long-term objectives, central to which was a process of gift and return.[33] Cuthbert Burbage, Richard Burbage, Shakespeare, Phillips, Pope, Heminges, and Kemp all took part in the lease of the land as individuals; their personal 'demises', however, were then assigned to a third party (in the first instance consisting of two men, William Levison and Thomas Savage). That third party then immediately returned ownership to them, but not as individuals but as holders of a *tenancy in common*.[34] The purpose of this arrangement was to prevent dispersal: it was impossible for individuals in the business to mortgage their joint asset (this had been a major problem with the running of the Theatre and it was also what was happening with Massey when he wrote his pleading letter to Henslowe at a later date). Following the Globe acquisition, the core of the Chamberlain's were locked, more firmly than other ensembles, to a collective enterprise. On the relatively rare occasions when there was a change in personnel the ritual of collective gift and re-grant was repeated: this, as Heminges explains, is what happened with the departure of Will Kemp.[35] Evidently the double-lock system of fellowship and playhouse partnership was felt to be working—that essential unity of the lead performers with the theatre would continue until the addition of Blackfriars in 1608.[36] Indeed, so strong was the contractual bond on the housekeepers that they were collectively bound to rebuild the Globe after its fire even when the existence of Black-friars no longer made this an immediate economic necessity.[37]

33. This is the case pressed by John Witter, who was the new husband of Augustine Phillips's widow and was claiming the share as a part of her inheritance. For a full transcript of the papers see Wallace, 'London Associates', 305–25). A lucid explanation of the gift and return process is given in Wallace, 'Money Interest'.

34. This process is explained in Heminges and Condell's answer to Witter, Court of Requests, 27 April, Regis Jacobi Angliae xvii. See Wallace, 'London Associates', 313, and also Chambers, *Facts and Problems*, II, 52–5.

35. Wallace, 'London Associates', 314.

36. Eventually, with the deaths of original actor–founders, ownership of the playhouse would devolve away from the performers. This was the complaint of the King's Men sharers in 1635 when they sued Cuthbert, the only survivor alongside Heminges (for the collection of these papers see Halliwell-Phillipps, *Outlines*, II, 286–93).

37. Heminges makes this point in his deposition in response to William Ostler, stating that each housekeeping share was called upon for a rebuilding contribution of £50 to £60 (Wallace, 'London Associates', 320).

This book makes the case for the unique company status of Shakespeare and nothing makes his exceptional position more palpable than the contrast between the Globe's foundation and the arrangements at other playhouses: the Rose, the Swan, the Fortune, the children at Blackfriars, and St Paul's Boys. None of the other playhouses had a comparable joint-equity arrangement, nor did any of them bind a writer into their framework in the way that Shakespeare was invested in the Globe. Certainly, the establishment of a third London adult company (Worcester's) offered new possibilities for playwrights and certain writers also gained power from the re-emergence of the boys' companies. Marston at Blackfriars, if he was for a spell a sharer in the performing company, may have come close to replicating the working conditions of John Lyly two decades earlier.[38] He, along with other writers, must have been in a stronger position than when the Admiral's and Chamberlain's had been the only serious purchasers in town. As I will argue in Chapter 10, those new institutional arrangements helped to foster a new kind of drama. But Shakespeare's categorical difference from his contemporaries (artistically and institutionally) did not lessen. Rather, with the construction of the Globe, it became still more pronounced. Shakespeare, being bound to the adult players, did not write for the children and thus did not adopt the crafted artificiality of their style.

After a period of relative two-company dominance, the turn of the century was one of theatrical expansion. Because the Chamberlain's did not move to Blackfriars (as was most likely planned) that indoor playhouse was sublet to Henry Evans, who revived a boys' company in this location. The residents who had blocked the arrival of an adult company objected less to the children. There was already a precedent for indoor children's performances given that the St Paul's boys had resumed playing by the winter of 1599.[39] It may well also have been the shift of the Chamberlain's across the river that prompted a move in the opposite direction from the Admiral's Men. Alleyn and Henslowe at any rate designed their new home, the Fortune, in response to the Globe playhouse, which soon established a

38. Evidence for John Marston having been a sharer in the Children of the Chapel/Queen's Revels comes from Robert Keysar's suit against the housekeepers of Blackfriars. Keysar claims that Marston 'did enter in' and received 'one full sixth part of and in Certain goods apparel for players, properties, play books, and other things then and still used by the Children of the Queen's Majesty's Revels' and that Keysar then bought this share for £100. Burbage and his fellow owners say they know nothing of this arrangement and that their agreement was solely with Evans. For documentation see Wallace, 'London Associates', 337–55.
39. Chambers, *Elizabethan Stage*, II, 367.

reputation as the most important London venue.[40] The contract for the Fortune's construction, to be completed by the same carpenter, repeatedly mentions this precedent. And while the vacated Rose was supposed to be pulled down, it was in fact left and thus facilitated the residence of a new London troupe.

There was, quite likely, a period of financial stress for the Shakespeare company, especially given the sudden expansion in theatrical provision. Cuthbert Burbage would later speak of 'sums of money taken up at interest which lay heavy on us many years' and of the risk of setting up, on speculation, an independent venture of this kind.[41] In Hamlet's speeches, written around 1600, about the 'little eyases' who draw audiences from the adults there is an inkling of this pressure, the most dramatic expression of which would come in the so-called 'war of the theatres'.[42] The Globe venture, like others, was potentially threatened. That such competition was damaging is confirmed by the fact that, at a later date, housekeepers were actually paying money to the manager of Paul's Boys to keep his playhouse closed.[43] Yet the crisis, exacerbated by the plague, affected the weakest syndicates the hardest. Ultimately, powerful outfits would consolidate their pre-eminence: Alleyn and Henslowe ended up with control not only of the Rose and Fortune but also of their indebted companies. The boys' troupes ceased trading, largely as a result of political scandal. Thus, alongside the Alleyn–Henslowe empire there was left standing the Chamberlain's/King's Men at the Globe.

As with the bold move of the 1594 fellowship, the success of the Globe investment soon made its mark in the wider spending that the winners in this competition were able to enjoy. Alleyn, following the success of the Fortune, diversified into tenement properties and was able to afford a spectacular down payment to buy the manor house of Sir Francis Calton. On a proportionately smaller, but still impressive scale we find Shakespeare's

40. For example, Prince Otto of Hesse-Cassel in 1611 writes of seven theatres (which include children's playhouses), describing the Globe as 'most important' (see Chambers, *Elizabethan Stage*, ii, 369).
41. See Burbage v. Eyllaerdt Swanston, in Stopes, *Burbage*, 132.
42. William Shakespeare, *Hamlet*, Folio Text (1623), 2.2.337, in *Hamlet: the Texts of 1603 and 1623*, ed. Ann Thompson and Neil Taylor, Arden3 (London: Cengage, 2006). The Folio text itself has 'Yases' and this passage does not appear in *Hamlet* Q2. See discussion in Chapter 10 below.
43. This fact is revealed under questioning in the Keysar v. Blackfriars Housekeepers case, in which the Burbages confirm that Blackfriars and Whitefriars are jointly paying Rochester's rent so as to keep Paul's Boys shut (Wallace, 'London Associates', 355).

fellow sharer, Augustine Phillips, buying a country house near Mortlake, which apparently functioned as a summer retreat for the company in 1603.[44] The evidence we have on the estates of the Globe housekeepers shows them to be doing exceptionally well. Thus Pope in his will of 22 July 1603 talks of multiple houses and tenements alongside his shares in the Globe, and we have similar reports of the wealth of Richard Burbage, Heminges, and Condell.[45] Shakespeare's fortunes went hand in hand with his company's: on 1 May 1602 he turned over £320 cash to purchase more land in Stratford, he purchased more five months later, and on 24 July 1605 he spent £440 on a lease of tithes.[46] In a time before high street banks such purchases were the equivalent of long-term deposits. These were very substantial investments converting immediate profit into ongoing security: they show men able to establish prosperity that will last across generations, not just serving their present needs.

The difference between Shakespeare's financial position and that of other playwrights remains curiously under-reported. Equivalent professionals in this decade—Heywood, Jonson, Dekker, Middleton, Fletcher, Daborne, Drayton, Marston, and Webster—had nothing approaching Shakespeare's income. Many were in debt and even those doing better were still essentially existing year to year. They (in spite of the efforts made by several of their number) were not asset-holders and this position had a direct economic consequence. The system that locked Shakespeare into the Globe venture also locked others out and as time went on theatrical property became increasingly more important, more so even than acting company shares. Because he stood alone as both a sharer and a housekeeper, Shakespeare pulled steadily ever further ahead.

44. On Mortlake see Charles Nicholl, *The Lodger: Shakespeare on Silver Street* (London: Penguin, 2008), 236. The Witter *v.* Heminges case also refers to £300, belonging to Phillips, which his executors attempted to keep out of the hands of his widow's spendthrift husband (Heminges's Answer, recorded in Wallace, 'London Associates', 318). Wallace, 'Money Interest', 501, records that Phillips left an estate worth somewhat more than £1100.
45. On Pope see Honigmann and Brock, *Playhouse Wills*, 68. Honigmann and Brock (8) note that wealth was sometimes hidden from wills through deeds of gift carried through just before death. This is likely to be the case with Burbage, who certainly had considerable property when he was burgled a few years before his death (see Stopes, *Burbage*, 151, for list of stolen goods) and who was reputed to have left more than £300 in land. In Witter's complaint against the Globe housekeepers great play is made on the wealth of Heminges and Condell and, by implication, the housekeepers more generally (see Wallace, 'London Associates', 311).
46. See Samuel Schoenbaum, *William Shakespeare: A Documentary Life* (Oxford: Clarendon Press, 1975), 188–94. For full transcripts of these deals see Halliwell-Phillipps, *Outlines*, II, 17–22.

1599 made Shakespeare, the Globe, and the Chamberlain's Men a unified entity. The partnership of genuine equals became smaller, more selective, and more securely bonded. There were soon only five of the founding company remaining; these men were joined by others, who were selected for artistic purposes and incorporated in the company on terms that the founding members set. With Kemp on his way out, Richard Burbage (as leading actor, largest performing shareholder, and brother to the lead financier of the enterprise) was soon dominant. Given that Shakespeare was by this time easily the nation's most celebrated playwright there can be no doubt that the Chamberlain's/King's company was now not just a partnership of equals, but also a personal partnership between the pre-eminent actor and the pre-eminent poet of the age.

9

Robert Armin

B etween 6 February and 23 March 1600 the two great comic actors of
Shakespeare's plays were both at work on celebrity publications.[1]
Robert Armin wrote *Quips upon Questions* and William Kemp, after his
celebrated dance to the city of Norwich, produced his *Nine Days Wonder* as
an account of that trip. These works were the product of the Lent closure of
the theatres and cashed in on the reputation of two famous players. In spite
of that outward resemblance, however, it is difficult to imagine two books
more radically opposed. *Quips upon Questions* has an entirely different mood
from that of *Nine Days Wonder*: the satirical 'fool', Robert Armin, is the
opposite of the indulgent 'clown', Will Kemp. In these rival publications
the two men stake their claim on competing visions of the world. Over the
course of 1600 Armin replaced Kemp as sharer and principal comic performer of the Chamberlain's Men. As is well known, Shakespeare, from this
point on, created diminutive 'fools' instead of bulky 'clowns' as his lead
comic characters. The pamphlets that would have lain close together on
booksellers' stalls in St Paul's churchyard thus provide a unique example of
the way that the character of other sharers shaped his choices as dramatist.

Kemp's travelogue is filled with the spirit of health and festivity. It
celebrates the author's physical prowess in having completed the journey
and is written throughout in a plain-speaking prose. The *Nine Days Wonder*

---

1. Edward Arber, ed., *A Transcript of the Registers of the Company of Stationers of London, 1554–1640
   AD* (London: privately published, 1875–94), III, 160, records that Kemp's *Nine Days Wonder* was
   entered on 22 April 1600 and the book itself records events during Lent. *Quips upon Questions*
   does not appear on the Register but is dated 1600 on its frontispiece, which tells us the book was
   'clapt by a clown of the town in this last restraint, having little else to do' (A1ᵃ). There were no
   plague closures during 1600, so the reference must be to the traditional Lent restraint. For
   details of closures see Leeds Barroll, *Politics, Plague, and Shakespeare's Theater* (Ithaca, NY:
   Cornell University Press, 1991), 212, 230–1. The title page's reference to Armin as the
   clown of the Curtain, rather than the Globe, confirms this dating.

revels in popular admiration. Its crowds are universally enthusiastic and all who meet Kemp are caught up in the holiday fun. The account concludes with a wild festival in Norwich, whose citizens 'from the highest to the lowest, the richest as the poorest' are united in an acrostic poem that spells 'WELCOME' to the arriving star (C4^{a-b}).

There is no such merriment in *Quips upon Questions*. Armin's self-presentation as a professional fool instead involves an uneasy mixture of the wise and nonsensical. In contrast to the life force Kemp, his style is obscure, riddling, and often preachy. The collection begins with the Fall of Adam 'from all grace hurled' and proceeds with a series of dark, almost surrealistic, verses that contrast men unfavourably with beasts. The second poem, for example, compares dogs to humans and reasons that 'a dog's skin serves for something when he's dead' (A4^{a-b}). Crowds in Armin's book are threatening rather than festive, so that in 'Who's the Fool Now?' they 'smile' to see a drunken man robbed at the playhouse where the author performs (B3^{b}–B4^{a}). Where Kemp is forgiving and apparently self-confident, Armin at once depicts and embodies a cosmic spirit of the absurd.

It has not previously been noticed that the publication of these books coincides with Kemp's resignation. While the exact details of the pivotal change in personnel in Shakespeare's company are irrecoverable, it occurred at the latest by the middle of 1600.[2] For all its festivity, then, the *Nine Days Wonder* is a book of leave-taking. At the close of the volume the author says that he will soon sail from Dover to Calais and hints at his plan to travel to Rome. In all likelihood he alludes directly to his departure from the Globe playhouse in saying that he has 'without good help danced myself out of the world' (A2^{a}). Having been a founding sharer in the company and a housekeeper, and having briefly performed at the new playhouse, Kemp

---

2. Kemp's *Nine Days Wonder* makes clear that in April 1600 the author was about to depart overseas (D4^{b}). In Lent 1600 Armin still presented himself as clown of the Curtain in his publications. The first reference to Shakespeare's *As You Like It* appears on the Stationers' Register as a staying entry on 4 August 1600, so Armin must have been available to play its clown, Touchstone, by that date. The handover, therefore, almost certainly occurred between these dates. It should be noted that there are dissenting voices on the question of when Armin joined the company, with some scholars arguing that the two comic performers could have performed together for the Chamberlain's for a time. For further debate see Martin Butler, 'Armin, Robert (1563–1615)', *Oxford DNB*, and Stanley Wells and Gary Taylor, *William Shakespeare: A Textual Companion Companion* (Oxford: Clarendon Press, 1987), 121–2.

lost these strong ties with his fellows within six months of their move to the south bank.[3]

It is probably no coincidence that Kemp and Armin published these competing comic books at the point of changeover. By 22 April 1600, when *Nine Days Wonder* was entered in the Stationers' Register, Kemp is likely to have known that Armin had taken his place in the company and would now be playing his parts. There are several suggestions of a personal hostility to his replacement. In the opening and closing epistles to his book Kemp expresses his anger about recent events, including an unspecified libel. He tells us that his account was written 'to reprove lying fools' and ends by warning a ballad maker to 'cross me no more I prithee with thy rabble of bald rhymes' because 'all men may know thee for a fool' (A2[b], D4[b]). The word 'fool' was closely associated with Armin, who used this persona in all of his published texts. Armin, moreover, had first gained fame as a composer of ballads.[4] Indeed, only months previously he had published *A Pill to Purge Melancholy*, which referred in the present tense to his popular ragged 'ditties and songs' (B4[b]).[5] Armin is thus a close fit with the unnamed author of 'beastly ballets' (D4[b]) who is attacked at the close of Kemp's text.

A Pill to Purge Melancholy may itself have been a cause of resentment. The pamphlet consists of an exchange of letters featuring Armin's well-known foolish alter ego, Snuff. For the most part it is singsong nonsense, but its final page brings things closer to home. Here the letter writer makes several jokes about 'the ass's burden' that seem to allude to Kemp's performance as

3. James Nielson, 'William Kemp at the Globe', *Shakespeare Quarterly* 44 (1993), 466–8, presents the evidence for Kemp's performance. His case is based on a sentence in *A Pill to Purge Melancholy* (1599), B4[b]. That pamphlet, as I note below, is near enough certain to be the work of Armin.

4. Thomas Nashe in *Strange Newes* (1592), D4[b], refers to Armin as a ballad maker in the tradition of William Elderton. Gabriel Harvey, responding to Nashe in *Pierces Supererogation* (1593), 2A1[a], also twice places Armin alongside Philip Stubbes and Thomas Deloney as one of 'the common Pamfletters of London'. Besides *A Pill*, none of this early material survives. As is argued by Charles S. Felver in 'Robert Armin's Fragment of a Bawdy Ballad of "Mary Ambree"', *Notes & Queries* 7 (1960), 14–16, however, the song by Tutch in Armin's *Two Maids of More-Clacke* is probably a fragment of an existing ballad by Armin that dates from this time.

5. Chris Sutcliffe, 'The Canon of Robert Armin's Work: An Addition', *Notes & Queries* 43 (1996), 171–5, presents evidence for the pamphlet's attribution to Armin. The pamphlet was printed by William White, who also printed *Quips upon Question* and *Fool upon Fool* in 1600. It uses the character Snuff, also the nominal author of these later publications, as well as several other nicknames associated with Armin.

Dogberry.[6] The case for an allusion is strengthened when Snuff concludes that his *Pill* may 'easily be digested with one pleasant conceit or other of Monsieur de Kemp on Monday next at the Globe' (D4[b]). The references are not necessarily insulting, but they do belittle the performer. There is the sense that Armin is already taking liberties with the new theatre where, after 1600, he would take great pride in having taken over the role of Dogberry from Kemp.[7]

The *Nine Days Wonder* never definitively pins down the source of the unspecified libel that has offended its author.[8] The principal suspect, however, remains a youth 'a little stooping in the shoulders', a 'penny poet' who has broadcast his abuse 'on a public stage' (D3[b]–D4[b]). All of this matches with what we know of Armin—he was proud to be a 'crank' poet, famously small and stooping, and the only known performer of this kind upon the stage.[9] In the circumstances it is difficult to imagine that he was untouched by the insults levelled in the *Nine Days Wonder*. Even if Kemp did not suspect Armin of libel, he was clearly hostile to everything that he embodied: in Kemp's book 'blunt mirth', 'merry jests', and 'mad jigs' (A2[b]) are pointedly set against their opposite: ribald 'abominable ballads', 'apish humour', and 'unreasonable rhymes' (D3[a]–D4[b]). When Kemp offers to bestow 'a leash of my cast bells to have crowned you with coxcombs' (D3[a]) his gesture effectively encapsulates this contrast: the clownish bells of his merry morris stood in profound opposition to the fool's motley and

---

6. The phrases 'I am very well content to bear the ass's burden, if she be as willing to wear the ears', and 'come up ass into a higher room' (*Pill*, D4[b]) may also suggest Bottom in *Midsummer Night's Dream*. Sutcliffe, 'The Canon', 175, picks up these allusions and suggests Armin may already have been playing these parts. This is conceivable but it would mean that the placement of Armin at the Curtain in *Quips* and *Fool* is erroneous. If Armin had already taken these roles in 1599 then the insult to Kemp would certainly be egregious.

7. See, for example, Armin's references to 'his Constableship' in *The Italian Tailor and his Boy* (1609), A3[a].

8. Kemp twice returns to the 'penny poet' as suspect and then tells us that the name of the libeller was 'brought out' by 'a book in Latin called *Mundus Furiosus*' (D4[a]). This would appear to be a reference to P. A. Jansonius (pseud.), *Mundi furiosi* (Cologne, 1600), which is a continuation of Jansonius's newsbook *Mundus furiosus* (Cologne, 1597). No issue of this book, however, gives any noticeable indication of Kemp's target.

9. Throughout his works Armin is unabashed about his status as a 'crank' poet (*Two Maids*, 2[a]) and by 1600, as *Quips upon Questions* makes clear, he was also well established as a stage performer. Armin repeatedly refers to his diminutive size in his publications. David Wiles, *Shakespeare's Clown* (Cambridge: Cambridge University Press, 1987), 148–51, makes the case that Armin actually suffered from a physical deformity. On this point it is difficult to be certain, but as the author of *A Pill* reports that 'I am not able to endure a pair of straight leather shoes on my feet, my heels being fore' (B4[b]), physical awkwardness was certainly part of his act.

jester's cap. The publications of Lent 1600 show the old and the new comic stars of Shakespeare's company in a public face-off that coincides with a radical shift in the playwright's style.

The impact of Kemp's replacement by Armin is widely acknowledged.[10] Having written a series of clownish roles for Kemp (such as Launcelot Gobbo, Bottom, Peter, and Dogberry) Shakespeare began in 1600 to write a series of very different characters with an explicitly foolish persona: these included Touchstone, Thersites, Feste, and the Fool in *Lear*. It is near enough certain that all of these roles were crafted specifically for Armin and we can have confidence in the identification of other major parts as well. There is a strong possibility, for example, that the diarist Simon Forman saw him as Autolycus in *The Winter's Tale* at the Globe in 1611. In his record of the visit Forman made the following note:

> Remember also the Rog[ue] that cam in all tottered like coll pixci and howe he feyned him sicke & to haue bin Robbed of all that he had and howe he cosened the por man of all his money.[11]

The ballad-selling Autolycus would be a fit part for the one-time ballad-writing Armin; there would also be a neat irony in his easy triumphs over a number of clowns. Forman's account, then, is likely to be an eye-witness description of Armin: a 'colt-pixie', also spelled 'coll-pixie', was a mischievous sprite or fairy, so it fits neatly with the short-statured Armin and his merciless teasing persona, for whom trickery was a constant pursuit.[12] Armin styled himself as a jester: a self-consciously witty and irrational figure who directed laughter at others much more than himself. Kemp, in contrast, was an athlete: an actor who specialized in physical humour and whose naive persona made him the willing object of jokes.[13] The alteration in the

---

10. For a recent survey of the practicalities see Christopher Sutcliffe, 'Kempe and Armin: the Management of Change', *Theatre Notebook* 50 (1996), 122–34. For other aspects of this transition—as identified, most famously, in James Shapiro's *1599: A Year in the Life of William Shakespeare* (London: Faber & Faber, 2005)—see Chapter 8 above.

11. Simon Forman, 'Booke of Plaies', Bodleian, MS Ashmole 208, fol. 202, printed in E. K. Chambers, *William Shakespeare: A Study of Facts and Problems* (Oxford: Clarendon Press, 1930), II, 341. Because Forman's spelling leaves room for interpretation I here transliterate directly from the manuscript. Wiles, *Clown*, 157, is very absolute about this identification although he does not examine the quotation itself.

12. *OED*, 'Colt-pixie, n.'

13. Wiles, *Clown*, 61–70, shows that the word 'clown' in early modern playtexts is used consistently to refer to a specific member of the company who took these roles. Within the world of the plays, however, the 'clown' and the 'fool' were fairly distinctive entities, the latter being an iconographic figure of folly dressed in a distinctive way (69).

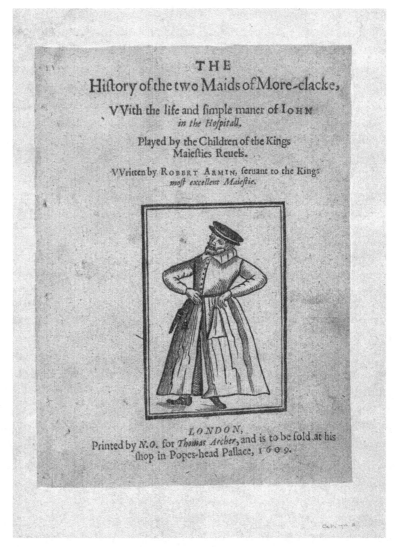

Figure 7. Title page of Robert Armin's *The History of the Two Maids of More-Clacke* (1609).

principal comic characters of Shakespeare's drama was thus immediate and stark.

Previous studies, most prominently the excellent work of David Wiles, have already treated this development in Shakespeare's writing.[14] We have a sound knowledge of Armin's biography, first as a goldsmith's apprentice, then as a writer of pamphlets, and finally as a player in Lord Chandos's and then the Lord Chamberlain's Men.[15] Nine of his roles can be securely identified, including a part in his own play, *The History of the Two Maids of More-Clacke*, which he appears to have written before he joined Shakespeare's company.[16] There is, then, material for a comprehensive picture of Armin. Given its understandable focus on performance, Shakespeare scholarship has tended to concentrate on the actor's physical qualities: his motley costume, diminutive size, and his probable skill as a mimic and singer. Yet, important though these are, there is a case for a more comprehensive impact. Of all the Chamberlain's Men, it is on Armin that we have greatest detail. He is the only sharer, besides Shakespeare, who demonstrated a sustained commitment to writing.[17] A competent poet, comfortable with

14. The basics of Armin's career and impact were already well known to critics in the nineteenth century—for example, through the Shakespeare Society's publication *Fools and Jesters* (1842). They are summarized in Chambers, *The Elizabethan Stage* (Oxford: Clarendon Press, 1923), II, 299–300. The subsequent major studies are Leslie Hotson, *Shakespeare's Motley* (London: Rupert Hart-Davis, 1952), Charles S. Felver, *Robert Armin, Shakespeare's Fool: A Biographical Essay*, Kent State University Bulletin 49 (Ohio, IL: Kent State University, 1961), and a section of Wiles, *Clown*, 136–63.

15. Emma Marshall Denkinger, 'Actors' Names in the Registers of St Bodolph Aldgate', *Proceedings of the Modern Language Association* 41 (1929), 91–109, first established Armin's residence amongst the community of actors, including Augustine Phillips. Further details of his biography are set out by Martin Butler in the *Oxford DNB*.

16. These are John of the Hospital in *Two Maids*, Touchstone in *As You Like It*, Feste in *Twelfth Night*, Lavatch in *All's Well that Ends Well*, Thersites in *Troilus*, Passarello in *The Malcontent* as revised for the King's Men, the Fool in *Lear*, Robin in George Wilkins's *Miseries of Enforced Marriage*, and Drugger in Ben Jonson's *The Alchemist*. Wiles, *Clown*, 144–63, lists most of these and makes the case for a number of additional roles. On Armin as Drugger, see Jane Belfield, 'Robert Armin as Abel Drugger', *Notes & Queries* 28 (1981), 146.

17. Kemp, it should be acknowledged, had his 'applauded merriments' published in *A Knack to Know a Knave* and is thought to have authored various lost entertainments. He stated, however, that *Nine Days Wonder* was the 'first pamphlet that ever Will Kemp offered the press' (D2^b), and by this point he was no longer a sharer. Nathan Field, who was the author of two plays, did not become a member of the company until after Shakespeare's death. Armin was well known as an author of ballads in the early 1590s. The surviving published works by him are *Quips upon Questions* (1600), *Fool upon Fool* (1600) and its revised later version *Nest of Ninnies* (1608), *The Italian Tailor and his Boy* (1609), and *The History of the Two Maids of More-Clacke* (1609). Other titles included in J. P. Feather's facsimile *Collected Works of Robert Armin* (New York: Johnson Reprint, 1972) are unlikely to be by the actor, on which see D. J. Lake, 'The Canon of Robert Armin's Work: Some Difficulties', *Notes & Queries* 222 (1977), 117–20.

Latin and Italian, he had literary connections of his own.[18] By beginning with Armin as a creative thinker, rather than simply as a player, a different perspective emerges as to his influence on Shakespeare's work.[19]

Quips upon Questions, unlike Kemp's *Nine Days Wonder*, was not published under the name of its author. Instead it is Armin's jester persona—the same Snuff who appears in *A Pill to Purge Melancholy*—who speaks a combative half-sense to his readership. The book's title page tells us it is 'a clown's conceit', and proceeds to address its audience as follows:

> Like as you list, read on and spare not,
> Clowns judge like Clowns, therefore I care not:
> > *Or thus,*
> Flout me, I'll flout thee; it is my profession,
> To jest at a Jester, in his transgression.

This was a disconcerting way for an author to address his readership. Unlike any other early modern performer we know of, Armin brought his stage identity into print. *A Pill to Purge Melancholy*, in fact, seems to have employed several of the jester's existing characters: not only Snuff, but also a Mr 'Baw-waw', and a natural fool in a 'blue vein' who may equate with another Armin favourite, the mentally retarded John of the Hospital.[20] These texts were themselves foolish productions: by defying the conventions of normal publication (such as a dedication, authorial name, or indication of content), Armin continued to play the fool on the page.

Armin's ludic persona, Snuff, is a controlling presence throughout *Quips upon Questions*. This voice is by turns intellectual, silly, and aggressive. It controls not just the poetry but also the absurd dedication of the book to the author's truncheon (Sir Timothy) and the strange alliterative address to its

As noted above, however, *A Pill to Purge Melancholy* (1599) can also be identified with some certainty as his.

18. The verse in *Quips upon Questions* is designedly rough, but *Two Maids* shows Armin writing workmanlike blank verse of a serious kind. In this play and in other works Armin skilfully employs Latin quotation and *The Italian Tailor* is a translation from the Italian. *Tailor*'s preface is decidedly literary, commending the poet Matthew Roydon. For possible connections with Nashe, see Sutcliffe, 'The Canon', 172.

19. To some extent Armin's role as writer is also emphasized in Richard Preiss's essay 'Robert Armin Do the Police in Different Voices', in Peter Holland and Stephen Orgel, eds., *From Performance to Print in Shakespeare's England* (Houndmills: Palgrave Macmillan, 2006), 208–30. Preiss argues that in presenting a version of clownish performance in print Armin put on record and also transformed a long tradition of roles that included those of Tarlton and Kemp. In this he took a lead, which Shakespeare followed (211).

20. See Sutcliffe, 'The Canon', 172.

'readers, revilers, or indeed what not' (A3ᵃ). The same persona is present in the other book that Armin published before joining the Chamberlain's Men: *Fool upon Fool*, which was also printed in 1600. Again, the text was pseudonymously published under the name Snuff and its character as the work of a fool was reinforced by a title page that declared it to be 'written by one seeming to have his mother's wit when some say he is filled with his father's foppery'. Still more so than *Quips upon Questions*, the book *Fool upon Fool* throws doubt on its author's sanity, so that as it describes the actions of six historical fools 'not so strange as true' it acknowledges the narrator's role as a seventh of that number.

The character of the Renaissance Fool is central to an understanding of Armin.[21] To say an author plays the fool in print might be one thing in the world of the modern novel. At the turn of the seventeenth century, however, 'playing the fool' was not a straightforwardly fictional act. The role of fool was an actuality at the courts of Tudor and Stuart monarchs and their wealthier subjects.[22] Such individuals could have genuine mental disability or affliction, or they might be self-conscious figures of fun. Often it was difficult to distinguish because the role of fool was not time-limited: it was not a performance that an actor turned on and off. The best-documented case is that of King James's fool, Archibald Armstrong, who was a practised comic famed for his witticisms, but also a licensed figure for whom conventional rules of court conduct did not apply. This meant, for example, that when he accompanied the Spanish embassy in the 1620s he alone was allowed access to the Infanta and her ladies, going 'blustering about them' as he wished. A fool could be whipped for crossing undefined boundaries, but (as Armstrong boasted) he could not be accused of libel, and could thus speak dangerous truths to courtiers and kings.[23]

The continuity of Armin's foolish persona between stage and text, then, is only part of the story: his was a mode of behaviour that could carry over into real-world interaction as well. That he himself exercised this privilege is evident in the expanded version of *Fool upon Fool*, which Armin published

---

21. The classic study here is Enid Welsford, *The Fool: His Social and Literary History* (London: Faber & Faber, 1935; repr. 1968), though see also John Southworth, *Fools and Jesters at the English Court* (Stroud: Sutton, 1998).

22. Welsford, *Fool*, 158–81, documents court fools in the households of all Tudor and Stuart monarchs until Charles II. Those with mental retardation generally appear on the record through their 'keepers' (158). On the history of keeping fools, and especially the history of Sir Thomas More's domestic fool Paterson, see also Robert Hillis Goldsmith, *Wise Fools in Shakespeare* (Liverpool: Liverpool University Press, 1958), 5–6.

23. See Welsford, *Fool*, 171–4.

in 1608 as *A Nest of Ninnies*. Its preface to the men of Oxford, Cambridge, and the Inns of Court seems to refer to a kind of licensed attendance at these institutions. Armin again speaks a kind of half-nonsense, but he is clearly referring to actual events:

> I have seen the stars at midnight in your societies and might have commenst like an ass as I was, but I lacked liberty in that, yet I was admitted in Oxford to be of Christ's Church, while they of All Souls gave aim, such as knew me remember my meaning. I promised them to prove mad and I think I am so, else I would not meddle with folly so deeply. (*Nest of Ninnies*, A2ᵃ)

There are references here to strange activity, perhaps at a Twelfth Night revels. Armin closes by reminding the gentlemen of his motley costume and of the pardon he carries from the figure of Folly herself.[24]

Well before he joined Shakespeare's company, Armin was fascinated by the conventions of fooling. His own *Fool upon Fool* is the most detailed Tudor account of the subject, so much so that it remains today a vital primary source. In spite of its foolish narrator, the work is a documentary record: its six fools are real people and the author calls attention to surviving portraits and living memory in support of that fact.[25] By the middle of 1600 Armin had made a specialism of the subject. He had completed not only *Fool upon Fool* and *Quips upon Questions* but also, in all probability, an early version of his play, *The Two Maids of More-Clacke*, which contained the first depiction of a 'natural fool' upon the English stage.[26] The childlike John of the Hospital (who seemingly also features in *A Pill to Purge Melancholy*) was a famous London simpleton, and in the preface to *Two Maids of More-Clacke* Armin explicitly tells us that he has played this part himself.[27]

Armin's game-playing with foolishness is an important element of *Two Maids of More-Clacke*. In this play one Armin character, John of the Hospital, is set against another in Tutch the Clown, a self-conscious comic. At the work's conclusion Tutch disguises himself as John and is then revealed as a 'counterfeit' (I1ᵃ), a moment that subtly pushes the boundaries of foolish performance. Very likely the parts of Tutch and John were doubled, thus making Armin a counterfeit at a second remove.[28]

---

24. Armin, *Nest of Ninnies*, A2ᵇ. The dedication apparently did cause offence to some as is evident from Armin's epistle to his readers in *The Italian Tailor*, A4ᵇ.
25. In the case of Henry VII's fool, Will Sommers, two portraits still survive today.
26. On John as the first natural stage fool see Felver, *Armin*, 20.
27. See Armin, *Two Maids*, 2ᵃ.
28. On the likelihood of the parts being doubled see Felver, *Armin*, 17.

The uncertain distinction between playing and being is also a pressing matter in *Quips upon Questions*, in which verses such as 'Who's the Fool Now?', 'He Plays the Fool', and 'Where's Tarlton?' challenge the distinction between jester and audience. This is likewise an issue in *Fool upon Fool*, whose subjects are self-conscious performers, even if most can be labelled as 'natural' fools. The characters in this book have a fatal drive to be the centre of attention, forcing their insanity upon others even if this commonly results in their being injured or punished for their deeds. They are intensely aware of a rivalry with professional entertainers and most of all with their effective opposite: the skilled clown of the minstrel tradition. The account of the first fool in Armin's book thus ends on a story that describes 'how a minstrel became a fool artificial, and had Jack Oates [the natural fool] his reward for his labour' (A4[b]). In this anecdote a trick is played by Jack's owner, Sir William, in which he tells the fool that he is being dismissed and will be replaced by a minstrel. A man is indeed hired to fulfil this 'artificial' function, but the joke, if such it is, turns out to be on him:

> By and by enters my artificial fool in his old clothes making wry mouths, dancing, looking asquint, who, when Jack beheld, suddenly he flew at him and so violently beat him that all the table rose, but could scarce get him off. Well off he was at length, [t]he knight caused the broken ones to be by themselves. My poor minstrel with a fall had his head broke to the scull against the ground, his face scratched, that which was worst of all his left eye put out, and with all so sore bruised that he could neither stand nor go.[29]

In celebration of this physical victory the book's foolish narrator composes a ditty of triumph. Through Jack's revenge on the minstrel for his presumption, therefore, we can see not only the fool's desire for public dominance, but also a dark premonition of Armin's confrontation with Kemp.

While Armin and Kemp were completing their publications in Lent 1600, Shakespeare's *As You Like It* was at the planning stage. That play first appears in the record on 4 August and it seems inconceivable that its lead comic role, the jester Touchstone, was not written with Armin in mind. Historical jesters had appeared previously in the commercial theatre: a Henslowe manuscript of 1598 makes mention of a suit for Henry VIII's fool, and a separate entry lists a 'fool's coat, cap, and bauble' which might

---

29. Robert Armin, *Fool upon Fool* (1600), B1[b].

have suited Raphe in Greene's *Friar Bacon*.[30] Armin, however, had made the fool's role a permanent feature of his public identity: it had been his idea to turn the jester—still a working reality within the early modern household—into a vehicle for commentary upon the world. The most conspicuous jester in a play for the English theatre had been Armin's own Tutch in *The Two Maids of More-Clacke* and the name 'Touchstone' seems deliberately to hark back to this earlier character.[31] Because a touchstone is a dark piece of quartz used to test the quality of gold and silver through rubbing, the name also alluded to Armin's first profession as a goldsmith and metaphorically hinted at his mode of comedy, which rubbed uncomfortably to test the mettle of men.[32] Never before had Shakespeare labelled one of his characters in this meta-theatrical manner. The role of jester did not appear in the play's sources and this would also be true of the comparable roles that Shakespeare produced in *All's Well that Ends Well*, *Twelfth Night*, and *Lear*.[33] Touchstone, therefore, not only heralded a new kind of Shakespearean comic character, he kick-started a transformation in the playwright's style.

Touchstone speaks nearly a third of the lines in *As You Like It* and many other speeches of the play, especially those of Jaques, are concerned purely

30. See the inventory lists, now lost, printed in Henslowe's *Diary* , ed. R. A. Foakes, 2nd edn (Cambridge: Cambridge University Press, 2002), 318. Alleyn's list of 'antic suits' also includes the coat but appears to date from around 1602 (see *Diary*, 291–4). The play that must have featured Sommers (or Somer) is lost. Raphe in *Friar Bacon* is clearly identified as the King's fool in the opening scene: there is mention of his cap and coat and later of coxcombs (Robert Greene, *Works*, ed. Collins, II, TLN 31–32; 546) but he does not otherwise conduct himself as a jester.

31. This is assuming, as almost all scholars do, that *Two Maids* was written before Armin became a Chamberlain's man. The play was printed in 1609 in a version that had been performed by the Children of the King's Revels, but in its preface Armin explains that there had been an earlier version 'sometime acted more naturally in the city' in which he himself played the fool, John of the Hospital. John Feather, 'Robert Armin and the Chamberlain's Men', *Notes & Queries* 19 (1972), 448–50, argues for an original composition date of 1597/8. For further debate see Nora Johnson, *The Actor as Playwright in Early Modern Drama* (Cambridge: Cambridge University Press, 2003), 46–7. As Robert Hillis Goldsmith demonstrates in *Wise Fools in Shakespeare*, 35–40, earlier clownish characters such as Shadow in Dekker's *Old Fortunatus* (1599) and Babulo in Haughton, Chettle, and Dekker's *Patient Grissil* (1600) are not fools by profession. After 1600 certain roles, such as Dondolo in Marston's *Parasitaster* (1604), follow Armin's model; Will Summers in Samuel Rowley's *When you See me, you Know me* (performed 1604) is actually based on the routines and exchanges of Armin's *Fool upon Fool*.

32. On Armin's career, see Jane Belfield, 'Robert Armin, Citizen and Goldsmith of London', *Notes & Queries* 27 (1980), 158–9, and also Martin Butler's entry in the *Oxford DNB*.

33. See Geoffrey Bullough, ed., *Narrative and Dramatic Sources of Shakespeare*, 8 vols. (London: Routledge and Kegan Paul, 1961–75), II and VII. Thersites does exist as a railing, deformed creature in George Chapman's translation, *The Seven Books of Homer's Iliads* (1598), which were the primary source for *Troilus* (see Bullough, *Sources*, VI, 122–3) but it was Shakespeare (recognizing the potential for an Armin role) who transformed him into a licensed jester.

with his character.[34] Having become a sharer and soon after this a housekeeper in the Globe, Armin was thus being fulsomely embraced by his new
company. The way in which his character is introduced in the play suggests
that Armin was thought of as a prize dramatic asset. In the Folio text there
are a dozen lines between the stage direction 'Enter Clown' and the first
speech by Touchstone. These lines are a kind of drum-roll of anticipation
for the character's introduction, highlighting Armin-like concerns with the
overlap between natural and artificial folly, wisdom and foolishness, that the
audience on the south bank would certainly have recognized. Touchstone's
concluding observation in this opening exchange ('the more pity that fools
may not speak wisely what wise men do foolishly') sounds not unlike
Armin's own 'fools talk like fools, while wise men sit,/ Wisely to descant
on an other's wit' in *Quips upon Questions* published earlier that year.[35]
Although we have but a patchy record of such audience recognition of
performers, it was unquestionably a resource on which Shakespeare could
draw.[36] By the time that John Davies came to write his epigram on the actor
it was a commonplace that Armin should 'wisely play the fool'.[37]

The scene in which Touchstone first appears is in some ways an expansion on
motifs from Armin's output. It is Jaques's report of his meeting with Touchstone, however, that constitutes a genuine paean to the ideas that drove the
author of *Quips upon Questions*, *Two Maids of More-Clacke*, and *Fool upon Fool*:

> A fool, a fool! I met a fool i'th' forest,
> A motley fool—a miserable world!
> As I do live by food, I met a fool,
> Who laid him down and basked him in the sun,
> And railed on Lady Fortune in good terms,
> In good set terms—and yet a motley fool!
>   . . . I must have liberty

34. This point plus a wider reading of the scene to which I am indebted is found in Felver, *Armin*,
    40–6.
35. William Shakespeare, *As You Like It*, ed. Juliet Dusinberre, Arden3 (London: Methuen,
    2006), 1.2.85–6; Armin, *Quips*, E2[b].
36. Tiffany Stern, *Rehearsal from Shakespeare to Sheridan* (Oxford: Clarendon Press, 2000), 14,
    making an inference based on later records of audience responses, describes how 'audiences
    who had attended to see a particular performer sometimes applauded when the player left the
    stage until the curtain was brought down "without suffering the whole to be regularly
    finished"' (account based on William Cooke, *Memoirs of Samuel Foote*, 3 vols. (1805), I, 86;
    V. C. Clinton-Baddeley, *It'll be Alright on the Night* (London, 1954), 43).
37. John Davies of Hereford, *Scourge of Folly* (1610) in *Works*, 2 vols, ed. Alexander B. Grosart
    (New York: AMS Press, 1967), II, 60–1 (cited by Felver, *Armin*, 70).

> Withal, as large a charter as the wind,
> To blow on whom I please, for so fools have,
> And they that are most galled with my folly,
> They most must laugh....
> Invest me in my motley. Give me leave
> To speak my mind, and I will through and through
> Cleanse the foul body of th'infected world.[38]

Jaques's speeches touch on many of Armin's characteristics: his motley, sense of licence, and moralism; his self-conscious witticism, his intellectual ambition, and the notion that he dispenses gall to a sinful world. All of these qualities are diametrically opposed to those of Shakespeare's earlier comic roles and *As You Like It* makes much of this contrast. Indeed the courtly status of Armin's fool is emphasized through a series of pointed juxtapositions between Touchstone and country clowns such as Corin and William— figures who function as a pastoral backdrop to offset the new player's skills.

Though striking in degree, there is nothing unique in the adaptation that Shakespeare made to Armin. Other writers for the company made similar adjustments. When Marston's *The Malcontent* transferred from the Children of the Chapel to the Globe, the playwright, in collaboration with Webster, added the fool's role of Passarello.[39] This too is a courtly character, wearing motley and enjoying a brand of coruscating paradoxical humour. Like Touchstone, Passarello was an addition not found in the play's sources—a figure given his own time and space within the drama to exhibit a set of witty routines. The same is true of the Armin fool in Wilkins's *Miseries of Enforced Marriage*, another motley entertainer whose name, Robin (a diminutive of Armin's own) had already been used by the actor on the stage.[40] Such gestures towards audience recognition were not uncommon in early modern theatre and Armin's jester persona seems especially to have encouraged them. Even where he did not play in jester's garb there was a tendency to highlight his identity as performer,

---

38. *As You Like It*, 2.7.12–17, 47–51, 57–60.
39. The date and auspices of first performance by a children's company are uncertain. For a careful examination of the evidence see John Marston, *The Malcontent*, ed. George K. Hunter, Revels (Manchester: Manchester University Press, 1999), xli–xlvi. The nature of the revisions is discussed by Hunter in the same volume, xlvii–liii; subsequent quotations are from this edition and sources appear in the text.
40. Robin in *Miseries* alludes several times to the actor's earlier role as Touchstone (see below). John Davies calls Robert Armin 'Robin', a shortened form of Robert, in *Scourge of Villany*, (see Davies, *Works*, II, 60–1).

as is the case with Armin's part of Drugger in Jonson's *Alchemist*, who tells the audience he has 'played the fool'.[41]

The role of Touchstone in *As You Like It* has much in common with these examples. It is unusual in its scope and still more so because it is the first in a series of roles that Shakespeare would produce for the actor, but even here there are parallels.[42] Probably the closest contemporary match for Shakespeare's relationship with Armin is that between Thomas Middleton and William Rowley: a literary dramatist and a comic writer–performer who, although they were not joint asset-holders, collaborated in the production of at least four plays.[43] The Middleton–Rowley partnership is instructive because it involves developing adaptation to a performer's characteristics across a series of characters. It shows that playwrights besides Shakespeare could develop more complex individuation when they had certainty about the actor who would perform the role.

Rowley often performed his own material and thus replicated the kind of control that Armin had in creating Tutch and John of the Hospital for *The Two Maids of More-Clacke*. In place of Armin's fools, he specialized in pleasure-seeking gluttons: archetypally the character Plumporridge in Middleton's *Masque of Heroes* (1616) who 'moves like one of the great porridge tubs, going to the counter'.[44] Over the course of several plays Middleton and Rowley experimented with the dramatic potential of this character. In their first collaboration, *Wit at Several Weapons* (1613), the romantic heroine pretends to fall in love with Rowley's character, the servant Pompey Doodle. This deception causes the fat clown to become horribly conceited: he is off-hand with his master, assumes the disposition of a gentleman, and attempts to starve himself for love. In *The Fair Quarrel* (1615–16) the joke of clownish conceit and

41. See Belfield, 'Robert Armin as Abel Drugger', 146.
42. Thomas Heywood's relationship with the comic actor Thomas Greene is another instance, although little evidence from playscripts survives. Collaboration with authors was pursued with particular success by the actor Nathan Field, who joined the King's Men soon after Shakespeare's departure: following a pattern he had already developed working under Henslowe, Field worked together with his dramatists and was listed as a co-author of *The Fatal Dowry* with Philip Massinger in 1632. The title page describes the work as 'acted at the private house in Blackfriars by his Majesty's servants' and 'written by P. M. and N. F.'
43. See Gerald Eades Bentley, *The Profession of Dramatist in Shakespeare's Time, 1590–1642* (Princeton, NJ: Princeton University Press, 1971), 215–18, who also reports on Rowley's co-authorship with Fletcher and Webster.
44. *Masque of Heroes* in Middleton, *Collected Works*, ed. Gary Taylor and John Lavagnino (Oxford: Clarendon Press, 2007), ll. 66–7. On the casting and likely date of this masque and the plays in which Middleton and Rowley collaborated, see the respective introductions in Middleton, *Works*.

futile ambition was further built upon, with Rowley playing Chough, a Cornishman come to town to be instructed in the ways of gentlemen in order to woo a young heiress. And in a third collaboration, *The Old Law* (1618–19), Rowley again played a lascivious gourmand whose excessive confidence gets its comeuppance at the close.

In some ways this partnership, grounded on co-authorship, was a more direct one than that of Shakespeare and Armin. At the same time, because Middleton was not a sharer, it still testifies to a practical separation between the jobs of literary author and performer. Rowley generally controlled the scenes in which he was appearing and felt at liberty to expand on a role where it proved successful. The second issue of the *Fair Quarrel* quarto thus contained 'new additions of Mr Chough's and Tristram's Roaring' for which Rowley alone was responsible.[45] Like other freelance playwrights, Middleton could have neither control nor income when it came to the long-term dramatic production of his output. His most celebrated collaboration with Rowley, *The Changeling*, for example, rapidly transferred in ownership between two newly amalgamated companies—its auspices were thus disrupted from the start.[46] This does remain the great point of contrast with Armin, who continued to perform Shakespeare roles for at least a decade and could, near the end of his career, still write proudly of his performance in *Much Ado About Nothing* and his joint possession of 'our Globe'.[47]

Touchstone is the role that introduced Armin's witty, intellectual, jester persona to the Globe audience and it was followed in the ensuing years by comparable licensed fools such as Thersites in *Troilus and Cressida* and Lavatch in *All's Well that Ends Well*.[48] This run of jesters illustrates Shakespeare's habit of constructing plays around the existing stage personae of his actors, but it also demonstrates something more profound and unusual. Across these roles Shakespeare can be seen to explore a world first depicted

---

45. See Suzanne Gossett in Middleton, *Works*, 1210.
46. See Annabel Patterson in Middleton, *Works*, 1634.
47. *Nest of Ninnies* (1608), A2ᵃ. In *The Italian Tailor* (1609), A3ᵃ, Armin refers to his fame as Dogberry in *Much Ado*, which was originally a Kemp role but one that the new clown evidently took to heart.
48. These roles are listed in Wiles, *Clown*, 144. Wiles here also claims Carlo Buffone in Jonson's *Every Man out of his Humour* (1599) as an Armin role, but that case is doubtful. Armin is not on the players' list in the 1616 Jonson folio and though he is, as Wiles points out (145), described as a 'jester' at the play's opening this is a derogatory comment rather than an actual description of Buffone's role. This character has nothing in common with Armin's conventional practice and in the absence of new evidence the title pages of Armin's 1600 publications are a strong indication that he had not yet moved to the Globe in Lent of that year.

by Armin in the works that he published before he joined the Chamberlain's Men. Armin's fascination with professional fools made him an influence much deeper than the earlier relationship with Kemp: more than simply a performer, he was a fellow creative thinker who introduced ways of thinking about comedy quite different from any that had earlier been evident in Shakespeare's plays. Cruelty, insanity, and absurdist poetry would—with increasing complexity—become an element in the drama that Shakespeare produced. Not only did Armin constitute a new element in Shakespeare's relational drama, he also changed the operating assumptions on which that relational drama worked.

The part of Touchstone highlights Armin's characteristics as a performer, but it is in his subsequent roles that Shakespeare more daringly exploits the sadistic quality that Armin brought to the depiction of fools. Some of this came from Armin's continual focus on the fool's dual role as victim and performer. In 'He Plays the Fool' Armin compares his own role to that of a carpenter who 'with his sharp tool,/ Cut his own finger oft, yet lives by't too'.[49] This mixture of pain and entertainment is a continual feature of the anecdotes in *Fool upon Fool*. In the case of Jack Miller, for example, an obsessively clean and decorous simpleton is introduced as a performer ('Sing he would much, and speak a player's part' (D3[a])) but is also punished again and again for vanity. Jack Leanard of Sherwood, 'now living well known of many' (C4[a]), not only attacks others but also repeatedly injures himself in his frenzies: he cracks his head, scratches his face, and breaks his own leg in anger; he eats his master's hawk alive and is nearly choked by the feathers; he sets fire to the barrow that serves as his bed and then burns the faces and legs of the household. Fools in Armin's volume are continually punished: they are fired at by cannon balls, stung by nettles, drugged, whipped, and burnt—all to the amusement of their masters. Fear and humiliation are not simply side-effects of the fool's chaos, they are central to its emotional and moral appeal.

Such queasy mirth will be familiar to those who know the parts that Shakespeare wrote for Armin. Ajax's fool is locked in a circle of mockery and violence: 'he beats me, and I rail at him' Thersites tells his audience as he recovers from the latest attack.[50] In *All's Well that Ends Well*, the Countess and Lavatch banter with apparent lightness on similar punishments:

---

49. Armin, *Quips*, B4[b].
50. William Shakespeare, *Troilus and Cressida*, ed. David Bevington, Arden3 (London: Cengage, 1998), 2.3.3.

COUNTESS: Do you cry 'O Lord, Sir!' at your whipping, and
  'spare not me'? Indeed 'O Lord, sir!' is very
  sequent to your whipping; you would answer very
  well to a whipping, if you were but bound to't.[51]

It can hardly be overstated how radically such exchanges differ from those that Shakespeare wrote when Kemp was the clown of the company—not only for the reason that Armin falls easily into the role of victim but also because he can turn so quickly to a persecutor of vice. Lavatch can depict himself as a kind of minor devil in the service of 'the prince of darkness' (*All's Well*, 4.5.39) and Thersites can rail with exhausting vehemence: 'lechery, lechery... A burning devil take them!' (*Troilus*, 5.2.201–3). Such characters have much in common with the speaker of Armin's earlier *Quips upon Questions*, who turns rapidly from such self-immolating verses as 'He Plays the Fool' to moral attacks like 'Where's the Devil?' and 'Why is he Drunk?'.[52]

Perhaps most powerfully it is Feste in *Twelfth Night* who encompasses the possibilities that Armin's perspective on fooling offered Shakespeare. Wisdom and folly, which had been key words endlessly twinned in Armin's own output, here combine with the thematic treatment of madness that had also haunted Armin's work. Feste is another motley entertainer. His tendency to turn the tables on those who surround him (such as 'proving' Olivia to be a fool through a catechism in 1.5) strongly recalls the motifs of Armin's writing.[53] In *Two Maids of More-Clacke*, for example, the Armin role, John of the Hospital, engages in the following dialogue with a boy:

BOY: I'll give thee a fool's head Jack. What wilt do with it?
JOHN: Carry't home to my nurse.
BOY: Carry a fool's head, what fool art thou?
JOHN: Should I go home without it? Who's the fool now?

(*Two Maids*, B4[b])

At his first appearance John had been casually threatened with a whipping, but his foolish wit wins out in this scene. Because Armin performed his role of fool both within and outside the world of the playhouse, such exchanges were

---

51. William Shakespeare, *All's Well that Ends Well*, ed. G. K. Hunter, Arden2 (London: Methuen, 1962), 2.2.48–51.
52. Armin, *Quips*, B4[b], E2[a], E2[b].
53. William Shakespeare, *Twelfth Night*, ed. Keir Elam, Arden3 (London: Methuen, 2008), 1.5.54–70.

tinged with irony. When Tutch later reveals himself as John of the Hospital's imitator, he revels in such doubling, telling the audience 'I am author of this shift: he's where he would be now, I'm where I should be too' (H2[b]).

Feste, as is always the case with Shakespeare's fools, is not there in the playwright's sources. While it would be crude to insist directly on *Two Maids* as an analogue, Armin's repertoire as a performer and body of work as a writer were surely an influence. The scam of Malvolio's supposed madness is powerfully redolent of the devices described by Armin. In *Fool upon Fool*, for example, Jemmy Camber is subjected to a series of absurd fictions: while asleep he is carried to a new location and then told he has run there, or is made to ride blindfold and then assured he has performed extraordinary feats (C1[a]–C3[a]). Shakespeare's Feste relishes the topsy-turvy world of such jesting. His visit to 'Malvolio the lunatic' while disguised as Sir Topas is a case in point:

FESTE: What ho, I say, peace in this prison.
SIR TOBY: The knave counterfeits well—a good knave.
MALVOLIO (*Within*): Who calls there?
FESTE: Sir Topas the curate, who comes to visit Malvolio
    the lunatic.
MALVOLIO: Sir Topas, Sir Topas, good Sir Topas, go to
    my lady.
FESTE: Out, hyperbolical fiend, how vexest thou this man!
    Talkest thou nothing but of ladies?
SIR TOBY: Well said, Master Parson.
MALVOLIO: Sir Topas, never was man thus wronged.
    Good Sir Topas, do not think I am mad. They have laid
    me here in hideous darkness.
FESTE: Fie, thou dishonest Satan! I call thee by the most
    modest terms, for I am one of those gentle ones that
    will use the devil himself with courtesy. Sayst thou that
    the house is dark?
MALVOLIO: As hell, Sir Topas.
FESTE: Why, it hath bay-windows transparent as
    barricadoes, and the clerestories toward the south-
    north are as lustrous as ebony, and yet complainest thou
    of obstruction?
MALVOLIO: I am not mad, Sir Topas. I say to you this
    house is dark.

FESTE: Madman, thou errest. I say there is no darkness
    but ignorance.

(Twelfth Night, 4.2.18–43)

The absurd logic of this exchange, in which brick walls can be declared transparent, is close to the world of Armin's writing. As Armin writes in the 'Incouragement' that prefaces *Quips upon Questions*: 'fools make rules for the wise to flout at' and 'fools have tools sharp in season,/ To wound and confound without reason' (A3^b): Malvolio is like the 'harebrained ass' of Armin's poem 'Why Looks he Angry' who refuses to bend to the absurdities of the jester's world (C2$^{a–b}$).

The projection of multiple identities was evidently an Armin specialism: in *The Two Maids* Tutch plays a Welsh knight, a servant, a famous natural fool, and also sings.[54] The account of the clown's act in *Fool upon Fool* is comparable: 'he would imitate plays doing all himself: king, clown, gentleman and all' (D4^b). This layering of performances in *Twelfth Night* helps to create a world of unreason. As Feste repeatedly switches between his song, his own voice, and the perverted academic logic of Sir Topas, Malvolio is eventually led into a very Armin-like trap:

MALVOLIO: Fool, there was never man so notoriously
    abused. I am as well in my wits, fool, as thou art.
FESTE: But as well? Then thou art mad indeed, if you be
    no better in your wits than a fool.

(Twelfth Night, 4.2.87–90)

At this point in the play the suffering becomes something more than simply comic. When Malvolio complains in response that 'they have here propertied me' (91) he appears to mean that he has been made a possession in the way that fools were—objects that could be donated, as was the case with the characters described in *Fool upon Fool*. Feste's unanswerable question 'but tell me true, are you not mad indeed, or do you but counterfeit?' (114–15) encapsulates the bind that holds Armin's foolish subjects, who are both mad and counterfeit. As Armin makes clear in his poem 'Are you There with your Bears?' there is a close analogy between jesting and baiting: 'were I bear ward I would learn to bite', he says of a questioner, and 'when I next

---

54. Wiles, *Clown*, 139, argues that the verses in *Quips upon Questions* were based on Armin's stage performance and involved the projection of multiple identities (with Armin's truncheon perhaps taking the 'quip' response). His case, however, is rejected by Nora Johnson, *Actor as Playwright*, 35, and remains speculative.

see him, I'll make his brains bleed' (C3^b). This link with the cruel sport is also there in *Twelfth Night*, where Sir Toby, planning Malvolio's humiliation, tells his companions 'to anger him, we'll have the bear again; and we will fool him black and blue' (*Twelfth Night*, 2.58–9). Such moments open up the absurd and threatening aspects of fooling, which Armin had placed directly in Shakespeare's sight.

Armin's foolish persona was never straightforwardly comic. It is little surprise, then, that his presence could be equally influential in other modes. When Marston's *The Malcontent* transferred to the company in 1604 the fool's part added for Armin sharpened rather than alleviated the play's satire. Passarello's cynical riddles on worldly corruption, which were the stock in trade of Armin's published writings, also served to heighten the tragicomic absurdity of Marston's creation. No doubt Shakespeare was present when the company decided to add the new scenes to accommodate the comic actor. He would also have observed the play's success in the theatre and could thus have seen the effect of the role in more serious drama. Because the fool was an integral part of the court he functioned differently from traditional clowns, who offered a comic alternative to the world of tragedy by means of a subplot. Passarello is not set apart in this manner: 'you are in good case since you came to court, fool,' says Malevole at their first meeting, and then proceeds with the crucial question 'why do great men beg fools?' (1.8.7, 22). The answer to Malevole's question foregrounds a productive ambiguity for the dramatist. Great men could 'beg' fools as a consequence of their power by claiming them as property.[55] Yet, as the exchange with Passarello makes clear, such men also proved oddly dependent on jesters. Malevole, himself a deposed duke, is asked to 'bear the burden' of Passarello's fooling by singing a chorus (1.8.1–2). His usurper, Jacomo, is likewise pulled into the jester's orbit: 'I am fain to fool him asleep every night', Passarello confides (1.8.11–12). In the corrupt court the jester is both a truth-teller and an emblem of the pervasive disorder. Thus Passarello is employed by his old lord 'to instruct him in the art of fooling' so he can thrive in the Duke's service (1.8.45–6) and is also the subject of a concluding lesson from the Malcontent:

55. Cardinal Wolsey's Patch, for example, was given to Henry VIII against his wishes, and Thomas More's fool, Henry Paterson, was passed to the Lord Mayor of London after his owner's fall (see Welsford, *Fool*, 159, 161).

> O world most vild, when thy loose vanities,
> Taught by this fool, do make the fool seem wise!
>
> (*Malcontent* 1.8.55–6)

This was essentially the message of *Quips upon Questions* and fitted seamlessly with the existing absurdities of Marston's play.

In *The Malcontent* Richard Burbage played the deposed ruler opposite Armin's jester. It is intriguing, therefore, that when, about a year later, Shakespeare began to work on *King Lear*, he introduced this same relationship between the company's most distinctive actors to his tragedy. Never before had Shakespeare made use of Armin's jester persona in his serious drama. The Fool in *Lear*, however, would test this character to its destruction—so much so that Shakespeare would never write for that figure again.

It would be absurd to claim that the world of Shakespeare's masterpiece was inspired by Armin. There is a case, however, for including Armin's *Quips upon Questions* and *Fool upon Fool* amongst the sources of the play. It is almost inconceivable that the dramatist was unfamiliar with the work of the only other member of his company to publish his own compositions. *Fool upon Fool* came out in a second edition in 1605, the year that *Lear* was being written; even if the playwright did not look at the volume, he could hardly have been unaware of its contents.[56] What we find in *Lear* is not only a fool role that directly imports Armin's performance characteristics, but also a pervasive mood of dark comedy, paradox, and purgative judgment that is there in the jester's published work. None of these elements are present in the play's conventionally acknowledged sources, but the line between sanity and madness had been the sustained interest of his lead comic actor for many years. Writing speeches for the Fool and also for the natural madman Poor Tom, who is impersonated by Edgar, the precedent of Armin's prose, poetry, and drama on this subject would have been impossible to ignore.

The Fool in *Lear* offers the most powerful and complex example of the influence that the actors had on Shakespeare. This role is the most extensively revised of Shakespeare's creations: across the two substantial texts of the play (that of the First Quarto and Folio) fifty-four, or almost a quarter, of

---

56. H. F. Lippincott, 'Bibliographical Problems in the Works of Robert Armin', *The Library* 30 (1975), 330–3, notes that this second edition was 'crudely truncated' and expresses his doubts about Armin's involvement in its publication. The book did, however, record Armin's new status as the clown of the Globe and was used by the author as the basis for his revised third edition, *A Nest of Ninnies* (1608).

the Fool's lines are changed. Many of these are subtle adjustments that alter the characterization: the jingle on the 'sweet and bitter fool' in Q1, for example, is removed in the Folio, which later adds a replacement in the verses on 'fathers that wear rags'.[57] Still more significant are the alterations that affect the Fool's interlocutors. For instance, in the Folio version of the storm scene two new lines by Lear are addressed to the Fool before he enters the hovel: 'In, boy, go first. You houseless poverty—/ Nay, get thee in. I'll pray and then I'll sleep' (3.4.26–7). These lines make the King's soliloquy— 'Expose thyself to feel what wretches feel'—a direct response to the Fool's condition.[58] Evidently Shakespeare tinkered extensively with this play and as he did so the role of Armin was foremost in his mind.

John Kerrigan has argued that the role of the Fool was made significantly more subtle as a result of Shakespeare's revisions between the Quarto and Folio versions.[59] To the extent that this is right it illustrates the effect of Shakespeare's close personal relationship with fellow sharers. The following alteration between Q and F, for example, requires key adjustments both to the specific cues and speeches of Armin's and Burbage's parts and to the psychological states of their characters. In the Quarto text the King's speech is rather grandly declamatory, ending on an accusation that the Fool endorses in a dry aside:

LEAR: Who is it that can tell me who I am?
   Lear's shadow? I would learn that, for by the marks
   Of sovereignty, knowledge, and reason
   I should be false persuaded I had daughters.
FOOL: Which they will make an obedient father.
LEAR: Your name, fair gentlewoman?
GONERIL: Come, Sir,
   This admiration is much of the savour
   Of other your new pranks.

(*Lear*, Q1 1.4.218–26)

In the Folio, however, this speech is broken up so that Armin can make a cutting intervention:

---

57. Compare Q1 1.4.130–7 to F 2.4.41–6 in *King Lear: A Parallel Text*, ed. René Weis (Harlow: Longman, 1993).
58. Compare Q 3.4.21–32 to F 3.4.25–36 in *Lear*, ed. Weis.
59. John Kerrigan, 'Revision, Adaptation, and the Fool in *King Lear*', in Gary Taylor and Michael Warren, eds., *The Division of the Kingdoms: Two Versions of 'King Lear'* (Oxford: Oxford University Press, 1983), 195–245.

LEAR: Who is it that can tell me who I am?
FOOL: Lear's shadow.
LEAR: Your name, fair gentlewoman?
GONERIL: This admiration, sir, is much o'th'savour
    Of other your new pranks.

(*Lear*, F 1.4.203–7)

The writing in the Folio is not only more economical, it also shifts to a more dialogic characterization in replacing the King's self-awareness with the Fool's sardonic gibe.[60] As is the case more widely in the Folio, Lear no longer appears fully conscious of the jester's presence, allowing this character to function as a kind of chorus. With the King losing his grip on reality, the Fool's responses become wilder and more prescient at the same time.

Key revisions to the Fool's role are testament to the depth of Shakespeare's engagement with Armin's thinking: his love of absurdity, riddles, and sadism are all more radically exploited in the Folio exchange. The key index of Armin's influence, however, is not revision but continuity across characters: the earlier roles of Touchstone, Thersites, Lavatch, and Feste all make their presence felt in the Fool in *Lear*. Comparison with Armin's first appearance at the Globe in *As You Like It* is revealing because (in contrast to his almost formal introduction to the audience on that occasion) in *Lear* the first mention of his existence precedes his actual arrival on stage by well over a hundred lines. It comes at the opening of Scene 3 when Goneril enters asking her steward, 'Did my father strike my gentleman for chiding of his fool?' (1.3.1–2).[61] By this point events are already well in train: the kingdom is divided, Kent and Cordelia banished, Edgar gulled, and Lear established in residence with his eldest daughter. First reference to the jester thus coincides with the earliest intimations of the old man's personal foolishness: Goneril concludes the short scene by observing 'Now by my life/ Old fools are babes again and must be used/ With checks as flatteries, when they are

---

60. On self-commentary and commentary by others as contrasting techniques of characterization see Manfred Pfister, *The Theory and Analysis of Drama*, trans. John Halliday (Cambridge: Cambridge University Press, 1988), 184–9.

61. In line with my practice throughout this book, I now return to the most recent Arden edition as my standard source for quotation, in this case William Shakespeare, *King Lear*, ed. R. A. Foakes, Arden3 (London: Cengage, 1997). Foakes, ed., *Lear*, 111–46, examines and critiques a straightforward thesis of revision across the Q1 and F variants and in the process makes a strong case for the utility of his text (which effectively uses F as copytext but also draws extensively on Q1). Subsequent references, unless otherwise indicated, are to his edition.

seen abused' (1.3.19–21). The Fool is mentioned by Lear himself at the end of his ensuing meeting with the disguised Kent: 'Where's my knave, my fool? Go you and call my fool hither' (1.4.42–3). When the King is then immediately slighted by Oswald the Steward, the absence of the Fool starts to become an indication of the household's unsettled state:

LEAR: What says the fellow there? Call the clotpoll back.
　Where's my fool? Ho, I think the world's asleep.

(*Lear*, 1.4.46–7)

Lear asks again for the Fool (1.4.69–70) and hears of his pining since Cordelia's departure. It is unprecedented for a character to be called upon so often and not enter. By the time Lear repeats his demand 'Go you; call hither my fool' (1.4.75) to a third servant the request begins to function like the tolling of an ominous bell.

These apparent cues for the entry of a well-known actor create a complex variant of the phenomenon that Susan Bennett terms 'double recognition': a theatre audience's pre-knowledge both of a famous performer and of the famous character that he or she plays.[62] The name of Armin and his jester persona were scarcely separable for the Globe audience and Shakespeare cements this association by naming the character simply 'Fool'. What happens with these unanswered calls is thus multi-layered in its implications: spectators must speculate about the nature of his role in the drama and the reasons for his delay. His failure to appear creates an especially awkward frisson in the theatre, leaving an audience conscious of the performer's presence back stage. As Bennett points out, such an effect is impossible in cinema (where a physical impediment cannot prevent an actor's scheduled arrival). On the stage, however, the character's delay lays the groundwork for his wider function in the creation of unease.

Even before his arrival, the latent possibilities of Armin's motley persona are a resource to draw upon and these are extended as the play goes on. Extraordinarily, at the moment where the mood of insanity hits fever pitch, and the Fool himself succumbs to madness, his character repeats phrases from the song on which he had concluded *Twelfth Night*:[63]

---

62. See Susan Bennett, *Theatre Audiences: A Theory of Production and Reception*, 2nd edn (London: Routledge, 1997), 152.
63. *Twelfth Night*, 5.1.366–85.

FOOL: He that has and a little tiny wit,
  With heigh-ho, the wind and the rain,
  Must make content with his fortunes fit,
  Though the rain it raineth every day.

(*Lear*, 3.2.74–7)

It is unprecedented for Shakespeare to echo his earlier work in this explicit manner, although Armin had used songs in this way more than once.[64] The actor had made such repetition a virtue, and Shakespeare's recollection of his earlier lines adds further pathos to the situation. As happens at several points in the drama, it moves the Fool away from the *locus* of the storm and towards the *platea* of the audience in the playhouse.[65] The deliberate allusion to another role for Armin's self-created jester thus both heightens the experience of distortion and strengthens the universal imperatives of the play.

To a degree, such expansion on existing character is also found in other playwrights and can prove especially effective where generic boundaries are crossed. Middleton and Rowley, like Shakespeare and Armin, worked together for more than a decade but it was in their late experiment with tragedy that they achieved greatest success. Across a number of works—*Wit at Several Weapons*, *Masque of Heroes*, and *A Fair Quarrel*—they had exploited Rowley's lascivious and greedy clown persona. Lollio of the joint-authored *The Changeling*, who was presumably played by Rowley, is a continuation of this figure. But because this play is more widely concerned with the sexual threat of servants (especially that of De Flores to Beatrice-Joana), the clown's ambition to woo his mistress, which was comic in *Wit at Several Weapons*, cuts much deeper when Isabella is confronted by Lollio. His

---

64. Tiffany Stern, *Documents of Performance in Early Modern England* (Cambridge: Cambridge University Press, 2009), 120–73, demonstrates that songs often had a textual existence separate from the play in which they featured and were not infrequently re-used. The fragmentary reference to 'the rain it raineth every day', however, is something much more character-specific than what occurs in those instances. As noted above, Felver, 'Robert Armin's Fragment', shows that the song by Tutch in Armin's *Two Maids of More-Clacke* is probably a fragment of Armin's own earlier composition. Feste's other song in *Twelfth Night* ('Hey Robin, jolly Robin' (4.2.71)) also looks very much like a self-referential gesture by Armin because it repeats the diminutive of his first name, which he used elsewhere both on stage and in print.

65. Robert Weimann, 'Playing with a Difference: Revisiting "Pen" and "Voice" in Shakespeare's Theater', *Shakespeare Quarterly* 50 (1999), 415–32 (at 430), writes powerfully about this quality in the performance of another Armin role, Thersites. On the fool's privileged position as regards *locus* and *platea* more generally, see Weimann, *Shakespeare and the Popular Tradition in Theater: Studies in the Social Dimension of Dramatic Form and Function*, ed. Robert Schwartz (Baltimore, MD: Johns Hopkins University Press, 1978), 77–9.

assault ('Thou hast a thing about thee would do a man pleasure.—I'll lay my hand on't' (3.3.255–7)) is perhaps ridiculous but, as Isabella's response makes clear, it is also genuinely frightening. When she saves herself by offering her body to Antonio (whose payment 'for enjoying me shall be to cut thy throat' (3.3.263)) Middleton and Rowley make a daring connection across the twin plots of their play.

Comparison with Middleton cuts two ways. It illustrates the possibilities of player–author collaboration, but it also exposes the unique nature of the Shakespeare–Armin partnership. Lady Elizabeth's Men, for whom *The Changeling* was first licensed, soon merged with Palsgrave's, so that later performances came under the auspices of a very different company.[66] As ever, Middleton lacked a continued interest in the play's dramatic life and did not have an institutional bond with Rowley. For Shakespeare, in contrast, the possibilities for development with his players ran deeper. In *The Changeling* the comic and tragic plots, in spite of thematic connections, largely remain separate; in *Lear* the dramatist does something much more extraordinary. As Susan Snyder puts it, he 'sets comic order side by side with comic chaos, and out of the dislocation that results he develops a special, devastating tragic effect'.[67]

The multiform influence of the Fool, even when he is not himself present, is a product or perhaps even the catalyst of that antagonistic conjunction. Once he enters and for as long as the King is still at court the Fool's songs and witticisms provide an insidious commentary on the old man's predicament. His quips often exhibit a cruel rationality, for example:

FOOL: Nuncle, give me an egg
  and I'll give thee two crowns.
LEAR: What two crowns shall they be?
FOOL: Why, after I have cut the egg i'the middle and eat
  up the meat, the two crowns of the egg.

(*Lear* 1.4.148–52)

This satirical riddling strain is the most straightforward element of Armin's creation. In *Quips upon Questions* some verses dramatize comparable exchanges in which the fool logic-chops with an unwary straight man. In 'What's a clock?', for example, Armin perversely interprets a query about

---

66. See Middleton, *Works*, 1634–5.
67. See 'Between the Divine and Absurd: *King Lear*', in Susan Snyder, *The Comic Matrix of Shakespeare's Tragedies* (Princeton, NJ: Princeton University Press, 1979), 137–79 (at 137).

the time of day as a matter of definition (what *is* a clock?) and then pivots from this into an accusation that the questioner must have avoided divine service: 'Wilt thou know what's a clock?', 'Go to the church and see' (C3ᵃ). Similar vaguely moralistic quibbles dominate the early scenes featuring the King and the Fool.

Once Lear is outside the boundaries of civilization the jester assumes a more natural madness in the speaking of nonsense:

> FOOL: Cry to it, nuncle, as the cockney did to the eels
> when she put 'em i'the paste alive: she knapped 'em
> o'the coxcombs with a stick, and cried 'Down, wantons,
> down!'

(Lear, 2.2.311–14)

This crazy concoction of the quotidian and the apocalyptic, too, had long been part of Armin's repertory. In *A Pill to Purge Melancholy*, for instance, 'She that scorns thee and thy puffy stuff: Snuff', comically rages in the following terms:

> Yell for mercy at the portal gates of my compassion or I will so chastise thee inflicting corrosives upon thy feigning soul, that thou shalt be enforced to vilify thy rotundities, the only storehouse for thy bread and cheese.[68]

As Lear curses ever more fiercely against his daughters, the Fool's strange rhymes and gnostic pronouncements blend with his encroaching insanity. By the time of the storm, Armin's well-worn maxim that rational men are fools becomes pervasive: 'this cold night', as the jester observes, 'will turn us all to fools and madmen' (3.4.77).

Once Edgar, in the role of Poor Tom, joins Lear and the Fool on the heath, the mood hits fever pitch. From this point on Armin's character is no longer the principal source of crazy pronouncements. This does not mean, however, that the possible influence of his writing declines. What connects Act 3 of *Lear* to Armin's writing is the language of riddles, deprivation, animal images, whipping, and half-sense. As has been noted, the *Quips* collection begins with verses in which a dog's skin and voice are humanized (A4ᵇ). The next, 'Who Sleeps in the Grass?', is still more disconcerting as it

---

68. Armin, *Pill*, A3ᵇ. The work of the compositor and the worn black-letter print of this pamphlet make the passage difficult to interpret: I here conjecturally amend 'castice' to 'chastise' and 'corasiues' to 'corrosives'.

invites the reader's simultaneous scorn and sympathy for a sleeping body
that may be an animal, a drunkard, a pauper, or an insane man:

> If he b'a beast, I know a number more,
> Thy self was one before thou hadst a bed.
> Take m'as I am, not as I was before:
> For now I have a pillow to my head.

(Quips, B1^a)

This verse seems to end on condemnation for the sleeper, yet its quip 'this
man's a worse beast, having worldly pelf,/ That thinks all beasts, and would
be none himself' cuts in the other direction. Such rhymes, like the obscure
riddle 'Where is Ginking Gone?', tend to blur the distinctions between
animal, man, and madman. Ginking is described as one who leaps, reaps,
sweeps, and weeps in rapid succession and 'must a beggar be . . . when every
bird her feather takes' (*Quips*, B2ᵇ). The subject would appear to be a
gleaner, who survives on what others have sown, and by the end of the
poem this 'fool' whose 'heart with sorrow aches' has 'gone', presumably
having starved to death (B2ᵇ). Armin concludes by asking 'are not all [men]
Ginkings then I pray thee judge,/ When one man doth become another's
drudge?' (B2ᵃ). The fate of these lonely figures is not far from that of *Lear*'s
Poor Tom, who is 'whipped from tithing to tithing' and 'drinks the green
mantle of the standing pool' (3.4.129–30).

    Quips upon Questions switches wildly in tone and perspective. Some of its
verses are starkly moralistic: for example, 'What Ails that Damsel?', which
describes the 'fat flesh' of a prostitute and urges the reader to 'let her feel the
whip' (D3ᵃ). Others are bawdy conceits like 'What's near her?', where the
narrator writes with sexual excitement about a girl's smock (C2ᵃ). There are
simple riddles such as 'Who's Dead?' (B1ᵃ), the answer to which is 'a dyer',
but also grander moral statements, like the long response given to the
question of a 'madman' in 'Where's the Devil?', which ultimately concludes
on 'the follies of a wavering mind' (E2ᵃ⁻ᵇ). In this, the collection comes
close to providing a model for Shakespeare's cacophonous union of the
Fool, Edgar, and Lear, in which bawdy songs like 'Pillicock sat on Pillicock
hill' (3.4.75) accompany outcries to 'the foul fiend' (3.4.112) and moments
of insight such as Lear's 'unaccommodated man is no more but such a poor,
bare, forked animal' (3.4.105–6). The ironies, of course, are vastly more
complex in Shakespeare: Lear is wrong to think Poor Tom is 'unaccommodated'—the disguised Edgar is a courtier and the man who offers this

homily upon him is himself insane. Such side-by-side comparisons will never flatter Shakespeare's sources. It should be acknowledged, however, that key raw materials of Shakespeare's masterpiece were the staples of Armin's art.

The strongest of all correspondences comes in the Fool's last scene: the mock trial of Lear's absent daughters, which is present only in the Quarto text. In *Fool upon Fool* Shakespeare would have found a number of comparable scenarios. In the opening tale, for example, we hear how 'Jack Oates played at cards all alone' and greeted the knaves, queens, and kings as if they were people: 'if he spied a Queen, Queen *Richard* art come quoth he; and would kneel down and bid God bless her Majesty' (A4ᵃ).[69] With Leanard of Sherwood the scenario is still more expansive, with Leanard locking himself in a room to play slide groat with a whole cast of imaginary characters and eventually coming to blows with these projected adversaries:

> As his manner was, pieces or counters he had none, yet casting his hand empty from him, 'fly' says he, short with a vengeance. Then 'play' says he to his fellow, when indeed there is none but himself, but thus with supposes he plays alone, swaggers with his game fellow, out-swears him with a thousand oaths, challenges him the field to answer him if he be man, appoints the place and all, that if any not knowing his conditions should stand without and hear him, [he] would think two swaggerers were swearing God from heaven.
> (*Fool upon Fool*, C4ᵇ)

There is an edge of the supernatural to this incident, with Leanard addressing a vacancy and being declared 'a play fellow for the devil' (D1ᵃ), so that the parallel with the Quarto feels strong:

LEAR: Arraign her first. 'Tis Goneril. I here take my oath
before this honourable assembly she kicked the poor
King her father.
FOOL: Come hither, mistress. Is your name Goneril?
LEAR: She cannot deny it.
FOOL: Cry you mercy, I took you for a joint-stool.

69. The odd title 'Queen *Richard*', incidentally, may be a case of the fool's licence to speak politically, given the suppression of John Hayward's *First Part of The Life and Reign of King Henry the Fourth* (1599) a year earlier; a book famously associated with the Queen's later public statement 'I am Richard II, know ye not that?' (for which see Chambers, *Facts and Problems*, II, 326).

LEAR: And here's another, whose warped looks proclaim
   What store her heart is made on. Stop her there.
   Arms, arms, sword, fire, corruption in the place!
   False justicer, why hast thou let her 'scape?

(Lear, Q1 3.6.43–52)

It is evident from his account of the clown Grumball (D4[b]) that Armin had already imagined the staging of such fantastical projection—most likely he had also already performed such scenes himself.

Even after his disappearance following the trial scene, the Fool continues to have an influence. 'Jesters do oft prove prophets' (5.3.72), Regan declares, and Lear, speaking to the blinded Gloucester, speaks of how 'when we are born we cry that we are come/ To this great stage of fools' (4.6.178–9) and considers himself 'the natural fool of fortune' (187). Most powerfully of all, the King's final speech conflates the absent Fool with his daughter:

LEAR: And my poor fool is hanged. No, no, no life!
   Why should a dog, a horse, a rat have life
   And thou no breath at all?

(Lear, 5.3.304–6)

The universalizing of the fool's fate had been the standard motif of Armin's writing. At the conclusion of *Fool upon Fool* the author contemplates the death of his last natural fool and addresses his readers as follows: 'Wise men and fools, all one end makes,/ God's will be done, who gives and takes' (F4[a]). To cite this as the core of Armin's influence on *Lear*, however, would be to undersell his contribution. Shakespeare's play cannot be reduced to such platitudes, but nor can Armin's writing. Much more than simply creating a role to accommodate an actor, Shakespeare embraced the caustic insanity we find in *Fool upon Fool* and *Quips upon Questions*. Before working with Armin, Shakespeare had produced nothing like *Lear*'s strange delusional drama, in which Edgar can fully embrace a hallucinatory madness and can lead Gloucester to an imaginary cliff to jump to his death.

More fully than any other player, Armin illustrates the effect of Shakespeare's position as a sharer and housekeeper. The two men were bound together in a close association that left its imprint on at least five plays. Armin himself was evidently proud of the partnership. Once a sharer, he claimed his roles in Shakespeare plays as part of his public character, so that his ballad *The Italian Tailor* (1609) was presented as the work of a 'poor petite of transformation' who 'hath been writ down for an ass'.[70] In the same way Armin's character Robin in Wilkins's *Miseries of Enforced Marriage* uses versions of Touchtone's riddles, rephrases *Lear* in 'nothing comes of nothing', and makes distinctions between fools 'by Art' and 'by Nature' in his opening scene.[71] The second edition of *Fool upon Fool* was billed as the work of 'Clonnico del mondo' and the third, revised under the title *A Nest of Ninnies*, proudly trumpets 'our Globe' and again evokes Shakespeare by telling readers 'love loses not his labour' and warning that 'there are as Hamlet says things called whips in store'.[72] Such allusions are testament to a collective sense of theatrical ownership and provide a tantalizing glimpse of the company as a cohesive unit.[73] Armin, as a performer and as a writer, had a personal influence on Shakespeare that was as great as that of major poets of the age.

70. Robert Armin, *The Italian Tailor and his Boy*, A3ᵃ. This reference to Dogberry in *Much Ado About Nothing* makes it evident that the role was taken over from Kemp.
71. George Wilkins, *The Miseries of Enforced Marriage*, ed. Glenn H. Blayney, Malone Society Reprints (Oxford: Oxford University Press, 1964), TLN 45–9. Robin's name clearly also foregrounds *Robert* Armin's presence on the stage. Although 'nothing comes of nothing' is proverbial, the link with Shakespeare's drama must have been evident to the audience.
72. Armin, *Nest*, A2ᵃ⁻ᵇ; G3ᵇ. Because it does not exactly match Hamlet's 'whips and scorns of time' (3.1.69) it has sometimes been thought that Armin's allusion must be to the lost Ur-*Hamlet*. There is little logic, however, in preferring a reference to an unknown work when the line works perfectly well in relation to a play with which Armin must have been familiar.
73. On Armin's alternative model of dramatic ownership see Johnson, *Actor as Playwright*, esp. 6–7, 16–47.

10

The children's companies

One consequence of Shakespeare's position as a sharer and house-keeper was his ability to adapt carefully over time to the performance characteristics of his actors. Another is what I have called the 'relational' quality of his drama—its tendency to place characters within social units in which there is an evolving power balance between protagonists. This tendency (which I relate to Shakespeare's presence at rehearsals and his ties to the fellowship as a collective) moved the playwright away from the conventional patterns of composition found amongst educated Renaissance writers: the courting of artifice, imitation, and the employment of existing (often classical) dramatic structures and types. A third consequence was the prosaic fact of Shakespeare's financial security. By the turn of the century he was already much richer than any contemporary dramatist. This wealth gave him greater freedom. He began to write more slowly and had the liberty to pursue the artistic ventures that attracted him most.

These consequences, which have been the concern of this study thus far, were artistic and financial. But Shakespeare's investment in the public theatre also had moral and ideological implications. These came out more strongly in the early 1600s, in part because of the so-called Poets' War, a conflict between leading dramatists that raged from 1599 to 1601 and has itself been the subject of much controversy.[1] From late 1599 onwards the boys'

1. Thomas Dekker, *Satiromastix*, in *Dramatic Works*, ed. Fredson Bowers, 4 vols. (Cambridge: Cambridge University Press, 1953–61), I, 'Preface', refers jokingly to 'that terrible Poeto-machia, lately commenc'd between Horace the second, and a band of leane-witted Poetasters'. The first significant critical account of this conflict was R. A. Small's *The Stage Quarrel Between Ben Jonson and the So-Called Poetasters* (Breslau: M. and H. Marcus, 1899). Developing from this, Robert Boies Sharpe, *The Real War of the Theaters: Shakespeare's Fellows in Rivalry with the Admiral's Men, 1594–1603*, Modern Language Association Monograph Series, 5 (Boston, MA: D. C. Heath, 1935), offered an elaborate thesis of encoded identities in plays of the period. Alfred Harbage, *Shakespeare and the Rival Traditions* (Bloomington: Indiana University Press, 1952), 90–119, considered the conflict instead through the competing ideologies of the indoor

companies (which had lain in abeyance since the 1580s) re-emerged in the London theatrical market. They performed at indoor theatres for an audience that was dominated by the educated young men of the Inns of Court.[2] Their plays were more self-consciously artistic, artificial, and sceptical than the material performed on public stages.[3] As a sharer in the Chamberlain's Men and the Globe playhouse, Shakespeare could not have contemplated writing for these companies and for this reason his financial and artistic investment may have turned into an ideological investment as well.

How did Shakespeare respond to this new drama? On one level he simply catered to current fashions by producing work in modes that were popular. This is the conclusion, most prominently, of Roslyn Knutson, who presents evidence that the Chamberlain's Men's repertory consistently matched that of the Admiral's in the 1590s.[4] That claim becomes, if anything, stronger in the new century: in the view of G. K. Hunter, the comedy that Shakespeare

and outdoor playhouses. Roslyn Lander Knutson, *Playing Companies and Commerce in Shakespeare's Time* (Cambridge: Cambridge University Press, 2001), 75–149, largely rejects what she calls a 'moribund' narrative of conflict, arguing that the 'war' was short lived and should not distract from a general picture of cooperation between companies. James P. Bednarz, *Shakespeare and the Poets' War* (New York: Columbia University Press, 2001), offers the most careful account thus far of a personal conflict involving Jonson, Marston, Dekker, and Shakespeare. He, like Knutson, rejects the idea of a strong conflict between adult and children's repertories, but is much more confident about the recoverability of a set of *ad hominem* attacks made through allusions in the works of Shakespeare, Jonson, Marston, and others.

2. The notion of a distinct coterie audience for the hall playhouses was propounded by Harbage, *Rival Traditions*, 29–57, and endorsed in more moderate terms by Michael Shapiro, *Children of the Revels: The Boy Companies of Shakespeare's Time and their Plays* (New York: Columbia University Press, 1977), 67–101. It was strongly rejected by Anne Jennalie Cook in *The Privileged Playgoers of Shakespeare's London, 1576–1642* (Princeton, NJ: Princeton University Press, 1981), which argues that most audience members in this period should be counted as part of the elite. Cook's conclusions are tentatively backed by Knutson, *Playing Companies*, 63, and Bednarz, *Poets' War*, 231. However, Martin Butler, *Theatre and Crisis, 1632–1642* (Cambridge: Cambridge University Press, 1984) and Andrew Gurr, *Playgoing in Shakespeare's London*, 2nd edn (Cambridge: Cambridge University Press, 1996), xv, 1–3, 60–80, offer extensive primary research to confirm the exclusivity of the hall playhouses and the contrasting mass audience that the outdoor amphitheatres enjoyed. As Gurr makes clear, elite playgoers certainly attended the amphitheatres in large numbers, but traffic the other way from a citizen audience was much more limited, and remarked upon when it occurred. Janette Dillon, *Theatre, Court and City, 1595–1610: Drama and Social Space in London* (Cambridge: Cambridge University Press, 2000) discusses the complex balance between court and city audiences and authorities that the companies needed to address.

3. This is again a position stated in the strongest terms by Harbage, *Rival Traditions*, 58–89, and restated less emphatically by Shapiro, *Children*, 103–38. Bednarz, *Poets' War*, 232, largely rejects the idea of a specific repertory whereas Gurr, *Playgoing*, 158–64, largely confirms it.

4. Knutson, *The Repertory of Shakespeare's Company, 1594–1613* (Fayetteville: University of Arkansas Press, 1991).

wrote after the reopening of the children's theatre is 'much more like' the work of contemporaries than that which he composed between 1595 and 1600.[5] As Hunter points out, after having written a series of distinctive romantic comedies, Shakespeare now wrote plays that catered to more gritty, urban, and satirical fashions. *Measure for Measure*, for example, sits as part of a cluster of plays in the period depicting disguised rulers, and *All's Well that Ends Well* matches a number of other dramas that deal with the vindication of a good wife. That observation is certainly valid. Yet to echo a theatrical fashion is not necessarily to endorse it: there is room for resistance alongside pragmatic imitation when Shakespeare responds to commercial trends. It is my argument in this chapter that the playwright's work in the early 1600s involves an ideological rejection of the new drama even as it adopts important parts of the content of this work.

The boys' companies are referred to in the Folio text of *Hamlet*, when the tragedians of the city are forced to visit Elsinore as a result of this recent innovation's success:

HAMLET: How chances it they travel? Their residence,
　both in reputation and profit, was better both ways.
ROSINCRANCE: I think their inhibition comes by the
　means of the late innovation.
HAMLET: Do they hold the same estimation they did
　when I was in the city? Are they so followed?
ROSINCRANCE: No, indeed they are not.
HAMLET: How comes it? Do they grow rusty?
ROSINCRANCE: Nay, their endeavour keeps in the wonted
　pace. But there is, sir, an eyrie of children, little eyases
　that cry out on the top of question and are most
　tyrannically claped for't. These are now the fashion,
　and so berattle the common stages (so they call them)
　that many wearing rapiers are afraid of goose-quills and
　dare scarce come thither.
HAMLET: What, are they children? Who maintains 'em?
　How are they escotted? Will they pursue the quality no
　longer than they can sing? Will they not say afterwards
　if they should grow themselves to common players—as

5. See George K. Hunter, 'Theatrical Politics and Shakespeare's Comedies, 1590–1600', in R. B. Parker and S. P. Zitner, eds., *Elizabethan Theater: Essays in Honor of S. Schoenbaum* (Newark: University of Delaware Press, 1996), 241–51 (at 242).

it is most like if their means are no better—their writers
do them wrong to make them exclaim against their own
succession?

ROSINCRANCE: Faith, there has been much to-do on both
sides, and the nation holds it no sin to tar them to
controversy. There was for a while no money bid for
argument unless the poet and the player went to cuffs
in the question.

HAMLET: Is't possible?

GUILDENSTERN: O, there has been much throwing
about of brains.

HAMLET: Do the boys carry it away?

ROSINCRANCE: Ay, that they do, my lord—Hercules and
his load too.[6]

There is a great deal of theatrical history caught up in this exchange.[7] Partly,
it involves a backward vision. In 1586 and 1587 (when an earlier ensemble of
boy players had entertained London) English actors had travelled to Elsinore
for employment.[8] Shakespeare's fellows in the Chamberlain's Men—
George Bryan, Thomas Pope, and William Kemp—had been part of this
group, so the appearance of the players, like so much else in *Hamlet*, bears a
nostalgic stamp.[9] Yet the relevance of this passage was also very immediate.
In 1601, when it is probable that Shakespeare's *Hamlet* had its first performance, the children's companies were at the height of their influence and there
was what Guildenstern calls 'much throwing about of brains' in the Poets'

---

6. William Shakespeare, *Hamlet* F (1623) in *Hamlet: The Texts of 1603 and 1623*, ed. Ann
   Thompson and Neil Taylor, Arden3 (London: Cengage, 2006), 2.2.328–60 (TLN 1376–
   1408). In the ensuing discussion I use the Folio version of the name Rosincrance/Rosencrantz.
7. The matter is further complicated by the fact that reference to the children appears only in the
   Folio version. The most straightforward explanation for this is that the passage was no longer
   considered relevant when Q2 was printed in 1604. Knutson, *Playing Companies*, 113–26,
   postulates that a lost, milder version of the exchange existed in 1600 and that this was cut in
   Q2 and then finally replaced by the Folio exchange around 1606. In her view the exchange is
   thus not a response to the emergence of the children but rather to their newly political plays in
   the years 1606–8. That theory, however, does not match well with the detail of the passage,
   which treats playing by children as a new phenomenon. For a full discussion see *Hamlet*, ed.
   Thompson and Taylor, Q2, 259n., 468–70.
8. On the activities of the first Children of Paul's and Blackfriars and the English travelling actors
   see E. K. Chambers, *The Elizabethan Stage* (Oxford: Clarendon Press, 1923; repr. 2009), III,
   17–18, 272–3.
9. Kemp and (judging from the acting list of *Every Man in his Humour* in Jonson, *Works* (1616))
   Bryan had already left the company; Pope was still a member and would die around 22 July
   1603 (E. A. J. Honigmann and Susan Brock, *Playhouse Wills: 1558–1642* (Manchester: Manchester University Press, 1993), 68).

War. According to Rosincrance, the indoor theatre drew the patronage of the young, educated, gentlemanly classes 'wearing rapiers'. That development was a threat to the adult companies and their suburban venues: 'Hercules and his load' meant Shakespeare's company and the Globe.[10]

Ironically, the crisis alluded to in *Hamlet* was in part the creation of Richard and Cuthbert Burbage. In 1596 their father had purchased a substantial property in Blackfriars liberty and had converted it to an indoor playhouse at his own expense.[11] At his death his sons had taken over the venue, had failed to make it the playhouse of the Chamberlain's, and had then leased it for twenty-one years from Michaelmas 1600 to Henry Evans for performances by boys.[12] Ben Jonson's *Cynthia's Revels* was performed by the Children of the Chapel at Blackfriars at this juncture, probably as the company's opening play. The threat to the Globe partnership, such as it was, was thus coming from the other half of the Burbage portfolio.

Boys' companies had not acted commercially since 1590. Before that time performances by children (either from schools or from chapels) had been an intermittent feature of court performance. From time to time their masters had also charged the general public for the privilege of attending rehearsals, a technically 'private' performance that worked to subsidize employment at court.[13] At the turn of the century this practice was revived in a more ambitious manner. First, in 1599, performances began to be held by the choirboys of St Paul's Cathedral. Seeing their success, Evans began a similar venture soon after at Blackfriars, using the child singers of the Chapel Royal. His was a more cut-throat operation. The chapel gave him a legal cover but his proceedings were hardly religious: Evans and his associates kidnapped boys for their service and set up a nakedly commercial venture. The boy players were their instruments: the very opposite of fellows in a stakeholder group. For this reason the boy

10. The same events are viewed from a different perspective in Jonson's *Poetaster*, performed by the Children of Blackfriars, where the adult player, Histrio, reports on the fashion for satire 'on the other side of Tiber' and complains that 'this winter has made us all poorer than so many starved snakes' (3.4.196–7, 327–8). For further discussion see Chapter 11 below.

11. For a transcription of the contract see C. C. Stopes, *Burbage and Shakespeare's Stage* (London: Alexander Moring, 1913), 170–2; for additional commentary see Chambers, *Elizabethan Stage*, II, 503.

12. On the nature of the contract and subsequent disputes around it see Charles William Wallace, 'Shakespeare and the Blackfriars', *The Century* 80 (1910), 742–52, and also Chambers, *Elizabethan Stage*, II, 509.

13. In theory this was no different from the justification for the adult companies (see Tiffany Stern, *Rehearsal from Shakespeare to Sheridan* (Oxford: Clarendon Press, 2000), 49) but the basis in scholarly or religious institutions made the arrangement less of a fiction than it was for the men.

companies were tools in the rivalry with the playing profession.[14] Not only were they competitors for custom, they were also mouthpieces that could articulate different moral and artistic values from those promulgated by adult troupes.

The exchange in *Hamlet* is revealing because it revives the poet–player opposition found in the prose complaints of dramatists such as Robert Greene and Stephen Gosson. With the same impressionability as print, the boys allowed authors to project their personal identities and ethos. As Hamlet observes, the boy actors might themselves be fated to become adult players, and indeed that proved to be so.[15] But this likelihood did not stop the children being used to voice the old anti-player prejudice, even if, in Hamlet's view, 'their writers do them wrong to make them exclaim against their own succession' (2.2.347–9).

Although the matter has been much debated, it is difficult to deny the commonsense understanding of Rosincrance's observation concerning the 'many wearing rapiers': elite, gentlemanly, educated audiences were attracted to the new hall playhouses and slacked off in their attendance at the amphi-theatres, where they had previously mingled with citizens and artisans.[16] Views from the Inns of Court transferred easily to the indoor theatre—literally so in the case of *Histrio-Mastix*, a satire on common players of which John Marston probably wrote a substantial part.[17] In all likelihood this play was first written for an amateur production at the Middle Temple's Christmas revels of

14. On this independence from the players see Gerald Eades Bentley, *The Profession of Dramatist in Shakespeare's Time, 1590–1642* (Princeton, NJ: Princeton University Press, 1971), 62.

15. Nathan Field, for example, came from the boys' troupe and eventually, after Shakespeare's time, joined the King's Men. In 1615 the Children of the Revels at Whitefriars seem to have merged with an adult company, Lady Elizabeth's, to form Prince Charles's Men.

16. For the debate about audience composition see note 2 above. Although Cook, in *Privileged Playgoers*, has argued that audience members at both kinds of playhouse were persons 'elevated to the upper levels of society' (11) that category, whose membership she estimates as numbering 'far in excess of 100,000' (50), is unhelpful in this context. Gurr's identification of the roughly eight hundred men who attended the Inns of Court (*Playgoing*, 52) is much more relevant to the Poets' War, although it clearly does not set the limit on the indoor playhouse audience.

17. The attribution first made by Richard Simpson in *The School of Shakespeare*, 2 vols. (London: Chatto & Windus, 1878), II, 1–4, was essentially confirmed by Alvin Kernan, 'John Marston's Play *Histriomastix*', *MLQ* 19 (1958), 134–40, who doubts the revision theory, and D. J. Lake, '*Histriomastix*: Linguistic Evidence for Authorship', *Notes & Queries* 28 (1981), 148–52, who argues for co-authorship. Roslyn Lander Knutson in 'Histrio-Mastix: Not by John Marston,' *Studies in Philology* 98 (2001), 359–77, and in *Playing Companies*, 75–102, has disputed Marston's authorship. The case for the Marston attribution was restated and strengthened by James P. Bednarz, 'Writing and Revenge: John Marston's *Histriomastix*', *Comparative Drama* 36 (2002), 21–51, and confirmed, on the balance of probability, by Charles Cathcart, '*Histriomastix, Hamlet* and the "Quintessence of Duckes"', *Notes & Queries* 50 (2003), 427–30.

1598 and was then revised by Marston for St Paul's Boys the following year.[18] Its characterization of the players will be familiar to those who have read *Greenes Groats-worth*. Incle, Belch, Gutt, and Posthaste are ignorant artisans who decide to 'make up a company of players'.[19] First, they attempt through Posthaste to produce their own material, and their fellow narrates his composition, 'The Prodigal Child', to the company's acclaim:

POSTHASTE [reading]: Enter the Prodigal Child. [drinks] Fill the pot I would say.
  Huffa, huffa, who callis for me?
  I play the Prodigal Child in Jollytie.
CLOUT: Oh detestable good.
POSTHASTE [reading]: Enter to him Dame Virtue:
  My son thou art a lost child.
  (This is a passion, note you the passion?)
  Oh prodigal child, and child prodigal.
  Read the rest sirs, I cannot read for tears.[20]

As in *Groats-worth*, the company, Sir Oliver Owlet's Men, become prosperous and arrogant, thinking themselves gentlemen. But they find 'their own stuff' no longer pleases their patrons and are thus forced to employ a scholar, Chrisoganus, even though they quibble about his 'lowest price' of 'ten pound a play'.[21]

As was also the case with *Groats-worth*, satire written by poets against the players produced collateral damage amongst the poets themselves. Just as Shakespeare had seen himself in 'Shake-shaft', so Jonson saw Chrisoganus as a personal attack by Marston.[22] As he later told William Drummond, Jonson had many quarrels with Marston, the origin of which was 'that Marston had represented him in the stage'.[23] The so-called Poets' War was thus a consequence of the conflict between the boys and the adult stages. In the early years of the seventeenth century, Marston, Jonson, and several other poets

18. See Philip J. Finkelpearl, 'John Marston's *Histrio-Mastix* as an Inns of Court Play: A Hypothesis', *Huntington Library Quarterly* 29 (1966), 223–34, and Bednarz, 'Writing and Revenge'.
19. John Marston, *Histrio-Mastix*, in *Works*, ed. H. Harvey Wood, 3 vols. (Edinburgh: Oliver and Boyd, 1939), I, 1.1.127 (p. 250).
20. Marston, *Histrio-Mastix*, in *Works*, I, 2.1.122–31 (p. 259). I have modernized from Wood's edition except in cases where a change would significantly affect pronunciation.
21. Marston, *Histrio-Mastix*, in *Works*, I, 3.1.198–9 (p. 273).
22. See James P. Bednarz, 'Representing Jonson: *Histriomastix* and the Origin of the Poets' War', *Huntington Library Quarterly* 54 (1991), 1–30.
23. *Conversations with Drummond*, in Ben Jonson, *Works*, ed. Ian Donaldson (Oxford: Oxford University Press, 1985), 601.

who had first written for the public theatre shifted their preference to the boy
players, a position from which they were able to express some old prejudices
about the artisan and minstrel origins of the acting class.[24] The plays they
wrote (in line with the coterie tastes of both poets and audience) were more
consistently ironic in their treatment of rhetoric, more classical and Italian in
structure, and more explicit in their allusions to other literary texts. They
tended to be satirical about mainstream citizen values and—perhaps most
importantly—placed the poet centre stage. Indeed, the interpersonal conflict
of their 'war' only became possible because child performers made authorial
representation, which was marginal in the public theatre, a much more
showy affair.[25]

It is telling that the first composition that Marston wrote specifically for
Paul's Boys, *Antonio and Mellida*, opens with a kind of rehearsal (a gesture that
for Shakespeare too had been a symptom of increased authorial control). The
boy actors enter 'with parts in their hands, having cloaks cast over their
apparel' full of nervous uncertainty about the roles that they 'must' play.[26]
This Induction subtly highlights the priority of composition over performance, something also achieved through the substance of the drama, which
continuously highlights its 'written' quality through its parody of high
rhetoric and romance absurdity. Indeed the final act opens literally on a
portrait of its author 'Anno Domini 1599' (*Antonio and Mellida*, 5.1.8).[27] *Jack
Drum's Entertainment*, composed around the same time and probably by the
same author, likewise highlights authorial agency.[28] This time the poet's
power is asserted in the very title, because the audience are warned they may

---

24. Tucca in Jonson's *Poetaster* is especially keen to revive those origins as he mocks Histrio's
    reduced circumstances: 'come, we must have you turn fiddler again, slave, get a bass violin at
    your back, and march in a tawny coat with one sleeve to Goose Fair' (*Poetaster*, ed. Tom Cain,
    Revels (Manchester: Manchester University Press, 1995), 3.4.137–40).
25. Various critics associated with career criticism (such as Patrick Cheney in *Shakespeare's Literary
    Authorship* (Cambridge: Cambridge University Press, 2008); Bednarz in *Poets' War*, and Jeffrey
    Knapp in *Shakespeare Only* (Chicago: University of Chicago Press, 2009)) argue that Shake-
    speare is persistently self-referential in his drama and in their readings discover an allegorical
    dimension in many dramatic episodes. If such allegorical episodes exist, however, they are a
    good deal more hidden than the kind of authorial representation we find in the children's
    repertory.
26. John Marston, *Antonio and Mellida*, ed. W. Reavley Gair, Revels (Manchester: Manchester
    University Press, 2004), IND SD and l. 4. Subsequent references are to this edition and appear in
    the text.
27. On this portrait see K. Gustav Cross, 'The Date of Marston's *Antonio and Mellida*,' *Modern
    Language Notes* 72 (1957), 328–32.
28. John Marston, *Jack Drum's Entertainment*, in *Works*, ed. H. Harvey Wood, 3 vols. (Edinburgh:
    Oliver and Boyd, 1939), III.

be given 'Jack Drum's entertainment' (i.e. be dismissed without ceremony) if the poet is not satisfied that his child actors are 'perfect' in their parts. The author's supposed threat to withdraw the playtext is linked to an insistence about the contrast between popular and elite entertainment. Thus Jack Drum is also a character in the play's action: a mass entertainer fond of jigs and clowning, bankrolled by Sir Edward Fortune (a patron whose name recalls that of Edward Alleyn, whose Fortune playhouse was under construction at the time). The play ridicules both citizens' and aristocrats' appetite for the fare of common players and commends the 'good gentle audience' at the indoor theatre (though even this is done with an edge of irony).[29]

John Marston (an Inns of Court man who inherited a decent income from his father) was above most playwrights in wealth and social status. He at some point bought a stake in the Blackfriars venture and from that time onwards wrote his plays for this rival indoor company, never returning to write for Henslowe, who had briefly employed him as 'the new poet' in 1599.[30] His investment in the culture of child performance was thus more absolute than that of other playwrights, a fact reflected in the ethos of his plays. Yet adaptation to the indoor culture was not unique to Marston. Ben Jonson and George Chapman had already written humoural comedies for the adult players, but they were attracted (at least initially) to the children's theatre, for which they wrote in a more exclusive literary tone. Jonson's *Cynthia's Revels*, produced at Blackfriars, opens, like Marston's *Antonio and Mellida*, on an assertion of authorial power, with a child actor insisting that he should be given a role that has been assigned to his rival 'if the author think I can speak it better'.[31] *Poetaster*, performed at the same venue a year later, is still more insistent in its focus on literary culture; it champions the ideal of the independent poet, and its hero, Horace, came notoriously close to being a portrait of the author himself.[32] The new indoor theatre encouraged authorial self-representation. So too George Chapman, in his early

29. See Marston, *Jack Drum's*, ed. Wood, 4.110–24 (p. 234), where Sir Edward discusses the previous night's visit to 'the Children of Paul's'.

30. Henslowe, *Diary*, ed. R. A. Foakes, 2nd edn (Cambridge: Cambridge University Press, 2002), 124; this is Marston's only appearance in the account book, interestingly receiving an advance double that paid to Ben Jonson in the entry above.

31. Ben Jonson, *Cynthia's Revels*, in *Works*, ed. C. H. Herford and Percy Simpson, 11 vols. (Oxford: Clarendon Press, 1925–52), IND 6–7.

32. The play, as Jonson insisted in the closing 'Apologetical Dialogue' featuring the author in his study, is not a straightforward allegory. Yet the Dialogue, performed only once, plus the 'armed' Prologue, enforces the intense poetic self-consciousness of the drama. A comparable frame is found in the Induction to Marston's *What you Will*.

Blackfriars play *Sir Giles Goosecap*, appears to present himself through his hero, Clarence, a poor, sonnet-writing scholar who is rewarded by marriage to a wealthy widow at the work's close.[33]

The indoor theatre's tendency to depict poet figures connects to its general bias in favour of self-conscious wit—what Gurr describes as a 'sophisticated artifice' as against the appeal of 'enchantment' on the popular stage.[34] In plays such as *Michaelmas Term*, *Your Five Gallants*, *A Trick to Catch the Old One*, and *A Mad World, my Masters* Middleton adopts the attitudes and aesthetic preferences of a sophisticated male audience (in the last case including a mock version of an adult travelling troupe).[35] Chapman's plays, like *May Day* and *Monsieur D'Olive*, share these 'wit' qualities—they celebrate the tricks of educated, impecunious, young gentlemen and laugh at the exposure of portentous establishment types.[36] What these plays eschew is sentiment and a nascent bourgeois propriety, both of which are mocked in the pastiche composition attributed to the journeyman poet in *Histrio-Mastix*, whose 'prodigal child' rejects the sensible life of a citizen and thus brings his mother and the audience to tears. Many adult productions of the period (such as *Shoemaker's Holiday* and *If you Know not Me, Part II*) explicitly endorsed the London civic establishment's values. Humoural plots involving wit heroes were not unknown on the public stages (for example, in plays such as Haughton's *Englishmen for My Money* or Chapman's *All Fools but the Fool*, which it seems was at first in the Admiral's repertory).[37] Yet such plays did little to critique the civic establishment and tended towards the romantic. In contrast, many compositions for the indoor

---

33. On the tradition of identifying Chapman with his hero see George Chapman, *Sir Giles Goosecap*, in *Works*, ed. Thomas Marc Parrott, 3 vols. (London: Routledge, 1914), II.

34. Gurr, *Playgoing*, 158.

35. For texts and performance history see Middleton, *Collected Works*, ed. Gary Taylor and John Lavagnino (Oxford: Clarendon Press, 2007); Follywit and his comrades' disguise as travelling players in order to rob Sir Bounteous (a foolish patron in the mould of Sir Fortune in *Jack Drum's Entertainment*) occurs in Act 5.

36. Of course not all the plays for the boys' companies follow the same pattern. *Eastward Ho*, co-authored by Chapman, Jonson, and Marston, is (at least in the form it exists after censorship) generally positive in its depiction of the guilds and aldermen and contemptuous of its would-be gallant, even if Gurr calls it a 'sophisticated burlesque of the citizen playhouse repertory' (*Playgoing*, 164). The offence it caused at court, however, is characteristic of the political edginess of many indoor plays. For details see *Eastward Ho*, ed. R. W. van Fossen, Revels (Manchester: Manchester University Press, 1979), 37–9, 218–25.

37. On the likelihood that *All Fools*, which in the form it was printed is a Blackfriars production, started as the 'All Fools' mentioned in Henslowe's *Diary* see George Chapman, *All Fools*, in *Works*, ed. Parrott, II, 701.

theatre exude a triumphalist pleasure in the defeat of these values. This is done not only through parody of mainstream genres (such as the class of plays based on the Prodigal Son story), but also through plots that depict empowered figures such as fathers, merchants, and creditors being outmanoeuvred by gentlemen wits. The satirical impulse was central to the culture of the children's companies; the depiction of English citizen virtue was thus all but impossible on the indoor stage.

Alfred Harbage, more than half a century ago, published the classic account of the opposition between the children's theatre and that of the adults in *Shakespeare and the Rival Traditions*. He insisted on a duality in Elizabethan drama, not between patricians and plebeians, but between the 'Theatre of a Coterie' and the 'Theatre of a Nation'.[38] Writing in the 1950s, he compared the culture of the indoor playhouses to that of 'little magazines' that attracted beatnik intellectuals: there was, he argued, the same 'sense of self-righteousness among the writers, in the proud refusal to go along with popular tastes' (56). Set against this there was a tradition that had its roots in the old moralities, patriotic and romantic, that one might call 'bourgeois' or 'Victorian'.[39]

While Harbage's account has been much criticized, its two cultures model remains useful.[40] If the boys' theatre had something of modern arthouse culture, the public stage bears comparison with Hollywood in its norms of co-authorship, its true loves and heroes, and broadly patriotic appeal. This was not a straightforward contrast between high and low culture: both sets of companies attracted a court audience and the young lawyers who frequented Paul's and Blackfriars were clearly familiar with adult repertories too. In rough terms, however, the combination of dominant audience composition and theatrical ownership did exert pressure. It is an overstatement to claim, as Harbage did, that the traditions of the two were 'as distinct as the size of their actors', but the tendencies are apparent, especially in the early years.[41] These connected with a differing status for the poet. Like print (with which the indoor playhouses had a strong connection), the boys'

38. Alfred Harbage, *Shakespeare and the Rival Traditions* (Bloomington: Indiana University Press, 1952).
39. Harbage, *Rival Traditions*, 296.
40. See notes 2, 3, and 16 above on this issue. Cook, *Privileged Playgoers*, 216–71, cites testimony relating to 'Plebeian Playgoers' and concludes they could have existed only in small numbers. Harbage, however, was not concerned with 'plebians' but with a larger citizen category that included very wealthy merchants. There is, moreover, much evidence to show that even the poor attended the public houses. For a further overview of the debate see Gurr, *Playgoing*, 3–5.
41. Harbage, *Rival Traditions*, 29.

theatre encouraged a conspicuous authorial presence.[42] Like film, the adult theatre tended to subsume the character of its writers and to emphasize a collective whole.

Such institutional imperatives are relevant to Shakespeare. It is, I suggest, these acquired attachments (rather than simply an innate sympathy with a moral tradition, as was concluded by Harbage)[43] that account for his actions in the Poets' War. Non-attached writers were not restricted to one outlet: Jonson, Middleton, Dekker, Chapman, and others swapped venues (and also shifted their ideological and aesthetic standpoint) in line with circumstance and market demand.[44] Attached writers, however, thought differently: Marston, who became an investor, stuck to the indoor theatre; Shakespeare and Heywood, as company sharers, remained fixed on the public stage. Again, the example of Heywood is instructive as a parallel to Shakespeare. His *Apology for Actors* (1612) is a remarkable document. It is the only substantial defence of the acting profession published in Renaissance England and it was written by a playwright whose first loyalty was to academic drama, of which Heywood saw a great deal while at Cambridge two decades before. It is a printed text by a playwright whose prefatory material features the names of professional actors, a theatrical patron, and a fellow author (in the

---

42. The connection between children's companies and print works in two ways. First, the cynicism of print publications such as Marston's *Scourge of Villanie* and *Certain Satires* (both 1598) or Middleton's co-authored *Penniless* and *Black Book* (both 1604) carried easily into the indoor theatre. Second, the percentage of transfer to print was much higher for children's productions than was the case with adult drama. The lack of clear authorial publications by Shakespeare and Heywood during their time as company members offers a telling contrast. Heywood famously declared his lack of ambition to be 'voluminously read' (*English Traveller* (1633), A3[a]) and his *If you Know not Me, Part I* is interestingly the only case of a playtext where an author complains of piracy by secret recording (on his complaints about this 'stenography' see Thomas Heywood, *If you Know not Me you Know Nobody, Part I*, ed. Madeleine Doran (Oxford: Malone Society, 1935), xv.). On the unreliable transfer to print of Admiral's plays see Andrew Gurr, *Shakespeare's Opposites: The Admiral's Company 1594–1625* (Cambridge: Cambridge University Press, 2009), 109–19.

43. See Harbage, 'Shakespeare's Tradition: Conclusion', in *Rival Traditions*, 290–318.

44. All of these writers were highly adept at such transitions; one particularly notable example is Dekker's involvement with the sentimental *Patient Grissil* for the Admiral's and the satirical *Northward Ho* and *Westward Ho* for Paul's Boys. Ian Donaldson, *Ben Jonson: A Life* (Oxford: Oxford University Press, 2011), 145–74, describes Jonson's easeful adaptation to the demands of individual theatres during this stage of his career. Of course, some playwrights tied themselves contractually for fixed periods. On poets' ongoing mobility and attachments see Knutson, *Playing Companies*, 48–60; Bentley, *Profession of Dramatist*, 26–37; and Grace Ioppolo, *Dramatists and their Manuscripts in the Age of Shakespeare, Jonson, Middleton and Heywood: Authorship, Authority, and the Playhouse* (London: Routledge, 2006), 16–17.

person of John Webster). The only printed book sharing these characteristics is the Folio of Shakespeare's plays published in 1623.

Three things are worth highlighting about the *Apology*. The first is the author's exceptional closeness to the actors. Dedicatory verses from established players address Heywood as 'my loving friend and fellow', 'my approved good friend', and 'my good friend and fellow'.[45] The only other places we find such sustained expressions of bonds between a literary playwright and the actors are in the last testaments left by Shakespeare and other members of the Chamberlain's Men. Heywood's sense of the profession's dignity also has much in common with Shakespeare's defence of the players through Hamlet. Heywood names great actors from recent history, including Kemp, Pope, Phillips, and Sly of the Chamberlain's Men. There is an insistence on training to produce lifelike performance: 'actors should be men picked out personable, according to the parts they present' and 'may by instructions be helped and amended' (E3ª); such strictures resemble Hamlet's 'suit the action to the word, the word to the action' (Q2 *Hamlet*, 3.2.16–17) and are remarkable for their emphasis on the player's craft.

Second, Heywood's closeness to the actors finds its corollary in a distance from the children. Hamlet in Elsinore has not previously heard of the 'little eyases' but is instinctively hostile towards them. The notion that the children are the instruments of their authors is the same in the two cases. Heywood, in 1612, complains of 'the liberty which some arrogate to themselves, committing their bitterness and liberal invectives against all estates to the mouths of children supposing their juniority to be a privilege for any railing' (G3ᵇ). The 'inveighing against the state, the court, the city, and their governments' that Heywood lays at the door of the children's companies stands in contrast to 'harmless mirth', which he contends the adult players produce (G3ᵇ, F3ᵇ).

Third, this rejection of the children and alliance with the actors links to Heywood's moralistic orientation. His investment in an acting company thus becomes symbolic of a wider investment in social stability, with the actors themselves being put forward as model citizens. 'Many amongst us', Heywood reports, 'I know to be of substance, of government, of sober lives, and temperate carriages, house-keepers, and contributory to all duties' (E3ª). The players, amongst whom Heywood at this point classes himself, address and are part of the general citizenry. Their plays, Heywood contends, also

45. Heywood, *Apology*, A2ᵇ–A3ᵇ.

work to enforce this social conformity: they are written 'to teach the subjects obedience to their king, to show the people the untimely ends of such as have moved tumults, commotions, and insurrections' (F3[b]). Linked to Heywood's endorsement of exemplarity is a heuristic function like that which is famously set out by Hamlet. The Prince, after meeting the players, remembers 'that guilty creatures sitting at a play/ Have by the very cunning of the scene/ Been struck so to the soul that presently/ They have proclaimed their malefactions' (*Hamlet*, Q2, 2.2.524–7). *An Apology for Actors* describes a number of such miraculous confessions; for Heywood, as for Hamlet, 'the play's the thing' through which the conscience may be caught.

Hamlet's views on the acting profession are no key to Shakespeare's personal opinion. The *Apology*, moreover, is hardly a failsafe guide to intention in Heywood's plays. All the same, the congruence between *Hamlet* and the *Apology* is significant as an expression of the proclaimed ethos of the public theatre, an ethos to which both dramatists at some level lay claim. What Hamlet says he has 'heard' about confessions elicited by players, in fact, directly recalls lines from the Chamberlain's Men's play *A Warning for Fair Women*, which was 'lately' acted in 1599. This domestic tragedy depicts the fall of an essentially good woman, the merchant's wife Anne Sanders, who becomes complicit in a cover-up following the murder of her husband. The play is strikingly self-referential about its status as a performance, and as the conspiracy begins to unravel a bystander recalls how 'a woman that had made away her husband/ And sitting to behold a tragedy' was moved by 'the passion written by a feeling pen/ And acted by a good tragedian' to a spontaneous admission of her guilt.[46] This memory, which is also reported in Heywood's *Apology* and credited to Sussex's company (G1[b]), thus functions as a kind of meta-theatrical signal for the moral tradition of the public play. It is a signal that connects Shakespeare and Heywood and which reveals a polemical element in the thinking of these two sharer–dramatists at the turn of the century.

Hamlet's defence of the common players at Elsinore is an idealized picture of royal patronage. He not only eulogizes their profession, he also works to improve it, and will have the players treated 'much better' than they strictly deserve (*Hamlet*, Q2, 2.2.467). The Prince is thus the perfect reversal of the patrons who are mocked in Marston's productions, such as

---

46. Anon., *A Warning for Fair Women*, ed. Charles Dale Cannon (The Hague: Mouton, 1975), TLN 2038–9, 2044–5.

the fickle Lord Mavortius and the absent Sir Oliver Owlet of *Histrio-Mastix* or the undiscerning Sir Edward Fortune in *Jack Drum's Entertainment*. Crucially, Hamlet defends the long-standing tradition of the adult players ('they are the abstract and brief chronicles of the time' (*Hamlet*, Q2, 2.2.462)) but also strives to reform it. It thus offends him to the soul 'to hear a robustious periwig-pated fellow tear a passion to tatters' and he insists that clowns must 'speak no more than is set down for them' and not 'set on some quantity of barren spectators to laugh' (*Hamlet*, Q2, 3.2.8–10, 37–9). There is here a delicate negotiation between the elite and the mainstream, one which Shakespeare's company—in the face of the children's innovation—itself pursued.[47]

Across a number of plays in the early 1600s we see Shakespeare interacting with the emerging culture of the children's theatre and, as a result, more clearly revealing an ethical and class allegiance to the world of the adult players. *Hamlet*, with its nostalgic recall of the travelling companies and (in its Folio version) its reference to competition with the boy performers, contains direct evidence of that friction. *Henry V*, written and performed on the eve of the new century, contains no explicit reference to a rival dramatic culture. But it is, much more than *Hamlet*, a dramatic production with a polemical edge. Thanks to Act 5's chorus, with its allusion to the Earl of Essex, the composition of *Henry V* can be dated with certainty between 25 March and 28 September 1599.[48] Quite probably it was the first work performed at the Globe playhouse in the summer of that year.[49] The prologue's apostrophe to 'this unworthy scaffold' and 'wooden O' would

47. This ties in with Gurr's judgement (*Playgoing*, 161) that Shakespeare's company took up a 'neutral' position between 'the polarized Blackfriars and the citizen companies', except that I think this apparent neutrality has a more polemical edge. Knapp sees a kind of meta-theatrical commentary in the play itself, in which 'through the instability of its genre as well as its title character, *Hamlet* transforms the author from a literary figure modelled on a king who issues "prescripts" to a histrionic prince who is pulled in irreconcilably diverse directions by his "distraction"' (*Shakespeare Only*, 32).

48. See William Shakespeare, *Henry V*, ed. T. W. Craik, Arden3 (London: Methuen, 1995), 1–6. This chorus, as is the case with over half of the play's line total, is not present in the Quarto printed that year and appears only in the 1623 Folio. As Craik's analysis makes clear, Q1 is not a good text on which to judge the nature of first performance, whereas F shows signs of being based on the authorial manuscript (19–32). Subsequent references are to this edition and appear in the text.

49. Whether the Globe was ready in time for its first production is uncertain. Melissa D. Aaron, 'The Globe and *Henry V* as Business Document', *Studies in English Literature* 40 (2000), 277–92, argues that while a first performance at the new playhouse was the intention it was not ultimately possible to carry this out.

thus have advertised a playhouse in which, for the first time, an author held a stake (*Henry V*, Prologue.10, 13). As a modest but quietly proprietorial statement it matches the company ethic of the play's epilogue, which describes how 'our bending author has pursued the story,/ In little room confining mighty men' (*Henry V*, Epilogue.2–3).

Without doubt, Shakespeare wrote *Henry V* with thoughts of his new position as housekeeper, but the play's unprecedented self-consciousness about its place of performance is likely also to have been coloured by an awareness of a coterie theatrical culture taking shape across the Thames within the city walls. By the time that *Henry V* was performed, St Paul's Boys may already have been in operation, because John Marston wrote *Antonio and Mellida* specifically for this company at some point in 1599.[50] Certainly Shakespeare knew of Marston's *Histrio-Mastix* with its satire on the common players. This play had been a success at the Inns of Court a year earlier and was one of the first productions on the children's stage. It is possible that Shakespeare was also aware of plans for the Blackfriars playhouse, which was to be leased by his leading actor, Richard Burbage, to the Children of the Chapel in the following year.[51] A new phase of performance at the indoor theatres was evidently coming and, no doubt, many gentlemen of Rosincrance's description 'wearing rapiers' were already shifting their allegiance to this more socially exclusive world. In this context the prologue, choruses, and epilogue of *Henry V* were a countervailing statement of intent.

James Shapiro has written brilliantly about Shakespeare's determination to produce a more sophisticated form of drama as he moved to the Globe playhouse and saw the departure of William Kemp.[52] As he points out, *Henry V* is a different kind of history play from its immediate predecessors: it is stronger in its legal content, more informed by Tacitean politics, and more controlled in its use of comic material. In certain ways, we might say, it shows Shakespeare returning to more academic traditions of drama, the kind of writing he had produced in *Richard III*. Yet although *Henry V* can rightly be seen as a move 'up market' it also contains an emphatic rejection of elite removal from the mainstream. Like *Hamlet*, the play is balanced in a careful negotiation: in part it streamlines, reforms, and connects to the

---

50. See Gair, ed., *Antonio and Mellida*, 21–4.
51. Chambers, *Elizabethan Stage* II, 508.
52. James Shapiro, *1599: A Year in the Life of William Shakespeare* (London: Faber & Faber, 2005), 23, 42–3.

sophisticated new fashion for politic history, but it also (more strongly than ever) stakes a claim to the adult playing tradition of the English stage.[53]

Writing *Henry V* was a defiant choice simply on the grounds of its genre. The chronicle play was the backbone of the public theatre. Both Hamlet and Thomas Heywood use 'chronicle' as a word to justify the moral function of players; this was a form of drama both practically and ideologically unsuited to the indoor stage. *Henry V* emphatically states its connection to this tradition, not only because its protagonists frequently recall events depicted in *Richard II* and *Henry IV*, but also because its concluding commentary (in a gesture that is both backward- and forward-looking) foregrounds the *Henry VI* trilogy 'which oft our stage hath shown' (Epilogue.13). The epilogue calls explicitly upon the loyalty of an existing audience: the possessive 'our' that describes its author thus unites company, playwright, and playgoer as one.[54]

The emphasis on social unity in *Henry V* no doubt responds in part to its political moment: the departure of the Earl of Essex to fight Tyrone's uprising in Ireland in the spring of 1599. The play's surface patriotism, however, cannot be separated from the more local politics of theatrical competition, in which a social collective stood in marked contrast to the emergent coterie culture of the indoor stage. Heywood, too, repeatedly makes call upon this collective, not only in the *Apology* (with its emphasis on players as citizens and royal servants) but also in his plays. Thus, Heywood's two *If you Know not Me* plays, on the life of Queen Elizabeth, make a central theme of the monarch's comfortable movement between poor men, wealthy merchants, and high aristocrats. Like King Henry of Shakespeare's play, 'Queen Bess' is on easy terms with plain-speaking commoners such as 'Honest Hobson', who at first fails to recognize her but still sees the heroine as a 'true maid'.[55] In *Part I* the common people keep faith with the Princess in her adversity and in *Part II* they share with the Queen in triumph over the Spanish Armada and the building of the Royal Exchange. Crucially, the

53. On the increasing prominence of political history on the stage during this period see Bart van Es, 'Historiography and Biography', in Patrick Cheney and Philip Hardie, eds., *The Oxford History of Classical Reception in English Literature*, vol. II: *The Renaissance: 1558–1660* (Oxford: Oxford University Press, *forthcoming*).

54. On the matter of prologues and epilogues, Susan Bennett, *Theatre Audiences: A Theory of Production and Reception*, 2nd edn (London: Routledge, 1997), 1–71, makes a useful distinction between inclusive and exclusive gestures towards an audience. Bennett is not specifically concerned with English theatres of this period but contrasts theories and practices of audience response from Greek drama to the *Verfremdung* of Brecht.

55. Thomas Heywood, *If you Know not Me you Know Nobody, Part II*, ed. Madeleine Doran (Oxford: Malone Society, 1935), TLN 2086, 2093.

villain of *Part II* is the figure who threatens this social partnership: the would-be gallant John Gresham, who plots to coney-catch Hobson and marry an aristocratic widow, failing in both attempts. Heywood thus reverses the common pattern of the gallant's triumph depicted on the indoor stages, offering instead a prosperous union of the monarch and the general citizen. That union, and the rejection of an exclusive gentlemanly culture, is relevant to Shakespeare, who in the early years of the new century was, like Heywood, strengthening his ties with the collective body of a fellowship.

The Poets' War, as Edward Gieskes has argued, was in part the product of a conflict between two emergent professional fields.[56] On the one hand, poets were increasingly willing to define playwriting as a profession, with that activity's status progressively rising over the decades of the new century. At the same time, players gradually claimed acting as a 'quality': a trade that bore comparison with other skilled specialisms and that constituted a fraternity on an equal footing with the established guilds. Thus, by the first decade of the 1600s, the housekeeper–players of the Globe, like the prosperous established actors lauded by Heywood in his *Apology*, were closely aligned with the merchant–magnates of London. We see this in the business dealings of the Burbage brothers, which involved, for example, property speculation with a leading member of the Brewers' Company.[57] The rich detail we have on the material lives of the Chamberlain's/King's Men's principal sharers, Richard and Cuthbert Burbage, shows them as comfortable operators in the city's institutions. Cuthbert was a citizen and a gentleman and a major operator amongst the merchants.[58] In documents like the account of a break-in at their neighbouring London homes (which lists the cloaks, gowns, aprons, and tableware that were 'burglariously'

---

56. Edward Gieskes, *Representing the Professions: Administration, Law, and Theater in Early Modern England* (Newark: University of Delaware Press, 2006). The gradual growth in the status of playwrights and players is recorded in Bentley's *Profession of Dramatist* and *Profession of Player* respectively.

57. See Mary Edmond, 'Yeoman, Citizens', 40.

58. Edmund, 'Yeomen, Citizens, Gentlemen, and Players: The Burbages and their Connections', in R. B. Parker and S. P. Zitner, eds., *Elizabethan Theater: Essays in Honor of S. Schoenbaum* (Newark: University of Delaware Press, 1996), 30–49, esp. 32–3, 37. For more detail on the guild connections of the Chamberlain's/King's sharers see Alexandra Mason, 'The Social Status of Theatrical People', *Shakespeare Quarterly* 18 (1967), 429–30, and for a suggestive reading of Shakespeare's *Merry Wives* as well as other early modern adult players' productions in this context see Phil Withington, *The Politics of Commonwealth: Citizens and Freemen in Early Modern England* (Cambridge: Cambridge University Press, 2005), esp. 44–7.

stolen) we see the solid prosperity of the Burbage brothers.[59] They, like John Heminges, who was a freeman of the Grocers' Company, were figures of the civic establishment who moved easily between court and city.[60] The social level of their interactions was thus decidedly different from those surrounding the children's stage.

In *Henry V* Shakespeare aligns two related collaborative ventures: that of a king and his nation and that of an audience and an acting fellowship. The overlap between the language of martial and imaginative endeavour is striking. In tandem with the King's speeches to his soldiers, spectators are called upon to 'follow, follow!/ Grapple your minds to sternage of this navy' and to 'work, work your thoughts' (3.0.17–18; 25). After the triumph of Agincourt, when 'London doth pour out her citizens' (5.0.24), the chorus explicitly draws together two audiences: the historical crowd that gathered to welcome Henry in 1415 and that which sees the players on the Bankside now. Like the army itself, this audience is characterized in the coming together of social strata: 'lords' and 'citizens'; 'senators' and 'plebeians' (5.0.17, 24–7). The play is remarkable for its language of social inclusion: 'good yeomen,/ Whose limbs were made in England' (3.1.25–26); 'none of you so mean and base/ That hath not noble lustre' (3.1.29–30); 'mean and gentle all' (4.0.45); 'we band of brothers' (4.3.60). King Henry's 'fellowship to die with us' is conspicuous in embracing the ordinary citizen: the common soldier who 'will yearly on the vigil feast his neighbours' and for whom great men shall be 'familiar in his mouth as household words' (4.3.39, 45, 52). That language matches the class compact that was required for the adult theatre to function—joining high aristocratic figures such as Baron Hunsdon, the Lord Chamberlain, to a tradition that had popular appeal. In a sense, the King's skill as a social chameleon (his ability to play all men to all classes on the eve of the battle) is metonymic of the company's achievement. King Henry's embrace of the common soldier and Prince Hamlet's acceptance of the common player are thus closely aligned.

Set against this army of national inclusion there is a group of outsiders defined entirely in terms of social exclusion. Even within Henry's speeches there is a touch of resentment about a class that withdraws itself from the

59. For a transcript of this bill, see Stopes, *Burbage*, 151–2.
60. On this and wider guild membership amongst players see Knutson, *Playing Companies*, 22. On the guilds as the cornerstone of social organization in the capital see Steve Rappaport, *Worlds within Worlds: Structures of Life in Sixteenth-Century London* (Cambridge: Cambridge University Press, 1989).

spirit of union: 'those men in England/ That do no work today' and 'gentlemen in England now abed' (4.3.17–18, 64). But the bulk of this language is applied to the French. In scenes that frame Henry's disguised mingling with the common soldiers, we are afforded a glimpse of the enemy camp where the Duke of Orleans and Constable of France boast of horses, armour, sonnets, mistresses, and gaming. The Dauphin, who also joins these conversations, takes pleasure in absurdly artificial rhetoric. 'Nay', he declares, 'the man hath no wit that cannot, from the rising of the lark to the lodging of the lamb, vary deserved praise on my palfrey' (3.7.31–3). These are the cadences of a rarefied coterie culture not so distant from the English Inns of Court. In a scene that comes immediately after Henry's famous double-edged statement 'I think the King is but a man, as I am' (4.1.102), the social aggression of this world becomes still more apparent:

> our French gallants shall today draw out
> And sheathe for lack of sport.
>
> (4.2.21–2)
>
> our superfluous lackeys and our peasants
>   . . . were enough
> To purge this field of such a hilding foe.
>
> (4.2.25–8)
>
> Shall we go send them dinners and fresh suits
> And give their fasting horses provender,
> And after fight with them?
>
> (4.2.56–8)

Such statements and others like them make the war a clash of social strata as much as of nations. There is thus a nasty irony to French complaints, after the battle, that 'our vulgar drench their peasant limbs/ In blood of princes' (4.7.76–7) because it so pointedly recalls and reverses King Henry's generous fellowship of blood (4.3.39, 61).

To characterize a foreign enemy as effete is, one might assume, not unusual, but precedents are in fact hard to find. In the play's sources it is, if anything, King Henry who is accused of being foppish (through the taunting gift of tennis balls, included also in Shakespeare's play).[61] It is an innovation to depict Henry's opponents as idle gentlemen, an innovation that can have

---

61. See Geoffrey Bullough, ed., *Narrative and Dramatic Sources of Shakespeare*, 8 vols. (London: Routledge and Kegan Paul, 1961–75), IV, 299–432. David Womersley, 'France in Shakespeare's *Henry V*', *Renaissance Studies* 9 (1995), 442–59, picks up on the lack of precedent for this characterization and relates it to Shakespeare's dismissal of the Salic law.

nothing to do with a war against Irish rebels, to which it very poorly applies. It does connect, however, to a defence of the common stages, in which cultural inclusiveness played an important role. *Histrio-Mastix* had been contemptuous in its depiction of the less educated classes, not just the players but also the townsfolk who are their customers. Above all, that play scoffs at the coming together of different strata of society in the hall of Lord Mavortius, where aristocrats and common citizens come together to enjoy the play. The declaration made here by its 'goosequillian' player–poet Posthaste—'A Gentleman's a Gentleman, that hath a clean/ shirt on, with some learning, and so have I'—is mocked as patently absurd.[62] It is this new gentlemanly fear of 'goose-quills' (*Hamlet*, F 2.2.341) that Prince Hamlet deplores.

In the first years of the 'controversy' reported by Rosincrance the opposition between the adult and the children's stages was strident. Marston, in plays such as *Antonio and Mellida*, made an appeal to the 'select and most respected auditors' whom he claimed for his faction.[63] Jonson, especially in *Poetaster* for Blackfriars, escalated this conflict—making it partly a personal fight. Shakespeare took part in this rivalry: his company performed Dekker's *Satiromastix*, which attacked Jonson's pretensions, especially his self-proclaimed distance from the players and his supposed elevation above the superficiality of certain elements at court.[64] According to the author of *The Second Part of the Return from Parnassus* Shakespeare also delivered a 'purge' to Jonson 'that made him beray his credit', and it is possible that, as James Bednarz and others have argued, this refers to a satirical portrait of the poet as Ajax in *Troilus and Cressida*.[65] This first period of contact between two distinctive venues for production exerted pressures that made personal allusions to poets (otherwise highly unusual on the public stages) for a time a possible thing.[66]

62. Marston, *Histrio-Mastix*, in *Works*, I, 3.1.202 (p. 273); 2.1.248–9 (p. 263).
63. Marston, *Antonio and Mellida*, Prologue.3.
64. See Thomas Dekker, *Satiromastix*, in *Dramatic Works*, ed. Bowers, I, esp. 1.2.353–58; 4.1.121–36; 4.3.202–7; 5.2.324–7.
65. The reference to Shakespeare's 'purge' of Jonson appears in one of the speeches given to William Kemp in *The Second Part* in *The Three Parnassus Plays*, ed. J. B. Leishman (London: Nicholson & Watson, 1949), TLN 1766–73 (4.3). For a cautious assessment of the passage's meaning see Leishman, ed., *Parnassus*, 59–60, 337n., 369–71. Bednarz, *Poets' War* (esp. 1–11, 35–48), argues that this is a reference to an extended personal intellectual battle between the two poets, encoded within their plays. He also argues that Jonson is represented in *As You Like It* and *Twelfth Night* (esp. 120–224).
66. The original attempt to read the plays of this period as a kind of *roman à clef* depicting poets is Sharpe, *The Real War*, but very few of his identifications in plays performed before 1599 can be said to hold weight.

The so-called Poets' War, which is remembered in *Hamlet*, was a feature of only the first few years of the children's theatre. *Henry V*, written on the eve or in the early stages of this conflict, may or may not be a direct response to the social exclusion projected in *Histrio-Mastix*, but it is certainly a work that projects values that were associated with the public stage. The long-term contention between the indoor and the outdoor stages was both more nebulous and more deep-rooted than the 'throwing about of brains' described by Rosincrance. There were no clear battle lines separating the two parties: playwrights, audiences, and playtexts could move between the camps.[67] Yet, if we examine the full run of the surviving repertories, there are foundational distinctions between the two cultures—British chronicle history and domestic tragedy, for example, were matter of the public theatre profoundly alien to the indoor stage.

At the core of the division, I suggest, lay competing concepts of sincerity. To be 'honest' in the world of the indoor stage's humoural comedies and politic tragedies was to be realist. The dominant ethic was a fusion of the stoic and the epicurean: it was honest to admit that men and women were subject to sexual disorders and that the political realm was a place of strategic calculation rather than high ideals.[68] The best men strove to know themselves and thus to recognize and master their humours; to claim anything as grand as 'virtue' was likely to prove hubristic and risked the dread charge of

67. W. Reavley Gair, *The Children of Paul's: The Story of a Theatre Company, 1553–1608* (Cambridge: Cambridge University Press, 1982) charts a blurring of the repertories after initial years of intense opposition, but still finds the mood of the two kinds of theatre to be distinct. One fascinating witness to the adaptability of texts to the two stages, dated around the turn of the century, is provided by the plays of William Percy. This playwright, a younger son of the Earl of Northumberland, was evidently eccentric but was nevertheless familiar with the London repertories. Repeatedly, he offers variations depending on the place of performance that indicate the indoor audience is resistant to populism. The manuscript of *Change is No Robbery*, for example, contains a prologue to be spoken by the ghost of the famous clown Richard Tarlton accompanied by a tabor, which is 'rather to be omitted if for Paul's, and another prologue, for him, to be brought in Place' (Alnwick Castle, MS Percy 507, 'Plays Volume 2', fol. 2ᵃ [foliation mine]). In a later volume covering this and other plays (Alnwick Castle, MS Percy 509, 'Plays Volume 3') Percy continues to suggest such variants, offering a more scholarly prologue plus a formal dance for the boys, as opposed to the spectacular storm and hell scene recommended for the outdoor stage.
68. For background see Christopher Tilmouth, *Passion's Triumph over Reason: A History of the Moral Imagination from Spenser to Rochester* (Oxford: Oxford University Press, 2007). Tilmouth's study is largely concerned with the elite tradition, but his location within *Hamlet* of a conflict between fury and asceticism (75–113) has relevance to that play's negotiation of a position between popular and coterie modes.

hypocrisy.[69] In contrast, passion was a source of authenticity on the public stages: patriotic fervour, the heart-warming conversion of the prodigal, and the trembling loyalty of the mistreated wife were keynotes of popular drama.[70] It is the embarrassing lachrymosity of such moments ('This is a passion, note you the passion? . . . Read the rest sirs, I cannot for tears') that is mocked in *Histrio-Mastix* and ironized in the spoof romance elements of such plays as *Jack Drum's Entertainment* and *Antonio and Mellida*. It was, in part, the unpalatable display of passion that made the history play unsuitable for the indoor stage. So too it proved an obstacle for domestic tragedy, above all in its treatment of less than aristocratic wives.

For the final part of this chapter I am concerned especially with the indoor and outdoor theatres in their treatment of women, but the division regarding passion applies more widely to Shakespeare's repertory in the years 1599 to 1608. In plays of the adult companies such as Worcester's Men's *Good Wife from a Bad*, the Admiral's *Patient Grissil*, or the Chamberlain's *London Prodigal* the affecting spectacle of a wronged but loyal wife provides an ethical holdfast. Conversely, across numerous boys' company productions—including Marston's *Parasitaster*, Chapman's *May Day*, and Middleton's *Michaelmas Term*—the readiness of young women to jettison their husbands is a fertile subject for the dramatist's wit. Plays such as Middleton's *Puritan Widow* and *Michaelmas Term* pour scorn on the idea of love that lasts beyond the death of a wealthy husband, making speeches of wifely devotion an object of fun. Marston's *What you Will*, which is full of references to cuckoldry, comically tortures its merchant protagonist (who is reported as dead at the play's opening) with the prospect of his wife's remarriage as he tries desperately to convince the world he is alive. In Chapman's *The Widow's Tears* (written around 1605 for Blackfriars) the husband's likely fate in such circumstances is still more ruthlessly laughed at.[71] Lysander (like Quomodo in *Michaelmas Term*) fakes his own death in

---

69. For contemporary presentations of this ethos see, for example, Ben Jonson's 'Induction' to *Every Man out of his Humour*, ed. Helen Ostovich, Revels (Manchester: Manchester University Press, 2001) and the address 'To My Equal Reader' in John Marston, *Parasitaster or The Fawn*, ed. David A. Blostein, Revels (Manchester: Manchester University Press, 1978).

70. Non-elite plays like Thomas Heywood's *The Fair Maid of the West, Parts I and II* or Heywood and William Rowley's *Fortune by Land and Sea* combine such elements liberally with adventure and exotic foreign locations.

71. On date and venue of first performance, see George Chapman, *The Widow's Tears*, ed. Akihiro Yamada, Revels (London: Methuen, 1975), xxxi–xxxiii. This play most directly parodies *How a Man May Choose a Good Wife from a Bad*, attributed to Heywood, in which the good wife fends off unwanted advances from Anselme as she lies in her tomb following

the expectation that his wife will be overcome with emotion. Inevitably he is disappointed: not only does Cynthia quickly move on to find a new lover, she decides that her husband's tomb is a convenient place in which to pursue the affair.[72] True, there are faithful women in plays for the indoor stages, but their passion almost always contains an element of parody (as is the case, for example, in the love plots of *Jack Drum's Entertainment* and *Antonio and Mellida*). The caustic atmosphere of satire that pervades the children's stages makes sentiment around marriage an impossible thing.

Of course, unfaithful wives are also found in the adult theatre—their seduction and fall is the subject of domestic tragedies like the Chamberlain's *Warning for Fair Women* or Worcester's *A Woman Killed with Kindness*. The difference is that marriage matters; just as much as in the patient wife dramas, its sacred status is the dominant assumption of the characters. Sentiment is thus easily sanctioned in fallen and faithful women alike. As with *Henry V* and class sympathy, it is revealing to examine Shakespeare's treatment of women in the context of this opposition between the public and the private stages. In particular, the pathos of a wronged woman, which is so powerful a feature of *All's Well that Ends Well* and *Othello*, is inconceivable as a serious subject for the indoor companies. There is a potential analogy here with the conflict between Samuel Richardson and Henry Fielding more than a century later. The indoor theatre's self-consciously learned, ironic form of writing was also Fielding's, as was its suspicion of lower-class women's tears. Shakespeare's drama from this period appeals to the populist side of that division: if *All's Well that Ends Well* anticipates *Pamela* then *Othello* is the pyrrhic triumph of feminine virtue that *Clarissa* would be. Yet to say that Shakespeare replicates the appeal of domestic drama is too simple. The King's Men's plays were not restricted to either a populist or an elitist medium: *All's Well* is not a standard 'patient wife' story and *Othello* is no conventional domestic tragedy. As with *Henry V* (which harnesses and transforms a genre central to the appeal of the public stages) the treatment, in these plays, of female passion and virtue involves a complex negotiation of social alliances.

Shakespeare's investment in the values of the public stage is evident when we compare his works with the more populist plays in his company's

---

her attempted murder by her husband (see Thomas Heywood (?), *How a Man May Chuse a Good Wife from a Bad*, ed. A. E. H. Swaen (Louvain: Librairie universitaire, Uystpruyst, 1912), TLN 1797–2010).

72. The lover, in fact, is her disguised husband; Quomodo in *Michaelmas Term* is less fortunate. Both men end the play forced to accept less quixotic notions of wifely honour.

repertory. As Knutson has shown, such non-elite drama must have remained commercially important, even if it was not shown at court.[73] *The London Prodigal*, of unknown authorship, was performed on the same stage as *All's Well that Ends Well*, quite possibly in the same year.[74] At first glance it is difficult to believe that the two plays have anything in common. Shakespeare's is set in France and Italy of the Middle Ages and concerns the deeds of dukes and monarchs; *The London Prodigal*, in contrast, depicts contemporary merchants in familiar settings in and around the nation's capital. The anonymous play is a conventional drama of decline and salvation. Young Flowerdale wastes the advantages of a good marriage and family and sinks to debt, gaming, coney-catching, and eventually highway robbery. It is only at the play's conclusion that his disguised father (thought dead by Flowerdale) intervenes with a spectacular display of financial power by doubling the wife's dowry and thus ensuring a happy end. This mercantile world, set forth in unornate writing, looks very different from the fabliau artifice of *All's Well that Ends Well*.

Beneath the surface, however, there are connections between *All's Well* and the citizen drama. For a start, the King of France, in persuading his ward Bertram to marry the physician's daughter, Helena, uses strikingly unaristocratic arguments. This low-born woman, he argues, has cured the monarch and deserves payment for this service. She is virtuous and the King can supply her with a title and a dowry. Nothing beyond this, it seems, sets this commoner and the Count of Roussillon apart:

73. For the relevant plays see Knutson, *Repertory*, 95–132, and also her alphabetical list of plays attributable to the company, 180–209. From the record of court payment it is evident that these plays were not considered suitable for performance there (see E. K. Chambers, *William Shakespeare: A Study of Facts and Problems*, 2 vols. (Oxford: Clarendon Press, 1930; repr. 1988), II, 319–45).

74. The play is ascribed on its title page to Shakespeare and is widely assumed to be correctly assigned to the Chamberlain's repertory. Stanley Wells and Gary Taylor, *William Shakespeare: A Textual Companion* (Oxford: Clarendon Press, 1987), 126–7, posited a date range of 1604–5 for *All's Well*, which would overlap with the date of *Prodigal* of 1604 in Alfred Harbage, *Annals of English Drama: 975–1700*, 3rd edn, rev. Sylvia Stoler Wagonheim (London: Routledge, 1989). Recently a later date for *All's Well*'s composition has gained favour. Support for this position is found, for example, in MacDonald P. Jackson, 'Spurio and the Date of *All's Well that Ends Well*', *Notes & Queries* 48 (2001), 298–9; Gary Taylor, "Divine [ ]sences,' *Shakespeare Survey* 54 (2001), 13–30 (at 24n.); Gordon McMullan, 'What is a Late Play?' in Catherine Alexander, ed., *The Cambridge Companion to Shakespeare's Last Plays* (Cambridge: Cambridge University Press, 2009), 5–27; and Lois Potter, *The Life of William Shakespeare: A Critical Biography* (Oxford: Wiley-Blackwell, 2012).

KING: 'Tis only title thou disdain'st in her, the which
    I can build up. Strange is it that our bloods,
    Of colour, weight, and heat, pour'd all together,
    Would quite confound distinction, yet stands off
    In differences so mighty.[75]

(All's Well, 2.3.117–21)

This happy mingling of bloods has much in common with Henry V's 'band of brothers'—amazingly it is an ethos that all members of the medieval court (besides Bertram, Count of Roussillon) appear to share. It is only through the mouthpiece of the fraud Paroles that we hear a defence of the gentlemanly ethos. His justification of Bertram's supposed seduction of Diana evidently shocks all who are present, even though it is hardly atypical for an aristocrat: 'tricks he hath had in him,/ which gentlemen have', 'he did love her, sir, as a gentleman loves a woman . . . he lov'd her, sir, and lov'd her not' (All's Well 5.3.238–9, 243–5). In All's Well that Ends Well all right-thinking characters reject such rakish conduct and invest profoundly in the virtues of prudence and sexual fidelity.

Like All's Well, The London Prodigal makes a rejected but resourceful wife the emotional centre of its story. Outraged though Flowerdale's father is by all of his son's behaviour, it is when he sees the suffering of his faithful spouse that he suffers most: 'it grieves me at the soul, to see her tears,/ thus stain the crimson roses of her cheeks'.[76] Shakespeare's heroine is likewise the subject of a parent-in-law's pity. The Countess, hearing of her son's abandonment of Helena, sounds exactly like the mother of a prodigal:

COUNTESS: What angel shall
    Bless this unworthy husband? He cannot thrive
    Unless her prayers, whom heaven delights to hear
    And loves to grant, reprieve him from the wrath
    Of greatest justice. . . .
    My heart is heavy, and mine age is weak;
    Grief would have tears and sorrow bids me speak.

(All's Well 3.4.25–30; 41–2)

---

75. William Shakespeare, *All's Well that Ends Well*, ed. G. K. Hunter, Arden2 (London: Methuen, 1962), 2.3.117–21. For the sake of simplicity, I have used Arden editions throughout as my primary reference text. The Oxford edition is more recent and has a thesis about the origin of the Folio's copy that is different from Hunter's (see William Shakespeare, ed. Susan Snyder, *All's Well that Ends Well* (Oxford: Oxford University Press, 1994), 52–65) but this has no significant impact in the case of the quotations I draw from this text.

76. Anon., *The London Prodigal*, in *The 'Doubtful' Plays of the Third Shakespeare Folio*, ed. John S. Farmer, Tudor Facsimile Texts (London: Early English Drama Society, 1911), E3ᵃ.

In the words of Marston's *Histrio-Mastix*: 'this is a passion, note you the passion?' (2.260). The parallels between *All's Well* and *The London Prodigal* are not limited to their speeches on prudence and wifely virtue; their plots have much in common too. Like Helena, Luce of *The London Prodigal* disguises herself in order to follow the husband who has cruelly dismissed her. The denouement of both plays is the sudden reappearance of wives who are thought to have died in penury—a reappearance that is a triumph because it rescues and converts an unworthy husband through a woman's love.

Such plots and sentiments anticipate what Mary Beth Rose has called 'the heroics of marriage', in which wifely obedience and the active pursuit of a husband are twinned. Rose describes a development of the 1620s and early 1630s when, she argues, private life began to be assigned a new centrality in dramatic art.[77] But marital heroics of a kind did already exist in the early years of the century in public stage depictions such as Heywood's *Fair Maid of the West* plays, *A Good Wife from a Bad*, and *The Wise-Woman of Hogsdon*. These works by the nation's other sharer–playwright are distinctive in their focus on women's fate and agency. That distinction is not necessarily polemical in origin, but it does reflect a popular sensibility that connected adult players with their audience.

All's Well that Ends Well and Heywood's composition of around the same period, *The Wise-Woman of Hogsdon*, provide a particularly intriguing parallel.[78] Both involve a socially elevated gallant whose lies are exposed in the final scene and both feature a disguised wife who comes to his rescue.[79] Neither Shakespeare nor Heywood writes conventional prodigal dramas: their plays are far more knowingly literary, for example, than *The London Prodigal*. In contrast to this populist writing, *The Wise-Woman of Hogsdon*, with its references to other plays and devices of classical New Comedy,

77. Mary Beth Rose, *The Expense of Spirit: Love and Sexuality in English Renaissance Drama* (Ithaca, NY: Cornell University Press, 1988), 96.
78. Neither play is easily dated, but, as noted above, *All's Well* is traditionally dated 1604–5 and *Wise-Woman* is usually placed in 1604. For debate see Harbage, *Annals*; Thomas Heywood, *The Wise-Woman of Hogsdon*, in *Thomas Heywood: Three Marriage Plays*, ed. Paul Merchant, Revels (Manchester: Manchester University Press, 1996), 6; and Wells and Taylor, *Textual Companion*; plus my Appendix on the dating of Shakespeare's plays.
79. Technically Second Luce, the 'wife' in Heywood's play, does not have a legal marriage to her 'husband' Chartley because he absconded on the night before their wedding. The match, however, is (a little like that of Marina and Angelo in *Measure for Measure*) considered to be an honourable obligation. Chartley's father laments his prodigal son's behaviour ('who should have married/ A fair, a modest and a virtuous maid' (5.1.14–15)) and considers Second Luce his 'loving daughter' (5.6.203).

and *All's Well* with its half-ironic title, have a 'knowing' quality of artistic removal. Yet, unlike plays for the children's companies, Heywood and Shakespeare could not be said to parody the prodigal husband and faithful wife motifs. Their heroic wives are celebrated and the gallant's world of broken promises is powerfully critiqued. *All's Well that Ends Well* and *The Wise-Woman of Hogsdon* sit uneasily between the ironic and the conventionally moral. That position gives both plays a 'problem play' status because the sudden conversions of their lying husbands remain difficult (at least for a modern audience) to accept.

All's Well that Ends Well employs the cadences, characters, and plot trajectory of the popular 'patient wife' plays of the public stages. Much like *Measure for Measure*, which is the product of roughly the same period, it focuses on complex issues of female chastity: not simply praising virginity but examining the acceptable conditions for its loss. Shakespeare's Globe plays also investigate the abuse of male power. In the comedies of this period, quite unlike those that come earlier, the nature and moment of marital commitment is a central issue. Dowries, pregnancy, and sexual gratification—almost untouched upon as serious topics in the earlier writing—are now the primary drivers of plot. Above all, marriage, which was previously a dramatic end point, is now a state whose material conditions are contemplated and portrayed. This phase in Shakespeare's development is widely acknowledged. What has not previously been acknowledged, however, is that at least a part of its origin must relate to the friction between the new cynical and misogynistic comedies of the boys' stage and the more gynocentric drama of the adults. Shakespeare, given his secure association with the players, was more consistently tied to this woman-centred drama than his contemporaries. At the same time, as a writer for the court and coterie circles he was also responding to trends in fashionable literary culture. The distinctive 'mixed' quality of Shakespeare's writing, in which the popular female voice often sits side by side with the expression of a new, harsher, misogynistic fear of sexual betrayal, may be traced to the competing pressures of the outdoor theatre's popular heroics of marriage and the indoor theatre's caustic cynicism about the fate of the married man.

Shakespeare's experimentation on this contested ground continues in *Othello*, a play that could be said violently to throw together the competing cultures of the indoor and outdoor stage. Nowhere is the raw emotional power of Shakespeare's investment in this world of female experience more present than in this drama. Yet the work takes Venice (the common hunting ground of gallants and courtesans in boys' plays such as Chapman's *May Day*) as its centre of civic order. That world of magnificos and braggart soldiers would seem, on the face of it, to be exceptionally unconducive to domestic tragedy, and critics, from the very beginning, have spotted a problematic aspect to this mixture of worlds. Most prominent amongst the early sceptics is Thomas Rymer, whose *Short View of Tragedy* (1693) famously savaged *Othello* and mocked its moral purpose as 'a warning to all good wives that they look well to their linen'.[80] For all its racist pigheaded-ness, Rymer's *Short View* is a useful point of departure because it gives access to attitudes that were also present at the time of the play's composition. He notes its popularity, with the persuasion of its hero by Iago being heralded 'the top scene, the scene that raises *Othello* above all other tragedies on our theatres' (118). Why, then, should this, more than any other play of the period, have been the work whose reputation Rymer should have sought to overthrow?

First, there is the issue of social standing. Rymer's phrase 'good wives' already has an edge of condescension, but his obsession with class becomes much more evident when we read the chapter on *Othello* as a whole. In the play's Venice he quickly spots a world of English middling citizens at 'the latitude of Gotham': 'a body must strain hard', Rymer tells his readers, 'to fancy the scene at Venice and not rather in some of our Cinq-ports, where the bailey and his fishermen are knocking their heads together on account of some whale' (100). The Senator's daughter, he scoffs, runs away to 'a carrier's inn' (95) and converses with common soldiers in the manner 'of any country kitchen maid with her sweet heart' (111). Of Desdemona's plea 'O good Iago, what shall I do to win my Lord again?' Rymer fulminates 'no woman bred out of a pigsty could talk so meanly'.[81] Worst of all is the handkerchief and the agency it gives to Emilia, 'the meanest woman in the play' (145). It is this world of women's business that truly connects the work with the civic origins of the public players 'beyond what all the parish clerks in London with their Old Testament farces . . . could ever pretend to' (146).

---

80. Thomas Rymer, *A Short View of Tragedy* (London, 1693), 89. Further references are to this edition and sources appear in the text.

81. Rymer, *Short View*, 131, here quotes Q1 or a later text based on it. F has 'Alas', which E. A. J. Honigmann's Arden3 edition conjecturally amends to 'God' on the basis that it must replace a censored profanity, a possibility still more likely to have excited Rymer's ire. References in the text are to Honigmann's edition, *Othello* (London: Thomas Nelson, 1997), in which Desdemona's line is spoken at 4.2.150.

Second, Rymer is concerned about the play's generic indeterminacy. Love and jealousy 'are no part of a soldier's character, unless for comedy' (93) and the play's gulling plot, its location, its Italian cast of characters, and the all-consuming language of cuckoldry prove this is so. Othello, as a gulled and jealous husband, is from this perspective an absurd humoural figure, for in the Italian tradition jealous husbands are stock dullards. Rymer calls him a 'booby' (128) as often as he can. This position is, of course, entirely at odds with the grandeur that the dramatist affords him: Shakespeare, he notes, 'styles him the Moor of Venice: a note of pre-eminence, which neither history nor heraldry can allow him' (87). Worse, Othello's language is much more dignified than the play's subject warrants: 'one might think', Rymer observes, 'the general should not glory so much in this action, but make an hasty work on't, and have turn'd his eyes away from so unsoldierly an execution: yet is he all pause and deliberation' (134–5). The 'booby's' rhetorical sophistication is, in his assessment, grotesquely misplaced.

A Short View of Tragedy is revealing because it responds to the competing theatrical traditions within Othello and makes telling connections between gender, subject matter, and class. Rymer spots the play's roots in the domestic tragedy of the common stages. Its actions and the language surrounding its women are of the kind reported in 'the last speeches and confessions of the persons executed at Tyburn' (139)—just the material that the King's Men were to perform in the Yorkshire Tragedy of 1606. But Rymer is equally struck by the play's elevated setting, political context, and protagonists, and the rhetorical splendour of its male speakers: it is the conjunction of these diametrically opposed elements that exercises him most.

More than any other play of the period, Othello brings together moral and generic expectations that ought to be kept separate. John Bayley, also responding to Rymer, notes that one of its key problems is a matter of genre: a 'problem not elsewhere encountered in the tragedies, or indeed in Shakespeare's works in general: the distinction between tragic and comic'.[82] To a degree, he historicizes his answer: men in the theatre, he argues, 'were the more inclined to see the Moor as a great booby', so that, 'historically speaking, half an audience might well have been disposed to see the play in terms of tragedy and love, the other in terms of comedy and sex' (202). There may be something in this, but I suggest that we can better apply

82. John Bayley, Shakespeare and Tragedy (London: Routledge, 1981), 201.

Bayley's answer to the indoor and outdoor theatre of the period. It is not that cynical frequenters of the boys' playhouses coming to see *Othello* on the Bankside would find it comic, but rather that they would recognize its allusion to an established set of comic conventions only to find those conventions challenged through a rival tradition: in *Othello* Shakespeare intentionally presented them with a generic shock.

As in *Henry V* and *All's Well*, virtue in this play is set against the hollow culture of the gallant. Iago presents cuckoldry as 'sport' in the feeble would-be rake Roderigo, whose night-roving of the streets of Venice would suit a humoural comedy. Iago's wit (such pat couplets as 'She never yet was foolish that was fair,/ For even her folly helped her to an heir' (2.1.136–7)) is likewise standard for that setting. And Iago's temptation of Cassio and Roderigo with drinking and lechery is of the same kind. The villain's much-vaunted 'honesty', in fact, is not so very distant from the moral realism of the indoor theatre's dramatists.

The 'heroics of marriage', whether of domestic tragedy or of patient wifely endurance, was, in the first decade of the seventeenth century, a mode suited exclusively to the public stages; it was both woman-centred and socially middling in sympathy. This is relevant to *Othello* because Desdemona is not an aristocrat, but instead the daughter of the prosperous senator of a city state. As Mary Beth Rose has noted, she has, even before her elopement, been granted a choice in marriage, a fact itself indicative of class. The close communion of Emilia and Desdemona helps to fashion a world redolent of the material density of domestic drama (the kind of detail we also find in Heywood's *A Woman Killed with Kindness* or in the anonymous *A Warning for Fair Women*, where the innocent Joan asks for a 'carnation ribbon to tie my smock sleeves' in the scene before her true love is killed).[83] The physical particularity of Desdemona's world is an exception to the dichotomy that Bert O. States sets up between scenic illusion in Shakespeare and that of later dramatists such as Ibsen and Chekhov, and the fact that a pattern is broken makes this all the more significant.[84] The audience sees Desdemona undressing, hears of her nightgown, and knows of her hand-

---

83. Anon., *A Warning for Fair Women*, ed. Cannon, TLN 1061–2.
84. Bert O. States, *Great Reckonings in Little Rooms: On the Phenomenology of Theatre* (Berkeley: University of California Press, 1985), 48–79. The element of symbolism to objects in Ibsen that States discusses is relevant to many objects in *Othello*, such as the wedding sheets and the handkerchief, but other objects in the play, such as the nightgown, are 'negligibly symbolic' in the same way as the objects States describes in Chekhov's rooms.

kerchief. Such details, combined with Emilia's great speech on the fate of women ('let husbands know/ Their wives have sense like them' (4.3.92–3)), help to level social distinctions. These are exactly the material aspects of the story that made Thomas Rymer certain that this was not fit matter for a tragedy. Yet this is also a tragedy of state, with its hero the general of an empire. In its sentimental but at the same time cataclysmic denouement the play refutes the conventional separation of kinds.

As Rymer recognized, the play's strongest oppositions lie in the competing strains of its language. As is well known, *Othello* is profoundly concerned with the arts of persuasion (it is for this reason that, already in 1693, it could be held 'above all other tragedies on our stage' (*Short View*, 118)). From the first, Iago's complaints about Cassio advertise this theme to erudite listeners: 'bombast circumstance/ Horribly stuffed with epithets of war', 'bookish theoric', 'mere prattle' (*Othello*, 1.1.12–25). The learned theatregoer (the kind of Blackfriars man gently mocked in the induction to *The Malcontent* who has already recorded 'most of the jests here in my table-book' (IND.17)) must prick his ears up at this warning. He is not to be disappointed, because a few lines later Iago deploys a spectacular range of rhetorical devices in order to rouse Desdemona's father, Brabantio:

> thieves, thieves, thieves!
> Look to your house, your daughter, and your bags!
>
> (1.1.78–9)

The grammar-school-trained reader used to spotting and organizing his tropes and figures will spot epizeuxis (repetition of words) and also ironic auxesis (where words are arranged in ascending order of importance: house, daughter, bags). Just so, a few lines later:

> Even now, now, very now, an old black ram
> Is tupping your white ewe!
>
> (1.1.87–8)

Iago concentrates metaphor, epizeuxis, and the deliberate ungrammatical amplification in 'very now' plus a daring synecdoche: 'the beast with two backs' (1.1.115). Brabantio, in response to Iago's goading hints, produces the kind of broken speech which we will later hear from Othello, including exclamatio and erotesis in the rhetorical question 'who would be a father?' (1.1.162). In a sense this scene sets a rhetorical paradigm for what is to be the whole shape of the drama, for over the course of the play Iago is repeatedly to use manipulative rhetoric in such a way as to elicit the rhetoric of real passion from his victims.

The central trick of Iago's rhetoric, as a subset of the Globe audience must have recognized, is mastery of an armoury of tropes and figures that fit loosely under the term 'significatio'. The *Ad Herennium* (the standard grammar-school authority on the subject) describes it as follows:

> Significatio is that which leaves more to be suspected than has been positively asserted: it is produced through hyperbole, ambiguity, logical consequence, aposiopesis, and analogy. (*Significatio est, que plus in suspicione relinquit, quam positum est in oratione: ea fit per exsuperationem, ambiguum, consequentiam, absciscionem, similitudinem.*)[85]

As the text goes on to spell out at a later stage 'it permits the hearer himself to guess what the speaker has not mentioned'.[86] Hearers repeatedly complain of not understanding Iago fully; this is, of course, a central plank of his rhetorical strategy.

Iago, as he gradually ensnares Othello in jealousy, makes use of a very large number of tropes and figures that form part of, or relate to, significatio. He thus makes continual use of ambiguity that invites complicitous completion from the hearer. Cassio, in Iago's description, thus repeatedly 'seems' honest—leaving a very open gap through which Othello's suspicions can enter (it is another trick of Iago's to *seem* to be using enormous understatement, when in fact he exaggerates). Iago is also a consistent master of aposiopesis (the deliberate breaking off of a sentence in order to invite its completion): 'Nothing, my lord; or if—I know not what' (3.3.36). Again and again, Iago deploys tropes that invite Othello to go much further than he has himself explicitly gone. Such as, for example, in the implied logical consequence 'She did deceive her father, marrying you' (3.3.209), adynaton (a declaration of the impossibility of expressing oneself adequately), and litotes (with which Puttenham's *Arte of English Poesie* deals immediately after emphasis or significatio). Thus, in his reluctant, stumbling coming forth about a drunken incident involving Cassio, Iago makes his effort of repression so obvious that he invites Othello to expand greatly on his report:

---

85. Marcus Tullius Cicero (?), *Rhetoricum ad C. Herennium libri quattuor* (1579) 167.
86. Cicero, *Ad Herennium*, 167. For discussion of the term see Richard A. Lanham, *A Handlist of Rhetorical Terms* (Berkeley: University of California Press, 1991), 138–40, and, for wider context, Brian Vickers, *Classical Rhetoric in English Poetry* (Carbondale, IL: Southern Illinois University Press, 1989).

> I know, Iago,
> Thy honesty and love doth mince this matter,
> Making it light to Cassio.
>
> (*Othello*, 2.3.242–4)

One of the great dramatic ironies of *Othello* is that its hero is so acutely aware of the qualities of Iago's speech, which, in line with rhetorical affective theory, he understands not as the effect of study but as an outpouring of nature:

OTHELLO: And for I know thou'rt full of love and honesty
    And weigh'st thy words before thou giv'st them breath,
    Therefore these stops of thine fright me the more.
    For such things in a false disloyal knave
    Are tricks of custom, but in a man that's just
    They're close delations, working from the heart
    That passion cannot rule.
IAGO: For Michael Cassio,
    I dare be sworn, I think, that he is honest.
OTHELLO: I think so too.
IAGO: Men should be what they seem,
    Or those that be not, would they might seem none.

> (*Othello* 3.3.121–30)

Othello's observation here, in what Rymer against his will acknowledged as the 'top scene' in English tragedy, strikes at the heart of the play's radically expansive treatment of rhetoric: persuasive speech can indeed involve the 'tricks of custom' but in a speaker who is just it is also the 'close delation' of the heart. In Iago, of course, 'these stops' are markers of a disloyal knave, but in the play's women we are soon to find them 'close delations, working from the heart,/ That passion cannot rule'.

OTHELLO: Thy husband knew it all.
EMILIA: My husband?
OTHELLO: Thy husband.
EMILIA: That she was false?
    To wedlock?
OTHELLO: Ay, with Cassio. Had she been true,
    If heaven would make me such another world
    Of one entire and perfect chrysolite,
    I'd not have sold her for it.
EMILIA: My husband?
OTHELLO: Ay, 'twas he that told me on her first;
    An honest man he is, and hates the slime

                    That sticks on filthy deeds.
EMILIA: My husband!
OTHELLO: What needs
       This iterance, woman? I say thy husband.

                         (*Othello*, 5.2.137–46)

Part of the emotional impact of this scene rests on the conjunction of modes
of speech that ought to be kept apart: the equipoise of Othello's rolling
polysyllabic 'perfect chrysolite' and Emilia's woman's 'iterance'. Emilia,
whom Rymer calls the play's 'meanest woman' (145), speaks a language
that is at times not far removed from the domestic tragedy of a play like *A
Warning for Fair Women*, which was (as Rymer scoffingly suggests could be
true of *Othello*) based on the depositions in a murder trial.[87] Joan's discovery
of her mortally wounded fiancé—'I shall sweb, I shall swound, cut my lace,
and cover my face, I die else, it is John Beane, killd, cut, slain; maister, and
ye be a man, help' (*Warning*, TLN 1500–1) bears comparison with Emilia's
uncontrolled outpouring of grief and rage:

              Villainy, villainy, villainy!
              I think upon't, I think I smell't, O villainy!
              I thought so then: I'll kill myself for grief!

                         (*Othello*, 5.2.187–90)

This concentration on an ordinary woman's passion, combined with the
background of domestic and urban violence, must remind the audience of
popular theatre—in no other play by Shakespeare does a character from outside
the ruling classes bear the burden of tragic discovery in this way. In the speeches
of Emilia, Shakespeare achieves a fusion of the learned and the demotic. Her
phrasing ('Thou hast not half that power to do me harm/ As I have to be hurt.
O gull, O dolt' (5.2.158–9)) sits on the edge of crafted constructions such as
chiasmus and ploche but also repeatedly tips to the quotidian.

   The crossing of generic and class boundaries and the bringing together of
linguistic registers in *Othello* is purposive. In the context of rival indoor and
outdoor theatrical cultures, Shakespeare's adoption of popular alongside
comic forms within high tragedy must have been striking. The play, through
its inclusion of an aggressive male language of cuckoldry and a feminine
language of suffering, is in this respect very different from his earlier love

87. This was Arthur Golding's *Brief Discourse of the Late Murther of Master George Saunders* (1573),
    dealing with an actual crime.

tragedy, *Romeo and Juliet*, which lacks *Othello*'s elevated political action as well as its stark focus on sexual acts. On the banal level of marketability, *Othello* could have appealed equally to the company's Bankside and court audiences. But in a deeper sense the work challenged its learned constituency by taking comic precepts to unexpected conclusions. Gentlemen 'wearing rapiers' and 'afraid of goose-quills' (to quote, for the last time, Rosincrance's description) must have been shocked at where the play's rhetoric took them. When *Othello* was performed at court in 1604 its depiction of a domestic murder was, as far as we can tell, unprecedented for a royal audience; the contrast with the productions from the children's companies, which were also staged for the monarch that year, must have been stark.[88]

In the years 1599 to 1608 Shakespeare consolidated his association with the public playhouse. Having become a housekeeper in the Globe, he also became, in 1604, a King's Man through James's adoption of his company. The existence, throughout this period, of a children's theatre with a more author-centred and satirical credo brought further definition to Shakespeare's position. He adopted many elements of the drama that they had brought into fashion, but he also offered a counter-narrative to their culture of wit. *Hamlet, Henry V, All's Well that Ends Well*, and *Othello*, though they differ greatly, all express their author's cultural investment in the Globe playhouse. Each strives to unite popular and elite traditions. Each also embraces histrionic passion: whether that of the travelling players in *Hamlet*, patriotic fervour in *Henry V*, or the spectacle of women wronged in *Othello* and *All's Well*. These qualities separated Shakespeare from the literary culture of the indoor stages, and they brought him closer to his players.

The parallel with Thomas Heywood as sharer–playwright is instructive, not only because his *Apology for Actors* uniquely mirrors this strong bond between author and performer, but also because it spells out something of the moral conventions of the public stage. An earlier generation of critics, most prominently E. M. W. Tillyard, found in Shakespeare a supreme model of moral order, a perspective that today looks naive. Yet Shakespeare's investment in certain normative public values during the middle stage of his career is at one level a statistical reality—the easy acceptance of women's suffering we find in *The Two Gentlemen of Verona* or *The Taming of*

---

88. For court performances see Court Calendar in Chambers, *Elizabethan Stage*, IV, 75–130 (at 119).

the Shrew is not found here.[89] In the Globe plays the gallants and tricksters are not the heroes; there are few if any incompetent or corrupt city governors; wives and daughters are consistently chaste. Shakespeare's work, like Heywood's, restrains its irony and cynicism; it retains something of the sense of a national collective that the acting companies could trace back to the old moralities. The Poets' War of 1599–1601 involved a challenge to those values and Shakespeare, across many of the works that he produced in that period, offered a challenge in return. Hamlet is not Shakespeare, but the Prince's views on the travelling players must be close to his company's: 'let them be well used, for they are the abstract and brief chronicles of the time' (*Hamlet* Q2, 2.2.461–2).

89. The concluding scenes of these two comedies are notoriously problematic for modern audiences: in *Two Gentlemen* Valentine blithely resigns 'all that was mine in Silvia' to his friend Proteus who has just attempted to rape her and Katherine counsels women to 'place your hands below your husband's foot'—these are sentiments not likely to resurface in the context of opposition to the children's stage. See William Shakespeare, *The Two Gentlemen of Verona*, ed. William C. Carroll, Arden3 (London: Thompson, 2004), 5.4.83, and *The Taming of the Shrew*, ed. Brian Morris, Arden2 (London: Methuen, 1981), 5.2.178.

II
Richard Burbage

There is but one recorded expression of grief upon the death of William Shakespeare: the epitaph by William Basse that places the poet beside Chaucer, Spenser, and Beaumont as a 'rare tragedian'.[1] Although these verses were quite widely distributed in manuscript it was not until seven years later, with the publication of the First Folio by the company's surviving founding fellows, that there came a broader public response to the nation's loss. The case of Shakespeare's leading actor was different—so voluminous were the declarations of regret that they caused a minor scandal because they reputedly dwarfed the recognition of the death of Queen Anne, which also occurred in 1619.[2] British Library manuscript Stowe 962, a miscellany largely put together in the 1620s and 1630s, contains the earliest of the surviving elegies for Burbage, which it attributes to John Fletcher.[3] It is an indication of the relative neglect of Shakespeare's actors as influences on the playwright that no direct transcription of this manuscript has been printed in full.[4]

1. See William Basse, 'On Mr Wm. Shakespeare he dyed in Aprill 1616' in E. K. Chambers, *William Shakespeare: A Study of Facts and Problems*, 2 vols. (Oxford: Clarendon Press, 1930; repr. 1988), II, 226.
2. See Edwin Nungezer, *A Dictionary of Actors* (Ithaca, NY: Cornell University Press, 1929), 73, who provides a detailed overview of the elegies.
3. 'An Elegy on the Death of the Famous Actor Rich: Burbage', British Library, MS Stowe 962, fols. 62ᵇ–63ᵇ. The manuscript also contains a version of Basse's epitaph on fols. 78ᵇ–79ᵃ. For commentary on the collection as a whole see Mary Hobbs, *Early Seventeenth-Century Verse Miscellany Manuscripts* (Aldershot: Scholar Press, 1992) 87–90, 94, and also Lara M. Crowley, 'Was Southampton a Poet? A Verse Letter to Queen Elizabeth [with text]', *English Literary Renaissance* 41 (2011), 111–45 (at 112–20). For a transcription of the elegy in its first printed version, plus confirmation of its authenticity, see G. P. Jones, '*A Burbage Ballad* and John Payne Collier', *Review of English Studies* 40 (1989), 393–7.
4. Jones, '*Burbage Ballad*', transcribes and validates the earliest printed copy, which excludes lines 13–17 of the Stowe 962 version, but, oddly, does not discuss the earlier manuscript. Glynne Wickham, Herbert Berry, and William Ingram, eds., *English Professional Theatre, 1530–1660* (Cambridge: Cambridge University Press, 2000), 181–3, transcribes Huntington HM 198, 99–101.

MS Stowe 962 is a sophisticated literary collection that probably emanates from Christ Church, Oxford. It contains reliable early copies of work by Donne, Carew, and Jonson, as well as speeches and letters on political topics that reflect an elevated coterie. The appearance of a lengthy and splendidly laudatory elegy on Richard Burbage in such company is noteworthy.[5] Although the poem is well known, its unique qualities are worth highlighting. No other early modern actor was the subject of such posthumous adulation.[6] Contemporary acknowledgement was made of the talents of important players such as Richard Tarlton, Edward Alleyn, William Kemp, Thomas Greene, and Robert Armin, but none was praised in such detail or by such a wide constituency. In his lifetime Burbage was depicted on stage in *The Second Part of the Return from Parnassus* at St John's College Cambridge and in the Induction to Marston's *The Malcontent* at the Globe. Jonson in *Bartholomew Fair*, performed at the Hope by Lady Elizabeth's players, called him the 'best actor'; Webster took him as the model for his prose description of 'an excellent actor'; and Middleton, in another obituary poem, termed Burbage 'that great master in his art'.[7] At the very highest level, the Earl of Pembroke, dedicatee of the First Folio, 'could not endure to see' another play soon after the loss of Burbage.[8] Middleton called this an 'eclipse of playing' and the memory of his excellence would live on in theatrical circles for generations to come.

The first point to note is Burbage's outstanding ability, a skill in performance rooted in verisimilitude—'so truly to the life' as the elegy stresses.[9]

---

5. Another instance is the elegy for Burbage found in the commonplace book of William Parkhurst (d. 1667), which is attributed to Ben Jonson. See Brandon S. Centerwall, '"Tell me Who Can when a Player Dies": Ben Jonson's Epigram on Richard Burbage, and How it was Lost to the Canon', *Ben Jonson Journal* 4 (1997), 27–34.

6. Jonson's epigram on Alleyn was written while its subject was still living and is also much more restrained. The closest parallel is Heywood's address to 'my entirely beloved Fellow' Thomas Greene, who was the lead comic actor of his company (see Heywood's preface to John Cooke, *Greenes Tu quoque, or The Cittie Gallant* (1614), A2ᵃ).

7. See Ben Jonson, *Bartholomew Fair*, ed. G. R. Hibbard, New Mermaids (London: A. & C. Black, 1977), 5.3.75. Webster's sketch appears in the expanded version of Thomas Overbury's *Characteristics* entitled *Sir Thomas Overburie his Wife* (1616), M2ᵃ–M3ᵃ, and can be linked to Burbage because of its reference to painting, for which the actor was also celebrated. On the attribution of this part of the text to Webster, see E. K. Chambers, *The Elizabethan Stage*, 4 vols. (Oxford: Clarendon Press, 1923; repr. 2009), IV, 257–8. For Middleton's elegy, see his *Collected Works*, ed. Gary Taylor and John Lavagnino (Oxford: Clarendon Press, 2007), 1889.

8. See Mary Edmond, 'Yeomen, Citizens, Gentlemen, and Players: The Burbages and their Connections', in R. B. Parker and S. P. Zitner, eds., *Elizabethan Theater: Essays in Honor of S. Schoenbaum* (Newark: University of Delaware Press, 1996), 30–49 (at 41).

9. 'An Elegy on the death', British Library, MS Stowe 962, fol. 62ᵇ.

Figure 8. Reputed portrait of Richard Burbage, Dulwich Picture Gallery, London.

Second, there is a marked emphasis on tragedy. Although Burbage was also a comic actor, taking the lead in Jonson's *Volpone* for example, his reputation was established above all through serious performance. MS Stowe 962 declares that 'no man can act so well/ This point of sorrow' and counsels poets to cease writing tragedies 'since tragic parts you see/ die all with him' (fols 62^b, 63^a). This matches the depiction in the *Parnassus* trilogy (where Burbage instructs a young hopeful) and is confirmed in the list of parts for which he was celebrated: Richard III, Othello, Lear, Ferdinand in *The Duchess of Malfi* and—most of all—Hamlet.[10] The actor's pre-eminence rested in the 'true' depiction of grief.

A third aspect of Richard Burbage's impact on Shakespeare is less commonly noted. This is his financial power and role in the attainment of

10. Burbage's fame as Richard III is recorded in John Manningham's celebrated anecdote in his diary (see Chambers, *Elizabethan Stage*, II, 308); Othello, Lear, and Hamlet (and perhaps also Romeo in the 'mad lover, with so true an eye' (fol 62^b)) are mentioned in 'An Elegy on the death', British Library, MS Stowe 962; Burbage is listed as the first Ferdinand in the 1623 quarto of *The Duchess of Malfi*, A2^b.

patronage. Richard and his brother Cuthbert had a family partnership that bore comparison with that of Alleyn and Henslowe. Their father James was, as Cuthbert proudly proclaimed, 'the first builder of playhouses' in England: not only the Theatre at Shoreditch but also the indoor stage at Blackfriars owed their construction to his sense of enterprise.[11] James made investments, based on substantial borrowing, that bore fruit for his children.[12] Equally important, he was, like Edward Alleyn, a theatrical insider. The family had performance experience dating back to the 1540s and James had been a leading member of the first truly famous travelling company, the Earl of Leicester's Men.[13] As with Alleyn's close connection with Lord Howard, this ability to call upon support from members of the high nobility was essential for the long-term success of a company. Cuthbert, the eldest son and chief financier, secured employment with Sir Walter Cope, Gentleman Usher to the Lord Treasurer, who was closely associated with the Cecils. Although Leeds Barroll has rightly cautioned against an overestimate of the closeness between players and court patrons, it was impossible for a dramatic enterprise to function without high-level support.[14] For the Burbage duo, just as with the Alleyn–Henslowe business, associations at court helped to smooth the way at moments of conflict, such as the time when Cuthbert was fighting a legal action for the survival of the Globe in the years 1599–1601.[15]

11. Cuthbert's account of his father comes as part of the case against a group of King's Men sharers heard in 1635; for a transcription see C. C. Stopes, *Burbage and Shakespeare's Stage* (London: Alexander Moring, 1913), 131–4, 237–9.

12. Cuthbert specifies 'many hundreds of pounds taken up at interest' in his dispute with the actors; they counter with claims about his great wealth (Stopes, *Burbage*, 233–42 (237–8)).

13. See Edmond, 'Yeomen, Citizens'. Details in the rest of this paragraph are partly drawn from Edmond's article.

14. Barroll, in *Politics, Plague, and Shakespeare's Theater* (Ithaca, NY: Cornell University Press, 1991), 23–69, argues that direct court patronage was limited, but in Barroll, 'Shakespeare, Noble Patrons, and the Pleasures of "Common" Playing', in Paul Whitfield White and Suzanne R. Westfall, eds., *Shakespeare and Theatrical Patronage in Early Modern England* (Cambridge: Cambridge University Press, 2002), 90–121, he also demonstrates how important a variety of input from aristocratic connections could be.

15. Alleyn MSS 9 (Diary and Account Book of Edward Alleyn) provides extensive documentary evidence for such lobbying. In this manuscript Alleyn records his movements and expenditure in the period from 29 September 1617 to 1 October 1622. He regularly meets with aristocratic patrons as well as players and business associates. In July 1622, for example, Alleyn is very busy consulting interested parties in a new contract for the Fortune playhouse and on the 12th of that month he records a meeting 'with my Lord of Arundel' in which he 'showed the Fortune plot' (MSS 9, fol. 59ª). For a full study, see S. P. Cerasano, 'The Patronage Network of Philip Henslowe and Edward Alleyn', *Medieval and Renaissance Drama in England* 13 (2000), 82–92; Cerasano, 'Cheerful Givers: Henslowe, Alleyn, and the 1612 Loan Book to the Crown', *Shakespeare Studies* 28 (2000), 215–19; and also Cerasano, 'The Geography of Henslowe's Diary', *Shakespeare Quarterly* 56 (2005), 328–53 (at 340, 347). There are many indications of

We get a glimpse of this occluded aspect of Shakespeare's professional life from a chance survival in the accounts of Francis Manners, sixth Earl of Rutland (whose brother, Roger, the fifth Earl, had been so obstructive to the Theatre): in 1613 Shakespeare designed an impresa for him, which was painted in gold by Richard Burbage, so it could be worn in the accession day tilts.[16] Such personal connection with the nobility evidently depended on the two brothers: in a surviving letter to Robert Cecil, for example, Cope reports as follows:

> Burbage is come and says there is no new play that the Queen hath not seen, but they have revived an old one called *Loves Labour Lost*, which for wit and mirth he says will please her exceedingly. And this is appointed to be played tomorrow night at my Lord of Southampton's, unless you send a writ to remove the *corpus cum causa* to your house in Strand. Burbage is my messenger ready attending your pleasure.[17]

The 'Burbage' in question here is most likely Cuthbert, but the brothers were first housemates and then immediate neighbours and evidently worked hand in glove.

The events of 1599–1600 made Richard Burbage much more important to Shakespeare. The departure of Kemp left him the undisputed leading performer of the company and this dominance was reinforced by a massive increase in his financial investment in his own acting career. Richard and Cuthbert owned the old materials that were used in the new playhouse and it was they who had organized the lease of the land. Together the brothers held a 50 per cent stake in the enterprise, whereas Shakespeare, like the other ordinary housekeepers, held only one-tenth. Thus the playwright, by becoming a Globe sharer, had made a personal commitment to Richard Burbage. From this point on he was a stakeholder in a company of which

comparable activity by the Burbage brothers. Giles Allen, the litigant against the Globe housekeepers, made wild claims about bribery of legal officials by Cuthbert Burbage. Though the accusations are improbable, the proceedings do bear witness to the extensive connections that Cuthbert could call on in the courts and city institutions. For transcripts see Stopes, *Burbage*, 217–27, and, more fully, Charles W. Wallace, 'The First London Theatre: Materials for a History', *University Studies of the University of Nebraska* 13 (1913), 1–297 (at 181–290).

16. For the impresa see Samuel Schoenbaum, *William Shakespeare: A Documentary Life* (Oxford: Clarendon Press, 1975), 220, and on the legal action see Earl of Rutland against Allen and Burbage, Mich. 42 Eliz, 1599, Exchequer Bills and Answers, Eliz. 369, printed in Stopes, *Burbage*, 184–90 (at 185).

17. Hatfield Hist. MSS iii.148, printed in Chambers, *Elizabethan Stage*, iv, 139. A similar record exists for a performance at Wilton, but as no manuscript survives its veracity is open to doubt (Chambers, *Facts and Problems*, ii, 329).

the Burbages had near majority ownership. It was the Burbage brothers who took the lead in the move to the Bankside and Shakespeare's decision to join them would prove a pivotal one.

One basic way of measuring the effect of Richard Burbage's new status is to measure the size of the roles that Shakespeare wrote for him. In the years 1594 to 1598, when the power balance between sharers was relatively equal, so too was the division of parts. In no play did the lead role take more than a quarter of the line total and on average the largest part had less than a fifth of the overall lines.[18] In plays that can be dated from 1599 to 1608, starting with *Henry V*, the division is very different: eight of the fourteen plays written in that period have a lead who speaks over a quarter of the line total, and major parts such as Henry V, Hamlet, Macbeth, Timon, and Duke Vincentio in *Measure for Measure* speak more than 30 per cent of the whole. The lead part from 1599 onwards, moreover, is almost always suited to Burbage. In the first five years of the fellowship the leading roles, in terms of line length, included Helena in *A Midsummer Night's Dream*, Portia in *Merchant of Venice*, and Falstaff in *Henry IV Part 1*, *Henry IV Part 2*, and *The Merry Wives of Windsor*—none of these are parts that Burbage could have played. Although we cannot always be sure of which parts were taken by him, the situation after 1599 was markedly different. There are eleven dominant roles in the plays dated 1599–1608, which on average take 29 per cent of the lines: of this total, nine are strongly suited to what we know of Richard Burbage's style.[19]

Such line counts are only one form of evidence, but they do confirm what is apparent simply from overview. In the second phase of the company's history, with the Globe as a permanent place of performance, the major male roles become both more dominant and more distinctive: Henry V, Hamlet, Othello, Lear, Macbeth, Timon, Antony, and Coriolanus are all a product of this time. There is not in all cases proof positive that these parts

---

18. All line counts are based on T. J. King, *Casting Shakespeare's Plays: London Actors and their Roles, 1590–1642* (Cambridge: Cambridge University Press, 1992); the calculation of percentages is mine.

19. These are Henry V (33.0%); Brutus in *Julius Caesar* (27.9%); Hamlet in Q2 (36.4%); Duke Vincentio in *Measure* (30.0%); Lear in Q1 (22.3%); Macbeth (30.8%); Timon (35.2%); Antony in *Antony and Cleopatra* (24.1%); and Coriolanus (24.3%). From the Stowe MS elegy it is clear that Burbage played Othello rather than Iago, the largest role in that play, but the eponymous hero's part nearly matches the villain's (it is 78.6% of Iago's, which is 31.9% of the whole). Only *Twelfth Night*, *Troilus*, and *All's Well* lack such a dominant speaker, although the role for Burbage is still likely to have been large.

were taken by Burbage, but the likelihood is overwhelmingly strong. Later company history shows us these roles were considered as a unit, to be taken by the ensemble's leading man.[20] Pre-eminence in major productions was evidently prized by the players;[21] so that even if we cannot trace it in every detail, the effect upon Shakespeare's writing of Burbage's strengthened position was immediate and profound.

One role that we can be certain was written for Burbage is Hamlet. At 1338 lines in the Second Quarto, it is by some measure the largest part in the Shakespeare canon and more than double the length of any play's leading role between 1594 and 1599. Even in Burbage's lifetime the role was legendary. In *Ratseis Ghost*, an anonymous pamphlet published in 1605, the 'one man' who plays Hamlet is presented as the apogee of his profession, a figure whose parts are the most demanding in the repertory and whose 'money', 'dignity', and 'reputation' are destined to earn him 'some place or lordship in the country'.[22] That prophecy, though tinged with anti-theatrical resentment, was not unrealistic: on a scale that was grander than that of Shakespeare and the other fellows in the Chamberlain's/King's Men the Burbage family acquired a country residence in addition to their London property and had strong bonds of connection with the higher echelons of power.[23] *Hamlet*, as the title page of the First Quarto reminded its readers, was 'diverse times acted by his highness' servants in the City of London as also in the two universities of Cambridge and Oxford and elsewhere'; it thus functioned in elite circles as the calling card of its leading man.

The character of Hamlet must have emerged as a corollary of Burbage's pre-eminence. More than this, when combined with external evidence on the actor's roles and reputation, it provides significant insight into the way that Burbage performed. At the heart of this stands the Prince's first oration, which Shakespeare penned in full knowledge of the capacities of the person for whom it was meant:

20. See King, *Casting*, 17–18, 48; Simon Palfrey and Tiffany Stern, *Shakespeare in Parts* (Oxford: Oxford University Press, 2007), 32; Stern, *Rehearsal from Shakespeare to Sheridan* (Oxford: Clarendon Press, 2000), 58.

21. See Stern, *Rehearsal*, and Palfrey and Stern, *Shakespeare in Parts*, 32, 46. As noted, James A. Riddell, 'Some Actors in Ben Jonson's Plays', *Shakespeare Studies* 5 (1969), 284–98, reports on a copy of Jonson's 1616 folio in which seventeenth-century manuscript annotations assign the leading roles of Volpone and Subtle to Burbage.

22. Anon., *Ratseis Ghost*, facsimile edition by H. B. Charlton (Manchester: Manchester University Press, 1932), A3[b].

23. For details see Edmond, 'Yeomen, Citizens', 41–9.

'Seems', madam—nay it is, I know not 'seems'.
'Tis not alone my inky cloak, cold mother,
Nor customary suits of solemn black,
Nor windy suspiration of forced breath,
No, nor the fruitful river in the eye,
Nor the dejected haviour of the visage,
Together with all forms, moods, shapes of grief,
That can denote me truly. These indeed 'seem',
For they are actions that a man might play,
But I have that within which passes show,
These but the trappings and the suits of woe.

(*Hamlet*, Q2 1.2.76–86)

These lines offer something different from the standard self-reflexivity
of Renaissance drama. It is usual for revenge tragedies to depict acts of
performance: we find this in Shakespeare's own *Titus Andronicus* and
seminally in Kyd's *Spanish Tragedy*, whose lead character Hieronimo
ends the play as an actor in a performance and tells his on-stage audience
'Haply you think, but bootless are your thoughts,/ That this is fabulously
counterfeit,/ And that we do as all tragedians do' (4.4.76–8). In plays of
this genre, including the Admiral's Men's *Lust's Dominion* and St Paul's
Boys' *Antonio's Revenge*, we find a 'play within a play' in which the revenger
suddenly reveals that his actions are real. It is logical that the lost original
Hamlet, which evidently featured a pretended madness, also contained
this element. But what Shakespeare's Hamlet opens by saying is almost
the reverse of this standard closing revelation: it is not that the performance is
real, but rather that an interior reality negates outward performance.[24]

In making this claim and in delivering his later reflections on the player's
speech about 'rugged Pyrrhus' (*Hamlet*, Q2 2.2.485–540) Burbage needed to
speak in a way that could be distinguished not just from the on-stage
'tragedians of the city' (2.2.292) but also from the words of his 'cold mother'
(as the Quarto text has it) or the portentous ranting of Laertes later in the
play. To dismiss all outward forms of grief as 'actions that a man might play'
(1.2.84) is a risky move in a tragedy, especially one like *Hamlet*, which does

---

24. There is, of course, a vast and rich tradition of commentary on Shakespeare's conception of
performance, especially in *Hamlet*. Excellent overviews highlighting some of the major studies
appear in Meredith Anne Skura, *Shakespeare the Actor and the Purposes of Playing* (Chicago:
University of Chicago Press, 1993), x–xi, and James P. Bednarz, *Shakespeare and the Poets' War*
(New York: Columbia University Press, 2001), 252.

not court the comic artificiality of *Antonio's Revenge*.[25] For the play to work the audience must at some level accept the idea that Hamlet's emotions are more real than those that are performed around him. That possibility as something achieved through Burbage's acting is clearly proclaimed in the elegy on his death:

> No man can act so well
> This point of sorrow, for him none can draw
> So truly to the life this map of woe;
> That grief's true picture.
>
> (MS Stowe 962, fol. 62[b])

This description is delivered specifically in reference to Hamlet and so cannot be dismissed as formulaic praise. It matches with the account of Richard Flecknoe, who is certainly a reliable authority and who may even have seen Burbage performing in his final years.[26] Alone among the actors of the period, Flecknoe praises Burbage at length as follows:

> He was a delightful Proteus, so wholly transforming himself into his part, and putting off himself with his clothes, as he never (not so much as in the tiring-house) assumed himself again until the play was done: there being as much difference betwixt him and one of our common actors as between a ballad singer who only mouths it and an excellent singer, who knows all his graces and can artfully vary and modulate his voice, even to know how much breath he is to give to every syllable.[27]

Not just a great orator, Burbage was, according to Flecknoe's account, a consistent embodiment of the character he was performing even when not directly involved in the action, 'never falling in his part when he had done speaking, but with his looks and gesture maintaining it still unto the

---

25. It is interesting that Bednarz (*Poets' War*, 232) should consider *Antonio's Revenge* as one of Marston's 'variations' on Shakespeare's generic choices, a reading that fits with his argument that the repertories of the indoor and outdoor playhouses were not distinct. To my understanding the modes of the plays are quite divergent. Marston, in line with the aesthetic preference of the St Paul's audience, plays up the artifice already inherent in the play's genre—for example, by making a spectacularly bloodthirsty hero (happy to kill innocent children) out of the feeble lover of *Antonio and Mellida*.

26. The poet and playwright Richard Flecknoe's date of birth is *c*.1605. Very little is known about his origins and early life, but travel to London in his teens is not inconceivable. His 'Short Discourse' is reliable on matters such as the location of the children's theatres and the first formation of acting companies.

27. Richard Flecknoe, 'A Short Discourse of the English Stage' appended to his *Love's Kingdom* (1664), G6[b]–G7[a].

height'.[28] Webster, who worked closely with Burbage and wrote while the actor was still performing, insisted that 'what we see him personate, we think truly done before us'.[29] Even more so for Thomas Bancroft, another likely contemporary witness, Burbage offers a case of total absorption in the present moment (the subject of his poem being vanity and the way material things come to obsess the worldly mind):

> Such, like our *Burbage* are, who when his part
> He acted, sent each passion to his heart;
> Would languish in a scene of love; then look
> Pallid for fear; but when revenge he took,
> Recall his blood; when enemies were nigh,
> Grow big with wrath, and make his buttons fly.[30]

It is important to be cautious of ascribing an ahistorical 'realism' to this form of acting, which is still connected to the rhetorical traditions of the age.[31] As Palfrey and Stern point out, Bancroft's praise highlights something different from straightforward verisimilitude, it is what they call the 'seemingly spontaneous change from one passion to another' that is the true mark of the actor's greatness in this account.[32] Still, the testaments to Burbage's acting do consistently credit him with an unprecedented emotional contact with the character he embodies.[33] This intensity, combined with the quality of rapid transition, sets Burbage apart from the formulaic and protracted single emotional state that is described in Hamlet's speech on 'seeming', or projected in the oration by the player that Polonius finds 'too long' (*Hamlet*, Q2 2.2.436).

28. Flecknoe, 'Short Discourse', G7[a].
29. See Overbury, *His Wife*, M2[b], and note 7 above.
30. Thomas Bancroft, *Time's Out of Tune* (1658), 44.
31. For a clear account of the connection between playing, rhetoric, and the passions in the period see Joseph R. Roach, *The Player's Passion: Studies in the Science of Acting* (Newark: University of Delaware Press, 1985).
32. Palfrey and Stern, *Shakespeare in Parts*, 312. They compare Bancroft's account with a section from Anthony Scoloker's *Daiphantus* (1604) in which the passionate lover 'Puts off his clothes; his shirt he only wears,/ Much like mad-Hamlet thus [at] passion tears' (E4[b]). Because Scoloker evidently saw Shakespeare's play in performance, it is suggested by them that these overblown histrionics may reflect those of Burbage, but it is more logical that they reflect Hamlet's action as reported by Ophelia.
33. John Russell Brown, 'On the Acting of Shakespeare's Plays', in G. E. Bentley, ed., *The Seventeenth Century Stage: A Collection of Critical Essays* (Chicago: University of Chicago Press, 1968), 41–54, argues that something approaching a new naturalism can be detected in accounts of performance at this time.

In *Hamlet* Shakespeare juxtaposes a series of different modes of acting: that of the newly revived children; the older rhyming moralities depicted in *The Murder of Gonzago*; the university drama in which Polonius 'was accounted a good actor' (Q2 3.2.96–7); and the grand pseudo-Marlovian cadences of the 'rugged Pyrrhus' (2.2.390) speech that Hamlet requests. Burbage's own performance stood alongside these and demanded attention, above all through the character's defining changeability in his interior state. To speak of Hamlet's indecision is, of course, amongst the oldest clichés of English literary criticism and Margreta de Grazia has recently offered a powerful counterblast to what can seem like a tired way of understanding this work.[34] Yet the notion of a 'transcendent inwardness' to Hamlet, which de Grazia decries as a modern invention, is not without its original historical context. The intense introspection of his soliloquies can be placed not only as a reaction to the surface artifice of the children's productions but also as a response to contrasting modes of delivery in the adult theatre world.

The Fortune playhouse, built unashamedly on the model of the new Globe, was under construction as Shakespeare wrote *Hamlet* and held its first performances while Shakespeare's new drama appeared on the stage. To launch his new theatre Edward Alleyn returned from retirement.[35] Thus, just as Shakespeare had begun to craft a new kind of role for his leading player–investor, the outstanding performer and theatrical impresario of the first half of the 1590s had re-emerged to public view. Alleyn was the original Tamburlaine, Faustus, Muly Mahamet, and mad Orlando.[36] He had also performed work by Shakespeare before the playwright joined the Chamberlain's Men and probably had a prominent role in the first performances of *Titus Andronicus*. Besides Burbage, Alleyn was the only celebrated tragic actor of this period. The two men had travelled together in 1593 during

34. Margreta de Grazia, *'Hamlet' without Hamlet* (Cambridge: Cambridge University Press, 2007).
35. For details see S. P. Cerasano, 'Edward Alleyn's "Retirement" 1597–1600', *Medieval and Renaissance Drama in England* 10 (1998), 98–112, who suggests that Alleyn may not have intended a permanent retirement when he 'left off playing' in 1597. Having established the new venue, the actor did fully retire in 1604.
36. For accounts of what is known about Alleyn's performances see S. P. Cerasano, 'Edward Alleyn, the New Model Actor, and the Rise of Celebrity in the 1590s', *Medieval and Renaissance Drama in England* 18 (2005), 47–58 and Andrew Gurr, *Shakespeare's Opposites: The Admiral's Company 1594–1625* (Cambridge: Cambridge University Press, 2009), 11–24. Alleyn's name appears in the Plot of *Battle of Alcazar* and his part as Orlando in *Orlando furioso* survives (see W. W. Greg, ed., *Henslowe Papers: Being Documents Supplementary to Henslowe's Diary* (London: A. H. Bullen, 1907),138–41, 155–71.

the closure of the theatres, but since 1594 they had been the central figures in two competing theatrical troupes.[37] Their capabilities must inevitably have been the subject of comparison, especially now that the heroic roles that had set the standard in the previous decade were to be seen anew on the London stage.

The speech that Hamlet requests from the First Player involves something more complicated than mere nostalgia because it so closely approximates the roles that Alleyn was reviving. At one point it becomes a virtual quotation from *Dido, Queen of Carthage*, a play that at some stage had been performed by the original Children of the Chapel but which was now in the repertory of the Admiral's Men.[38] In Nashe and Marlowe's play Aeneas's lengthy oration describes this part of Troy's destruction as follows:

> At last came Pyrrhus, fell and full of ire,
> His harness dropping blood, and on his spear
> The mangled head of Priam's youngest son . . .[39]

Hamlet remembers very similar lines as a prompt to the player for a speech he 'chiefly loved':

HAMLET: *The rugged Pyrrhus like th' Hyrcanian beast* . . .
—'Tis not so. It begins with Pyrrhus.
The rugged Pyrrhus, he whose sable arms,
Black as his purpose, did the night resemble . . .

(*Hamlet*, Q2 2.2.388–91)

This is not straightforward parody and it is also something different from the casual 'Marlovian' rhetoric that Shakespeare commonly deployed in his

---

37. Burbage, judging from the *Seven Deadly Sins* plot (see Greg, *Henslowe Papers*, 129–32) was at this point a hired man with Lord Strange's Men, with whom Alleyn travelled that year (see Gurr, *Opposites*, 14; Chambers, *Facts and Problems*, I, 45). As regards subsequent competition, Roslyn Lander Knutson, *Playing Companies and Commerce in Shakespeare's Time* (Cambridge: Cambridge University Press, 2001), 1–42, argues against an assumption of outright hostility, noting factors such as cooperation in performance at court.

38. Its presence in the repertory is evident from the stage properties listed for its production in Henslowe's *Diary*, for details of which see Gurr, 'The Great Divide of 1594', in *Words that Count: Essays on Early Modern Authorship in Honor of MacDonald P. Jackson*, ed. Brian Boyd (Newark: University of Delaware Press, 2004), 29–48, (at 31).

39. Christopher Marlowe (with Thomas Nashe?), *Dido, Queen of Carthage*, in Marlowe, *Complete Plays and Poems*, ed. E. D. Pendry (London: Everyman, 1976), 2.1.213–15.

Figure 9. Portrait of Edward Alleyn, Dulwich Picture Gallery, London.

pre-1594 dramas. The Prince's endorsement of the speech's quality stands curiously alongside Polonius' scepticism, making a role that must have been associated with Alleyn appear both antiquated and refined. The scene is intriguingly different from a comparable one in Jonson's *Poetaster*, which was likewise written at the highpoint of the conflict between the rival playhouses: in this play a young boy performs 'the rumbling player' as he acts out various roles associated with Alleyn, leaving the custom-starved sharer, Histrio, looking on.[40] As a comedy performed by the Children of

40. Ben Jonson, *Poetaster*, ed. Tom Cain, Revels (Manchester: Manchester University Press, 1995), 3.4.240. His speeches as the Moor (3.4.224–6; 293–9) echo Peele's *Battle of Alcazar* in which Alleyn had taken the lead role. Gurr, *Opposites*, 22n., asserts that Histrio represents

Blackfriars, *Poetaster*'s approach is essentially parodic, but *Hamlet* (a tragedy written for adults) takes a subtly different tack.

Hamlet's second great soliloquy, which is prompted by the player's oration, juxtaposed Burbage's acting with Alleyn's. As Susan Cerasano has shown, Alleyn's abilities were widely admired—his roles were marked by charismatic self-projection and the skilful delivery of heroic blank verse.[41] Edward Guilpin, who saw him perform as Cutlack the Dane (a role with particular resonance for Shakespeare's tragedy), remembered him possessed by humours, with eyes of lightning and words of thunder.[42] Hamlet offers admiration and even envy for such qualities as performed by the player:

> Tears in his eyes, distraction in his aspect,
> A broken voice, and his whole function suiting
> With forms to his conceit.
>
> (*Hamlet*, Q2 2.2.490–2)

If we accept that the 'rugged Pyrrhus' speech must bring Alleyn to mind then the allusion is partly deferential, yet the word 'forms' must also remind the audience of the first speech by Hamlet concerning 'forms, moods, shapes of grief' as 'actions that a man might play' (1.2.82, 84). Were the player to have Hamlet's cause, we are told, he would 'drown the stage with tears,/ And cleave the general ear with horrid speech' (2.2.497–8), a description that edges dangerously close to the oratorical whirlwind later condemned by the Prince in his instructions to the actors (Q2 3.2.1–43). As with the earlier speech on 'seeming', Hamlet's description of acting serves as a point of contrast that differentiates Burbage:

> Yet I,
> A dull and muddy-mettled rascal, peak
> Like John-a-dreams, unpregnant of my cause,
> And can say nothing.
>
> (*Hamlet*, Q2 2.2.501–4)

There is at this point a doubleness in operation: for while the Prince can say 'nothing', the actor who embodies him must be eloquent to an unprecedented

---

Alleyn; Bednarz, *Poets' War*, 233, thinks him 'a likely proxy' for Augustine Phillips of the Chamberlain's Men.

41. Cerasano, 'Alleyn, the New Model Actor'. On Alleyn's 'fustian' roles and his ability himself to parody them see also Gurr, *Opposites*, 22–3.

42. See Cerasano, 'Alleyn, the New Model Actor', 50.

degree, moving from indecision to sudden rage. The strange shifts of logic in this soliloquy make the representation of a conflicted interiority possible. This happens, for example, when the speaker reaches a point of break-down in his self-accusation for cowardice and comes up with the plan of testing the King's guilt by means of a play:

> Oh, vengeance!
> Why, what an ass am I! This is most brave,
> That I, the son of the dear murderèd,
> Prompted to my revenge by heaven and hell,
> Must like a whore unpack my heart with words,
> And fall a-cursing like a very drab,
> A scullion!
> Fie upon't, foh! About, my brains. Hum, I have heard
> That guilty creatures sitting at a play
> Have by the very cunning of the scene
> Been struck so to the soul . . .
>
> (*Hamlet* (conflated text), 2.2.534–44)[43]

At one level this speech fails utterly to give an adequate account of Hamlet's interior. Is he, as he proclaims, a coward? If so, then the invention of a need to test Claudius is a characteristic ploy to delay. Or is the test a sensible precaution? If this is the case then the earlier self-admonition about his cowardice has been insincere. This soliloquy forces on the audience that which de Grazia finds supremely ahistorical in critical responses to Hamlet: the notion of 'self-deceit'.[44] Her forensic scepticism on this point is useful because it highlights the innovativeness of Shakespeare's characterization. Yet to declare self-deception an impossibility is to make history close down rather than open up the joint achievement of Shakespeare and Burbage. The dysfunctional grammar of Hamlet's soliloquies is precisely what allows the speaker to move beyond mere 'seeming'. As Hamlet puts it after his meeting with the Captain from Young Fortinbras's army:

> Now whether it be
> Bestial oblivion or some craven scruple

---

43. I quote here from Philip Edwards's edition of *Hamlet* (Cambridge: Cambridge University Press, 1985), which conflates F and Q2, neither of these being in themselves sufficiently reliable at this point. Edwards includes the Folio text's 'Oh Vengeance!' (TLN 1622) set apart as a short line, which, as he says, 'emulates the Player' (142n.). On the visual distinctiveness of short lines as presented to players, see Stern and Palfrey, *Shakespeare in Parts*, 347, 370.
44. De Grazia, *Without Hamlet*, 163 (158–204).

> Of thinking too precisely on the th'event
> (A thought which quartered hath but one part wisdom
> And ever three parts coward) I do not know
> Why yet I live to say this thing's to do,
> Sith I have cause and will and strength and means
> To do't.

(Hamlet, Q2 4.4.38–45)

In this final great soliloquy (which exists only in the Quarto) Hamlet not only propounds the notion of self-deception but also shows it in action. It is plainly contradictory that he should have 'cause and will and strength and means' to perform the murder and yet fail to do it—thus his sentence never settles to express a clear meaning. This speech functions instead to go beyond mere 'seeming' because these are actions that a man, ordinarily speaking, cannot play.

In *Hamlet* Burbage went definitively beyond even the great speeches of self-doubt in Alleyn's role of Faustus. The primary achievement is of course Shakespeare's, but it should not therefore be detached from the material circumstances of his leading performer and the specific pressures on his acting company. Hamlet was and remained a defining character for Burbage, a moment of professional self-definition that set a marker for subsequent writing, not only by Shakespeare but also by other playwrights who worked for the company. It was inevitable, for example, that the philosophical, skull-contemplating heroes Vindice (of Middleton's *Revenger's Tragedy*) and Charlemont (of Tourneur's *Atheist's Tragedy*) would be written for the lead actor with Shakespeare's earlier creation in mind.[45] Burbage alone was celebrated by contemporaries specifically for his true-to-life performance. From this point on Shakespeare would write a string of plays in which the internal state of the central protagonist was an open question: the Duke in *Measure for Measure*, Othello, Lear, Macbeth, Timon, Antony, and Coriolanus. It is almost certain that all of these were written for Burbage. The great tragedian was now Shakespeare's primary partner and by the middle of the decade the dramatist would entirely abandon the writing of comedies.

---

45. Both *The Revenger's Tragedy* (1606) and *The Atheist's Tragedy* (1611?) appear to have been written for the King's Men; the lead role in each is constructed through repeated allusion to Hamlet, largely in a parodic vein.

With Burbage still more so than with Armin it was possible for Shakespeare to develop devices and characters over many years of partnership. Their names are conjoined in over a dozen theatrical documents and Burbage was one of only three London acquaintances remembered in the playwright's will.[46] A few months after the playwright's death, Burbage named what would be his only surviving son 'William'.[47] This closeness must have enabled a new level of authorial adaptation, one obvious feature of which is that Shakespeare's leads age over the course of the canon, so that eventually we come to fathers such as Pericles, Cymbeline, Leontes, and Prospero. Although we do not always have proof of the roles taken by Burbage this should not blind us to his influence. The external evidence offers coherent witness to his talents and an almost unbroken history of the plays in performance—from Joseph Taylor to Thomas Betterton through Garrick, Kean, Olivier, and beyond—is testament to his line.[48]

46. See Schoenbaum, *Documentary*, 136, 142, 150, 152, 154, 195–6, 214, 220, and 223.
47. See Edmond, 'Yeomen, Citizens', 43.
48. See, for example, *Hamlet*, ed. Robert Hapgood, Shakespeare in Production (Cambridge: Cambridge University Press, 1999), 1–96, and other books in this series for an account of continuities. Peter Holland, 'A History of Histories: From Flecknoe to Nicoll' in W. B. Worthen, ed., *Theorizing Practice: Redefining Theatre History* (Houndmills: Palgrave Macmillan, 2003), 8–29, amongst other essays in that volume, considers the difficulties and uses of the record of performance.

PHASE IV

Shakespeare in the company of playwrights again (1608–1614)

12

The events of 1608

The change in Shakespeare's style around the year 1608 has been an established dictum of criticism since a reliable chronology of the plays was established in the late nineteenth century.[1] In late plays such as *Cymbeline*, *The Winter's Tale*, and *The Tempest* the playwright seems to embrace a new dramaturgy: sudden transformations of character become common; there is more investment in spectacle; the verse is evenly lyrical; and plots tend to turn on the last-minute revelation of facts. Numerous critics have written brilliantly on these qualities. While Kenneth Muir's contention that change came 'suddenly in 1608' has been nuanced by subsequent studies, rapid stylistic change remains a point of consensus: even in the assessment of Gordon McMullan (the most sceptical of analysts) there is 'undoubtedly a Shakespearean late style'.[2] It is Russ McDonald who has most recently characterized the distinctive qualities of the late plays and his treatment of the transition is worth citing at length:

> That Shakespeare learned, as he reached professional maturity in the mid-1590s, to make his speakers sound like themselves is one of the triumphs of his craft, one of the talents for which he is celebrated and by which he is differentiated from lesser dramatists. Prince Hal, Falstaff, King Henry, Hotspur, Owen Glendower—none of these speakers will be confused with the others. Indeed, so confident of their distinctive voices is their creator that he even allows some speakers to parody others with the certainty that the audience will get the joke. Such verbal differentiation obtains throughout the middle plays, allowing the listener to distinguish among the various speakers in *Othello*, for example. However, about 1607 or so Shakespeare begins to weaken the link between

1. For a brief overview see Russ McDonald, *Shakespeare's Late Style* (Cambridge: Cambridge University Press, 2006), 9–15.
2. Kenneth Muir, *Shakespeare's Comic Sequence* (Liverpool: Liverpool University Press, 1979), 148; Gordon McMullan, *Shakespeare and the Idea of Late Writing: Authorship in the Proximity of Death* (Cambridge: Cambridge University Press, 2007), 120.

speech and speaker. The most persuasive articulation of this principle is Anne Barton's elegant analysis: 'Shakespeare has adjusted his language and dramatic art to the demands of a new mode: one in which plot, on the whole, has become more vivid and emotionally charged than character.'[3]

In place of character-based composition, McDonald argues, Shakespeare now writes in a way that is attuned to genre, above all the genre of romance. The late style, he observes, exists as much for tonal effect as for the convey-ance of meaning. Often sentences are obscurely elliptical and veer a long way from their subject only to return to a literal truth in the end. There is frequent repetition of letters, words, phrases, and rhythms, so that the overall sound of the play can have a kind of incantatory effect. Tone and the phenomenon of enchantment take priority over, indeed at times overwhelm, the articulation of specific ideas. Metaphors are introduced only to be succeeded rapidly by others, so are not articulated at length—this is what Simon Palfrey, in an earlier study, called Shakespeare's 'new world of words'.[4]

While the fact of change is widely acknowledged, its origins remain an open question. Dowden, first on the scene, attributed the 'late style' to a new contemplative wisdom in the poet: having suffered the spiritual crisis evinced in the tragedies, Shakespeare reached 'the heights' at the end of his life when he discovered a providential unity in the order of nature. Strachey, reversing this analysis (but sticking to its biographical premise) instead pictured a late, bored, disenchanted Shakespeare: a man no longer interested in character and instead toying listlessly with poetic conceits.[5] This first generation of 'late style' analysts was succeeded by a more practically minded school of theatre historians. Most prominently, Gerald Eades Bentley pressed the case for the importance of the Blackfriars playhouse: from late 1608 onwards, he pointed out, Shakespeare had the prospect of his plays being performed at this indoor venue, which his company had now acquired.[6] This meant that

3. McDonald, *Late Style*, 33–4, with quotation from Anne Barton, *Essays, Mainly Shakespearean* (Cambridge: Cambridge University Press, 1994), 168.
4. Simon Palfrey, *Late Shakespeare: A New World of Words* (Oxford: Clarendon Press, 1997), xviii, comments that in the late plays 'characters are built out of metaphoric patterns: unlike the appropriative masteries of a Mercutio, Rosalind, Falstaff, of a Hamlet or Iago, speech is now manipulated in the service of Shakespeare's supra-characterological ambitions'.
5. G. L. Strachey, 'Shakespeare's Final Period', *The Independent Review* (August 1904), 401–18 (at 415).
6. The seminal argument for this view was provided by Gerald E. Bentley, 'Shakespeare and the Blackfriars Theatre', *Shakespeare Survey* 1 (1948), 38–50. Although Bentley noted that the period of plague after August 1608 would have delayed the inception of playing he imagined

he addressed a more elite audience and composed for a space that demanded a different kind of dramaturgy. Bentley's explanation, like Dowden's, remains influential, but since the 1980s it has also become common to highlight political factors.[7] By 1608, as Jonathan Goldberg amongst others has argued, the King's Men were much more frequently involved in court employment—James I being an enthusiast for drama, with a particular passion for music, masque, and spectacle.[8] The submerged politics of the late romances (with their fortuitous discoveries and their supernatural endorsement of the established order) held a logical appeal for the sovereign, who was a more consistent theorist of monarchy than his predecessor. Instead of the religious and contemplative philosopher envisaged by Dowden, therefore, the New Historicism of Goldberg and others imagined a more starkly political Shakespearean old age.

The personal, architectural, and political explanations for the late style offered by different generations of critics remain important and must contain strands of the truth. Recent work, however, has made such explanations feel less than the whole picture. Gordon McMullan has critiqued the projection of a self-conscious 'lateness' onto Shakespeare's writing after 1608, showing such biographical readings to be not only anachronistic but also impractical given the commercial conditions of the early modern stage.[9] Likewise, although the historical context of affairs of state remains vital to our understanding, there has been a reaction against a picture of early modern literature that is too nakedly political: the idea of Shakespeare constructing a *mythos* for the consumption of James I now holds less currency than it did in previous years.[10] Most important, for my purpose, there has been a strong reaction amongst theatre historians to Bentley's ideas

a series of hypothetical 'conferences' (47) that year in which the company would have planned a change in repertory to cater for the more elite audience that had frequented the indoor stage.

7. Strong readings in this vein include Jonathan Goldberg, *James I and the Politics of Literature: Jonson, Shakespeare, Donne, and their Contemporaries* (Baltimore, MD: Johns Hopkins University Press, 1983) and Leonard Tennenhouse, 'Family Rites: Patriarchal Strategies in Shakespearean Romance', in Kiernan Ryan, ed., *Shakespeare: The Last Plays* (London: Longman, 1999), 43–60.
8. See Gary Schmidgall, *Shakespeare and the Courtly Aesthetic* (Berkeley: University of California Press, 1983).
9. McMullan, *Idea of Late Writing*.
10. David Norbrook, '"What cares these roarers for the name of king?": Language and Utopia in *The Tempest*', in Kiernan Ryan, ed., *Shakespeare: The Last Plays* (London: Longman, 1999), 245–78, critiques colonial and royalist readings, seeing a more dissenting politics in the late work. For critiques of some of New Historicism's assumptions about early modern theatre's political orientation, plus a subtly different approach to the playwright's relation to his monarch, see David Scott Kastan, *Shakespeare after Theory* (London: Routledge, 1999),

about adaptation to Blackfriars.[11] True, greater emphasis on the effect of music, plus the introduction of act divisions are perceptible developments; it is also arguable that Shakespeare worked to address the more gentlemanly audience that frequented this place. Yet the record we have of post-1608 performance still gives the Globe primacy. It was there that Simon Forman saw *Cymbeline* and *The Winter's Tale* and where *Henry VIII* had its calamitous first performance, which led to the fire that burned down the first incarnation of this theatre. Although the set that frequented Blackfriars as a children's venue may have enjoyed artifice and satire, this does not mean that the King's Men lacked experience with elite audiences: even the distinguished foreign dignitary Prince Lewis Frederick of Württemberg was happy to go to the Bankside to see *Othello* when he visited London in the spring of 1610.[12]

Shakespeare's plays after 1608, then, were not necessarily pitched at a Blackfriars audience; indeed the majority of the acknowledged 'late plays' were written before this playhouse became operational for the King's Men.[13] No playtext before *The Tempest*, Gurr has argued, was written by Shakespeare specifically for the indoor theatre, and even it was most memorably performed at the Globe.[14] William Percy, writing in 1601, thought spectacle and magic physically unsuited to the indoor theatre: in the manuscript of one of his plays, *Mahomet and his Heaven*, he offered the restrained alternative of a 'dance of the winds' to replace a storm scene in case the work was taken up for performance by boys.[15] *The Tempest*'s spectacular opening scene and other magical stage

esp. 109–47, 165–97, and Colin Burrow, 'Reading Tudor Writing Politically: The Case of *2 Henry IV*', *Yearbook of English Studies* 28 (2008), 234–50.

11. See, for example, Roslyn Lander Knutson, 'What if there wasn't a "Blackfriars Repertory"?', in Paul Menzer, ed., *Inside Shakespeare: Essays on the Blackfriars Stage* (Selinsgrove, PA: Susquehanna University Press, 2006), 54–60, which argues against the distinctiveness of the King's Men's Blackfriars plays.

12. For a recent account of these performances see Leeds Barroll, 'Shakespeare and the Second Blackfriars Theater', *Shakespeare Studies* 33 (2005), 156–70 (at 165).

13. See Barroll, 'Blackfriars Theater', which shows how late Blackfriars became available to Shakespeare.

14. Andrew Gurr, '*The Tempest*'s Tempest at Blackfriars', *Shakespeare Survey* 41 (1989), 91–102, notes that the play is not only musical but also the first of Shakespeare's dramas conceived unequivocally with act breaks in mind. This point about act divisions is endorsed by Gary Taylor and John Jowett, *Shakespeare Reshaped: 1606–1623* (Oxford: Clarendon Press, 1993), 21.

15. See Alnwick Castle, MS Percy 507, *Mahomet and his Heaven*, fol. 38ᵇ–fol. 39ᵇ [foliation mine] and also William Percy, *Mahomet and his Heaven*, ed. Matthew Dimmock (Aldershot: Ashgate, 2006), 166. Although Percy is hoping to have his play performed at the smaller stage at St Paul's, it is evident that he thinks more broadly about a distinction between the indoor stage and production values 'for actors' (as opposed to boys) outdoors.

tricks are therefore very far from being conventional fare for Blackfriars. Looking back at the successes of the preceding years of the boys' stages one would not logically recommend Shakespeare to begin at this venue with romances, but rather with satiric comedy or burlesque revenge. It is difficult to argue, therefore, that the marked change in Shakespeare's writing in 1608 has its origins in a physical change of scene.

If the shift in Shakespeare's style just before the turn of the decade cannot adequately be accounted for by the existing explanations, what else changed for the playwright? One answer that presents itself is an alteration in his daily patterns of work. It was, I have argued, a new connection with the players that first facilitated what McDonald calls the 'professional maturity [of] the mid-1590s'. So if the late plays evince a weakening of 'the link between speech and speaker', might the cause be a weakening of the link between the players and Shakespeare himself? Although neat, this suggestion feels at first sight like an absurd one, because Shakespeare, by investing in Blackfriars, is generally thought to have reached the apotheosis of his investment as a company man. Given the correlation between the change of style and change of circumstance, however, that assumption is worth examining afresh.

To begin with, it is important to establish the nature of the Blackfriars venture. As is often observed, it appears that James Burbage (Richard's father) had always intended the old monastic hall in this liberty of the city as the site for an adult playhouse.[16] In 1596 he had bought the building (which by then had been subdivided into multi-purpose apartments) for £600. He had stripped out seven residential sets to create a space not unlike a modern theatre: it had galleries and also floor-level seating and its audience sat in semi-darkness watching a small stage that was illuminated by candles as well as by natural light from above.[17] The playhouse was thus a

16. The whole history of the Blackfriars as a venue for playing is covered in Charles William Wallace, *The Evolution of the English Drama up to Shakespeare with a History of the First Blackfriars Theatre* (Berlin: Georg Reimer, 1912), which transcribes many original documents. Irwin Smith, *Shakespeare's Blackfriars Playhouse: its History and its Design* (London: Peter Owen, 1966) is clearer in its narrative and incorporates some new work by Chambers and others. Very largely, however, he and other scholars remain dependent on Wallace as a primary source. Herbert Berry, *Shakespeare's Playhouses* (New York: AMS Press, 1987), 19–44, has made a survey of Wallace's transcriptions and finds him very reliable. Much of the account below is based on Wallace, *Evolution*, although I reference other sources where relevant. Where Berry, in Wickham, Berry, and Ingram, eds., *English Professional Theatre* (Cambridge: Cambridge University Press, 2000), provides a document transcription I make citations to his text.
17. A detailed description complete with floor plans is given in E. K. Chambers, *The Elizabethan Stage* (Oxford: Clarendon Press, 1923; repr. 2009), II, 475–515.

bigger, grander version of the venue used by the boys in the grounds of St Paul's Cathedral.[18] It was situated in an established centre for up-market entertainment near the Inns of Court, where fashionable young men resided. An earlier children's playhouse had been a success in this area (its old premises were now occupied by the Pipe Office, where important legal documents of the Chamberlains of the Exchequer were kept).[19] The large suite of connecting rooms that Burbage purchased also housed the fencing academy founded by the Italian master Rocco Bonetti, and Blackfriars had been the home of a dance school in the recent past.[20] The whole precinct was thus a prestige location for legal business, residence, and recreation— the ideal site for a theatre to house the Chamberlain's Men.

James Burbage's venture, however, was immediately blocked by a local petition, and Richard, who inherited it soon after, rented the space to Henry Evans for performances by the Chapel Boys.[21] This, then, was the playhouse where the children performed Jonson's *Cynthia's Revels* and *Poetaster* and Chapman's *Widow's Tears* and *Monsieur D'Olive*. It was also the enterprise that Marston joined after Evans first hit trouble and which put on his *Dutch Courtesan* and *Insatiate Countess*. The venue thus had pedigree but also a history of scandal, including productions of the politically disastrous *Philotas* by Samuel Daniel and the co-authored *Eastward Ho*. Evans himself was perhaps the greatest liability because in 1601 he had been castigated in Star Chamber for child kidnap after imprisoning the son of a well-to-do Norfolk gentleman, Henry Clifton, and forcing the child, under the threat of a beating, to appear on the stage.[22] Clifton, who was persistent and had

---

18. On the cathedral space see W. Reavley Gair, *The Children of Paul's: The Story of a Theatre Company, 1553–1608* (Cambridge: Cambridge University Press, 1982), 10–50.
19. Wallace, *Evolution*, 195.
20. Wallace, *Evolution*, 187–94. C. C. Stopes, *Burbage and Shakespeare's Stage* (London: Alexander Moring, 1913), 170–4, provides a transcript of the contract, from which it is evident that the fencing school still has a tenant and that various other respectable tenants remain in the property that James Burbage has bought.
21. Both Evans and Lord Hunsdon had a history as property speculators in the precinct. Hunsdon's signing of the petition, an oddity given his position as patron, may well have been the result of his frustrated ambitions as a purchaser. Wallace, *Evolution*, 164–95, traces the complex history of financial competition in this area involving Hunsdon, Evans, the Burbages, and others. For additional information see M. E. Smith, 'Personnel at the Second Blackfriars: Some Biographical Notes', *Notes & Queries* 25 (1978), 441–4, and Barroll, 'Blackfriars Theater'.
22. For the clearest account of these events see Joseph Quincy Adams, *Shakespearean Playhouses* (Boston, MA: Houghton Mifflin, 1917), 210–14.

contacts, pursued a campaign against Evans that eventually forced him to withdraw his public association with the performing company—a point of crisis at which Marston probably joined. There were, however, soon other causes for outrage and, following complaints from the French ambassador about the performance of Chapman's *Charles, Duke of Byron* in March 1608, King James determined that the boys 'should never play more but should first beg their bread'.[23] Apparently without the prospect of an income from the property, Evans was now prepared to surrender his lease to Burbage and this occurred in August of that year.

It is often said that Shakespeare became a sharer or co-owner of the Blackfriars playhouse, but this is not strictly accurate.[24] At the Globe he owned part of the fabric of the building and also had a stake in the long-term lease of the ground. Blackfriars, however, always remained a Burbage property. What happened in 1608 is that Shakespeare and six others, including Richard Burbage (who thus became his own tenant), took over Evans's rental agreement.[25] Quite possibly he was not required to pay up front for this transaction: in a later set of legal papers we hear that Heminges and Condell, at least, had their portions 'for nothing'.[26] If so, this was not an act of wild generosity, because although at times a lease could be tradable it was also a potential liability.[27] Not only did Shakespeare and his co-signatories agree to share payment of a rent of £40 per annum to Burbage, they were also responsible for the property's upkeep.[28] With Blackfriars about to lose its

23. For details see George Chapman, *The Conspiracy and Tragedy of Charles Duke of Byron*, ed. John Margeson, Revels (Manchester: Manchester University Press, 1988), 4, and also Chambers, *Elizabethan Stage*, II, 53–5. Chambers's account shows that the case was a little more complicated: in fact two separate plays caused offence and the company may possibly have been allowed to return to Blackfriars for a spell.

24. Andrew Gurr, 'London's Blackfriars Playhouse and the Chamberlain's Men', in Paul Menzer, ed., *Inside Shakespeare: Essays on the Blackfriars Stage* (Selinsgrove, PA: Susquehanna University Press, 2006), 17–30, for example, refers to 'equivalent shares in the Blackfriars' (27) for the Globe housekeepers.

25. Smith, *Shakespeare's Blackfriars*, 245, lists the seven original lessees as Richard Burbage, John Heminges, William Shakespeare, Cuthbert Burbage, Henry Condell, William Sly, and a new man named Thomas Evans. 'Thomas', in the hand of the scribe, may be an error for 'Henry' or this may have been a relative acting as proxy for the original tenant. On the difference between the Blackfriars and Globe deals see Richard Berry, 'Playhouses, 1560–1660', in Wickham, Berry, and Ingram, eds., *English Professional Theatre*, 287–674 (at 502–3).

26. See Stopes, *Burbage*, 133.

27. Wallace, *Evolution*, 186–7, transcribes documents that refer to John Lyly's sale of leases in Blackfriars, but it is evident that these leases were nevertheless a financial burden on Lyly at this time. Evans had signed a £400 bond on commencement of occupation and that arrangement is likely to have been maintained (see Berry, 'Playhouses', 502).

28. Adams, *Playhouses*, 225.

protected status as a liberty this was a risky commitment.[29] While ultimately Blackfriars would become London's most prestigious and profitable theatre, with actors clamouring to join the partnership, this was not inevitable at the point when Shakespeare signed up. Indeed if, as is sometimes suggested, the playwright dropped out of the syndicate within a year and a half of the agreement, then he must have made a substantial loss on the deal.[30]

It might seem logical that signing the lease increased Shakespeare's personal connection with his actors. This, however, was not necessarily the case. William Sly, one of the Chamberlain's founding fellows, died within a week of joining the venture and was not replaced.[31] Of the six remaining signatories, four (the playwright included) had been performers, but two of these were at or near the end of their days on the stage. Shakespeare had long since ceased appearing in acting lists and his fellow John Heminges was listed only twice in the Blackfriars period, for the last time in 1611.[32] This meant that only half of the Blackfriars tenants were regular performers—a situation very different from that of 1599 at the Globe.

The Blackfriars investment, in fact, crystallized a separation between house-keepers and mere actors that had been in progress for some time. For while the group of player–housekeepers had dwindled, the acting fellowship had got larger and younger. In 1604 the number of company sharers had expanded from eight to a dozen, so that by the time the new theatre syndicate was put together only a quarter of its members were founding Chamberlain's men.[33]

29. Blackfriars was subsumed under the authority of the city barely a month after the rental agreement, a prospect of which the signatories were surely aware (see Barroll, 'Blackfriars Theater', 166). The financial danger of the situation was genuine. Edward Alleyn eventually made similar deals involving members of the Admiral's/Palsgrave's Men for the lease of the Fortune, first in October 1618 and then again after a fire destroyed it in December 1621. In both cases the lessees suffered as a result of disaster. In the case of the second syndicate, the outbreak of the Civil War brought an end to playing in London, yet Dulwich College (to which Alleyn assigned the bulk of his assets) continued to pursue members for the payment of rent (see Alleyn Papers, MSS 18, fols. 140–218). The nature of these deals and the likely decline of Palsgrave's Men as a consequence is analysed in G. E. Bentley, *The Jacobean and Caroline Stage*, 7 vols. (Oxford: Clarendon Press, 1941–68), I, 137–54.

30. On this possibility, given his absence as a name in the February 1610 court case, see E. K., *William Shakespeare: A Study of Facts and Problems*, 2 vols. (Oxford: Clarendon Press, 1930; repr. 1988), II, 68.

31. Smith, *Shakespeare's Blackfriars*, 245.

32. See Chambers, *Facts and Problems*, II, 72–4; Shakespeare's last recorded appearance is in Jonson's *Sejanus* of 1603. It is generally concluded that the 'stuttering' Heminges of the Globe fire ballad of 1613 is a man no longer likely to act.

33. See Chambers, *Facts and Problems*, I, 76–82, and II, 71–87. The royal patent of 1603 lists eight sharers (Laurence Fletcher's name being considered honorific) but by the summer of 1604 the list of Grooms of the Chamber had increased to twelve (Chambers, *Facts and Problems*, I,

In 1608 former boys from Blackfriars were, as Cuthbert Burbage put it, 'taken to strengthen the King's service'.[34] Cuthbert's phrase is revealing. Technically he meant that the new arrivals were made sharers, but, under the new financial structure of the company, sharing in the King's Men was not quite the privileged position that it had formerly been.

At a personal level Shakespeare is less likely to have had an intimate acquaintance with players like William Ostler and John Underwood, who joined from the Chapel Boys in 1608: in contrast to the founding fellows of 1594, these late arrivals never make an appearance in the poet's transactions and they were not remembered in his will.[35] Financial power, moreover, now resided with housekeepers much more than it did with mere sharers (a pattern that is also in evidence in other companies at this time). There are signs that the new men felt alienated from their elders. Many years later, in 1635, the younger actors would launch a legal appeal against the housekeepers in the Globe and Blackfriars, accusing them of exploiting their labour. 'Actors', they reasoned, had their income diluted into twelve parts and had to bear the costs of wages to hired men, apparel, play-purchases, lighting, and other charges; 'housekeepers', in contrast, were but six in number and made unreasonable profits at the players' expense.[36] The origins of this conflict can be traced back to the 1608 lease of Blackfriars. This deal broke the performers' majority stakeholding, which had been a foundational principle of the Chamberlain's Men.

The formation of the new playhouse syndicate and the incorporation of new actors distanced Shakespeare from the majority of the working players. Plague, also starting in August 1608, is certain to have strengthened that tendency. From that date until February 1610 the theatres were closed because of the high level of mortality; it proved the longest unbroken prohibition of Shakespeare's career.[37] Even in February 1610, when playing briefly resumed,

79–80). Andrew Gurr, *The Shakespearean Stage, 1574–1642*, 3rd edn (Cambridge: Cambridge University Press, 1992), 44, suggests a two-stage process and dates the expansion to twelve to 1603 on the questionable authority of T. W. Baldwin, *The Organization and Personnel of the Shakespearian Company* (Princeton, NJ: Princeton University Press, 1927), 52. The remaining founding sharers in late 1608 were Burbage, Shakespeare, and Heminges (Condell having first joined the company as a hired man).

34. Stopes, *Burbage*, 132.

35. See Samuel Schoenbaum, *William Shakespeare: A Documentary Life* (Oxford: Clarendon Press, 1975), 224–7; 242–9.

36. For a transcript of this action see Stopes, *Burbage*, 230–40. On this dispute see also Smith, *Shakespeare's Blackfriars*, 276.

37. Records on theatre closings are lacking for some parts of the period, but comparison of death toll figures with those during inhibitions in other plague years suggests that the London

the playwright was not there when members of the syndicate were involved in legal action, so presumably he was away from London at this time.[38] Throughout that year playing was fitful: Lent was always a time of restriction and, after a short reopening, there was again a period of closure from July until December of 1610.[39] Touring was also highly restricted.[40] August 1608, therefore, marked the beginning of a two-year stretch during which Shakespeare would have little involvement in the production of plays.

The lower level of involvement of players in the Blackfriars syndicate; the 50 per cent dilution of the King's Men's acting shares; and the sustained period of pestilence—all these taken together, must greatly have lessened Shakespeare's practical engagement with the acting profession. No doubt he was on hand in 1610 for spells when the theatres reopened, thus bringing *Cymbeline* and *The Winter's Tale* to the stage. These plays, however, had been composed at a distance from the actors—probably physically and certainly in an institutional sense. *The Tempest*, written in 1611, was the product of a year that was largely plague-free and conceivably its stronger relational element was the result of a reconnection. On the whole, however, the earlier tight connection between the playwright and a small core of well-known actors would have been impossible to restore.

By 1611 there are signs of Shakespeare's semi-permanent residence in Stratford (Chambers concluded that this move had probably already happened by the end of 1610).[41] The playwright's name appears near the top of a list of subscribers for a bill promoting highway maintenance compiled in September 1611 (suggesting he was by then considered a resident) and in May the following year 'William Shakespeare' was recorded as 'of Stratford upon Avon' when he testified at the Court of Requests.[42]

playhouses remained closed until at the very least December 1609 (Smith, *Shakespeare's Blackfriars*, 248). Leeds Barroll, *Politics, Plague, and Shakespeare's Theater* (Ithaca, NY: Cornell University Press, 1991), 183, concludes that playing was suppressed until February 1610.

38. In the suit of Robert Keysar only the Burbages, Heminges, Condell, and Evans are mentioned, and Shakespeare (who had previously taken an active role in the proceedings of the company) is not. See Chambers, *Facts and Problems*, II, 64, who also (68) entertains the possibility that the playwright had surrendered his lease. For a thorough account of the case see William Ingram, 'Robert Keysar, Playhouse Speculator', *Shakespeare Quarterly* 37 (1986), 476–85.

39. Barroll, 'Blackfriars Theater', strengthening the claims of his earlier monograph, states that 'any search for beginnings [of adult performance] must work backwards from 1611 (N.S.), the year for which I have found the first record clearly indicating that plays were being performed in the Blackfriars space' (164).

40. Barroll, *Politics*, 108–16.

41. Chambers, *Facts and Problems*, I, 86.

42. Schoenbaum, *Documentary*, 229, 212.

The poet frequently returned to the capital.[43] Yet when he bought the Blackfriars Gatehouse in 1613 it was again as a man 'of Stratford' and, given the evidence that this property had a sitting tenant, the acquisition is more likely to have been an investment for rental than a London pied-à-terre.[44] Shakespeare, unlike the other fellows of the company, had rented rather than bought a residential property in London and this would have made him more mobile once London was no longer a place where he needed regularly to coach actors or to perform. It may be significant that Malone could find no indication of his residence in the capital after 1608.[45] If so, then in the Blackfriars years Shakespeare's position may be compared to that of Samuel Daniel, a poet who, from around 1606, resided partly in the country while retaining contacts at court.

Does this mean that we should think of 1608 as the beginning of Shakespeare's retirement? A century after the event of the Blackfriars partnership Nicholas Rowe penned the following bucolic account of his final years:

> The latter part of his life was spent, as all men of good sense will wish theirs may be, in ease, retirement, and the conversation of his friends. He had the good fortune to gather an estate equal to his occasion, and, in that, to his wish; and is said to have spent some years before his death at his native Stratford.[46]

The 'latter part' of Shakespeare's life could be said in retrospect to have started with the tenancy at Blackfriars, and Rowe's testimony is not without value. All the same, this account sounds a little too much like an Augustan projection of gentlemanly removal from politics and commerce to ring true when applied to an early sixteenth-century poet and theatre entrepreneur. Withdrawal from the daily routines of production after 1608 is a likely scenario: the intimate connection between writing and playing that had

---

43. Schoenbaum, *Documentary*, 228–32.
44. See Schoenbaum, *Documentary*, 221. The Burbage brothers had bought up several properties for rental in the area and Cuthbert maintained these interests even when he had moved to the suburbs himself. Subsequent legal papers involving the gatehouse refer to its sitting tenant, who may well be the same John Robinson recorded as a resident of Blackfriars in the petition of February 1596 (Smith, *Shakespeare's Blackfriars*, 252).
45. Edmond Malone's *Inquiry into the Authenticity of Certain Miscellaneous Papers* (London: T. Cadell Jr & W. Davies, 1796), 216–17, referred to a 'curious document' that 'affords the strongest presumptive evidence that he continued to reside in Southwark to the year 1608' (216–17). This paper was not printed and does not survive and conflicts with the certain testimony of Shakespeare's residence in Silver Street in 1604 provided by the Belott-Mountjoy court case. It remains possible, however, that Malone's date has significance, because the other documents discussed in this section of the *Inquiry* are extant and genuine.
46. Schoenbaum, *Documentary*, 228.

been possible since the formation of the fellowship cannot have continued as before. After this point Shakespeare is much less likely to have composed with the image in his mind of a full set of distinctive individual performers or to have been present as those performers worked on their roles. Some of the conditions, therefore, that I have argued helped to distinguish Shakespeare's way of writing from that of his contemporaries were beginning to disappear.

Yet Shakespeare in 1608 was not removing himself from the theatre— quite the reverse. Work on at least half a dozen plays still lay before him; he was not old at the age of forty-five when he signed a twenty-one-year lease.[47] He and his fellow housekeepers were making a daring innovation in committing to a London theatrical operation that was designed to run for twelve months a year.[48] This was up-scaling, not downsizing, in a big way. What changed, then, was not the fact but the nature of Shakespeare's investment. The events of 1608 distanced him from the ordinary actors and in this sense involved a reversal of the watershed of 1594. But more of Shakespeare's money and prestige than ever was tied up in the business of commercial plays. What altered artistically is that he was now working more as a poet than as a director of actors. It is my contention that the late style is closely connected to that shift in material circumstance.

47. Berry, 'Playhouses', 502.
48. Gurr, 'London's Blackfriars Playhouse', 27, argues that summer and winter playing was possibly something that London companies had practised before the 1594 suppression of city performance, but these were not places of permanent residence as would be the case for the King's Men.

13
Shakespeare's late style

S o if, after 1608, Shakespeare moved away from day-to-day contact with the actors, what group came closer? Partly, no doubt, it was his family and Stratford connections: there is evidence for this in the correspondence of local men such as the poet's cousin Thomas Greene.[1] Professionally, however, the answer would seem to be 'writers'. Around half a century after Shakespeare's death the Stratford vicar, John Ward, recalled a story about his last night, on which the poet enjoyed an evening of celebration with some eminent literary friends: 'Shakespeare, Drayton, and Ben Jonson had a merry meeting and it seems drank too hard, for Shakespeare died of a fever there contracted.'[2] It is impossible to verify the truth of this incident, but it is not an absurd one: Ward was acquainted with Shakespeare's daughter Judith and his other observations on the poet's life are broadly based in fact. The truth of Drayton's connections with Shakespeare's Stratford circle is certainly confirmed by the fact that he was later a patient of the poet's son-in-law, who entered details of his treatment in his medical diary, recording that the *'poeta laureatus'* was prescribed an emetic infusion mixed with syrup of violets.[3] Whether for medical treatment, merry meetings, or literary transactions it is quite possible that Drayton and other poet-playwrights came to visit New Place over the years.

Whether literally true or not, the picture of Shakespeare sitting in the company of poets carries weight as an emblem of the final years of his

---

1. Samuel Schoenbaum, *William Shakespeare: A Documentary Life* (Oxford: Clarendon Press, 1975), 228–34, records Greene's correspondence on a case of enclosure, which involves frequent reference to Shakespeare. On Greene's use of the term 'cousin' see Schoenbaum, *Documentary*, 231.
2. Ward's memorandum book is now MS 2073.5 at the Folger Shakespeare Library; relevant passages are printed as 'Diary of the Reverend John Ward (1629–1681)', *Shakespeare Quarterly* 8 (1957), 460, 520, 526, 553. See also Schoenbaum, *Documentary*, 241–2.
3. Schoenbaum, *Documentary*, 236.

literary workmanship because his late plays are alive with the presence of other writers. Partly, this is evident in the re-emergence of co-authorship as a common working practice, a development that I will consider in the final chapter of this book. It is also there in the persistent representation of author figures, ranging from Gower as on-stage narrator in *Pericles* to the apostrophe to Chaucer in the prologue to *The Two Noble Kinsmen*. This depiction of poets relates to a wider tendency in the late plays to make artifice conspicuous, whether through ekphrasis (as in the extended description of art on the walls of Imogen's chamber in *Cymbeline*), through pageantry (for example the masque of Ceres in *The Tempest*), or through the exposure of fiction's mechanism (as in the entry of Time as a formal commentator in *The Winter's Tale*). In Shakespeare's drama from 1607 onwards, literary agency is pressed consistently to the fore.[4]

The self-reflexive quality of Shakespeare's work in the last five years of his career is well attested, but what is less acknowledged is the influence of contemporary playwrights on this development. Shakespeare's late work (with its poet-figures and pleasure in rhetorical surface) is still often characterized as distant and dreamy—the product of a kind of Wordsworthian retreat into the natural world. Critics such as Dowden, Traversi, and Wilson Knight found a gratifying correspondence between what they considered Shakespeare's concluding philosophical vision and the thinking of the romantic poets on art, nature, and divinity.[5] Above all it is solitude that such critics emphasized in their study of late Shakespeare. Physically they imagined him ambling beside brooks in the Warwickshire countryside; intellectually and spiritually they claimed he was loosening ties to material things. True to their convictions, this generation of commentators took pride in isolating themselves from the corrupting influence of contextual scholarship: they worked away from academic libraries, neglected critical citation, and (in Wilson Knight's phrasing) laboured 'to avoid side-issues of Elizabethan and Jacobean manners, politics, patronage, audiences and explorations; to fix attention solely on the poetic quality and human interest of the plays concerned'.[6] This notion of a spiritual retreat, best examined

---

4. Fitting this trend are the co-authored *Pericles* and *Timon of Athens* (with its poet and painter figures), both conventionally dated no later than 1607 and thus composed before the acquisition of Blackfriars. For discussion see Chapter 14.
5. See, for example, Edward Dowden, *Shakspere: A Critical Study of his Mind and Art* (London: 1875; repr. Routledge, 1948), 40.
6. G. Wilson Knight, *The Crown of Life: Essays in Interpretation of Shakespeare's Final Plays* (London: Methuen, 1965), 9; see also Derek Traversi's preface to *Shakespeare: The Last Phase* (New York: Harcourt, 1953).

through scrutiny of the late plays as a coherent unit, proved influential. Even today, critics entertain such narratives of withdrawal: Greenblatt, for example, suggests that Shakespeare had perhaps 'wearied of his popular success or had come to question its worth' and 'would finally be able to turn from the crowd'.[7]

Contrary to such psychological readings, however, Shakespeare's late work is in many ways more modish and intellectually sociable than that which preceded it. Not only did the playwright frequently collaborate with other writers, he can also be seen to imitate them much more closely than before. For the first time since the early 1590s it is meaningful to say that Shakespeare's work is 'like' that of his contemporaries; in this (and in the embrace of a more formal aesthetic) there are intriguing parallels between the early and the late style. The phenomenon is multiform, but one obvious instance is the shaping influence of John Fletcher. Although very different in kind, the presence of this playwright in the late plays is comparable to that of Marlowe in the early 1590s in that, for the first time in one and a half decades, it becomes possible to point to substantial passages in which Shakespeare strives for effects that another playwright has made his own.

Fletcher graduated with an MA from Cambridge in 1598. He had strong courtly and ecclesiastical connections, moved to London, and became part of Ben Jonson's circle. As we might expect given this background, he first wrote plays for the children's theatre, being best remembered for his collaborations with Francis Beaumont, a poet who, like him, enjoyed a prosperous youth and was placed at the more gentlemanly end of the profession.[8] The two can be credited with the introduction of pastoral tragicomedy to England, first in *Cupid's Revenge* and then in *The Faithful Shepherdess*, which Fletcher wrote single-handed.[9] This work stood alongside, and was coloured by, a mode of romance that had its origins in the work of Miguel de Cervantes. The Spaniard's *Don Quixote* was published in 1605 and had, by 1607, been translated into English, bringing to the public a

7. Stephen Greenblatt, *Will in the World: How Shakespeare Became Shakespeare* (London: Jonathan Cape, 2004), 377.
8. Fletcher's family were high achievers: his father had been a bishop, his uncle was a diplomat and author, and his cousin was the poet Phineas Fletcher. Personal and political scandals, however, brought financial trouble and laid the Fletchers low by 1601 (see Gordon McMullan, 'Fletcher, John (1579–1625)', *Oxford DNB*).
9. The key influence here was Guarini's *Il pastor fido*, which had been translated into English in 1602, on which see J. J. Lievsay, 'Jacobean Stage Pastoralism' in Richard Hosley, ed., *Essays on Shakespeare and Elizabethan Drama in Honour of Hardin Craig* (London: Routledge, 1963).

new knowing appreciation of the absurdities of the ancient storybook form.[10] Fletcher (alongside the other late Shakespearean collaborators Middleton and George Wilkins) was quick to exploit its dramatic potential. The ideas of *Don Quixote* were presented in the most spectacular way in Beaumont's *Knight of the Burning Pestle* (1607), in which the conventional tastes of the citizen audience were satirized and the assumptions of romance narrative made a constant subject of fun.[11] It was only *The Knight of the Burning Pestle* that fully adopted the Cervantean concept of an individual who is trapped (through excessive consumption) into understanding the world through literary conventions: its hero, Rafe, like Don Quixote, is fated to mistake every alehouse tapster for a castle squire. Yet this self-conscious and knowing attitude to genre became a more widespread feature of Fletcher's writing, not least in *The Faithful Shepherdess*, where an essentially non-dramatic set of literary assumptions is transferred, with an edge of irony, onto the stage. Fletcher was thus associated with an aestheticized, experimental movement in drama, albeit one that had (even with his restricted audience at the indoor playhouse) only mixed success.

Fundamentally, Fletcher was concerned with foregrounding artistic conventions. In plays such as *Cupid's Revenge*, *The Faithful Shepherdess*, and *Philaster*, he and Francis Beaumont reined in the artificiality of *The Knight of the Burning Pestle*'s high-concept satire, but they still aimed for a dramatic world that was 'bookish' in feel. *Cupid's Revenge*, which was probably their first full collaboration, turned to Sidney's *Arcadia* as a source and thus made romance a more artful form than it had been in the popular tradition of plays like *Clyomon and Clamydes* and *Mucedorus*. With its reigning deity of love, the play presents a world of abstract, slightly absurd, moral questions. It combines this with another constant of Fletcher's writing: sexual piquancy and pathos. In the *Arcadia* Sidney had toyed with the erotic vulnerability of his perfect virginal princesses and, alongside this, had made the jealous

---

10. Thomas Shelton produced the first English translation in 1607 but the work was not printed until 1612. On the early reception of Cervantes see Lee Bliss, 'Don Quixote in England: The Case for *The Knight of the Burning Pestle*,' *Viator* 18 (1987), 161–80 (at 168–80), and also Edwin B. Knowles, 'Thomas Shelton, Translator of *Don Quixote*', *Studies in the Renaissance* 5 (1958), 160–75. On the wider significance of Cervantes for Shakespeare see Bart van Es, 'Late Shakespeare and the Middle Ages' in Helen Cooper, Peter Holland, and Ruth Morse, eds., *Medieval Shakespeare: Pasts and Presents* (Cambridge: Cambridge University Press, *forthcoming*).

11. For details on the play's date, sources, and reception see *The Knight of the Burning Pestle*, ed. Michael Hattaway, New Mermaids (London: A. & C. Black, 1969). As Hattaway notes, the play's claim to greater antiquity than *Don Quixote* is not to be taken literally: the publisher imagines the two texts breaking lances like rival knights.

passions of his male protagonists a driver of plot. Spenser's *Faerie Queene* had likewise constructed a landscape of sexual tribulations, in which moralism and titillation intermix. In *Cupid's Revenge* this conjunction, which was familiar in prose and narrative poetry, was transferred into the province of drama. The play gives us a quasi-classical landscape that is governed by oracles, gods, and magical transformations. It is inhabited by implausibly good and absurdly evil characters: the play's heroine, Urania (a name familiar from the *Arcadia*), thus suffers constant trials as she is pursued by a violent and lustful mother and ends the play in a cave in the wilderness, disguised as a boy.

Fletcher's *Faithful Shepherdess* presents an equivalent world that is still more magical and artificial in its make-up. The work is most often cited for its prefatory defence of the play's objectives, which was written following its failure on the stage. Although, as McMullan notes, it is sometimes indiscriminately used as a description of all tragicomic drama, it contains a rare and therefore important artistic statement of purpose and so needs, still, to be quoted at length:[12]

> A tragi-comedy is not so called in respect of mirth and killing, but in respect it wants deaths, which is enough to make it no tragedy, yet brings some near it, which is enough to make it no comedy: which must be a representation of familiar people, with such kind of trouble as no life be questioned, so that a god is as lawful in this as in a tragedy, and mean people as in a comedy.[13]

In terms of plot (especially the use of 'a god', meaning *deus ex machina*) this manifesto is of obvious import for Shakespeare's late romances, but equally striking is the removed artistic ethos of this credo and of the text as a whole. Fletcher describes his work as a 'poem' and relates it to literary as opposed to popular convention: the 'reader' is reminded that his shepherds are such 'as all the ancient poets and modern of understanding have received them'. In the first quarto this preface is anticipated by verses from three poet–playwrights— Jonson, Beaumont, and Chapman—who all, to quote Chapman, praise a 'pastoral, being both a poem and a play' (p. 492). If *Cupid's Revenge* set out to stage the artificiality of Sidney's *Arcadia*, then *The Faithful Shepherdess* does the

---

12. On the origins and context of the preface see Gordon McMullan and Jonathan Hope, eds., *The Politics of Tragicomedy: Shakespeare and After* (London: Routledge, 1992), 2–5.

13. John Fletcher, *The Faithful Shepherdess*, ed. Cyrus Hoy, in *The Dramatic Works in the Beaumont and Fletcher Canon*, ed. Fredson Bowers, 10 vols. (Cambridge: Cambridge University Press, 1976), III, 497. Subsequent references are to this edition and appear in the text.

same for pastoral, a genre which, as Empson famously argued, is always premised on the 'gentle irony' of putting complex literary thoughts into the mouths of simple, rustic characters.[14] That irony in Fletcher's play is driven by the disparity between a formal presentation (of songs and masque-like movement) and the naive actions and thoughts of his protagonists. The odd conjunction of artificiality with simplicity is heightened in its effect when it is combined with Fletcher's plotting, which, as he states in his 'Preface to the Reader', depends on strong authorial intervention for the effect of surprise.

Several things, then, come together in the works that Fletcher had written for the boys' companies before his move to supply the King's Men. First, a significant interest in Cervantes combined with a wider conspicuous engagement with genre, specifically pastoral and romance. Second, his work focused strongly on sexuality, above all the anticipated loss of virginity, so that there is repeated emphasis on the need for purity set in tension with the burlesque representation of forces that put it at risk. Third, there is emphasis on artifice, effected through formal poetry, song, magic, and masque-like movement. Finally, Fletcher works to achieve sudden dramatic revelations, on the one hand surprising but on the other conspicuously fictional and thus anticipated by an audience aware of the genre within which he works.

To be sure, plays like *Cupid's Revenge* (1607–8) and *The Faithful Shepherdess* (1608) do not read like Shakespeare—their schematic formalism is a product of the boys' stages and was apparently too synthetic in its construction to be welcomed wholeheartedly even there. Yet when Beaumont and Fletcher shifted, after the collapse of the Children of the Queen's Revels, to write for the King's Men, they produced *Philaster*, *The Maid's Tragedy*, and *A King and No King*, works that were commercially successful and take us much closer to *Cymbeline* or *The Winter's Tale*.[15] As Andrew Gurr says of the first of these dramas, Beaumont and Fletcher were 'dramatizing not a story but a whole genre, the traditional prose romance': as he puts it, 'instead of a plot serving as vehicle for the "personation" of character . . . characters are set in patterns to serve the plot'.[16] The key influence is

14. William Empson, *Some Versions of Pastoral* (1935; repr. London: Chatto & Windus, 1950), 11.
15. On the popular success of the play see Francis Beaumont and John Fletcher, *Philaster, or Love Lies a-Bleeding*, ed. Andrew Gurr (Manchester: Manchester University Press, 2003), xlviii.
16. Beaumont and Fletcher, *Philaster*, ed. Gurr, xxix.

Sidney's *Arcadia* (with its abstract moral questions, its excitement over feminine virtue, its sudden revelations, and its pleasure in the power of rhetoric) but the drama draws conspicuously on fictional resources of many kinds.

The study of Fletcher's influence on Shakespeare has always foundered on the uncertainties of dating. *The Knight of the Burning Pestle* (1607), *Cupid's Revenge* (1607–8), and *The Faithful Shepherdess* (1608–9) are of the same period as *Pericles*, which was probably composed in 1607.[17] *Philaster* (1608–9), *The Maid's Tragedy* (1610), and *A King and No King* (1611) sit in a window of composition that overlaps with *The Winter's Tale* (1609–10), *Cymbeline* (1610), and *The Tempest* (1611).[18] Many works by Fletcher, therefore, could have been preceded by a comparable Shakespeare play. Traditional source study balks at such a hurdle; if we are interested, however, in relating Shakespeare's practice to that of his contemporaries the problem does not loom so large. *Pericles* was already full of elements that one could call Fletcherian, but these were possibly originated by Shakespeare's co-author George Wilkins (another early reader of Cervantes): here too there was an attempt to transfer Sidneyan poetics to drama, a foregrounding of authorial agency, an emphasis on wonder, and a focus on feminine sexual virtue that had erotic appeal.[19] Like the early 1590s fashion for overreaching grand rhetoric, the taste for tragicomic artifice cannot be traced to an individual playwright: this was a widespread literary phenomenon in which Fletcher was a leading participant with close ties to Shakespeare. As it happens, there can be no doubt that in several instances Shakespeare plays

17. For the dates of Fletcher's plays I here use the table provided by Gordon McMullan, *The Politics of Unease in the Plays of John Fletcher* (Amherst: University of Massachusetts Press, 1994), 267–9, although I have also consulted Alfred Harbage, *Annals of English Drama: 975–1700*, 3rd edn, rev. Sylvia Stoler Wagonheim (London: Routledge, 1989) and the relevant editions and scholarship. For Shakespeare I am using the most recent Arden edition (in this case William Shakespeare and George Wilkins, *Pericles*, ed. Suzanne Gossett, Arden3 (London: Methuen, 2004), 2), again in consultation with relevant other authorities. The dates cited are a matter of consensus.

18. See note above. Arden references here are *Cymbeline*, ed. J. M. Nosworthy, Arden2 (London: Methuen, 1955), xv; *The Winter's Tale*, ed. John Pitcher, Arden3 (London: Methuen, 2010), 88–9; *The Tempest*, ed. Virginia Mason Vaughan and Alden T. Vaughan, Arden3 (London: Methuen, 1999), 1. As Nosworthy's text is an old one, consistent comparison has also been made with Roger Warren's more recent edition, William Shakespeare, *Cymbeline* (Oxford: Oxford University Press, 2008).

19. The primary source for *Pericles* is, of course, Gower and not Sidney, but the tonal qualities of the *Arcadia* are undoubtedly a strong influence and the hero's name, which is not found in *Confessio amantis*, is probably a version of Sidney's 'Pyrocles'. On the likely division of labour in this play see Gossett, ed., *Pericles*, 1–75; 161–3, and discussion in Chapter 14 below.

do follow Fletcher's precedent; the important point, however, is much less a matter of influence than it is of parallel tracks.

Fletcher, then, provides a reference point through which to judge the normative qualities of Shakespeare's late plays: influence (as with Marlowe in the first phase of the playwright's composition) is a useful principle on which to begin this examination, but it does not set the limit on the significance of his work. On this front the conclusions of Thorndike's *The Influence of Beaumont and Fletcher on Shakespeare*, written well over a century ago, are still worth citing. Like subsequent critics, Thorndike noted a sharp divergence in the late romances from the earlier Shakespearean habits of composition enumerated by Coleridge, with characteristics such as 'expectation in preference to surprise' and 'inferred' rather than stated characterization dropping away. In bold terms, he attributed this shift to the influence of Beaumont and Fletcher, in whose works a string of stylistic features, including 'emphasized dénouements, characterization sacrificed to convention and situation, a versification perceptibly sacrificed for stage effect, and considerable pageantry taken from the court masques', were all to be found.[20] Later critics such as Wilson Knight and Traversi (understandably struck by a qualitative difference between these playwrights) resisted this inference, replacing it with a more elevated metaphysical structure of moral and artistic development, but parallels between Fletcher and Shakespeare are strong.

First, these elements are evident in the building blocks of their drama: character, plot, and location. Thus, in Fletcher's *The Faithful Shepherdess* the tragicomic action is governed by a wise, magically learned figure named Clorin, who is served by a powerful satyr. This situation is comparable not simply in outline but in scenic effect to that of Prospero and Ariel in *The Tempest*, a play written several years later. It is thus, for example, that the satyr addresses Clorin near the play's conclusion:

> What new service now is meetest
> For the satyr? Shall I stray
> In the middle air and stay
> The sailing rack or nimbly take
> Hold by the moon and gently make
> Suit to the pale Queen of the night

20. Ashley H. Thorndike, *The Influence of Beaumont and Fletcher on Shakespeare* (Worcester, MA: Oliver B. Wood, 1901), 149–50.

For a beam to give thee light?
Shall I dive into the sea
And bring thee coral, making way
Through the rising waves that fall
In snowy fleeces?

(*The Faithful Shepherdess*, 5.5.243–53)

It is not far-fetched to see this as anticipating the speeches of Shakespeare's Ariel:

All hail, great master; grave sir, hail! I come
To answer thy best pleasure, be't to fly,
To swim, to dive into the fire, to ride
On the curled clouds. To thy strong bidding, task
Ariel and all his quality.

(*The Tempest*, 1.2.189–93)

Such parallels are not restricted to single speeches. In *The Faithful Shepherdess* Fletcher creates a fictional realm of pastoral–romance that proves a partial template for Prospero's island, notably in the mixing of earthly persons and classical gods. The Fletcherian quality of lyric in Shakespeare's late plays is immediately evident when episodes are placed alongside one another. The song of the River God in *The Faithful Shepherdess*—'Do not fear to put thy feet,/ Naked in the river sweet' (3.1.429–30)—for example, bears comparison with Ariel's 'Come unto these yellow sands,/ And then take hands' (1.2.376–7) in tone, in imagery, and in creating an atmosphere of enchantment and supernatural calm. Pastoral songs of *The Faithful Shepherdess* and *The Tempest* are almost interchangeable, and the same is true of the masques. To point to just one instance, the shepherd's song to Pan 'All ye woods and trees and bowers,/ All ye virtues and ye powers,/ That inhabit in the lakes,/ In the pleasant springs or brakes' (5.5.218–21) anticipates almost phrase for phrase the enchantments that Iris speaks in Shakespeare's masque of Ceres:

You nymphs, called naiads, of the windring brooks,
With your sedged crowns and ever-harmless looks,
Leave your crisp channels, and on this green land
Answer your summons, Juno does command.

(*Tempest*, 4.1.128–31)

It is possible to list tens of comparable parallels that tie together *The Faithful Shepherdess* and *The Tempest* and which also connect Fletcher's early drama with *Cymbeline* and *The Winter's Tale*. Such similarity of character, plot, and location is highly unusual in the plays that Shakespeare wrote in the first decade and a half of his time with his company and it is striking that it should occur so consistently across the plays after 1608.

Second, more specifically, we may look to the pursuit of 'wonder' as an experience for protagonist and audience. Anne Barton has written brilliantly on a curious feature of Shakespeare's late plays in which disbelief is both asserted and denied.[21] Again, this is an effect conspicuous in earlier work by Fletcher, notably in the recovery of characters who are supposed to be lost. It is thus, for example, that Amarillis, thinking to have brought about the death of her rival, responds on finding her magically restored:

> What men call
> Wonder, or more than wonder, Miracle,
> For sure so strange as this the Oracle
> Never gave answer of. It passeth dreams
> Of madmen's fancy, when the many streams
> Of new imagination rise and fall.
>
> (*Faithful Shepherdess*, 4.3.32–7)

The reform of evil natures through such orchestrated spectacle is evident in all the reconciliations that unify the final actions of Fletcher's drama. Clorin's woodland cabin in *The Faithful Shepherdess* is for this purpose a similar space to Prospero's cell in *The Tempest* or Paulina's secluded house in *The Winter's Tale*. Thus in the final act of *The Faithful Shepherdess* 'the curtain is drawn' to reveal Clorin with the miraculously saved Cloe and Alexis. There is no precedent for this use of the discovery space in the English commercial theatre, but it is echoed with notable closeness by Shakespeare, both in *The Winter's Tale*, where Paulina draws a curtain and reveals Hermione, standing like a statue (5.3.21SD), and in *The Tempest*, where 'Prospero discovers Ferdinand and Miranda playing at chess' (5.1.171SD).[22] This is not simply a

---

21. Anne Barton, '"Enter Mariners Wet": Realism in Shakespeare's Last Plays' (1986), in *Essays, Mainly Shakespearean* (Cambridge: Cambridge University Press, 1994), 182–203.
22. Neither *The Winter's Tale* nor *The Tempest* has stage directions that are directly authorial: for the former the book was lost and had to be reassembled from actors' parts and for the latter the Folio text was based on a presentation copy written up by Ralph Crane (see John Jowett, 'New Created Creatures: Ralph Crane and the Stage Directions in *The Tempest*', *Shakespeare Survey* 36 (1983), 107–20). These interventions, however, cannot have altered the nature of the reported action; indeed, being based on report, they are likely to be especially accurate. Although Paulina's action in revealing Hermione is not reported as a stage direction in the Folio it is evident that this has happened because in the subsequent dialogue both she and Leontes refer to the curtain that has been drawn (*Cymbeline* F, TLN 3255, 3267).

matter of congruence between the wording of stage directions—the nature and dramatic function of these revelations are entirely alike. In each case a downcast wrongdoer is forgiven and reformed through this act of spectacular restoration, an event accompanied by music and expressions of mystical delight.

Gesturally and rhetorically the scenes of reconciliation between Perigot and Amoret and Leontes and Hermione have much in common. Like Leontes, Perigot approaches a woman who looks exactly like the loved one for whose death he thinks himself responsible. Set now on a life of classically religious penitence, he approaches her figure with awe. His words—'what e'r thou be,/ Be'st thou her sprite, or some divinity,/ That in her shape thinks good to walk this grove' (*Shepherdess*, 5.5.42–4)—have clear parallels with the mixture of the real and the unearthly in the speech of Leontes as he regards Hermione's supposed statue:

> O royal piece!
> There's magic in thy majesty, which has
> My evils conjured to remembrance, and
> From thy admiring daughter took the spirits,
> Standing like stone with thee.

> (*Winter's Tale*, 5.3.38–42)

The gradual recognition in Leontes of the return of a woman who seemed impossibly lost appears closely modelled on the same sequence in Fletcher's earlier drama. It provides a compelling instance of a new willingness on Shakespeare's part to orchestrate an experience of literary estrangement: making his characters not so much individuals but rather centres of spectacle. Fletcher, in common with many other literary playwrights, had always been content to do this, so Shakespeare is following where others have led.

Third, related to this, is Fletcher's and late Shakespeare's treatment of sexuality, in which a more schematic and moralistic perspective than was evident in plays like *Othello* or *All's Well that Ends Well* comes to the fore. In *The Faithful Shepherdess* mortal women are repeatedly taken for divine agents and have a transformative moral effect on men. This happens earlier, for example, where Clorin is declared a 'deity' and 'goddess' by the satyr, who is, we are told, tamed by the virgin's mystic power (1.1.67–8). Such elevated treatment of the feminine (alternating with an often misogynistic loathing of concupiscence) is a keynote of Fletcher's drama that also comes up repeatedly in Shakespeare's late plays. We might think, for instance, of

Ferdinand's first encounter with Miranda, whom he declares 'most sure the goddess/ on whom these airs attend' and whose virginity stands in pointed contrast to 'the foul witch Sycorax, who with age and envy/ Was grown into a hoop'.[23] In the same way, *Pericles*'s Marina is set against the daughter of Antiochus, a 'fair viol...played upon before [her] time'.[24] In the case of *Cymbeline* and *Philaster*, plays which Thorndike described as 'strikingly similar', there are numerous connections around this topic, running to sustained parallels between characters and scenes.[25]

The language of sexual obsession, switching rapidly from purity to corruption, pitching an innocent and timid voice against dominant out-bursts of obsession, was a core constituent of the younger playwright's drama. *The Faithful Shepherdess* had engineered such contrasts in a series of ways, setting Clorin beside Amarillis; Cloe beside Amoret; Daphnis beside the Sullen Shepherd; and creating numerous scenarios of resistance and pursuit. Subsequent plays for the adult companies, such as *Philaster*, *The Maid's Tragedy*, and *A King and No King*, reduced the number of such confrontations and made them less artificial, but the dominant patterns of threatened, uncomprehending chastity remained the same. Shakespeare likewise adopted this more schematic characterization, abandoning the more earthy language he had earlier drawn from domestic tragedy. The anger, sexual disgust, and bovine imagery of sudden jealousy in Fletcher's *Philaster* ('bulls and rams will fight/ To keep their females, standing in their sight;/ But take 'em from them, and you take at once/ Their spleens away;/ and they will fall again/ Unto their pastures, growing fresh and fat' (*Philaster*, 3.1.145–49)) is thus very close to the moment when obsession takes hold of Leontes in the later *Winter's Tale*:

> Come, captain,
> We must be neat—not neat, but cleanly, captain.
> And yet the steer, the heifer and the calf
> Are all called neat.
>
> (*Winter's Tale*, 1.2.122–5)

23. *The Tempest*, 1.2.422–3, 258–9.
24. *Pericles*, ed. Gossett, 1.1.82–5.
25. Compare, for example, the exchanges on the word 'stranger' in *Philaster*, 1.1.77–9, and *Cymbeline*, 2.1.32–6; Philaster and Iachimo's reflections on their defeat by simple countrymen (*Philaster*, 4.5.103–4, and *Cymbeline*, 5.2.2–6) are also closely aligned. Thorndike, *Influence*, 152–60 (quoted, 152), provides an excellent account that argues for the likelihood that Beaumont and Fletcher were the innovators. Gurr, ed., *Philaster*, xlv–l, also gives an account of various points of overlap, but is more cautious about the chronology, and rightly points out (xlix–l) that the plays do differ in fundamental ways.

At such moments it is not merely the words but also the scenic arrangement that is similar: in this case an obsessive adult addressing his anger to a childish totem of submissive innocence.

In three areas, then, there is sustained linkage between Shakespeare and Fletcher, but this is more than a simple personal tie. Ultimately, what the connection with Fletcher amounts to is the embrace of conscious literary artifice. At times, this is evident in direct allusion. There can be little doubt, for example, that the following episode in *Philaster* (which had been performed by his own company) made an impression on Shakespeare's mind. Escaping in the pastoral fourth act (disguised as Bellario) Euphrasia apostrophizes as follows to a bank of flowers where she intends to rest:

> Bear me, thou gentle bank,
> For ever if thou wilt. [*Lies down*] You sweet ones all [*indicating the flowers*],
> Let me unworthy press you; I could wish
> I rather were a corse strewed o'er with you
> Than quick above you.[26]

In *The Winter's Tale* Shakespeare likewise conspicuously shifts the action in the fourth act from a courtly to a pastoral setting. Yet, reversing Euphrasia's desire to be buried below the 'sweet ones', his heroine wishes instead to take her 'sweet friend' and 'strew him o'er and o'er' so that it is he who becomes a mound of flowers. Florizel, responding, appears directly to pick up on Fletcher's precedent:

> FLORIZEL: What, like a corse?
> PERDITA: No, like a bank, for love to lie and play on,
>   Not like a corse—or if, not to be buried,
>   But quick and in mine arms. Come, take your flowers.
>   Methinks I play as I have seen them do
>   In Whitsun pastorals.[27]

'Corse', 'strew', 'sweet', 'quick', 'gentle', 'bank': the repetitions are striking—at a moment like this, Shakespeare seems to be offering a quiet homage to Fletcher, whose 'Preface to the Reader' in *The Faithful Shepherdess* had

---

26. Fletcher, *Philaster*, 4.6.2–6 (I here include both Gurr's stage direction and his note at the foot of the page).

27. I quote here from F1 (TLN 1944–9) rather than the Arden3 *Winter's Tale*, 4.4.129–34, whose modernization to 'corpse' obscures the connection with Fletcher. The link between these passages is pointed out in E. M. W. Tillyard, *Shakespeare's Last Plays* (London: Chatto & Windus, 1964), 9.

mocked the 'Whitsun' expectations of his audience, who had thought the work 'a play of country hired shepherds, in grey cloaks, with curtailed dogs in strings, sometimes laughing together, and sometimes killing one another'.[28] In Act 4 of *The Winter's Tale* Shakespeare foregrounds pastoral in a more exclusively literary way than he had ever done previously and in doing so he forges connections and knowing points of difference not just with Fletcher but also with Beaumont and Jonson and other writers who conceptualized their plays as 'poems'.[29] Homage and pastiche blend easily together, for while Shakespeare follows precedent in the adoption of pastoral in the fourth act he simultaneously mocks the classical unities that are constantly referenced in *The Faithful Shepherdess*. The absurd entry of the figure of Time at the beginning of Act 4 of *The Winter's Tale* (like the magical constriction of time, place, and action on the island in *The Tempest*) makes authorial agency prominent. The late plays are full of such interventions, which collectively function to bring art to the fore.

Granville-Barker, working in the biographical tradition, was of the view that 'this art that displays art is a thing very likely to be the taste of the mature and rather wearied artist'.[30] Yet in Stuart England it was the young, new dramatists, such as Marston and Fletcher, who were doing this kind of writing. Shakespeare's late plays are replete with metaphors and allegories that represent the literary creator, but these are the very opposite of lonely, contemplative episodes looking back on a career that is ending. Polixenes' opinions about 'that art,/ Which you say adds to Nature' or Prospero's thoughts about his 'charms' that 'are all o'erthrown' undoubtedly nod towards the playwright's workmanship, but the same is true of speeches in Fletcher's *The Faithful Shepherdess* where Clorin examines 'what my best art hath done' or in Jonson's *Alchemist* in which Subtle apostrophizes on 'mine own great art'.[31] When we place Shakespeare beside his contemporaries this supposed phase of introspective maturity comes to look much more like a return to the literary mainstream: we come to a narrative that does not

---

28. Fletcher, *Shepherdess*, in *Dramatic Works*, ed. Bowers, III, 497.
29. Jonson's commendatory poem, added in the 1629 edition of *The Faithful Shepherdess*, commends the work specifically as a 'poem' (A3ᵃ); Chapman's praise for 'his pastoral, being both a poem and a play' (A3ᵇ) makes the same point.
30. Granville-Barker, quoted in Tillyard, *Shakespeare's Last Plays*, 1.
31. *Winter's Tale*, 4.4.90–1; *Tempest*, Epilogue.1; *The Faithful Shepherdess*, 2.2.1; Ben Jonson, *The Alchemist*, ed. F. H. Mares, Revels (Manchester: Manchester University Press, 1967), 1.1.77.

require what McMullan rightly critiques as an ahistorical concept of artistic arrival; it is something less personally expressive and more provisional in kind.

Both in its parallels with the work of contemporaries and in its more formal, patterned quality, Shakespeare's late work bears comparison with the poet's output in the years before he became a sharer in 1594. 'Fletcherian' aspects of these plays, like 'Marlovian' elements in the first phase of his career, can be understood as an index of the playwright's closeness to the common working conditions of his contemporaries. The personal influence of Fletcher on Shakespeare was a factor, but many features of Fletcher's style were more widely distributed, such as the fashion for Cervantean irony or for tragicomedy. Shakespeare, after 1608, seems more directly interested in what his literary contemporaries are doing or is at least more willing to make that interest an explicit presence in his plays. The appearance in 1609 of Shakespeare's *Sonnets* with *A Lover's Complaint* strengthens this impression. This was the first significant release of non-dramatic work since *Venus and Adonis* (1593) and *The Rape of Lucrece* (1594). It also revisited many of the concerns of that period, including homo-eroticism and difficulties surrounding the rhetoric of praise. True, the *Sonnets* did not have the high production values in print that had marked the earlier non-dramatic poems and they cannot therefore definitively be called an authorial publication; they were also the product of many preceding years.[32] But if Shakespeare acquiesced in their being printed he was making a statement: here was a collection that repeatedly alluded to rival poets and made its claim to originality through the imitation and twisting of existing forms. Like the late plays, this is work focused more on writers than on individual actors— in the absence of daily contact with the players, it is apparent, the company of poets was making its presence felt.

---

32. See Shakespeare, *Complete Sonnets and Poems*, ed. Colin Burrow (Oxford: Oxford University Press, 2002), 91–3, 103–7.

14

Shakespeare and co-authorship

Harleian MS 7368, the manuscript of the play *Sir Thomas More*, is amongst the very greatest treasures of the British Library. As a physical object it is not, on the face of it, impressive. The crudely boxed title 'The Booke of Sir Thomas Moore' is written on an upside down re-used piece of vellum, still covered with an old black-letter script, and the 'volume' consists of loose pieces of paper, written in various hands.[1] The name 'foul papers', used of working dramatic manuscripts in this period, feels entirely appropriate, even if the Book of *Sir Thomas More* is nothing so simple as an author's first draft.[2] As the sole example of a surviving playhouse document that shows co-authorship in action, the grubbiness of the Book is itself a piece of evidence.[3] It would be a treasure of the British Library, albeit an unlovely one, even without the talismanic presence of Shakespeare's hand.

There are few things about the play *Sir Thomas More* that are uncontested. Even Shakespeare's participation (attested by a mass of evidence including handwriting, orthography, and word use) is a logical deduction rather than an absolute fact.[4] The playwright's presence is now a matter of

1. As is noted in Peter W. M. Blayney, '*The Booke of Sir Thomas Moore* Re-examined', *Studies in Philology* 69 (1972), 167–91 (at 171), a scrap of the same vellum was used to bind the MS of Munday's *John a Kent*, dating from 1590. Although not conclusive, this fact suggests an early 1590s date.
2. Vittorio Gabrieli and Giorgio Melchiori, eds., Anthony Munday and others, *Sir Thomas More*, Revels (Manchester: Manchester University Press, 1990), 3, observe that the original script is a 'fair' copy. That text is marked up with additions, but this is not technically a case of foul papers.
3. Some other manuscripts could be forwarded as candidates—for example, the Alnwick playtext of *John of Bordeaux*, probably originally a play by Greene in which Chettle's hand also appears. There are five hands in this manuscript, one or more of which may be authorial. See *John of Bordeaux or The Second Part of Friar Bacon*, ed. W. L. Renwick (Oxford: Malone Society, 1935).
4. A standard defence of the attribution is provided in G. Blakemore Evans, ed., *The Riverside Shakespeare* (Boston, MA: Houghton Mifflin, 1974), 1683–5.

consensus.[5] But the same degree of confidence does not apply to the date of his additions and important scholars are still at variance over the sequence of events.[6] Some recent editors of the play date the creation of the original manuscript to 1593, with subsequent alterations running possibly to the first months of the following year.[7] Others have insisted, on grounds of vocabulary and metrics, that Shakespeare's additions must have come later.[8]

5. Carol Chillington, 'Playwrights at Work: Henslowe's, Not Shakespeare's, Book of Sir Thomas More', *English Literary Renaissance* 10 (1980), 439–79, questioned the attribution to Shakespeare and proposed Webster, but her theory has not won favour. For a rejection see, for example, Charles R. Forker, 'Webster or Shakespeare? Style, Idiom, Vocabulary, and Spelling in the Additions to *Sir Thomas More*', in T. H. Howard-Hill, ed., *Shakespeare and 'Sir Thomas More': Essays on the Play and its Shakespearian Interest* (Cambridge: Cambridge University Press, 1989), 151–70. Taylor, in the same volume, finds 'manifest deficiency' (101) in her methods, but is positive about her redating of the additions.

6. W. W. Greg, ed., *The Book of Sir Thomas More* (Oxford: Malone Society, 1911), the first thorough scholarly editor, suggested a date range of 1592–3. Blayney, '*Moore* Re-examined', constructed a seminal case, based on manuscript evidence and possible echoes of *Sir Thomas More* in Chettle's *Kind-Harts Dreame* (1592), that offered a 'a fairly certain' date range of August to November 1592 for Shakespeare's additions. Blayney suggested two stages of censorship, fairly close together, with Shakespeare taking part in response to the first. The reaction against this consensus for an early date has its roots in stylometrics. Gary Taylor, 'The Date and Auspices of the Additions to *Sir Thomas More*', in Howard-Hill, ed., *Shakespeare and 'Sir Thomas More'*, 101–30, offered the thesis that the additions were made for a late revival around 1603, either by the Admiral's or by the Chamberlain's Men. Other contributors to Howard-Hill's volume continued to support the early-date theory for Shakespeare's part of the manuscript, but came to different conclusions about the other participants.

7. See Gabrieli and Melchiori, eds., *More*, 11–29. They plausibly argue that Shakespeare's additions date from a revision that occurred before official censorship.

8. D. J. Lake, 'The Date of the *Sir Thomas More* Additions by Dekker and Shakespeare', *Notes & Queries* 222 (1977), 114–16, on grounds of metrics, and MacDonald P. Jackson, 'Linguistic Evidence for the Date of Shakespeare's Additions to *Sir Thomas More*,' *Notes & Queries* 223 (1978), 154–6, on grounds of colloquial word use, concluded that Shakespeare's additions must have been made after 1600. This case was accepted in Stanley Wells and Gary Taylor, *William Shakespeare: A Textual Companion* (Oxford: Clarendon Press, 1987), 124–5, which offers a date range of 1603–4 on the basis of this stylometric evidence and parallels with Chettle's *Tragedy of Hoffman*, which is dated by them as 1602–4. Brian Vickers, amongst others, is supportive of these methods (based on rare word use, prosody, and pause patterns) and offers a positive assessment in '*The Troublesome Raigne*, George Peele, and the Date of *King John*', in Brian Boyd, ed., *Words that Count: Essays on Early Modern Authorship in Honor of MacDonald P. Jackson* (Newark: University of Delaware Press, 2004), 78–116 (106). The sample of Shakespeare's writing, however, is small and also compromised by the fact that it is a rewriting of another's original. This makes the stylometric evidence less strong. The most powerful reason for supporting an early date is the fact that the scribal hand correcting Shakespeare's is also that of the plot of *2 Seven Deadly Sins* and several other early manuscripts. The actor's name that the scribe inserted also appears in the *2 Seven* plot, which was made for Strange's Men. While it is possible to construct a case around this (and Taylor does so ingeniously), the string of hypotheticals becomes very long. (As noted in Chapter 2 above, the date of the *2 Seven Plot* has also been disputed: see David Kathman, 'Reconsidering *The Seven Deadly Sins*', *Early Theatre* 7 (2004), 13–44, and Andrew Gurr's response in 'The Work of Elizabethan Plotters, and *2 Seven Deadly Sins*', *Early Theatre* 10 (2007), 67–87.)

I accept the arguments of Gabrieli and Melchiori and believe that Shakespeare wrote his scenes for *Sir Thomas More* in early 1594. While that date remains conjectural what is almost beyond doubt is that he wrote them for a company in which he was not a shareholder. The play was sold to Strange's Men or perhaps the Lord Admiral's, so Shakespeare was never an owner of this text.[9] What the manuscript gives us is a witness to a process: whatever its point of completion, it is testament to working conditions that are relevant to both the first and the final phase of Shakespeare's career.

All scholars agree that the play was written out as a complete fair copy no later than 1595 by Anthony Munday, who presented it to an acting company. Quite possibly it was at this point already a collaborative project, with Munday acting in a scribal capacity as he brought together work by himself and another professional playwright.[10] Munday's hand makes up the majority of the manuscript. The acting company, however, greatly increased the complexity of the script by inviting other authors to adapt it to company requirements. These were partly political (replacing controversial material with a more palatable alternative) but they were also practical (being designed to produce a more exciting and performable text). The playwrights involved can be identified with a reasonable degree of certainty: Henry Chettle, Thomas Heywood, Thomas Dekker, William Shakespeare, and an anonymous playhouse scribe or bookkeeper who tried to pull the entire effort together. What now survives in the British Library is their composite text.[11]

---

9. Scott McMillin, '*The Book of Sir Thomas More*: Dates and Acting Companies', in Howard-Hill, ed., *Shakespeare and 'Sir Thomas More'*, 57–76 (at 57–60), notes Shakespeare's ignorance of the changes made by other hands to the manuscript. He therefore proposes that Shakespeare was part of a team that originally presented the text to Strange's Men around 1592 and that the play was subsequently adapted by Dekker and others for the Admiral's around 1603. Shakespeare's ignorance about the wider revision seems an absolute bar to his having worked on the play for a Chamberlain's revival. Work on an Admiral's revival remains a possibility; if so, this must have been what Taylor calls a 'favour' (111) for Henslowe's company.

10. John Jowett, 'Henry Chettle and the Original Text of *Sir Thomas More*', in Howard-Hill, ed., *Shakespeare and 'Sir Thomas More'*, 131–49, presents evidence that Chettle wrote substantial parts of the manuscript that now appears in Munday's hand.

11. At a certain point (or in some accounts, on two separate occasions) a version of *Sir Thomas More* was also sent to the government censor, Edmund Tilney. He can be seen to have worked through the text making deletions but he soon gave up on this process, finding the play to be fundamentally problematic. His rejection of performance 'at your perils' must be the reason for the manuscript's ultimate survival (even though G. Harold Metz, '"Voice and Credyt": The Scholars and *Sir Thomas More*', in Howard-Hill, ed., *Shakespeare and 'Sir Thomas More'*, 11–44, notes we cannot be certain that the play *wasn't* performed).

The practice of Hand C (the bookkeeper, an experienced professional who was also involved in the production of other theatrical documents) is revealing. Sometimes he fully transcribes scenes that have been written by the playwrights (making changes as he sees fit). At other points he is content simply to make alterations on their sheets of paper: adding stage directions, regularizing speech prefixes, and noting a minor actor's name. Shakespeare's portion is treated no differently from the others: he is a working playwright in the company of fellow professional authors. The three sides of paper in his hand re-write part of a crowd scene in which Thomas More calms a group of Londoners, who are at the point of attacking the city's immigrants.[12] Shakespeare wrote a fine speech for the play's hero, but in sketching the response of the citizens he held back from specifics, evidently because he was unaware of the players' larger plans for the text.

The company in question had decided, for example, that the play needed a stronger comic element, and they commissioned Thomas Heywood to introduce a part that would suit their clown.[13] Heywood therefore determined to give George Betts (one of the rioting citizens) a brother, whom he named Ralph. He then worked through the text, sometimes re-writing entire sections to accommodate his additions and at other times just squeezing new lines into Munday's original script. The second half of the scene on which Shakespeare worked (which remained in Munday's hand but was passed over to Heywood) contains an example of the latter practice: Heywood added a quip on dealing 'double honestly' to be spoken by Ralph.[14] Shakespeare, however, was not involved in this part of the revision. The name Betts, in his half of the scene, remained a featureless entity with short functional lines such as 'We'll hear the Earl of Surrey'.[15] Shakespeare was evidently unaware that George Betts had now been given a brother. It was

12. British Library, Harleian MS 7368, fol. 7^b, fol. 8^b, fol. 9^a. Probably Shakespeare also supplied More with a new soliloquy (pasted onto the manuscript at the bottom of fol. 11^b) but that speech was subsequently copied (and, in the process, further altered) by the company scribe.

13. This and other anomalies are discussed in Brian Vickers, *Shakespeare, Co-Author: A Historical Study of Five Collaborative Plays* (Oxford: Oxford University Press, 2002), 438–9. See also Blayney, '*Moore* Re-examined', 167–8. Giorgio Melchiori, '*The Book of Sir Thomas More*: Dramatic Unity', in Howard-Hill, ed., *Shakespeare and 'Sir Thomas More'*, 77–100, argues that these revisions were concurrent. McMillin, in the same volume, suggests Heywood's additions came later, with Shakespeare working alongside Munday at an earlier stage. Hands A, B, C, and E, he notes, were 'concerned about such specific matters of casting as eliminating three apprentices and Sir John Munday from the insurrection, building up a new role for a clown, and providing patches of additional time at points where costume changes were proving difficult' (McMillin, 'Dates and Acting Companies', 60).

14. Munday et al., *More*, ed. Gabrieli and Melchiori, 2.3.187–8.

15. For ease of reference, as noted above, I here quote the modernized transcript in Evans, ed., *Riverside Shakespeare*, which appears on pp. 1683–1700. In this case (line 31) the bookkeeper inserted 'Ge' before Shakespeare's speech prefix, thereby assigning the line to George.

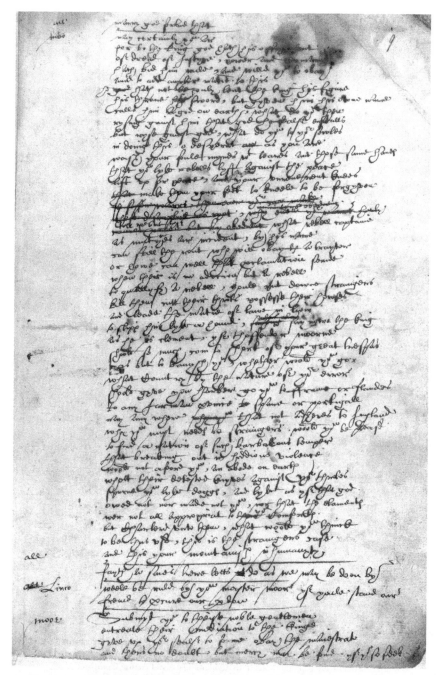

Figure 10. William Shakespeare's authorial holograph in the book of *Sir Thomas More*, British Library, Harleian MS 7368, fol. 9ᵃ.

Hand C, the company bookkeeper, who subsequently inserted this new character, 'Ralph Betts the clown', into Shakespeare's sections. This, for instance, was the opening exchange of the scene as Shakespeare left it:

LINCOLN: Peace, hear me! He that will not see a red herring at a Harry
    groat, butter at elevenpence a pound, meal at nine shillings a
    bushel, and beef at four nobles a stone, list to me.
OTHER: It will come to that pass if strangers be suffer'd. Mark him.
LINCOLN: Our country is a great eating country, argo they eat more in our
    country than they do in their own.
OTHER: By a halfpenny loaf a day, troy weight.[16]

The bookkeeper found the last of these lines amusing, so he altered the prefixes as follows:

LINCOLN: Peace, hear me! He that will not see a red herring at a Harry
    groat, butter at elevenpence a pound, meal at nine shillings a
    bushel, and beef at four nobles a stone, list to me.
GEO[RGE] BETT[S]: It will come to that pass if strangers be suffer'd. Mark him.
LINCOLN: Our country is a great eating country, argo they eat more in our
    country than they do in their own.
R[ALF] BETTS CLOW[N]: By a halfpenny loaf a day, troy weight.[17]

'Betts', 'all', and 'other', were largely interchangeable for Shakespeare. These and other prefixes were altered as the bookkeeper saw fit. By originally designating these speeches as words to be delivered simply by 'other' the playwright showed himself content to leave their physical embodiment open: within the culture of professional theatre, character was something that the company, rather than an individual author, set in stone.

The book of *Sir Thomas More* survives as a compelling testament to Shakespeare's involvement with the common professional practice of collaboration. The vast majority of scholars now accept that the poet was, at certain points, a collaborative writer.[18] At the beginning of his career

16. Modernized text in Evans, ed., *Riverside*, 1687, ll. 1–7, restoring Shakespeare's original. The Riverside defends 'alevenpence' as Shakespearean useage, but I have followed Gabrieli and Melchiori, eds., *More*, in conjecturally emending to 'elevenpence'.
17. To make the changes clear I here combine elements of the diplomatic and modernized transcriptions in Evans, ed., *Riverside*, 1686–7, ll. 1–7.
18. The conclusions of Samuel Schoenbaum's classic *Internal Evidence and Elizabethan Dramatic Authorship* (London: Edward Arnold, 1966) remain salutary: internal evidence can point to a likelihood in attribution, but it cannot constitute proof. On this basis only *The Two Noble Kinsmen*, produced with John Fletcher, qualifies as an absolute certainty. The evidence that Hand D in *Sir Thomas More* is Shakespeare's is, however, exceptionally strong. Brian Vickers's

Shakespeare was conversant—at both a literal and a figurative level—with men practised at co-authorship including Henry Chettle, Thomas Dekker, and Thomas Heywood. As one of many working as a freelance in the early 1590s he is quite likely to have been asked to contribute to a number of such projects: for example, *Edward III*, in portions of which his style has been detected and which was assembled around 1592.[19] Judging from the evidence, his position here was again not one of privilege. Just as for other writers collaborating on *Edward III*, the layered contributions of scribes, company bookkeepers, and later adaptors and printers, make Shakespeare's contributions difficult to pin down. This blurring of agency also applies in several early plays in which Shakespeare was the major creative presence. Most notably in the cases of *Henry VI Part I* and *Titus Andronicus*, other writers seem to have been commissioned to collaborate or provide additions to his work.

After 1594, however, the picture becomes sharper. For some dozen years (the time that saw Shakespeare write the core of his dramatic oeuvre) collaboration was totally or almost totally absent. If the additions to *Sir Thomas More* were the product of this period they constitute an oddity: a moment where Shakespeare agreed (perhaps in a political crisis) to add some

landmark study *Shakespeare, Co-Author: A Historical Study of Five Collaborative Plays* (Oxford: Oxford University Press, 2002) adds *Titus Andronicus*, *Timon of Athens*, *Pericles*, and *Henry VIII* to this tally. Few scholars would now question the list presented in *Shakespeare, Co-Author*, even if *Timon* and *Pericles* remain difficult cases because they do not survive in a finished state. That said, stylometrics (the computerized search for an authorial 'DNA' as a method of attribution) remains in its infancy and may perhaps never prove a failsafe method for determining authorship in works as difficult as the dramatic texts of this period. Brian Boyd, ed., *Words that Count: Essays on Early Modern Authorship in Honor of MacDonald P. Jackson* (Newark: University of Delaware Press, 2004) assembles state-of-the-art scholarship in this area and includes a valuable bibliography of the work of MacDonald Jackson, the scholar who has done most to develop a scientific methodology for attribution. The numerous disagreements on attribution between the contributors to this volume, however, shows that the technical problems are far from being solved.

19. Timothy Irish Watt, 'The Authorship of *The Raigne of Edward the Third*', in Hugh Craig and Arthur F. Kinney, eds., *Shakespeare, Computers, and the Mystery of Authorship* (Cambridge: Cambridge University Press, 2009), 116–33, backs Shakespeare's authorship of the King's scenes with the Countess of Salisbury, a case to which Jonathan Hope, *The Authorship of Shakespeare's Plays* (Cambridge: Cambridge University Press, 1994), is also sympathetic. The evidence is far from conclusive but the playwright's authorship of 2.1, obscured by subsequent intervention, is a viable thesis. For an overview of recent scholarship see William Shakespeare and others, *King Edward III*, ed. Giorgio Melchiori (Cambridge: Cambridge University Press, 1998). His date range for the play's composition is 1592–3.

speeches to another company's play.[20] At no point in the middle two phases did Shakespeare allow another literary writer to make alterations or additions to one of his plays.[21] Of course all Shakespeare's texts, as they made their way into the printed forms that survive today, were subject to a degree of alteration: sometimes they were shortened for production; some were modified after 1606 to comply with legislation on offensive language; and for all plays there was a degree of interference at the hands of scribes, bookkeepers, or printers.[22] None of these processes, however, involved Shakespeare in collaboration with other poets. *Macbeth* and *Measure for Measure* can easily be discounted as counter-examples: these are single-author creations. True, as reproduced after Shakespeare's death in the 1623 Folio they possibly contain additions by Middleton, but this was modification after Shakespeare's retirement and should not be confused

20. As noted above, the possibility of such a favour is muted in Taylor, 'Auspices', 111. Hugh Craig, 'The 1602 Additions to *The Spanish Tragedy*', in Craig and Kinney, eds., *Shakespeare, Computers, and the Mystery of Authorship*, 162–80, further proposes that the alterations to *The Spanish Tragedy* were Shakespeare's. The computational evidence here is controversial but, if correct, it presumably means that this play transferred to the Chamberlain's Men and that Burbage's performance of 'old hieronimo' recorded in the anonymous elegy BL, MS Stowe 962, fol. 62ᵇ, is correct. Brian Vickers, 'Shakespeare and Authorship Studies in the Twenty-First Century', *Shakespeare Quarterly* 62 (2011), 106–42, finds the methods in Craig and Kinney's volume to be inadequate, but does provisionally endorse their conclusions about the Shakespearean authorship of the scenes in *The Spanish Tragedy*.
21. Were one to accept the case of Laurie Maguire and Emma Smith, 'Many Hands: A New Shakespeare Collaboration?', *TLS*, 19 April 2012, that *All's Well that Ends Well* is collaborative it would still not constitute an exception because these authors tie their argument to the theory that the play was written after 1606. As with *Pericles* and *Timon*, the status of *All's Well* is difficult to determine on account of an unusually poor text.
22. This process is the focus of Gary Taylor and John Jowett's *Shakespeare Reshaped: 1606–1623* (Oxford: Clarendon Press, 1993) and also Grace Ioppolo, *Revising Shakespeare* (Cambridge, MA: Harvard University Press, 1991). A comprehensive overview is provided by Wells and Taylor, *Textual Companion*, the monumental work of scholarship from which *Shakespeare Reshaped* derives. The extent to which Shakespeare's texts were shortened in performance (either by himself or in collaboration with other members of the company) remains a matter of controversy. Lukas Erne, *Shakespeare as Literary Dramatist* (Cambridge: Cambridge University Press, 2003), 23 and *passim*, proposes separate performance and literary texts as a standard practice. Some printed texts (for example, Q1 *Henry V*, or Q1 and, to some extent, F *Hamlet*) do vary from other versions (in this case F *Henry V* and Q2 *Hamlet*) in a way that, to some, suggests purposive cutting. Yet long texts of this period (e.g. the B text of Marlowe's *Faustus*) also occasionally contain traces of production and it remains uncertain to what extent shorter ones can be taken as a record of what appeared on the stage. For a learned analysis of the way performance and manuscript versions may have differed for Shakespeare as a 'company man' see Richard Dutton, 'The Birth of an Author', in Cedric C. Brown and Arthur F. Marotti, eds., *Texts and Cultural Change in Early Modern England* (New York: St. Martin's Press, 1997), 153–78.

with collaborative authorship.[23] Assimilation into a company made Shakespeare a lone operator rather than one of the crowd.[24]

It is often supposed that Shakespeare, as the attached playwright of his company, must have adapted texts by other authors when these became part of the Chamberlain's repertory. Yet while this is a logical supposition, there are few signs that it occurred in reality.[25] *Sir Thomas More*, whatever its date, would not qualify: as we have seen, Shakespeare was not in this case working with a special knowledge of performance demands. Playwrights including Jonson, Marston, and Middleton wrote plays that were performed by the Chamberlain's/King's Men and it is evident that these were modified by the company. No study of co-authorship, however, has found evidence of a Shakespearean presence in these plays. As far as we can tell, Shakespeare retained sole responsibility for the work he produced for the first twelve years of the partnership, and for that work alone. Where his plays were revised for new productions (as was the case with *Henry IV Part 1*, *Othello*, *King Lear*, and *Hamlet*) it is evident that he himself was in charge of the changes.[26] Sole responsibility for the dramatic revision of his playtexts is

---

23. It is widely accepted that two songs, 'Come away, Come away' and 'Black Spirits' from Middleton's *The Witch*, were added for performances of Shakespeare's *Macbeth* after he left the company. These were not printed in full in the 1623 Folio and are generally omitted from modern editions of Shakespeare's play. It is also probable that Middleton cut Shakespeare's text of this play and modified and occasionally augmented portions of Shakespeare's drama. Middleton, *Collected Works*, ed. Gary Taylor and John Lavagnino (Oxford: Clarendon Press, 2007), 1165–201, provides a comprehensive introduction describing this process and offers a speculative genetic version of the text as Middleton might have adapted it. Taylor and Lavagnino's edition of Middleton's *Works*, 1542–85, also introduces and presents a genetic text of *Measure for Measure* as adapted by Middleton. That adaptation, it is argued, involved various minor changes, the addition of a song, a new passage involving Lucio and two gentlemen at 2.1, and possibly a change of setting from Ferrara to Vienna. In neither case do Taylor or his editors suggest that Shakespeare was alive to witness these alterations (the changes to *Macbeth* are thought to have been made around 1616; those to *Measure* are precisely dated to 1621).

24. It may simply be that Shakespeare, as actor and principal playwright, had no time to collaborate with other authors. In all likelihood, however, his position as sharer also somewhat removed him from the social orbit of other playwrights.

25. For the possible exception of *The Spanish Tragedy* see note 20 above.

26. On Shakespeare's involvement with the change of name of the comic lead from Oldcastle to Falstaff in *1 Henry IV* see David Scott Kastan, 'Killed with Hard Opinions: Oldcastle, Falstaff, and the Reformed Text of *1 Henry IV*', in *Textual Formations and Reformations*, ed. Laurie E. Maguire and Thomas L. Berger (Newark: University of Delaware Press, 1998), 211–27. John Kerrigan, 'Shakespeare as Reviser', in *On Shakespeare and Early Modern Literature: Essays* (Oxford: Oxford University Press, 2001), 3–22, makes a compelling case for purposive authorial revision in *Othello* and *Lear* and John Jones, *Shakespeare at Work* (Oxford: Clarendon Press, 1995) offers complementary readings of the same works and others. While it is not universally accepted that what we find in these plays is programmatic rewriting, there is no

another thing that makes Shakespeare's case special; becoming part of a company of actors, it seems, moved Shakespeare out of the working company of authors—thus changing the way that he worked.

From 1594 to 1605 there is no respectable evidence that Shakespeare co-authored his playtexts, but hereafter the picture begins slowly to change.[27] *Timon of Athens* was probably written between 1606 and 1607, and Thomas Middleton, who had up until then been working for the now-defunct St Paul's Boys, seems to have contributed substantial parts of this play. Around a year later Shakespeare's *Pericles* was performed by the King's Men and in 1608 it was published in a pirated edition in which Acts 1 and 2 were put together by George Wilkins, a playwright who (like Middleton) had recently begun to work for the Globe company. As texts, *Timon of Athens* and *Pericles* are difficult to deal with because neither survives in a version that could have been acted. *Timon* may never have made it to theatrical production and it was not intended, initially, to appear in the Shakespeare Folio at all. *Pericles* was altogether excluded (possibly for copyright reasons) so that only the pirate copy remains. This awkward textual history means that neither *Timon* nor *Pericles* provides incontestable evidence that Shakespeare had returned to co-writing: it is possible that in both cases the younger playwrights obtained Shakespeare scripts that were not finished and that they then worked independently to produce the two-author playtexts that now remain.[28] The likelihood is, however, that

doubt that the only comprehensive case of restructuring, that of *Lear*, was controlled by Shakespeare. That fact is confirmed by stylometric evidence set out by Kinney, 'Transforming *King Lear*', in Craig and Kinney *Shakespeare, Computers*, 181–201.

27. I disagree with Craig and Kinney's conclusion in *Shakespeare, Computers*, that Shakespeare was a collaborator 'throughout his career' (206). Their instances of 'collaboration' in the middle period (*Measure* and *Macbeth*) are cases where changes were made to a text after Shakespeare had left the company (on which see Jowett and Taylor, *Shakespeare Reshaped*). Even supposing that Shakespeare did write additions for *The Spanish Tragedy* and *Sir Thomas More* between 1602 and 1604, these cases would not constitute co-authorship; this would, instead, be play-patching of works composed more than a decade before.

28. On *Timon* the most important early study is MacDonald P. Jackson, *Studies in Attribution: Middleton and Shakespeare* (Salzburg: University of Salzburg, 1979). John Jowett, 'The Pattern of Collaboration in *Timon of Athens*', in Boyd, ed., *Words that Count*, 181–205, backs Jackson's case for joint authorship, although he observes that doubts do remain. Jowett's view, *contra* Jackson, is that Middleton worked separately after Shakespeare had finished with the manuscript. While Jowett does not believe that Middleton simply took up an abandoned manuscript and worked without the original author's permission, this remains a scenario that we cannot rule out. On *Pericles* the stand-out study is MacDonald P. Jackson, *Defining Shakespeare: 'Pericles' as Test Case* (Oxford: Oxford University Press, 2003) and its case for active collaboration has been widely accepted. Still, it should be acknowledged that the evidence is not

Shakespeare was part of the planning for these joint-authored projects and that *Timon of Athens* in particular was, by the year 1607, intentionally under production as a co-authored work.[29] If this is correct then Shakespeare, just before he signed the Blackfriars contract, was beginning to return to a method of writing that he had abandoned after becoming a sharer in the Chamberlain's Men.

The cases of *Timon of Athens* and *Pericles* remain open to interpretation, but there can be no doubt that in the final years before his full retirement Shakespeare did return to co-authorship as a favoured method. *Cardenio*, performed by the company in 1613, is reported with some reliability as composed 'by Mr Fletcher & Shakespeare'.[30] That play is lost, but good texts survive of *Henry VIII* and *The Two Noble Kinsmen*. These plays are rock-solid evidence of collaboration with Fletcher in or around 1613.[31] The long middle period of Shakespeare's career as a playwright, then, is book-ended by several years in which co-authorship was common. How do we account for this career pattern and how does it correlate with our understanding of Shakespeare's late style?

conclusive. Jackson's limited textual sample (using only Wilkins's *Miseries of Enforced Marriage* and Shakespeare's *The Tempest*) is, he admits, problematic (*Test Case*, 203). It remains possible that there existed at some point a completely Shakespearean *Pericles* and that what we have in Q1 is an attempt by someone (possibly Wilkins or possibly an individual using material supplied by Wilkins) to construct a pirated version of that text. Hope, *Authorship*, concluded that 'memorial reconstruction by Wilkins of a Shakespearean original is consistent with the evidence' (113) and although Jackson finds full collaboration 'much more likely' he does not dismiss this alternative (see especially *Test Case*, 215–16).

29. Vickers, *Shakespeare, Co-Author*, 142, 448–9, 476, writes about both plays as planned collaborations initiated by Shakespeare, not merely as texts that had, in their final version, the work of more than one hand.

30. Payments for court performances of 'Cardenno' or 'Cardenna' by the King's Men were recorded on 20 May and 9 July 1613; the attribution was made by Moseley in a Stationers' Register entry on 9 September 1653 (see Wells and Taylor, *Textual Companion*, 132–3). Brean Hammond's Arden3 edition of *Double Falsehood* (London: Methuen, 2010) makes the case for a connection between Theobald's eighteenth-century forgery and an original work by Shakespeare and Fletcher. Tiffany Stern, '"Whether one did Contrive, the Other Write, /...": Fletcher and Theobald as Collaborative Writers', in David Carnegie and Gary Taylor, eds., *The Quest for Cardenio: Shakespeare, Fletcher, Cervantes, and the Lost Play* (Oxford: Oxford University Press, 2012), 115–79, gives a powerful case for scepticism on this front and, more tentatively, expresses caution about the reliability of Moseley's claim.

31. For these dates and attributions see William Shakespeare, *The Two Noble Kinsmen*, ed. Lois Potter, Arden3 (London: Cengage, 1997) and William Shakespeare, *King Henry VIII*, ed. Gordon McMullan, Arden3 (London: Methuen, 2000). McMullan, though long a sceptic on the co-authorship question, comes out strongly in favour of it for *Henry VIII* and offers a table of attribution for specific scenes in his edition (448–9). Subsequent references are to these editions and appear in the text.

As the stock of the actor shares was diluted, as the founding fellows died or retired, as the plague interrupted performance, and as Shakespeare himself lessened his commitments as an actor, connections between the playwright and the players are likely to have weakened. Burbage remained a close friend, the outstanding talent of the company, and the dominant financial influence on Shakespeare's affairs. Armin, likewise, was a conspicuous presence. Shakespeare, like other playwrights composing work for the company, must have continued first and foremost to think of these players as he set about planning new work. Beyond this, however, the network was now more loosely constructed. The events at the end of 1608 broke lines that were already more stretched than they had been for the first twelve years of the fellowship's history. *Coriolanus*, written in 1608 and surviving in a text that was set from Shakespeare's personal hand-written manuscript, was the playwright's last comprehensively relational play.

This did not mean, however, that Shakespeare ceased to be interested in drama. Quite the opposite, his writing after this date comes alive, more conspicuously than it had since his earliest compositions, to the literary influence of other plays. This was a marked change for a playwright who had been fairly resistant to direct imitation for one and a half decades. Late Shakespeare is, like early Shakespeare, a playwright who draws energy from collaboration with other writers. The difficult cases of *Timon of Athens* and *Pericles* (whether originally co-authored or not) show a new self-consciousness about agency in artistic creation, whether through the poet and painter figures in the former or through the latter's antiquated narrator, Gower, who orchestrates the dumb shows and acts as a chorus. Both plays tend to place their audience at a critical distance through their conspicuous artifice. Their lead characters are also profoundly unconnected, at an emotional level, to the protagonists who surround them. There are radical breaks of locale that leave complete sets of characters abandoned: once the action moves from Athens to the wild woods (in *Timon*) or from Tharsus to Tyre (in *Pericles*) there is no going back. These are plays actually *about* their own genre (the satirical morality tale in *Timon*; in *Pericles*, romance): they are the first of a series of works in which Shakespeare responds (often collaboratively) to the tension between bookish sources and spectacle on the stage.

Even in *Henry VIII*, where a return to the genre of English history would license the playwrights to employ a less artificial palette, there is this same tendency towards abstraction. Speakers whom we might expect to become distinctive in their tactics and motivation, such as Suffolk, Norfolk, and Sir Thomas More as Chancellor, function almost as a chorus. The play is full of characters whose very names in the playbook signal their anonymity: Porter, Man, and gentlemen marked simply '1', '2', and '3'.[32] This is not neglect but rather a joint authorial strategy: exactly what we see in Shakespeare's scene for the much earlier *Sir Thomas More*. There are notable parallels between the two compositions. As Foakes observed, for example, the character of Sir Thomas More in *Henry VIII* becomes, in the final council scene, simply an unspecified 'Chancellor'—a stripping of individuality that was implemented, he argues, 'to avoid the intrusion of a personality'.[33] The play is extraordinarily even-toned in its depiction of the protagonists. Even in the case of Cardinal Wolsey we see little in the way of decadence or manipulative politics: it is only through the report of others that such claims are heard. Wolsey's fall is related at a double remove through a report on the contents of a letter. Although the Cardinal admits his faults by means of soliloquy we have not seen them in action and by the time he is willing to make a confession he is a wise stoical philosopher in line with almost all other speakers in the play. Indeed, Wolsey's great oration on his 'many summers in a sea of glory' bears a close resemblance to the hero's soliloquy in *Sir Thomas More* on the same subject, which was probably written by Shakespeare two decades before.[34] As in this early play, Shakespeare in *Henry VIII* is explicitly moralistic and makes the impersonal force of history (rather than individuals) the controller of events. The effect is one of staged chronicle rather than active drama. Characters whom we might expect to become emotional centres, such as Anne Bullen, are restricted to a single scene.

No doubt such emotional reticence is in part a consequence of the play's politically sensitive subject matter (another quality that connects it to *Sir Thomas More*). It is surely also a consequence, however, of a relative distance from the actors. In this respect, *Henry VIII* bears comparison not just with

---

32. See, for example, *Henry VIII*, 4.1, Folio TLN 2377–546.
33. William Shakespeare, *King Henry VIII*, ed. R. A. Foakes, Arden2 (London: Methuen, 1957).
34. *Henry VIII*, 3.2.350–71; *Sir Thomas More*, ed. Gabrieli and Melchiori, 3.1.1–21. Both these speeches are traditionally identified as Shakespeare's. Although in the manuscript of *Sir Thomas More* the soliloquy is in Hand C, that of the bookkeeper, he is generally considered to be transcribing Shakespeare's lines. Blayney, 'Moore Re-examined', 179, agrees the speech is by Shakespeare but thinks it was not originally intended for this position. John W. Velz, 'Sir Thomas More and the Shakespeare Canon: Two Approaches', in Howard-Hill, ed., *Shakespeare and 'Sir Thomas More'*, 171–95, explores further parallels between *More* and *Henry VIII* in their structural principles of 'coherence-through-contrast'; obviously he finds the latter the 'closer collaboration' (190).

Sir Thomas More but also with *Edward III*. This play, too, is episodic in structure, with characters often restricted to a particular episode or, where they are not, showing no 'memory' of earlier action when confronted by new events. The King of Act 3 of *Edward III*, for example, is immensely proud of his son the Black Prince, and shows no apparent recall of his expression of loathing for the same character in the previous act.[35] While the examples are not as extreme in *Henry VIII*, which is a much more sophisticated creation, that play likewise progresses episode by episode, with minimal emphasis on evolving mental states or power relations. Act V's conspiracy against Cranmer is a good example. Here Suffolk (hitherto a wise observer) suddenly becomes a plotter in league with Gardiner—a switch for which no previous action allows the audience to prepare.

Instead of character interaction, then, *Henry VIII* draws its audience's attention to moments of spectacle and revelation that bear comparison with the romances: a series of courtly processions; Katherine of Aragon's dying vision; Cranmer's revealing of the King's ring that gives him a quasi-magical protection; and Cranmer's great prophecy of Elizabeth as virgin monarch in the final act. Such spectacles not only distract from evolving character interaction, they actively resist it, because obtrusive distinctiveness would undermine the play's welling strains of Providence. The forbidding edict in what is probably Fletcher's prologue that banishes 'a fellow/ In a long motley coat guarded with yellow' (*Henry VIII*, Prologue 15–16) shuts the door on an author–actor collaboration that could have taken this play in a different direction. Shakespeare's fellow Robert Armin had made a specific study of King Henry's fool Will Sommers, the subject of this dismissal, who had already been a hit in Rowley's earlier play.[36] Had Shakespeare initiated the *Henry VIII* project six years earlier, his day-to-day contact with Armin would surely have led him to retain and personalize this part.

Shakespeare's last play, *The Two Noble Kinsmen*, written jointly with Fletcher, is the apotheosis of a new way of working. Co-authorship, it seems, lessens Shakespeare's emphasis on the evolution of character in

<hr/>

35. Act divisions are taken from *King Edward III*, ed. Melchiori. Melchiori claims that the scenes featuring the attempted seduction of the Countess are by Shakespeare, conclusions which are endorsed by Watt, 'The Authorship of *The Raigne of Edward the Third*', in Craig and Kinney, eds., *Shakespeare, Computers*, 116–33.
36. Will Sommers is the penultimate and most celebrated of the fools of Armin's *Fool upon Fool*, which Rowley had used as a source for the principal comic part of his play on the reign, *When you See me, you Know me* (c.1603–5).

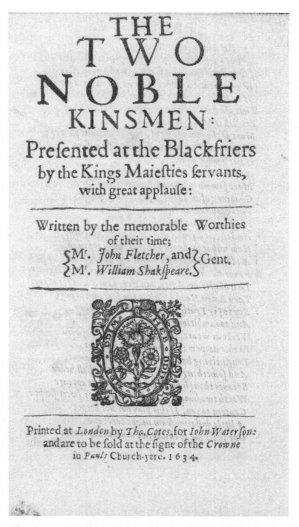

**THE
TWO
NOBLE
KINSMEN:**
Prefented at the Blackfriers
by the Kings Maiefties fervants,
with great applaufe:

Written by the memorable Worthies
of their time;
{M^r. *John Fletcher*, and}Gent.
{M^r. *William Shakfpeare*.}

Printed at *London* by *Tho. Cotes*, for *Iohn Waterfon*:
and are to be fold at the figne of the *Crowne*
in *Pauls* Church-yard. 1 6 3 4.

Figure 11. Title page of William Shakespeare and John Fletcher's *The Two Noble Kinsmen* (1634).

favour of a more choreographic interest in visual impact and rhetorical effect. In part this is, no doubt, a practical matter, because consistency is harder to achieve between authors who work at some distance on different portions of a text. This explains, for example, the confusion in *The Two Noble Kinsmen* over Palamon's offer of a dowry for the jailor's daughter, which is reported by the Second Friend at the beginning of the fourth act and then occurs again, to the apparent surprise of her father, in the play's final scene.[37] Although the division of labour in this play is no straightforward matter, Shakespeare and Fletcher can here be seen to be working without intimate knowledge of each other's writing (a fact of co-authorship that is also frequently evident in the book of *Sir Thomas More*).[38] Brian Vickers has catalogued such problems in Shakespeare's co-authored output and has shown how classically inspired ideals of unity came under strain when Renaissance playwrights worked together to the production schedules of the commercial stage.[39] As Vickers demonstrates, most technical slips could be corrected by the players in production, but alternative principles of unity (for example the complementarity of a plot and subplot) could also make diversity of input a driver of creativity in itself.[40]

Shakespeare's awareness of a co-author, it seems, fosters an aesthetic of primary colours. Opacity of character is thus a structural constant in *The Two Noble Kinsmen*—a fact again borne out by the proliferation of numbered types in its list of *dramatis personae*: two Friends, five Countrymen, five Countrywomen, two Messengers, three Queens, plus three Knights apiece for Palamon and Arcite.[41] In this play even the lead characters share in the opaque uniformity of these numbered minor protagonists. It is evident that the playwrights thought more about local scenic effect than they did about internal development and were willing to sacrifice consistency in this cause. In Act 1 Scene 2 and Act 2 Scene 2 (attributed to Shakespeare and Fletcher respectively), for example, the two kinsmen present themselves as sexual innocents as they pursue the triumph of the battlefield or the higher calling

---

37. *Two Noble*, ed. Potter, 4.1.23–4; 5.3.25–36. The consensus of scholarship (as recorded in Potter, ed., 25) attributes the first of these scenes to Fletcher and the second to Shakespeare.
38. Vickers, *Shakespeare, Co-Author*, 402–32, gives a critical account of attempts to divide the play between the two authors. The conventional division (as summarized in Potter's Arden3 edition, 24–35) was given by Cyrus Hoy, 'The Shares of Fletcher and his Collaborators in the Beaumont and Fletcher Canon (V)', *Studies in Bibliography* 13 (1960), 77–108. Hoy's division (89) gives Acts 1 and 5 (minus 5.1.1–33 and 5.2) to Shakespeare, as well as 2.1 and 3.1–2. Others are doubtful about the authorship of 1.4–5, and 3.2, but Hope, *Authorship*, 150, concludes both are by Shakespeare. Thomas B. Horton, 'Distinguishing Shakespeare from Fletcher through Function Words', *Shakespeare Studies* 22 (1994), 314–35, while supporting most of the traditional divisions, adds 2.3 and 4.3 to the scenes that Shakespeare might have written. In the discussion below I refer to Hoy's as the traditional division, but with the caution that Fletcher seems to have had responsibility for putting the final version together and that individual lines, therefore, may have a blurred attribution.
39. Vickers, *Co-Author*, 433–500.
40. Vickers, *Co-Author*, 433–8, 440–1.
41. No list of roles was supplied in the 1634 Quarto, but these numbered type names are used in the text.

of male friendship. In the drinking scene of Act 3 Scene 3 (credited to Fletcher), however, they speak of the women they have conquered with the swagger of seasoned gallants. Here it seems not so much a matter of the dramatist's forgetting earlier action but instead, more fundamentally, of an attitude to character that is scene-specific: the atmosphere of a drinking scene demands masculine bravado, whereas the mood-music of perfect chastity adds pathos to the scenes that envisage death in battle or a lifetime of imprisonment. Change in behaviour can thus be both instant and absolute, as we see at the moment when the drinking scene ends. Similar sharp divergences are found in *Pericles* and *Timon of Athens*, where past action is little guide to a character's future intent.

Such relative simplicity of characterization is a consistent feature of the co-authored drama. This is strikingly true of *The Two Noble Kinsmen*, irrespective of the authorship of individual portions of the text. In this respect the rehearsal scenes in Athenian woods that are found in *A Midsummer Night's Dream* (3.1) and *The Two Noble Kinsmen* (3.5) could scarcely be more different. The first is a foundational moment for Shakespeare's use of physical distinctiveness in character composition; the second, in contrast, depends for its effectiveness on symmetry between participants, with the countrywomen perfectly matching the countrymen. *The Two Noble Kinsmen*'s rehearsal scenes are attributed to Fletcher, but their aesthetic qualities are also found in scenes written by Shakespeare. His Act 1 Scene 1, for example, features the arrival of the petitioning queens, whose gesture and rhetoric alike are immensely repetitive. They each kneel in turn to Theseus, even after their appeal has been granted, and their action and mode of phrasing is then echoed by Hippolyta and Emilia. Throughout the play requests are marked by this synthetic quality, whether it be the kneeling women of Act 3 Scene 6 (written by Fletcher) or the prayers at the altar in Act 5 Scene 1 (always credited as Shakespeare's work).

Not since *Titus Andronicus* had Shakespeare been involved in the creation of such aestheticized action. The connection with that earlier work is significant because it ties up with important characteristics of the late style. Language in *The Two Noble Kinsmen* is, like plot and action, often driven by the logic of pattern: structural elements of rhetoric, such as stichomythia, are thus used to mark out a continuous principle of harmony and counterpoint. The reported scenes of combat, for example, employ patterns of reversal: thus cries of '*Palamon!*' marking this kinsman's apparent victory are neatly succeeded by opposing calls of '*Arcite!*' (5.3.71, 89).

Vickers, writing on *Titus Andronicus*, observes that George Peele (whom both he and Jackson identify as Shakespeare's co-author) tends to compose with an eye to balance and repetition. 'The symmetrical patterning', as Vickers puts it, 'has an operatic quality, as if the characters were engaged in a trio or quartet'.[42] This is true of Peele, but this is also a quality that Shakespeare was prone to adopting in his sections of *Titus Andronicus*—for example, in the macabre balletic exchanges as Titus, Lucius, and Marcus offer their hands for amputation in Act 3 Scene 1.[43] Such a preference for stylization, though no doubt a marker for Peele's authorship, is also a general feature of erudite penmanship. It is equally found in Fletcher's work in *The Two Noble Kinsmen* and is again echoed by Shakespeare in that drama as the writers collaborate.

In both the first and the final stage of his career Shakespeare tends to emphasize artifice and that tendency overlaps with his participation in co-authorship. These are two separate phenomena but they are not unrelated. Co-authorship, of course, did not always produce a more artificial style of writing: there is nothing artful about most of the collaborative productions of the Henslowe stable, such as *Sir John Oldcastle* or the Robin Hood trilogy. Ambitious poet-playwrights, however, often encouraged each other to move in a more knowing literary direction. In their tendency to foreground artifice and in their allusions to literary precedent writers as far apart as George Peele and John Fletcher are united. Peele, in *Titus Andronicus*, advertises Ovid's *Metamorphoses* with its 'tragic tale of Philomel' as a mutual point of reference; correspondingly, Fletcher begins *The Two Noble Kinsmen* with a prologue addressing 'Chaucer, of all admired'—thus trumpeting a close connection with his source text that runs throughout the play.[44] Paradoxically, such signals of indebtedness in the Renaissance often sit alongside assertions of creative independence: they demonstrate originality not through a complete departure from common practice, but rather

42. Vickers, *Co-Author*, 456; see also Jackson, *Test Case*, 195–203.
43. For further analysis of the play's dramaturgy in the light of contemporary dramatic conventions see John Kerrigan, *Revenge Tragedy* (Oxford: Clarendon Press, 1996), 193–208.
44. *Titus*, 4.1.47; *Two Noble*, Prologue.13. Vickers, *Co-Author*, 470, identifies *Titus*, 4.1, as Peele's and the Prologue of *Two Noble Kinsmen* is always credited as Fletcher's. The complex pattern of allusion to Ovid in *Titus* is widely recognized and examined, for example, in Jonathan Bate, *Shakespeare and Ovid* (Oxford: Oxford University Press, 1993), 103–8, 115–17, and *passim*. Bate's work is also important for my discussion below. On the pervasive engagement with Chaucer in *Two Noble Kinsmen* see, for example, Ann Thompson, *Shakespeare's Chaucer: A Study in Literary Origins* (Liverpool: Liverpool University Press, 1978), 165–213, and Helen Cooper, *Shakespeare and the Medieval World* (London: Arden, 2010), *passim*.

through the bending of that practice to the poet's individual ends.[45] This twisting of tradition is what Shakespeare does so spectacularly in his late drama (for example, through reworking the unities of time and place in *The Tempest* through magic, trumping what Fletcher had done before him in *The Faithful Shepherdess*). Such self-expression as a poet is quite compatible with the ethos of collaborative authorship; it is the *collaborative* production of individuality that unites Shakespeare's earliest and last works.

I argued in the first part of this monograph that the patterned quality of Shakespeare's pre-company writing (including its recurrent parallels with classical precedent and contemporary drama) reflects the playwright's close integration with other professional poets in that period. The publication of poetry and the practice of co-authorship were both features of that cultural milieu. These factors are once again present in the final phase of Shakespeare's development, including the sustained mutual exploration of literary conceits. In this respect, late works such as *The Two Noble Kinsmen*, *The Winter's Tale*, and *Cymbeline*, just like the early *Titus Andronicus*, *Richard III*, and *The Comedy of Errors*, are conspicuously literary plays. Co-authorship, then, was not necessarily a product of the practical deadlines of the commercial theatre; it could also be pursued as a sophisticated literary activity in its own right. Jeffrey Masten, in a study of the culture of co-authorship, has characterized these exchanges (including quotation, imitation, and parody) as part of a mode of interaction that he terms 'textual intercourse'.[46] His study is relevant because it shows how authors including Beaumont, Fletcher, and Shakespeare figured their individuality in a way that is fundamentally different from the modern. In both dramatic and non-dramatic writing they co-opted other authors (either contemporaries or venerable names such as Ovid and Chaucer) in games concerning textual production. Often, as Masten's term implies, this competitive *jouissance* had a sexual dimension.

---

45. The scholarship that sets out this proposition will be familiar to students of this period. Essential here is Thomas M. Greene's magisterial study *The Light in Troy: Imitation and Discovery in Renaissance Poetry* (New Haven, CT: Yale University Press, 1982). See also such outstanding contributions as A. J. Smith, 'Theory and Practice in Renaissance Poetry: Two Kinds of Imitation', *Bulletin of the John Rylands Library* 47 (1964), 212–43; G. W. Pigman III, 'Versions of Imitation in the Renaissance', *Renaissance Quarterly* 33 (1980), 1–32; Stephen Orgel, 'The Renaissance Artist as Plagiarist', *English Literary History* 48 (1981), 476–95; and David Quint, *Origin and Originality in Renaissance Literature: Versions of the Source* (New Haven, CT: Yale University Press, 1983).
46. See Jeffrey Masten, *Textual Intercourse: Collaboration, Authorship, and Sexualities in Renaissance Drama* (Cambridge: Cambridge University Press, 1997), esp. 12–66.

One example of 'textual intercourse' is the sharing of pastoral vocabulary between Fletcher and Shakespeare, which extends across their single-authored and collaborative work and frequently centres on female virginity. To characterize the virginal heroine of *The Winter's Tale*, Shakespeare had thus picked up on Fletcher's flower analogies from *The Faithful Shepherdess* and *Philaster*, allusive passages that themselves had a classical pedigree.[47] Fletcher, in turn, imitates his co-author in *The Two Noble Kinsmen*, again on the feminine topos of flowers. His scenes about the mad jailor's daughter have irritated critics because of what looks, from one perspective, like grating plagiarism of *Hamlet*.[48] The heartbroken girl, it is reported, gathers flowers to bury her father and seats herself upon a riverbank, contemplating thoughts of love and death:[49]

> The place
> Was knee-deep where she sat; her careless tresses
> A wreath of bullrush rounded; about her stuck
> Thousand fresh water-flowers of several colours,
> That methought she appeared like the fair nymph
> That feeds the lake with waters, or as Iris
> Newly dropped down from heaven. Rings she made
> Of rushes that grew by and to 'em spoke
> The prettiest posies: 'Thus our true love's tied',
> 'This you may loose, not me,' and many a one.
> And then she wept, and sung again, and sighed,
> And with the same breath smiled and kissed her hand.

(Two Noble Kinsmen, 4.1.82–93)

The closeness to the last moments of Ophelia's life as reported in *Hamlet* is obvious. Rather than what Dyce called 'plagiarism', however, the composition of this scene is perhaps better understood as an explicit act of creative reversal—an activity that Shakespeare surely encouraged, especially given Fletcher's earlier wholesale inversion for the company of one of his first creations, continuing *The Taming of the Shrew* with *The Tamer Tamed*

---

47. See Chapter 13 above.
48. For accusations of plagiarism see Francis Beaumont and John Fletcher, *Works*, ed. Alexander Dyce, 11 vols. (London: Edward Moxton, 1843–6), I, lxxxvi. Dyce's extensive comparison across a series of contemporary writers remains very valuable.
49. *Two Noble*, 4.1.95; compare with *Hamlet* Q2, ed. Ann Thompson and Neil Taylor, Arden3 (London: Thompson, 2006), 4.5.16–73, 160–92; 4.7.164–89.

around 1609.[50] Fletcher's catalogue of flowers, which ends in rescue from the river and eventual marriage rather than death by drowning, is a homage to the older playwright that has an edge of parody.

Physically, the interchange between Fletcher and Shakespeare must have been conducted both in person and through manuscript. They seem certain to have met to construct the plot-scenario of the play together: creating a document that established the narrative, the genre, and a scene-by-scene outline of how the action would unfold.[51] Yet composition thereafter would be individual, at least in the first instance, so there was also room for surprising the other poet and drawing attention to one's art. As Stern has demonstrated, the nature of plot-scenarios tended to encourage a scene-specific mode of composition: in the sub-genre created by such documents 'scenic rather than narrative integrity is a source of generative and creative power'.[52] We see this potential in the surviving manuscript scenario of the play *Philander, King of Thrace*, in which Sir Edward Dering makes plans for a series of episodes that echo one another across the play. In each of the completed acts, for example, the play's hero, Aristocles, has a scene in which he is banished from a kingdom, every time in a different form of emotional entanglement.[53] The wit of responding creatively to such a document lay in subtle patterns of parallel and antithesis.

Such patterns are evident in *The Two Noble Kinsmen*. The playwrights, for example, expanded on a hint in Chaucer to give Emilia a long, sexually charged, scene in a garden—a pastoral setting that they had explored through mutual allusion in the past. The scene was assigned to Fletcher, who gave the heroine a lengthy speech of self-comparison with a rose, 'the very emblem of a maid' (2.2.137). A series of evolving scenes that connected

---

50. For date and context see John Fletcher, *The Tamer Tamed, or, The Woman's Prize*, ed. Celia R. Daileader and Gary Taylor, Revels Student Editions (Manchester: Manchester University Press, 2006), 1–41.

51. Tiffany Stern, *Documents of Performance in Early Modern England* (Cambridge: Cambridge University Press, 2009), 22–3, shows that clear plot-scenarios were essential in co-authored compositions. They need not necessarily be written by the play's collaborators, but in this case that was the logical option. Vickers, *Co-Author*, 495–6, suggests a joint effort at constructing 'a coherent story line' but fairly separate composition; Potter, ed., *Two Noble*, 32, concludes that it was only Fletcher who overviewed the final draft, a text that may then have been worked over at a later date by the company bookkeeper (26).

52. Stern, *Documents*, 15.

53. Sir Edward Dering, Scenario of a play set in Thrace and Macedon (*c.*1620), Folger Shakespeare Library, MS X.d.206, pp. 4–6. For attribution see Stern, *Documents*, 13; a full transcription is provided by Joseph Quincy Adams, 'The Author-Plot of an Early Seventeenth Century Play', *The Library*, 4th series, 26 (1945), 17–27.

young women to flowers was no doubt something that the two men had discussed at their meeting, but playful embellishments could have been added as the playwrights worked apart. Fletcher's scene is thus flamboyantly self-reflexive about his action as a poet, not only re-telling a myth from Ovid but also picturing the process of artistic creation as Emilia asks her woman if she can 'work such flowers in silk' so that 'art can come near their colours' (2.2.127, 150).[54] This network of ideas and images had a strong pedigree in Renaissance poetry. In Spenser's sonnet sequence *Amoretti*, for example, his beloved's needlework is 'woven all about,/ with woodbynd flowers'—an object on which the poet comments through Ovidian tales. Shakespeare, working on a later part of the play, was thus also thinking about flowers, Ovid, and Spenser. In the scene assigned to him, set before the altar, he introduced a 'rose tree' not there in the source, and allowed the heroine ('her hair stuck with flowers') to contemplate how Diana's 'female knight' shall 'be gathered' or like 'a virgin flower,/ Must grow alone, unplucked'.[55] The scene has multiform connections with Fletcher's. This eroticized literary femininity, shared between male poets, is close in mood to what we find in Shakespeare's early poems, in which he, in common with many contemporaries, plays inventively with a restricted set of images and myths.[56]

The prologue to *The Two Noble Kinsmen* begins by comparing new plays to maidenheads and poets to breeders. We should be careful to avoid crude allegorization, but the competition between the kinsmen for the 'rose', Emilia, does offer a fictive shadow for the interaction of the authors. Like Palamon and Arcite, Shakespeare and Fletcher are often virtually inter-changeable in their modes of composition—indeed, they merge together all the more strongly as they assert their claims through inventive metaphors. Emilia's speech before the altar, for example, although always credited to Shakespeare, has a strong Fletcherian aspect—for example, in its masque-like formality, its exploitation of the erotic appeal of vulnerability,

54. See Edmund Spenser, *The Shorter Poems*, ed. Richard A. McCabe (London: Penguin, 1999), *Amoretti* LXXI, 9–10.

55. *Two Noble*, 5.1.162SD, 136SD, 140, 170, 167–8. For further exploration of this network see J. B. Lethbridge, ed., *Shakespeare and Spenser: Attractive Opposites* (Manchester: Manchester University Press, 2008).

56. Some of this field of reference is set out in John Kerrigan's *Motives of Woe: Shakespeare and 'Female Complaint': A Critical Anthology* (Oxford: Clarendon Press, 1991).

and its hypnotic rhetorical sheen.[57] Any uncertainty about attribution in this passage only confirms the extent to which Shakespeare was reabsorbed into the mainstream of literary discourse, thus mirroring his earliest work. Under the pressures of a culture of imitation and the practicality of the working theatre, distinct lines of authorial expression merge almost to a vanishing point.

For Shakespeare, the practice of co-authorship is difficult to detect, in part, because it co-exists with a stronger tendency towards imitation. This development cannot be linked with iron laws of determination to a growing distance between the playwright and his actors, but there is an overlap between these trends. Shakespeare in his co-authored plays starts to look more like his contemporaries, not just in the practicalities of his working conditions but also in his style of authorship. The influence of Fletcher, in particular, is not restricted to specific passages in *Henry VIII* and *The Two Noble Kinsmen*, but extends broadly across the late plays. Imitation and individual expression are not opposites. Ironically the moments at which Shakespeare asserts his agency as poet are also those at which he conforms most closely to the norms of Renaissance authorship. This is true, for example, of the instant when *Cymbeline*'s Imogen is pictured holding a copy of Ovid's *Metamorphoses*, in which 'the leaf's turn'd down/ Where Philomel gave up'.[58] The ekphrastic tableau here conjured by Iachimo pointedly recalls Shakespeare's *The Rape of Lucrece*, both through its Ovidian allusion and through the villain's self-comparison with 'our Tarquin' who 'thus/ Did softly press the rushes, ere he waken'd/ The chastity he wounded' (*Cymbeline*, 2.2.12–14). What can seem to modern sensibilities like a credo personal to the artist, however, can in fact be aligned with a much more orthodox humanist poetics, which was shared by all poet–playwrights of the age.[59] As a rule, this humanist poetics was something

57. See Michael D. Bristol, '*The Two Noble Kinsmen*: Shakespeare and the Problem of Authority', in Charles H. Frey, ed., *Shakespeare, Fletcher and 'The Two Noble Kinsmen'* (Columbia: University of Missouri Press, 1989) for a thoughtful essay on the difficulties of attribution in this play.

58. *Cymbeline*, 2.2.45–6. For a reading of this passage that relates it more widely to fictions of Shakespeare's authorship see Patrick Cheney, *Shakespeare's Literary Authorship* (Cambridge: Cambridge University Press, 2008), 234–64; Cheney, in this book and others, argues that shrouded career commentaries are a consistent feature of Shakespeare's work and that of others in the early modern period.

59. Gordon McMullan, *Shakespeare and the Idea of Late Writing: Authorship in the Proximity of Death* (Cambridge: Cambridge University Press, 2007), 22, notes that late style is presented as transhistorical but is in fact constructed by Romanticism and would have been 'incompre-

that excluded the players. In *Cymbeline* or *Two Noble Kinsmen*, unsurprisingly, we find little or nothing that connects with the personal characteristics of Shakespeare's actors. At some point in the 1610s the dramatist sold his shares in both the King's Men and the playhouses: his unique position, therefore, was not permanent.[60] The late plays evince a gradual loosening of his acting-company connections. The poet's farewell to the stage was something less romantic than the drowning of Prospero's book and retreat into contemplation. Shakespeare simply changed the company he kept.

hensible to Shakespeare and his contemporaries' and would, moreover, have been very difficult to articulate by means of the early modern theatrical system.

60. As is often observed, the shares are not mentioned in Shakespeare's will whereas shares do appear in the wills of many professional actors. The costly rebuilding of the Globe following the fire of 1613 is suggested by many as a likely catalyst for Shakespeare's departure but there can be no certain knowledge of the date.

Conclusion

'**N**ot a company keeper', wrote John Aubrey in some preliminary jottings about 'W. Shakespere' some sixty-five years after the dramatist's death. He 'would not be debauched and if invited to, writ: he was in pain'.[1] This note, found on an untidy sheet of paper and based on the report of the actor William Beeston, is hardly to be relied upon as definitive biography. Yet it does tally with other pieces of evidence (such as the poet's withdrawal, after 1594, from the conventional search for literary patronage in printed dedications) that suggest Shakespeare was not straightforwardly part of the early modern theatrical community, either of actors or of writers for the stage. Accounts of Shakespeare's working life offer disparate alternative contexts: they veer from myths of life as a travelling player on the one hand to legends of wit contests with Jonson at the Mermaid Tavern on the other.[2] For this reason the company that the poet kept has been difficult to pin down.

As a physical document Aubrey's note provides equivocal testimony. It was at some later stage cancelled by its author: his heavy pen lines cut the page vertically and several large crosses further obscure the text. Aubrey made

1. Biographical Scrap including details of Jonson, Fletcher, and Shakespeare, Bodleian Library, MS 8 & 4° L62 Art. (12). See Figure 12. The way in which this 'scrap' is preserved for posterity further illustrates the difficulty of contextualizing the life record. Samuel Schoenbaum's *William Shakespeare: A Documentary Life* (Oxford: Clarendon Press, 1975) cropped the facsimile, thus removing from view the anecdotes about John Fletcher and Ben Jonson that sit above and below 'W. Shakspere', thereby presenting a solitary figure on the page.

2. For a recent picture of Shakespeare as a stranger arriving in London in a troupe of actors 'in their gaudiest clothes, beating drums and waving flags' see Stephen Greenblatt, *Will in the World: How Shakespeare Became Shakespeare* (London: Jonathan Cape, 2004), 172; on the myth of the Mermaid Club see I. A. Shapiro, 'The "Mermaid Club"', *Modern Language Review* 45 (1950), 6–17, and James P. Bednarz, *Shakespeare and the Poets' War* (New York: Columbia University Press, 2001), 20. The 'wit combats' between Jonson and Shakespeare are first reported in John Fuller's *History of the Worthies of England* (1662), 'Warwickshire', 126, which describes Shakespeare as the combination of 'three eminent poets', Martial, Ovid, and Plautus, but thinks 'his learning was very little' in comparison with Jonson's 'great galleon'.

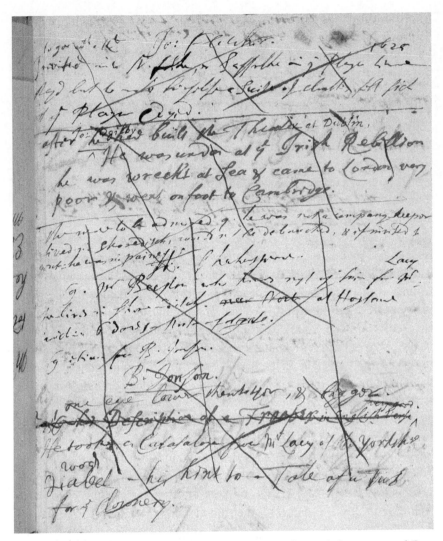

Figure 12. John Aubrey's note on John Fletcher, William Shakespeare, and Ben Jonson, Bodleian Library, MS Aubrey 8, fol. 45^b.

a statement about Shakespeare's lack of social engagement and then withdrew it. In doing so he presented a foundational problem for Shakespeare studies: how can the poet's literary achievement be contextualized? The daily routines of Shakespeare's life have proved stubbornly difficult to integrate with his writing: biographers and literary critics alike have found that the dry record of financial transactions, legacies, tributes, and company lists stands a long way apart from the life of the plays. Should we think of Shakespeare, in his creative life, as being 'not a company keeper'? Or is this a mistaken impression that should be crossed out? This book has confronted the binary of these two positions: on the one hand an acknowledgement of the unique achievement of Shakespeare's creation, which often seems unlike that of his contemporaries; on the other, a deep awareness of his integration with the working patterns of early modern theatre, practical commerce, and the stylistic habits of educated Renaissance art. It has forwarded a thesis in which both of these polarized positions are correct ones. Thereafter it has followed the history of their combination over two decades of professional authorship from 1592 to 1614.

It is useful to begin with a brief sketch of critical history because the isolation of Shakespeare as an artist was for a long time axiomatic. Samuel Taylor Coleridge, the first to provide what could be called a sustained close reading of the playwright, was profoundly struck by the difference between Shakespeare's writing and that of his contemporaries. This was not simply an assertion of faith from a Romantic poet. Examining the collected works of the playwright's contemporaries, Coleridge again and again commented on what he observed as Shakespeare's 'still remaining uniqueness'.[3] In the margins of his copy of the works of Beaumont and Fletcher, for example, he scribbled the rhetorical question 'why is Shakespeare an exception?'[4] Comparison with contemporaries, for Coleridge, was a method for discovering the character that set the playwright apart.[5] His eventual answer to his own question in the *Biographia Literaria* was rooted in Kantian metaphysics. The difference, Coleridge concluded, lay in Shakespeare's lack of spiritual investment in either fame or fortune: 'the utter *aloofness* of the poet's own feelings', his 'inward' nature, 'either indifferent or resigned':

> Shakespeare ... first studied patiently, meditated deeply, understood minutely, till knowledge become habitual and intuitive wedded itself to his

3. Samuel Taylor Coleridge, Letter to Thomas Allsop (30 March 1820), in *Works*, ed. H. J. Jackson, Oxford Authors (Oxford: Oxford University Press, 1985), 529. For wider discussion see *Coleridge's Criticism of Shakespeare: A Selection*, ed. R. A. Foakes (London: Athlone Press, 1989).
4. Coleridge, Marginalia on Beaumont and Fletcher, *Dramatic Works* (1811), IV, 166–7 (*The Noble Gentleman*) in *Works*, ed. Jackson, 567.
5. See, for example, Coleridge's commentary on the flyleaf of his copy of Ben Jonson, *Dramatic Works*, I: 'those who have read *Shakespeare only*, complain of occasional grossness in *his* plays— Compare him with his Contemporaries' (Coleridge, *Works*, ed. Jackson, 573).

habitual feelings, and at length gave birth to that stupendous power, by which he stands alone, with no equal or second in his own class; to that power, which seated him on one of the two glory-smitten summits of the poetic mountain, with Milton as his compeer not rival.[6]

In this conception, Shakespeare stood alone on a Parnassian hill because he transcended the material. Focused as he was on the unity of 'dramatic poems', Coleridge thus concluded that the drama, albeit produced on a physical stage, was the product of an interior experience and should be analysed as such: it finds its 'proper place, in the heart and in the closet'.[7]

Coleridge's insight into what he called the 'organic unity' of Shakespeare's plays had a formative effect on the practice of criticism. The idealization of the poet as a separated genius thus continued through Hazlitt to neo-Romantic critics such as Dowden and Wilson Knight and helped to establish 'Shake-speare Studies' as a distinct discipline, somewhat removed from the conventions of other Renaissance scholarship. A fixed canon of great plays, set apart from the commercial hubbub of company politics, continued to set the agenda for New Criticism from the 1920s till beyond the mid-century. While extraordinary scholarship was pursued at the same time in theatre history and bibliography (producing such monuments as the Arden editions), it had relatively little impact on the close reading that was practised by literary critics, whose instincts were humanistic and aesthetic and who tended still to think of Shakespeare as a mind on his own. Romantic convictions about the separate category of Shakespearean achievement thus remained important and found expression, for example, in Harold Bloom's passing observation, in 1976, that Shakespeare alone did not feel the anxiety of influence, absorbing Marlowe with ease as a 'very much smaller' creative power.[8]

From the mid-1970s, however, new movements in criticism began to approach Shakespeare's work through radically different methodologies. Deconstruction, Marxism, gender criticism, Lacanian psychoanalysis, New Historicism, the big schools of the last quarter of the century, all repudiated a Romantic tradition that saw human nature (and therefore artistic achievement)

---

6. Coleridge, *Biographia Literaria*, II and XV, in *Works*, ed. Jackson, 173, 322, 325.
7. Samuel Taylor Coleridge, 'Lectures on the Characteristics of Shakespear' (1813), in Jonathan Bate, ed., *The Romantics on Shakespeare* (London: Penguin, 1992), 140.
8. In the original text of 1976 Bloom was concerned primarily with Romantic and modern poets and only briefly excluded Shakespeare as belonging to 'the giant age before the flood'. In the revised edition two decades later, struck by a change in the critical climate, he considered the question more deeply; see Bloom, *The Anxiety of Influence: A Theory of Poetry*, 2nd edn (Oxford: Oxford University Press, 1997), xxiv–xlvii, 11.

as based in transcendent truths. It is a fool's errand to summarize their radical contribution, but these ways of reading all related Shakespeare to larger, less individuated, systems of significance, from semiotics to the oppressive power structures of his age. They challenged the notion that Shakespeare existed in some sense 'above' the age that produced him and thus also destabilized any Parnassian conception of his greatness. The twin pillars of the artist's moral and aesthetic elevation above the quotidian (both of which were central to Coleridge's beliefs about the poet) were shaken by this great wave of thought.[9]

In 1997, when Bloom wrote the preface to the second edition of *The Anxiety of Influence*, he reacted violently against the principles of this new thinking. The 'entire movement of our current School of Resentment', he argued, was 'towards eradicating Shakespeare's uniqueness': 'Neo-Marxists, New Feminists, New Historicists, French-influenced theorists', in his conception, 'all demonstrate their cultural materialism by giving us a reduced Shakespeare, a product of the "social energies" of the English Renaissance'.[10] In a series of works, most notably *The Western Canon* and *Shakespeare: The Invention of the Human*, Bloom returned to this fundamental point of opposition; setting up a dichotomy between his 'unique Shakespeare', rescued from cultural relativism, and a modern critical 'reduced Shakespeare', made simply one of the crowd. Such polemic hardly did justice to the complex critical revolution of the preceding two decades, but it was testimony to frustration about an oppositional gridlock between 'theory' and aesthetic judgement that was felt by many more traditional critics at this time.[11] Eminent thinkers thus continued to provide original accounts of the poet's development, one outstanding example being *Shakespeare's Language* by Frank Kermode. Such books, with an edge of resistance, retained an interior focus in their assessment of the evolving thought of a great genius. Their Shakespeare was emphatically not an intellectual company keeper and they themselves felt estranged from

---

9. It was Cultural Materialism that formulated this argument most directly; see, for example, Alan Sinfield, 'Give an account of Shakespeare and education, showing why you think they are effective and what you have appreciated about them; support your comments with precise references', in Jonathan Dollimore and Alan Sinfield, eds., *Political Shakespeare: New Essays in Cultural Materialism* (Manchester: Manchester University Press, 1985), 158–81, and Alan Sinfield, *Faultlines: Cultural Materialism and the Politics of Dissident Reading* (Oxford: Clarendon Press, 1992).
10. Bloom, *Anxiety*, xv.
11. A more comprehensive critique was delivered, for example, in Brian Vickers, *Appropriating Shakespeare: Contemporary Critical Quarrels* (New Haven, CT: Yale University Press, 1993).

the horde of modern critics whose instrumentalism, in their perception, did violence to an artist they loved.

The culture wars of the 1980s and 1990s were interesting times for Shakespeare studies—they generated light as well as heat. In the last decade and a half, a period often characterized as existing 'after theory', scholars and critics have been picking over the pieces. The major theoretical movements that were at their heyday in the 1980s are now much less readily identifiable and the concomitant defence of liberal humanist values is less stark. Formal discussion of style, which was neglected for a period, has returned to the mainstream. At the same time a new kind of historicism has taken shape as a practice, one dominated by questions, in the words of David Scott Kastan, 'about the forms in which Shakespeare's plays circulated, about the imaginative and institutional circumstances in which they were produced, and about what kinds of meanings were generated as the plays were experienced by their audiences and readers'.[12] Such questions have opened up an interest in fragments, both textual and historical, and facilitate the combining of critical methodologies that were previously distinct. They have enabled the rediscovery of Shakespeare's particularity without recourse to an essentialist mantra about 'human nature' or a rigid grading that separates genius from 'second rate' art.

Within theatre history this has, as a result, been a rich period of discovery. Scholars such as Gurr, Cerasano, Stern, Knutson, Dutton, and Ingram, to name but a few, have pursued a myriad of enquiries about the specific nature of institutions and contexts. Topics such as theatre finance, company identity and repertory, patronage, and the working practices of individual players and authors, have in this manner been substantially renewed. The great project of the Records of Early English Drama has given new access to theatrical activity at a national level, and the digitization of the Henslowe–Alleyn manuscript collection at Dulwich College, under the leadership of Grace Ioppolo, has made the material culture of the playhouse more approachable than before. Distinctions between playhouses, theatrical entrepreneurs, and audiences are now understood as vital to the way in which the period's drama was produced and received by consumers. The editorial methodology of the New Bibliography, which dominated for much of the twentieth century, has been superseded. In place of a focus on ideal texts and single authorial intentions, there is now an emphasis on variants.[13]

---

12. David Scott Kastan, *Shakespeare after Theory* (London: Routledge, 1999), 15.
13. Important studies here include Margreta de Grazia, *Shakespeare Verbatim: The Reproduction of Authenticity and the 1790 Apparatus* (Oxford: Clarendon Press, 1991) and Leah S. Marcus,

As a result, there is a new focus on the practicalities of Shakespeare's theatre: his dramatic works are not just recognized but celebrated as material entities that reflect the constraints on a particular author and a particular company at a particular time.

The culture wars have breached any remaining walls between 'Shakespeare' and 'Renaissance' studies, so that the playwright is now understood in more thorough ways as a product of specific educational and cultural institutions. Influential work includes that of Kastan and Loewenstein on print; Barroll and Dutton on the role of government; and Bate, Burrow, and Miola on Shakespeare's classicism. These critics and others like them are all informed by a large body of new research on the period's customs of composition and interpretation. Shakespeare's reception at learned institutions like the court, the Inns of Court, and the universities makes his connections with that culture more evident.[14] Above all it is apparent that Shakespeare responds to the ideals and anxieties of Renaissance humanism, which suffused high-status cultural production in his age.

Finally, life writing has also gained focus as a genre and a topic for enquiry. Biographical work aimed at a more general audience has demonstrated how a conjoined focus on literary text and material context can highlight the significance of a particular location or moment. This is true, for example, of Charles Nicholl's *The Lodger*, which investigates Shakespeare through the lens of Silver Street in London's Cripplegate, or James Shapiro's *1599*.[15] Simultaneously, recent writing on authorship has sharpened awareness of limits on the recoverability of personal identity in this period.[16] Jackson, Jowett, Vickers, and Taylor, amongst others, have done important empirical work to uncover practices of authorial collaboration, while a more theoretical grouping (including Johnson, Masten, and

Unediting the Renaissance: Shakespeare, Marlowe, Milton (London: Routledge, 1996). The 1986 Oxford *Works* of Shakespeare edited by Wells and Taylor and the Arden3 series edited by Proudfoot, Thompson, and Kastan have introduced an entirely new frame of reference for editors and readers.

14. An excellent example of this kind of focus on reception is found in the essays on 'Other Playing Spaces' collected in Richard Dutton's *Oxford Handbook of Early Modern Theatre* (Oxford: Oxford University Press, 2009), 263–344.
15. Nicholl, *The Lodger: Shakespeare on Silver Street* (London: Penguin, 2008); Shapiro, *1599: A Year in the Life of William Shakespeare* (London: Faber & Faber, 2005).
16. See, for example, Takashi Kozuka and J. R. Mulryne, eds., *Shakespeare, Marlowe, Jonson: New Directions in Biography* (Aldershot: Ashgate, 2006) and Kevin Sharpe and Steven N. Zwicker, eds., *Writing Lives: Biography and Textuality, Identity and Representation in Early Modern England* (Oxford: Oxford University Press, 2008).

Weimann) has questioned the fixity of theatrical authorship itself. Alongside them there are critics (such as Bednarz, Knapp, and Cheney) who think of Shakespeare as a strategist in authorial self-representation, even proposing (as Erne has done) his interest in the printing of his plays. In none of these accounts does Shakespeare emerge as entirely normative. As Knapp makes clear in his preface to *Shakespeare Only*, the playwright's reputation in his own age was unusual—a reputation that reflected the unrivalled quality of his writing, but also the unparalleled material circumstances that he enjoyed.

Scholarship at the beginning of the twenty-first century, then, does not place Shakespeare on a 'glory-smitten summit' but nor does it reduce him uncritically to the 'social energies' of the Elizabethan and Jacobean theatrical world. This book has set out a history of Shakespeare's writing that is based on his evolving material circumstances and institutional affiliations. It is therefore indebted to a great deal of the historical scholarship and criticism of recent decades, as well as the pioneering work of earlier historians such as Chambers, Bentley, and Greg. It could be said to bring together two separate strands of current thought on the playwright. On the one hand there is the work of theatre historians, doing more and more to uncover the practical realities of early modern performance: for instance, Stern and Palfrey's recent study *Shakespeare in Parts*. On the other there is a more literary criticism that explores the classically informed wit of the playwright and connects him to a Renaissance culture of imitation: this is what Kerrigan did, for example, in comparing Shakespeare with Kyd and Seneca in his study *Revenge Tragedy: Aeschylus to Armageddon*. This book has attempted to provide a narrative of how these separate aspects of Shakespeare's art came together and of how the balance between them changed over time.

The Shakespeare who emerges from this study is a product of circumstance. To state a counterfactual conditional: if he had not joined the Chamberlain's Men on their foundation, the consequences for his art would have been profound. He might, for example, have anticipated Jonson's trajectory by committing to print, striving for literary patronage, and pursuing more exclusively classical models for the structure of his plays. Without his intimate knowledge of his company's members, the distinctive dramaturgy of the post-1594 drama (based on individuated, evolving characters) could not have emerged. The extent of Shakespeare's separation from the mainstream, therefore, was not inevitable, even if his talents were always unparalleled. Examination of the late plays provides support for this theory. These works were written under conditions in which Shakespeare must have had a more distant contact with the actors. As a result they are, in their techniques of characterization, more like the plays written by Shakespeare's contemporaries and also more like the style of his earliest compositions, which were written before he was a sharer in the Lord Chamberlain's Men.

Shakespeare's work, then, is different from that of his fellow playwrights in part because of his different material situation. This conclusion is the opposite of that drawn by Coleridge, but it does acknowledge the uniqueness that Romantic criticism observed. Comparison of Shakespeare's working conditions and writing style with those of his contemporaries is doubly revealing. It is evident that no other early modern playwright had such a long association with a stable group of performers or composed so consistently with a focus on character. Yet other playwrights did for short periods work in a way that was comparable to Shakespeare's and this did have an impact on the way that they wrote. Heywood, most notably, also became a sharer (albeit in a less successful company) and because of this he promoted the ethos of the public theatre and developed aspects of what could be called a 'Shakespearean' style. Middleton, likewise, although never a sharer, collaborated closely with actors: his play *The Changeling*, for example, is one of a series of works produced through co-authorship with the comic performer William Rowley. Such examples illustrate the effect of performer contact on a dramatist's style. Shakespeare, therefore, is different but contingently different, and his circumstances (like those of other playwrights) changed over time.

Reading Shakespeare's plays and poems chronologically, it is evident that they develop as a result of his personal connections. This has always been recognized, but this impact from individuals has been irregularly noted and is often underplayed. I have argued here for the consistent, pressing importance of this multiform company. It makes sense, for example, to think of the work that Shakespeare produced before 1594 as the product of his close contact with fellow poet–playwrights: men such as Marlowe, Peele, and Heywood, whose work he imitated and with whom he probably co-wrote. This was not an immature period or one marked by an outsider's anxiety of influence, but instead a relatively conventional example of professional success. Things changed in 1594 and Shakespeare became less focused on other writing professionals. He now concentrated in the first instance on fellow actors, but this did not mean that his situation was entirely stable. Major developments like the replacement of Kemp with Armin, the restart of the children's companies, or the growing pre-eminence of Burbage all made their mark on the way that he wrote. Of course, the playwright was not insulated from other commercial or political influence, but his position as a company playwright did modify the extent to which he was borne on such tides.

Coleridge was right when he observed in Shakespeare an unparalleled breadth and consistency of characterization, a relative absence of scurrility, and a more sympathetic portrayal of women than is found in most other playwrights of the age. Such characteristics, however, can all be understood as products of his investment in the public theatre (and hence his move away from a certain kind of classicism, from print publication, and his avoidance of the children's stage). Shakespeare's material stake in a commercial enterprise had both artistic and ideological implications. The grubby world of the playhouse, which Coleridge believed the poet transcended, was in fact a daily reality, not least in the form of the payments for admission that mounted up over the years. The poet's extraordinary financial gain, also unparalleled, cannot be separated from some pure element of art that went to produce it. What Coleridge thought of as indifference was closely allied to the profit that the company made.[17]

Aubrey revised his first note, based on Beeston's visit, about Shakespeare's being 'not a company keeper'. He produced instead a more polished, less edgy version in which the playwright was 'very good company, and of a very ready and pleasant smooth wit'.[18] Still more than the original note, this is questionable evidence on which to judge character, but the palimpsest created by this alteration creates a useful paradigm. Shakespeare both does and does not fit into easy companionship with his contemporaries. By examining his plays alongside the work of his immediate associates, both actors and poets, this book has tried to focus on that combination of integration and difference. As a humanist-educated poet who joined a group of players, Shakespeare became a 'company keeper' in multiple senses; his decision precipitated both a kind of removal from the mainstream and a much deeper fellowship with other men.

17. Coleridge, *Biographia Literaria* in *Works*, ed. Jackson, 173, thinks of Shakespeare's indifference to print as a product of his 'inward assurance'. Yet, as Dutton makes clear in a strong overview of the evidence, acting companies in this period continued to resist publication because they considered it a threat to their commercial property in plays (see Richard Dutton, 'Birth of an Author', in Cedric C. Brown and Arthur F. Marotti, eds., *Texts and Cultural Change in Early Modern England* (New York: St. Martin's Press, 1997), 153–78).
18. Schoenbaum, *Documentary*, 205; see also John Aubrey, *Brief Lives*, ed. Oliver Lawson Dick (Harmondsworth: Penguin, 1972), 334–5.

Appendix: Dates of composition for Shakespeare's works

This table represents the consensus of scholarly opinion on Shakespeare's compositional chronology. For the date range of Shakespeare's works I rely in the first instance on the conclusions of Stanley Wells and Gary Taylor's *William Shakespeare: A Textual Companion* (1987), which provides a comprehensive analysis of the evidence in each case. For all plays I have also checked the discussion on dating in the most recent Arden edition as well as in other relevant scholarship, but I reference this only where a significant conflict arises. Cases where I differ from Wells and Taylor's dating are underlined and footnoted. The date listed for the *Sonnets and Lover's Complaint* is that of publication (for an account of their likely extended period of composition see *Complete Sonnets and Poems*, ed. Colin Burrow (2002)).

1590–1	*The Two Gentlemen of Verona*
1590–1	*The Taming of the Shrew*
1591	*2 Henry VI*
1591	*3 Henry VI*
1592	*1 Henry VI*
1592–3	*Richard III*
1592–3[1]	*Titus Andronicus*

1. Bate's Arden3 edition (1995) significantly changed the critical appreciation of *Titus Andronicus*, which was previously still often characterized as 'a piece of crude and embarrassing juvenilia' (3). His argument that the play was 'written in late 1593 and first performed in January 1594' has gained a great deal of support.

1592–3	*Venus and Adonis*
<u>1593–4</u>[2]	Additions to *Sir Thomas More*
1593–4	*The Rape of Lucrece*
1594	*The Comedy of Errors*
1594–5	*Love's Labour's Lost*
1595	*Richard II*
1595	*Romeo and Juliet*
1595	*A Midsummer Night's Dream*
1596	*King John*
1596–7	*The Merchant of Venice*
1596–7	*1 Henry IV*
1597–8	*The Merry Wives of Windsor*
1597–8	*2 Henry IV*
1598	*Much Ado About Nothing*
1598–9	*Henry V*
1599	*Julius Caesar*
1599–1600	*As You Like It*
1600–1	*Hamlet*
1601	*Twelfth Night*
1602	*Troilus and Cressida*
1603	*Measure for Measure*
1603–4	*Othello*
1604–5	*All's Well that Ends Well*[3]
1605–6	*King Lear*[4]
1606	*Macbeth*

2. Wells and Taylor date the additions 1603–4 but their judgement differs radically from the preceding scholarly consensus. Gabrieli and Melchiori's Revels edition (1990) re-asserts and strengthens W. W. Greg's case for an early period of composition and sets the limits to 1593–4. For discussion see Chapter 14 above.
3. Wells and Taylor support this date range for *All's Well That Ends Well* as their headline conclusion, although they think it possible the play was written as late as 1607. In the light of MacDonald P. Jackson, 'Spurio and the Date of *All's Well that Ends Well*', *Notes & Queries* 48 (2001), 298–9, the critical consensus has shifted somewhat towards endorsement of the later date.
4. Both Wells and Taylor and Foakes's Arden3 edition (1997) give this date range for the play's composition. Wells and Taylor separate *The History of King Lear* (1605–6) from *The Tragedy of King Lear*, for which they suggest the year 1610. Foakes is more sceptical about such a definitive separation. *Lear*'s two versions are discussed in Chapter 9 of this monograph.

1606	*Antony and Cleopatra*
1605–7[5]	*Timon of Athens*
1607	*Pericles*
1608	*Coriolanus*
1609	*Sonnets and Lover's Complaint*
1609–10[6]	*The Winter's Tale*
1610	*Cymbeline*
1611	*The Tempest*
1612–13	*Cardenio* [lost]
1613	*Henry VIII*
1613–14	*The Two Noble Kinsmen*

5. Wells and Taylor date the play 1605, which is certainly the earliest date possible, but Dawson and Minton's Arden3 edition (2008) makes a very strong case for the year 1607.
6. Wells and Taylor date the play 1609; Pitcher's Arden3 edition (2010) pushes the time of composition forward to late 1610.

Works cited

The list below includes only items that have been cited directly. Primary works discussed without mention of a specific edition (for example, Ovid's *Metamorphoses*) are not listed. Where the main text cites a work as it is printed in an anthology or in the collected works of an author (such as *Michaelmas Term* in the Oxford Middleton) it is only the edited volume that is listed below. Works of unknown, multiple, or disputed authorship are attributed according to the consensus of modern scholarship. *The London Prodigal* is thus listed as anonymous (in spite of its attribution to William Shakespeare on the title page) and *Histrio-Mastix* as 'Marston, John (?)' (in spite of ongoing debate about its authorship and the absence of an author's name on the title page).

PRIMARY

Manuscripts

All Alleyn and Alleyn–Henslowe manuscripts are in Dulwich College, London

Alleyn MSS 1, Letters and Papers Relating to the English Drama and Stage during the Life of Edward Alleyn and to the Subsequent History of the Fortune Theatre, 1559–1662

Alleyn MSS 2, Letters and Papers of Philip Henslowe and Edward Alleyn as Joint Masters of the Royal Game of Bears, Bulls, and Mastiff Dogs, 1598–1626

Alleyn MSS 3, General Correspondence of Edward Alleyn and Philip Henslowe, 1577–1626

Alleyn MSS 5, Legal and Miscellaneous Papers of Edward Alleyn and his Family, 1612–1626

Alleyn MSS 7, Diary and Account Book of Philip Henslowe, 1592–1609

Alleyn MSS 8, Memorandum Book of Edward Alleyn, 1594–1616

Alleyn MSS 9, Diary and Account Book of Edward Alleyn, 29 September 1617–1 October 1622

Alleyn MSS 19, The 'Platt' (or Plot) of *The Second Part of the Seven Deadly Sins*

Alleyn MSS 20, The Manuscript of *The Telltale*

Alleyn–Henslowe Muniments Series 1, Relating to Theatres and Theatrical Matters

Alleyn–Henslowe Muniments Series 3, Relating to Dulwich Manor and the Foundation of Dulwich College

Anon., *Dick of Devonshire*, British Library, MS Egerton 1994, fols 30–52

——*Edmund Ironside*, British Library, MS Egerton 1994, fols 96–118

——'An Elegy on the Death of the Famous Actor Rich: Burbage' and 'Epitaphium Gulielm Shakspeare', British Library, MS Stowe 962, fols 62^b–63^b, 78^b–79^a

——*The Faithful Friends*, Victoria and Albert Museum, MS Dyce 25.F.10

——fragmentary addition to Christopher Marlowe's *Massacre at Paris*, Folger Shakespeare Library, MS J.b.8

——*The Lady Mother*, British Library, MS Egerton 1994, fols 186–211

—— 1*Richard II*, or *Thomas of Woodstock*, British Library, MS Egerton 1994, fols 161–85

——*The Tragedy of Nero*, British Library, MS Egerton 1994, fols 245–67

Aubrey, John, Biographical scrap including details of John Fletcher, William Shakespeare, and Ben Jonson, Bodleian Library, MS Aubrey 8, fol. 45^b

——Brief Life of Shakespeare, Bodleian Library, MS Arch.F.c.37

Daborne, Robert, *The Poor Man's Comfort*, British Library, MS Egerton 1994, fols 268–93

Dekker, Thomas, Receipt for loan, Folger Shakespeare Library, MS X.d.319

Dering, Sir Edward, Scenario of a play set in Thrace and Macedon (*c.*1620), Folger Shakespeare Library, MS X.d.206

Fletcher, John, *Bonduca*, British Library, MS Additional 36758

Forman, Simon, *Casebooks*, Bodleian Library, MS Ashmole 411 and MS Ashmole 219

Heywood, Thomas, *Calisto, or, The Escapades of Jupiter*, British Library, MS Egerton 1994, fols 74–95

——*The Captives*, British Library, MS Egerton 1994, fols 52–73

Killigrew, Thomas, *The Second Part of Cecilia and Clorinda, or, Love in Arms*, Folger Shakespeare Library, MS V.b.209

Massinger, Philip, *Believe as You List*, British Library, MS Egerton 2828

Mountfort, Walter, *The Launching of the Mary* or *The Seaman's Honest Wife*, British Library, MS Egerton 1994, fols 317–49

Munday, Anthony, and others, *Sir Thomas More*, British Library, Harleian MS 7368

Percy, William, *Plays*, Alnwick Castle, MS Percy 507, MS Percy 508, and MS Percy 509

Rowley, Samuel, Note to Philip Henslowe (undated), Folger Shakespeare Library, MS X.d.261

Ward, John, Diary, Folger Shakespeare Library, MS 2073.5

Wilson, Arthur, *The Inconstant Lady*, Folger Shakespeare Library, MS J.b.1

Editions printed before 1700

Titles of plays are modernized in line with those in Alfred Harbage, *Annals of English Drama: 975–1700*, 3rd edn, rev. Sylvia Stoler Wagonheim (London: Routledge, 1989). Place of publication, unless otherwise stated, is London

Alfield, Thomas (?), *A True Report of the Death and Martyrdom of M. Campion* (1582)

Anon., *Defence of Conny Catching* (1592)
—— *The Famous Victories of Henry V* (1598)
—— *King Leir* (1605)
—— *Locrine* (1595)
—— *The London Prodigal* (1605)
—— *Mucedorus* (1610)
—— *The Taming of a Shrew* (1594)
—— *The True Tragedy of Richard III* (1594)
Armin, Robert, *Fool upon Fool* (1600)
—— *Fool upon Fool* (2nd edn 1605)
—— *The History of the Two Maids of More-Clacke* (1609)
—— *The Italian Tailor and his Boy* (1609)
—— *A Nest of Ninnies* (1608) [rev. 3rd edn of *Fool upon Fool*]
—— (?), *A Pill to Purge Melancholy* (1599)
—— *Quips upon Questions* (1600)
Bancroft, Thomas, *Time's Out of Tune* (1658)
Bavande, William, *Touching the Ordering of a Commonweal* (1559)
Chapman, George, *Bussy D'Ambois* (1641)
Chettle, Henry, *Kind-Harts Dreame* (1592)
—— *The Tragedy of Hoffman* (1631)
Cicero, Marcus Tullius (?), *Rhetoricum ad C. Herennium libri quattuor* (1579)
Cooke, John, *Greenes Tu quoque, or The Cittie Gallant* (1614)
Daniel, Samuel, *Delia* and *The Complaint of Rosamond* (1592)
Day, John, William Rowley, and George Wilkins, *Three English Brothers* (1607)
Dekker, Thomas, *The Gull's Hornbook* (1609)
—— *If it Be not Good, the Devil is In It* (1612)
Erasmus, Desiderius, *De copia verborum ac rerum* (1512)
—— *De ratione studii* (1512)
Field, John, *Godly Exhortation* (1583)
Flecknoe, Richard, 'A Short Discourse of the English Stage', appended to *Love's Kingdom* (1664)
Fletcher, John, *The Faithful Shepherdess* (1610)
—— *The Faithful Shepherdess* (1629)
Fuller, John, *History of the Worthies of England* (1662)
Gascoigne, George, *Supposes*, in *A Hundred Sundry Flowers* (1573)
Golding, Arthur, *Brief Discourse of the Late Murther of Master George Saunders* (1573)
Gosson, Stephen, *Plays Confuted in Five Actions* (1582)
Greene, Robert (?), *Friar Bacon and Friar Bungay* (1594)
—— (?), *George a Greene, the Pinner of Wakefield* (1599)
—— (?), *Greenes Groats-worth of Wit* (1592)
—— *Never Too Late* (1590)
—— *Orlando furioso* (1594)
—— *Quip for an Upstart Courtier* (1592)

——(?), *The Tragical Reign of Selimus* (1594)

Greene, Robert, and Thomas Lodge (?), *A Looking Glass for London and England* (1594)

Guarini, Battista, *Il pastor fido, or, The Faithful Shepherd* (1602)

Harington, Sir John, *Orlando furioso* (1591)

Harvey, Gabriel, *Pierces Supererogation* (1593)

Hayward, Sir John, *First Part of the Life and Reign of King Henry IIII* (1599)

Heywood, Thomas, *An Apology for Actors* (1612)

——*The English Traveller* (1633)

——*Nine Books of Various History Concerning Women* (1624)

Jansonius, P. A., *Mundi furiosi continuatio ab anno 1597–1600* (Cologne, 1600)

Jonson, Ben, *Sejanus* (1605)

——*Works* (1616)

Kemp, William, *Nine Days Wonder* (1600)

Lodge, Thomas, *Wit's Misery* (1596)

Marlowe, Christopher, *Edward the Second* (1594)

——*Tamburlaine the Great* (1590)

——and Thomas Nash (?), *Dido, Queen of Carthage* (1594)

Marston, John (?), *Histrio-Mastix, or, The Player Whipt* (1610)

——(?), *Jack Drum's Entertainment* (1601)

——*The Metamorphosis of Pygmalion's Image* (1598)

Massinger, Philip, and Nathan Field, *The Fatal Dowry* (1632)

Munday, Anthony (?), *Second and Third Blast of Retrait* (1580)

Nashe, Thomas, *Strange News* (1592)

Northbrooke, John, *Dicing, Dancing, Vain Plays or Interludes, with Other Idle Pastimes* (1577)

Overbury, Sir Thomas, *Characteristics*, printed as *Sir Thomas Overburie his Wife* (1616)

Puttenham, George, *The Arte of English Poesie* (1589)

Rowlands, Samuel, *The Letting of Humours Blood* (1600)

Rowley, Samuel, *When you See me, you Know me* (1605)

Rymer, Thomas, *A Short View of Tragedy* (1693)

Scoloker, Anthony, *Daiphantus* (1604)

Shakespeare, William, *Hamlet* [Q1] (1603)

——*Hamlet* [Q2] (1604)

——*The History of Henry the Fourth* [1 Henry IV] [Q2] (1598)

——*The Second Part of Henry the Fourth* [Q1] (1600)

——*The Chronicle History of Henry the Fifth* [Q1] (1600)

——*The First Part of the Contention* [2 Henry VI] (1594)

——*The Chronicle History of King Lear* [Q1] (1608)

——*Loves Labours Lost* [Q1] (1598)

——*The Merry Wives of Windsor* [Q1] (1602)

——*A Midsummer Night's Dream* [Q1] (1600)

——*Much Ado About Nothing* [Q] (1600)

——*Othello* [Q1] (1622)

——*Pericles* [Q1] (1608)

——*The Rape of Lucrece* (1594)

——*The True Tragedy of Richard Duke of York* [*3 Henry VI*] (1595)

——*The Tragedy of King Richard the Second* [Q1] (1597)

——*The Tragedy of King Richard the Third* [Q1] (1597)

——*Romeo and Juliet* [Q2] (1599)

——*Sonnets* and *A Lover's Complaint* [Q1] (1609)

——*Titus Andronicus* [Q] (1594)

——*Troilus and Cressida* [Qa] (1609)

——*Troilus and Cressida* [Qb] (1609)

——*Venus and Adonis* (1593)

——*Works* [F] (1623)

——and John Fletcher, *The Two Noble Kinsmen* [Q] (1634)

Sidney, Sir Philip, *The Countess of Pembroke's Arcadia* (1598)

Spenser, Edmund, *The Faerie Queene* (1596)

Tarlton, Richard (?), *Tarlton's Jests* (1613)

Taylor, John, *Works* (1630)

Webster, John, *The Duchess of Malfi* (1623)

Wilson, Robert, *The Cobbler's Prophecy* (1594)

——*The Three Ladies of London* (1584)

——*The Three Lords and Three Ladies of London* (1588)

Editions printed after 1700

Anon., *English Mystery Plays*, ed. Peter Happé (London: Penguin, 1975)

——*Fair Em: A Critical Edition*, ed. Standish Henning (New York: Garland, 1980)

——*The Faithful Friends*, ed. G. M. Pinciss (Oxford: Malone Society, 1975)

——*The Honest Man's Fortune*, ed. J. Gerritsen, Groningen Studies in English 3 (Groningen: J. B. Wolters, 1952)

——(Robert Greene?), *John of Bordeaux, or The Second Part of Friar Bacon*, ed. W. L. Renwick (Oxford: Malone Society, 1936)

——*A Knack to Know a Knave*, ed. G. R. Proudfoot (Oxford: Malone Society, 1964)

——*A Knack to Know an Honest Man*, ed. Henry de Vocht (Oxford: Malone Society, 1910)

——*Larum for London* (Oxford: Malone Society, 1913)

——*Locrine* (Oxford: Malone Society, 1908)

——*The London Prodigal*, in *The 'Doubtful' Plays of the Third Shakespeare Folio*, ed. John S. Farmer, Tudor Facsimile Texts (London: Early English Drama Society, 1911)

——*Look About You* (Oxford: Malone Society, 1913)

——*Lust's Dominion*, ed. J. Le Gay Brereton, Materials for the Study of Old English Drama (Louvain: Librairie universitaire, Uystpruyst, 1931)

Anon., *Ratseis Ghost (1605)*, ed. H. B. Charlton (Manchester: Manchester University Press, 1932)

—— *The Three Parnassus Plays*, ed. J. B. Leishman (London: Nicholson & Watson, 1949)

——*A Warning for Fair Women*, ed. Charles Dale Cannon (The Hague: Mouton, 1975)

—— *The Weakest Goeth to the Wall* (Oxford: Malone Society, 1912)

Arber, Edward, *A Transcript of the Registers of the Company of Stationers of London, 1554–1640 AD*, 5 vols. (London: privately published, 1875–94)

Armin, Robert, *Collected Works*, ed. J. P. Feather, 2 vols. (New York: Johnson Reprint, 1972)

Aubrey, John, *Brief Lives*, ed. Oliver Lawson Dick (Harmondsworth: Penguin, 1972)

Bale, John, *King Johan*, ed. Barry B. Adams (San Marino, CA: Huntington Library, 1969)

Beaumont, Francis, *The Knight of the Burning Pestle*, ed. Michael Hattaway, New Mermaids (London: A. & C. Black, 1969)

Beaumont, Francis, and John Fletcher, *Works*, ed. Alexander Dyce, 11 vols. (London: Edward Moxton, 1843–6)

—————*The Dramatic Works in the Beaumont and Fletcher Canon*, ed. Fredson Bowers, 10 vols. (Cambridge: Cambridge University Press, 1966–89)

—————*The Maid's Tragedy*, ed. T. W. Craik, Revels (Manchester: Manchester University Press, 1988)

—————*Philaster, or Love Lies a-Bleeding*, ed. Andrew Gurr, Revels (Manchester: Manchester University Press, 2003)

Bullough, Geoffrey, ed., *Narrative and Dramatic Sources of Shakespeare*, 8 vols. (London: Routledge and Kegan Paul, 1961–75)

Chapman, George, *The Blind Beggar of Alexandria* (Oxford: Malone Society, 1929)

—— *Bussy D'Ambois*, ed. Nicholas Brooke, Revels (Manchester: Manchester University Press, 1964)

—— *The Conspiracy and Tragedy of Charles Duke of Byron*, ed. John Margeson, Revels (Manchester: Manchester University Press, 1988)

——*An Humorous Day's Mirth*, ed. Charles Edelman, Revels (Manchester: Manchester University Press, 2010)

—— *The Widow's Tears*, ed. Akihiro Yamada, Revels (London: Methuen, 1975)

—— *Works*, ed. Thomas Marc Parrott, 3 vols. (London: Routledge, 1914)

—— Ben Jonson, and John Marston, *Eastward Ho*, ed. R. W. van Fossen, Revels (Manchester: Manchester University Press, 1979)

Coleridge, Samuel Taylor, *Works*, ed. H. J. Jackson, Oxford Authors (Oxford: Oxford University Press, 1985)

Davies, John (of Hereford), *Works*, ed Alexander B. Grosart, 2 vols. (New York: AMS Press, 1967)

Dekker, Thomas, *Dramatic Works*, ed. Fredson Bowers, 4 vols. (Cambridge: Cambridge University Press, 1953–61)

—— *The Gull's Hornbook*, ed. R. B. McKerrow (New York: AMS Press, 1971)

—— *The Shoemaker's Holiday*, ed. Anthony Parr, New Mermaids (London: A. & C. Black, 1990)

Drayton, Michael, *Works*, ed. William Hebel, 5 vols. (Oxford: Basil Blackwell, 1961)

Fletcher, John: *see also* Beaumont, Francis

Fletcher, John, *The Tamer Tamed, or, The Woman's Prize*, ed. Celia R. Daileader and Gary Taylor, Revels Student Editions (Manchester: Manchester University Press, 2006)

Greene, Robert, *The Scottish History of James the Fourth*, ed. Norman Sanders, Revels (London: Methuen, 1970)

—— (?), *The Tragical Reign of Selimus*, ed. W. Bang (Oxford: Malone Society, 1909)

—— *Works*, ed J. Churton Collins, 2 vols. (Freeport: Books for Libraries Press, 1905; repr. 1970)

Greg, W. W., *Dramatic Documents from the Elizabethan Playhouses: Stage Plots, Actors' Parts, Prompt Books*, 2 vols. (Oxford: Clarendon Press, 1969)

—— ed., *Henslowe Papers: Being Documents Supplementary to Henslowe's Diary* (London: A. H. Bullen, 1907)

Haughton, William, *Englishmen for My Money* (Oxford: Malone Society, 1913)

Henslowe, Philip, and others, *Diary*, ed. R. A. Foakes, 2nd edn (Cambridge: Cambridge University Press, 2002)

—— and others, *Documents of the Rose Playhouse*, ed. Carol Chillington Rutter, rev. edn (Manchester: Manchester University Press, 1999)

Heywood, Thomas, *The Captives*, ed. Arthur Brown (Oxford: Malone Society, 1953)

—— *The Fair Maid of the West, Parts I and II*, ed. Robert K. Turner Jr, Regents Renaissance Drama (London: Edward Arnold, 1968)

—— *The First and Second Parts of King Edward IV*, ed. Richard Rowland, Revels (Manchester: Manchester University Press, 2005)

—— (?), *How a Man May Chuse a Good Wife from a Bad*, ed. A. E. H. Swaen (Louvain: Librairie universitaire, Uystpruyst, 1912)

—— *If you Know not Me you Know Nobody, Part I*, ed. Madeleine Doran (Oxford: Malone Society, 1935)

—— *If you Know not Me you Know Nobody, Part II*, ed. Madeleine Doran (Oxford: Malone Society, 1935)

—— *The Wise-Woman of Hogsdon*, in *Thomas Heywood: Three Marriage Plays*, ed. Paul Merchant, Revels (Manchester: Manchester University Press, 1996)

—— *A Woman Killed with Kindness*, ed. R. W. van Fossen, Revels (Manchester: Methuen, 1961)

—— *A Woman Killed with Kindness*, ed. Brian Scobie, New Mermaids (London: A. & C. Black, 1985)

Heywood, Thomas, and others, *The Famous History of the Life and Death of Captain Thomas Stukeley*, in *The Stukeley Plays*, ed. Charles Edelman, Revels (Manchester: Manchester University Press, 2005)

Honigmann, E. A. J., and Susan Brock, *Playhouse Wills: 1558–1642: An Edition of Wills by Shakespeare and his Contemporaries in the London Theatre* (Manchester: Manchester University Press, 1993)

Jonson, Ben, *The Alchemist*, ed. F. H. Mares, Revels (Manchester: Manchester University Press, 1967)

——*Bartholomew Fair*, ed. G. R. Hibbard, New Mermaids (London: A. & C. Black, 1977)

——*Every Man in his Humour*, ed. Robert S. Miola, Revels (Manchester: Manchester University Press, 2000)

——*Every Man out of his Humour*, ed. Helen Ostovich, Revels (Manchester: Manchester University Press, 2001)

——*Poetaster*, ed. Tom Cain, Revels (Manchester: Manchester University Press, 1995)

——*Sejanus: His Fall*, ed. Philip J. Ayres, Revels (Manchester: Manchester University Press, 1990)

——*Volpone, or, The Fox*, ed. Brian Parker, Revels (Manchester: Manchester University Press, 1999)

——*Works*, ed. C. H. Herford and Percy Simpson, eds., 11 vols. (Oxford: Clarendon Press, 1925–52)

——*Works*, ed. Ian Donaldson (Oxford: Oxford University Press, 1985)

Kyd, Thomas, *The Spanish Tragedy*, ed. Philip Edwards, Revels (London: Methuen, 1959)

Lodge, Thomas, *Scylla's Metamorphosis*, in Sandra Clark, ed., *Amorous Rites: Elizabethan Erotic Verse* (London: Everyman, 1994)

——*The Wounds of Civil War*, ed. Joseph W. Houppert, Regents Renaissance Drama (London: Edward Arnold, 1969)

Lyly, John, *Campaspe* and *Sappho and Phao*, ed. G. K. Hunter, Revels (Manchester: Manchester University Press, 1991)

——*Endymion*, ed. David Bevington, Revels (Manchester: Manchester University Press, 1996)

——*The Woman in the Moon*, ed. Leah Scragg, Revels (Manchester: Manchester University Press, 2006)

Manningham, John, *The Diary of John Manningham of the Middle Temple, 1602–1603*, ed. Robert Parker Sorlien (Hanover, NH: University Press of New England, 1976)

Marlowe, Christopher, *Collected Poems*, ed. Patrick Cheney and Brian J. Striar (Oxford: Oxford University Press, 2006)

——*Doctor Faustus, A- and B-Texts (1604, 1616)*, ed. David Bevington and Eric Rasmussen, Revels (Manchester: Manchester University Press, 1993)

—— *Edward II*, ed. Charles R. Forker, Revels (Manchester: Manchester University Press, 1994)

—— *Tamburlaine the Great*, ed. J. S. Cunningham, Revels (Manchester: Manchester University Press, 1981)

—— *The Jew of Malta*, ed. N. W. Bawcutt, Revels (Manchester: Manchester University Press, 1978)

—— *Works*, ed. E. D. Pendry (London: Everyman, 1976)

Marston, John, *Antonio and Mellida*, ed. W. Reavely Gair, Revels (Manchester: Manchester University Press, 2004)

—— *The Dutch Courtesan*, ed. David Crane, New Mermaids (London: A. & C. Black, 1997)

—— (?), *Histrio-Mastix*, in *Works*, ed. H. Harvey Wood, 3 vols. (Edinburgh: Oliver and Boyd, 1939)

—— *The Malcontent*, ed. George K. Hunter, Revels (Manchester: Manchester University Press, 1999)

—— *Parasitaster, or, The Fawn*, ed. David A. Blostein, Revels (Manchester: Manchester University Press, 1978)

—— (?), *Jack Drum's Entertainment*, in *Works*, ed. H. Harvey Wood, 3 vols. (Edinburgh: Oliver and Boyd, 1939)

Massinger, Philip, *Believe as You List*, ed. Charles J. Sisson (Oxford: Malone Society, 1927)

Middleton, Thomas, *Collected Works*, ed. Gary Taylor and John Lavagnino (Oxford: Clarendon Press, 2007)

Munday, Anthony, *The Death of Robert, Earl of Huntington* (Oxford: Malone Society, 1967)

—— *The Downfall of Robert, Earl of Huntingdon* (Oxford: Malone Society, 1965)

—— *John a Kent & John a Cumber* (Oxford: Malone Society, 1923)

—— and others, *The Life of Sir John Oldcastle* (Oxford: Malone Society, 1908)

—— and others, *Sir Thomas More*, ed. Vittorio Gabrieli and Giorgio Melchiori, Revels (Manchester: Manchester University Press, 1990)

Nashe, Thomas, *The Unfortunate Traveller and Other Works*, ed. J. B. Steane (London: Penguin, 1972)

Peele, George, *The Battle of Alcazar*, in *The Stukeley Plays*, ed. Charles Edelman, Revels (Manchester: Manchester University Press, 2005)

—— *The Hunting of Cupid* [fragment], in *Collections IV & V* (Oxford: Malone Society, 1911), 307–15

—— *The Old Wives Tale* (Oxford: Malone Society, 1908)

—— *Works*, ed. Charles Tyler Prouty, 3 vols. (New Haven, CT: Yale University Press, 1952–70)

Percy, William, *Mahomet and his Heaven*, ed. Matthew Dimmock (Aldershot: Ashgate, 2006)

Plautus, Titus Maccius, *Plays*, ed. and trans. Paul Nixon, 5 vols. (Cambridge, MA: Harvard University Press, 1961)

Porter, Henry, *The Two Angry Women of Abington* (Oxford: Malone Society, 1913)

Rowley, William, and John Heywood, *Fortune by Land and Sea*, ed. William Doh (New York: Garland, 1980)

Seneca, Lucius Annaeus, *Tragedies*, ed. John G. Fitch, Loeb, 2 vols. (Cambridge, MA: Harvard University Press, 2002–4)

Shakespeare, William, *All's Well that Ends Well*, ed. G. K. Hunter, Arden2 (London: Methuen, 1962)

——*All's Well that Ends Well*, ed. Susan Snyder (Oxford: Oxford University Press, 1994)

——*Antony and Cleopatra*, ed. John Wilders, Arden3 (London: Methuen, 1995)

——*As You Like It*, ed. Juliet Dusinberre, Arden3 (London: Methuen, 2006)

——*The Comedy of Errors*, ed. R. A. Foakes, Arden2 (London: Methuen, 1962)

——*Complete Sonnets and Poems*, ed. Colin Burrow (Oxford: Oxford University Press, 2002)

——*Cymbeline*, ed. J. M. Nosworthy, Arden2 (London: Methuen, 1955)

——*Cymbeline*, ed. Roger Warren (Oxford: Oxford University Press, 2008)

——(attributed), *Double Falsehood*, ed. Brean Hammond, Arden3 (London: Methuen, 2010)

——*Hamlet*, ed. Robert Hapgood, Shakespeare in Production (Cambridge: Cambridge University Press, 1999)

——*Hamlet*, ed. Ann Thompson and Neil Taylor, Arden3 (London: Thompson, 2006)

——*Hamlet: The Texts of 1603 and 1623*, ed. Ann Thompson and Neil Taylor, Arden3 (London: Cengage, 2006)

——*Henry V*, ed. T. W. Craik, Arden3 (London: Methuen, 1995)

——*Julius Caesar*, ed. David Daniel, Arden3 (London: Cengage, 1998)

——*King Henry IV, Part 1*, ed. David Scott Kastan, Arden3 (London: Thompson, 2002)

——*King Henry IV, Part 2*, ed. A. R. Humphreys, Arden2 (London: Methuen, 1981)

——*King Henry VI, Part 1*, ed. Edward Burns, Arden3 (London: Thompson, 2000)

——*King Henry VI, Part 2*, ed. Richard Knowles, Arden3 (London: Thompson, 2001)

——*King Henry VI, Part 3*, ed. John D. Cox and Eric Rasmussen, Arden3 (London: Thompson, 2001)

——*King Henry VIII*, ed. R. A. Foakes, Arden2 (London: Methuen, 1957)

——*King Henry VIII*, ed. Gordon McMullan, Arden3 (London: Methuen, 2000)

——*King John*, ed. E. A. J. Honigmann, Arden2 (London: Methuen, 1954)

——*King Lear*, ed. R. A. Foakes, Arden3 (London: Cengage, 1997)

——*King Lear: A Parallel Text Edition*, ed. René Weis (Harlow: Longman, 1993)

——*King Richard II*, ed. Charles R. Forker, Arden3 (London: Thompson, 2002)

——*King Richard III*, ed. Antony Hammond, Arden2 (London: Methuen, 1981)

——*King Richard III*, ed. James R. Siemon, Arden3 (London: Methuen, 2009)

——*Love's Labour's Lost*, ed. H. R. Woudhuysen, Arden3 (London: Cengage, 1998)

—— *Macbeth*, ed. Kenneth Muir, Arden2 (London: Methuen, 1951)

—— *Measure for Measure*, ed. J. W. Lever, Arden2 (London: Methuen, 1965)

—— *The Merchant of Venice*, ed. John Drakakis, Arden3 (London: Methuen, 2010)

—— *The Merry Wives of Windsor*, ed. T. W. Craik (Oxford: Oxford University Press, 1990)

—— *The Merry Wives of Windsor*, ed. Giorgio Melchiori, Arden3 (London: Methuen, 2000)

—— *A Midsummer Night's Dream*, ed. Harold F. Brooks, Arden2 (London: Routledge, 1979)

—— *Much Ado About Nothing*, ed. A. R. Humphreys, Arden2 (London: Methuen, 1981)

—— *Much Ado About Nothing*, ed. Claire McEachern, Arden3 (London: Methuen, 2007)

—— *Othello*, ed. E. A. J. Honigmann, Arden3 (London: Thomas Nelson, 1997)

—— *Romeo and Juliet*, ed. Brian Gibbons, Arden2 (London: Methuen, 1980)

—— *The Taming of the Shrew*, ed. Brian Morris, Arden2 (London: Methuen, 1981)

—— *The Tempest*, ed. Virginia Mason Vaughan and Alden T. Vaughan, Arden3 (London: Methuen, 1999)

—— *Timon of Athens*, ed. Anthony B. Dawson and Gretchen E. Minton, Arden3 (London: Cengage, 2008)

—— *Titus Andronicus*, ed. Jonathan Bate, Arden3 (London: Routledge, 1995)

—— *Troilus and Cressida*, ed. David Bevington, Arden3 (London: Cengage, 1998)

—— *Twelfth Night*, ed. Keir Elam, Arden3 (London: Methuen, 2008)

—— *The Two Gentlemen of Verona*, ed. William C. Carroll, Arden3 (London: Thompson, 2004)

—— *The Two Noble Kinsmen*, ed. Lois Potter, Arden3 (London: Cengage, 1997)

—— *The Winter's Tale*, ed. John Pitcher, Arden3 (London: Methuen, 2010)

—— *The Riverside Shakespeare*, ed. G. Blakemore Evans (Boston, MA: Houghton Mifflin, 1974)

—— *Works*, ed. John Jowett, William Montgomery, Gary Taylor, and Stanley Wells, 2nd edn (Oxford: Oxford University Press, 2005)

—— and George Wilkins, *Pericles*, ed. Suzanne Gossett, Arden3 (London: Methuen, 2004)

—— (?), and others, *King Edward III*, ed. Giorgio Melchiori (Cambridge: Cambridge University Press, 1998)

Sidney, Sir Philip, *Complete Works*, ed. A Feuillerat, 4 vols. (Cambridge: Cambridge University Press, 1912–26)

Spenser, Edmund, *The Shorter Poems*, ed. Richard A. McCabe (London: Penguin, 1999)

Udall, Nicholas, *Dramatic Writings*, ed. John S. Farmer, Early English Dramatists (London: Early English Drama Society, 1906)

Wilkins, George, *The Miseries of Enforced Marriage*, ed. Glenn H. Blayney (Oxford: Malone Society, 1964)

Wilson, Robert (?), *The Pedlar's Prophecy* (Oxford: Malone Society, 1914)

326 WORKS CITED

SECONDARY

Aaron, Melissa D., 'The Globe and *Henry V* as Business Document', *Studies in English Literature* 40 (2000), 277–92

Adams, Joseph Quincy, 'The Author-Plot of an Early Seventeenth Century Play', *The Library*, 4th series, 26 (1945), 17–27

——'The Housekeepers of the Globe', *Modern Philology* 17 (1919), 1–8

——'*The Massacre at Paris* Leaf', *The Library*, 4th series, 14 (1934), 447–69

——*Shakespearean Playhouses* (Boston, MA: Houghton Mifflin, 1917)

Anon., 'Diary of the Reverend John Ward (1629–1681)', *Shakespeare Quarterly* 8 (1957), 460, 520, 526, 553

Baker, J. H., *An Introduction to English Legal History*, 4th edn (London: Reed Elsevier, 2002)

Bald, R. C., 'Arthur Wilson's *The Inconstant Lady*', *The Library*, 4th series, 18 (1937), 287–313

Baldwin, T. W., *The Organization and Personnel of the Shakespearean Company* (Princeton, NJ: Princeton University Press, 1927)

——*William Shakspere's Petty School* (Urbana: University of Illinois Press, 1943)

——*William Shakspere's Small Latine and Lesse Greeke*, 2 vols. (Urbana: University of Illinois Press, 1944)

Barroll, Leeds, *Politics, Plague, and Shakespeare's Theater* (Ithaca, NY: Cornell University Press, 1991)

——'Shakespeare and the Second Blackfriars Theater', *Shakespeare Studies* 33 (2005), 156–70

——'Shakespeare, Noble Patrons, and the Pleasures of "Common" Playing', in Paul Whitfield White and Suzanne R. Westfall, eds., *Shakespeare and Theatrical Patronage in Early Modern England* (Cambridge: Cambridge University Press, 2002), 90–121

——Alexander Leggatt, Richard Hosley, and Alvin Kernan, eds., *The Revels History of Drama in English*, vol. III: *1576–1613* (London: Methuen, 1975)

Bartels, Emily C., *Spectacles of Strangeness: Imperialism, Alienation, and Marlowe* (Philadelphia: University of Pennsylvania Press, 1993)

Barton, Anne, *Essays, Mainly Shakespearean* (Cambridge: Cambridge University Press, 1994)

Bate, Jonathan, ed., *The Romantics on Shakespeare* (London: Penguin, 1992)

——*Shakespeare and Ovid* (Oxford: Clarendon Press, 1993)

——*Soul of the Age: The Life, Mind, and World of William Shakespeare* (London: Penguin, 2008)

Bawcutt, N. W., 'Documents of the Salisbury Court Theatre in the British Library', *Medieval and Renaissance Drama in England* 9 (1997), 179–91

Bayley, John, *Shakespeare and Tragedy* (London: Routledge, 1981)

Beckerman, Bernard, *Dynamics of Drama: Theory and Method of Analysis* (New York: Knopf, 1970)

Bednarz, James P., 'Representing Jonson: *Histriomastix* and the Origin of the Poets' War', *Huntington Library Quarterly* 54 (1991), 1–30

——*Shakespeare and the Poets' War* (New York: Columbia University Press, 2001)

——'Writing and Revenge: John Marston's *Histriomastix*', *Comparative Drama* 36 (2002), 21–51

Belfield, Jane, 'Robert Armin as Abel Drugger', *Notes & Queries* 28 (1981), 146

——'Robert Armin, Citizen and Goldsmith of London', *Notes & Queries* 27 (1980), 158–9

Bennett, Susan, *Theatre Audiences: A Theory of Production and Reception*, 2nd edn (London: Routledge, 1997)

Bentley, Gerald Eades, *The Jacobean and Caroline Stage*, 7 vols. (Oxford: Clarendon Press, 1941–68)

——*The Profession of Dramatist in Shakespeare's Time, 1590–1642* (Princeton, NJ: Princeton University Press, 1971)

——*The Profession of Player in Shakespeare's Time, 1590–1642* (Princeton, NJ: Princeton University Press, 1984)

——ed., *The Seventeenth Century Stage: A Collection of Critical Essays* (Chicago: University of Chicago Press, 1968)

——'Shakespeare and the Blackfriars Theatre', *Shakespeare Survey* 1 (1948), 38–50

Berry, Herbert, 'Greene, Thomas (*bap.* 1573, *d.* 1612)', *Oxford DNB*

——*Shakespeare's Playhouses* (New York: AMS Press, 1987)

Bethell, S. L., 'Shakespeare's Actors', *Review of English Studies*, new series, 1 (1950), 193–205

Bevington, David M., *From 'Mankind' to Marlowe: Growth of Structure in the Popular Drama of Tudor England* (Cambridge, MA: Harvard University Press, 1962)

Bland, D. S., 'The "Night of Errors" at Gray's Inn, 1594', *Notes & Queries* 13 (1966), 127–8

Blayney, Peter W. M., '*The Booke of Sir Thomas Moore* Re-examined', *Studies in Philology* 69 (1972), 167–91

Bliss, Lee, '*Don Quixote* in England: The Case for *The Knight of the Burning Pestle*', *Viator* 18 (1987), 161–80

Bloom, Harold, *The Anxiety of Influence: A Theory of Poetry*, 2nd edn (Oxford: Oxford University Press, 1997)

——*Shakespeare: The Invention of the Human* (New York: Riverhead Books, 1998)

——*The Western Canon: The Books and School of the Ages* (Basingstoke: Macmillan, 1994)

Boas, Frederick S., *University Drama in the Tudor Age* (Oxford: Clarendon Press, 1914)

Bowers, Fredson, ed., *Jacobean and Caroline Dramatists* (Detroit, MI: Gale, 1987)

Boyd, Brian, 'Kind and Unkindness: Aaron in *Titus Andronicus*', in Brian Boyd, ed., *Words that Count: Essays on Early Modern Authorship in Honor of MacDonald P. Jackson* (Newark: University of Delaware Press, 2004), 51–77

Boyd, Brian, ed., *Words that Count: Essays on Early Modern Authorship in Honor of MacDonald P. Jackson* (Newark: University of Delaware Press, 2004)

Bradbrook, M. C., *English Dramatic Form: A History of its Development* (London: Chatto & Windus, 1965)

—— *The Rise of the Common Player: A Study of Actor and Society in Shakespeare's England* (London: Chatto & Windus, 1964)

—— 'Shakespeare's Recollections of Marlowe', in Philip Edwards, Inga-Stina Ewbank, and G. K. Hunter, eds., *Shakespeare's Styles* (Cambridge: Cambridge University Press, 1980), 191–3

Bradley, David, *From Text to Performance in the Elizabethan Theatre: Preparing the Play for the Stage* (Cambridge: Cambridge University Press, 1992)

Bristol, Michael D., '*The Two Noble Kinsmen*: Shakespeare and the Problem of Authority', in Charles H. Frey, ed., *Shakespeare, Fletcher and 'The Two Noble Kinsmen'* (Columbia: University of Missouri Press, 1989), 78–92

Brook, Peter, *The Empty Space* (New York: Macmillan, 1968)

Brunvand, Jan Harold, 'The Folktale Origin of *The Taming of the Shrew*', *Shakespeare Quarterly* 17 (1966), 345–9

Burrow, Colin, 'Reading Tudor Writing Politically: The Case of *2 Henry IV*', *Yearbook of English Studies* 28 (2008), 234–50

Butler, Martin, 'Armin, Robert (1563–1615)', *Oxford DNB*

—— 'Brome, Richard (c.1590–1652)', *Oxford DNB*

—— 'Kemp, William' (d. in or after 1610?), *Oxford DNB*

—— *Theatre and Crisis, 1632–1642* (Cambridge: Cambridge University Press, 1984)

Carson, Neil, *A Companion to Henslowe's Diary* (Cambridge: Cambridge University Press, 1988)

Cathcart, Charles, '*Histriomastix*, *Hamlet* and the "Quintessence of Duckes"', *Notes & Queries* 50 (2003), 427–30

Centerwall, Brandon S., '"Tell me Who Can when a Player Dies": Ben Jonson's Epigram on Richard Burbage, and How it was Lost to the Canon', *Ben Jonson Journal* 4 (1997), 27–34

Cerasano, S. P., 'Anthony Jeffes, Player and Brewer', *Notes & Queries* 31 (1984), 221–5

—— 'The "Business" of Shareholding, the Fortune Playhouses, and Francis Grace's Will', *Medieval and Renaissance Drama in England* 2 (1985), 231–51

—— 'Cheerful Givers: Henslowe, Alleyn, and the 1612 Loan Book to the Crown', *Shakespeare Studies* 28 (2000), 215–19

—— 'Competition for the King's Men?: Alleyn's Blackfriars Venture', *Medieval and Renaissance Drama in England* 4 (1989), 173–86

—— 'Edward Alleyn, the New Model Actor, and the Rise of Celebrity in the 1590s', *Medieval and Renaissance Drama in England* 18 (2005), 47–58

—— 'Edward Alleyn's Early Years: His Life and Family', *Notes & Queries* 34 (1987), 237–43

—— 'Edward Alleyn's "Retirement" 1597–1600', *Medieval and Renaissance Drama in England* 10 (1998), 98–112

——'The Geography of Henslowe's Diary', *Shakespeare Quarterly* 56 (2005), 328–53

——'Henslowe's "Curious" Diary', *Medieval and Renaissance Drama in England* 17 (2005), 72–85

——'The Master of the Bears in Art and Enterprise', *Medieval and Renaissance Drama in England* 5 (1991), 195–209

——'New Renaissance Players' Wills', *Modern Philology* 82 (1985), 299–304

——'The Patronage Network of Philip Henslowe and Edward Alleyn', *Medieval and Renaissance Drama in England* 13 (2000), 82–92

——'Revising Philip Henslowe's Biography', *Notes & Queries* 32 (1985), 66–72

——'Revising Philip Henslowe's Biography: A Correction', *Notes & Queries* 32 (1985), 506–7

Chambers, E. K., *The Elizabethan Stage*, 4 vols. (Oxford: Clarendon Press, 1923; repr. 2009)

——*William Shakespeare: A Study of Facts and Problems*, 2 vols. (Oxford: Clarendon Press, 1930; repr. 1988)

Cheney, Patrick, *Marlowe's Counterfeit Profession: Ovid, Spenser, Counter-Nationhood* (Toronto: University of Toronto Press, 1997)

——*Shakespeare: National Poet-Playwright* (Cambridge: Cambridge University Press, 2004)

——*Shakespeare's Literary Authorship* (Cambridge: Cambridge University Press, 2008)

Chillington, Carol: *see* Rutter, Carol Chillington

Clark, Ira, 'Shirley, James (*bap.* 1596, *d.* 1666), *Oxford DNB*

Coleridge, Samuel Taylor, *Criticism of Shakespeare: A Selection*, ed. R. A. Foakes (London: Athlone Press, 1989)

Cook, Anne Jennalie, *The Privileged Playgoers of Shakespeare's London, 1576–1642* (Princeton, NJ: Princeton University Press, 1981)

Cooper, Helen, *Shakespeare and the Medieval World* (London: Arden, 2010)

Craig, Hugh, and Arthur F. Kinney, eds., *Shakespeare, Computers, and the Mystery of Authorship* (Cambridge: Cambridge University Press, 2009)

Cross, K. Gustav, 'The Date of Marston's *Antonio and Mellida*', *Modern Language Notes* 72 (1957), 328–32

Crowley, Lara M., 'Was Southampton a Poet? A Verse Letter to Queen Elizabeth [with text]', *English Literary Renaissance* 41 (2011), 111–45

de Grazia, Margreta, '*Hamlet' without Hamlet* (Cambridge: Cambridge University Press, 2007)

——*Shakespeare Verbatim: The Reproduction of Authenticity and the 1790 Apparatus* (Oxford: Clarendon Press, 1991)

Denkinger, Emma Marshall, 'Actors' Names in the Registers of St. Bodolph Aldgate', *Proceedings of the Modern Language Association* 41 (1929), 91–109

Dessen, Alan C., *Elizabethan Stage Conventions and Modern Interpreters* (Cambridge: Cambridge University Press, 1984)

Dillon, Janette, *Theatre, Court and City, 1595–1610: Drama and Social Space in London* (Cambridge: Cambridge University Press, 2000)

Donaldson, Ian, *Ben Jonson: A Life* (Oxford: Oxford University Press, 2011)

Dowden, Edward, *Shakspere: A Critical Study of his Mind and Art* (London: 1875; repr. Routledge, 1948)

Duncan-Jones, Katherine, *Shakespeare: Upstart Crow to Sweet Swan, 1592–1623* (London: Arden, 2011)

——'Shakespeare's Dancing Fool', *TLS*, 13 August 2010

——*Ungentle Shakespeare: Scenes from his Life* (London: Arden, 2001)

——'Was the 1609 *SHAKE-SPEARES SONNETS* Really Unauthorized?', *Review of English Studies* 34 (1983), 151–71

Dutton, Richard, 'The Birth of an Author', in Cedric C. Brown and Arthur F. Marotti, eds., *Texts and Cultural Change in Early Modern England*, (New York: St. Martin's Press, 1997), 153–78

——ed., *The Oxford Handbook of Early Modern Theatre* (Oxford: Oxford University Press, 2009)

——'Shakespearean Origins', in Takashi Kozuka and J. R. Mulryne, eds., *Shakespeare, Marlowe, Jonson: New Directions in Biography* (Aldershot: Ashgate, 2006), 69–83

Edmond, Mary, 'Heminges, John (*bap.* 1566; *d.* 1630)', *Oxford DNB*

——'Yeomen, Citizens, Gentlemen, and Players: The Burbages and their Connections', in R. B. Parker and S. P. Zitner, eds., *Elizabethan Theater: Essays in Honor of S. Schoenbaum* (Newark: University of Delaware Press, 1996), 30–49

Empson, William, *Some Versions of Pastoral* (1935; repr. London: Chatto & Windus, 1950)

Erne, Lukas, *Beyond The Spanish Tragedy: A Study of the Works of Thomas Kyd* (Manchester: Manchester University Press, 2001)

——*Shakespeare as Literary Dramatist* (Cambridge: Cambridge University Press, 2003)

Feather, John, 'Robert Armin and the Chamberlain's Men', *Notes & Queries* 19 (1972), 448–50

Felver, Charles S., *Robert Armin, Shakespeare's Fool: A Biographical Essay*, Kent State University Bulletin 49 (Ohio, IL: Kent State University, 1961)

——'Robert Armin's Fragment of a Bawdy Ballad of "Mary Ambree"', *Notes & Queries* 7 (1960), 14–16

Finkelpearl, Philip J., 'John Marston's *Histrio-Mastix* as an Inns of Court Play: A Hypothesis', *Huntington Library Quarterly* 29 (1966), 223–34

Forker, Charles R., 'Webster or Shakespeare? Style, Idiom, Vocabulary, and Spelling in the Additions to *Sir Thomas More*', in T. H. Howard-Hill, ed., *Shakespeare and 'Sir Thomas More': Essays on the Play and its Shakespearian Interest* (Cambridge: Cambridge University Press, 1989), 151–70

Frey, Charles H., ed., *Shakespeare, Fletcher and 'The Two Noble Kinsmen'* (Columbia: University of Missouri Press, 1989)

Gair, W. Reavley, *The Children of Paul's: The Story of a Theatre Company, 1553–1608* (Cambridge: Cambridge University Press, 1982)

Garber, Marjorie, 'Marlovian Vision/Shakespearean Revision', *Research Opportunities in Renaissance Drama* 22 (1979), 3–9

Gieskes, Edward, *Representing the Professions: Administration, Law, and Theater in Early Modern England* (Newark: University of Delaware Press, 2006)

Goldberg, Jonathan, *James I and the Politics of Literature: Jonson, Shakespeare, Donne, and their Contemporaries* (Baltimore, MD: Johns Hopkins University Press, 1983)

Goldsmith, Robert Hillis, *Wise Fools in Shakespeare* (Liverpool: Liverpool University Press, 1958)

Greenblatt, Stephen, *Will in the World: How Shakespeare Became Shakespeare* (London: Jonathan Cape, 2004)

Greene, Thomas M., *The Light in Troy: Imitation and Discovery in Renaissance Poetry* (New Haven, CT: Yale University Press, 1982)

Gurr, Andrew, 'The Chimera of Amalgamation', *Theatre Research International* 18 (1993), 85–93

—— 'The Great Divide of 1594', in Brian Boyd, ed., *Words that Count: Essays on Early Modern Authorship in Honor of MacDonald P. Jackson* (Newark: University of Delaware Press, 2004), 29–48

—— 'London's Blackfriars Playhouse and the Chamberlain's Men', in Paul Menzer, ed., *Inside Shakespeare: Essays on the Blackfriars Stage* (Selinsgrove, PA: Susquehanna University Press, 2006), 17–30

—— *Playgoing in Shakespeare's London*, 2nd edn (Cambridge: Cambridge University Press, 1996)

—— *The Shakespearean Stage, 1574–1642*, 3rd edn (Cambridge: Cambridge University Press, 1992)

—— *The Shakespeare Company: 1594–1642* (Cambridge: Cambridge University Press, 2004)

—— *The Shakespearian Playing Companies* (Oxford: Clarendon Press, 1996)

—— *Shakespeare's Opposites: The Admiral's Company 1594–1625* (Cambridge: Cambridge University Press, 2009)

—— 'The Tempest's Tempest at Blackfriars', *Shakespeare Survey* 41 (1989), 91–102

—— 'The Work of Elizabethan Plotters, and 2 *The Seven Deadly Sins*', *Early Theatre* 10 (2007), 67–87

Hall, G. K., *Catalogue of Manuscripts of the Folger Shakespeare Library*, 3 vols. (Boston, MA: G. K. Hall, 1971)

Halliwell-Phillipps, J. O., *Outlines of the Life of Shakespeare*, 6th edn, 2 vols. (London: Longmans, Green, & Co., 1886)

Hammer, Paul E. J., 'Shakespeare's *Richard II*, the Play of 7 February 1601, and the Essex Rising', *Shakespeare Quarterly* 59 (2008), 1–35

Hapgood, Robert, *Shakespeare the Theatre-Poet* (Oxford: Clarendon Press, 1988)

Harbage, Alfred, *Annals of English Drama: 975–1700*, 2nd edn, rev. S. Schoenbaum (London: Methuen, 1964)

Harbage, Alfred, *Annals of English Drama: 975–1700*, 3rd edn, rev. Sylvia Stoler Wagonheim (London: Routledge, 1989)

——*Shakespeare and the Rival Traditions* (Bloomington: Indiana University Press, 1952)

Hobbs, Mary, *Early Seventeenth-Century Verse Miscellany Manuscripts* (Aldershot: Scholar Press, 1992)

Holland, Peter, 'A History of Histories: From Flecknoe to Nicoll', in W. B. Worthen, ed., *Theorizing Practice: Redefining Theatre History* (Houndmills: Palgrave Macmillan, 2003), 8–29

——and Stephen Orgel, eds., *Redefining British Theatre History* (Houndmills: Palgrave Macmillan, 2004)

Honan, Park, *Shakespeare: A Life* (Oxford: Oxford University Press, 1999)

Honigmann, E. A. J., *Shakespeare: The 'Lost Years'* (Manchester: Manchester University Press, 1985)

Hope, Jonathan, *The Authorship of Shakespeare's Plays* (Cambridge: Cambridge University Press, 1994)

Horton, Thomas B., 'Distinguishing Shakespeare from Fletcher through Function Words', *Shakespeare Studies* 22 (1994), 314–35

Hotson, Leslie, *Shakespeare's Motley* (London: Rupert Hart-Davis, 1952)

Howard-Hill, T. H., ed., *Shakespeare and 'Sir Thomas More': Essays on the Play and its Shakespearian Interest* (Cambridge: Cambridge University Press, 1989)

Hoy, Cyrus, 'The Shares of Fletcher and his Collaborators in the Beaumont and Fletcher Canon (V)', *Studies in Bibliography* 13 (1960), 77–108

Hunter, G. K., *Dramatic Identities and Cultural Tradition: Studies in Shakespeare and his Contemporaries* (Liverpool: Liverpool University Press, 1978)

——'Theatrical Politics and Shakespeare's Comedies, 1590–1600', in R. B. Parker and S. P. Zitner, eds., *Elizabethan Theater: Essays in Honor of S. Schoenbaum* (Newark: University of Delaware Press, 1996), 241–51

Ingram, William, 'Arthur Savill, Stage Player', *Theatre Notebook* 37 (1983), 21–2

——*The Business of Playing: The Beginnings of the Adult Professional Theater in Elizabethan London* (Ithaca, NY: Cornell University Press, 1992)

——'The Closing of the Theatres in 1597: A Dissenting View', *Modern Philology* 69 (1971), 105–15

——'The "Evolution" of the Elizabethan Playing Company', in John H. Astington, ed., *The Development of Shakespeare's Theater* (New York: AMS Press, 1992), 13–28

——'Laurence Dutton, Stage Player: Missing and Presumed Lost', *Medieval and Renaissance Drama in England* 14 (2001), 122–43

——'"Neere the Playe Howse": The Swan Theater and Community Blight', *Renaissance Drama* 4 (1971), 53–68

——'Robert Keysar, Playhouse Speculator', *Shakespeare Quarterly* 37 (1986), 476–85

Ioppolo, Grace, *Dramatists and their Manuscripts in the Age of Shakespeare, Jonson, Middleton and Heywood: Authorship, Authority, and the Playhouse* (London: Routledge, 2006)

——*Revising Shakespeare* (Cambridge, MA: Harvard University Press, 1991)

Jackson, James L., 'The Fencing Actor-lines in Shakespeare's Plays', *Modern Language Notes* 57 (1942), 615–21

Jackson, MacDonald P., *Defining Shakespeare: 'Pericles' as Test Case* (Oxford: Oxford University Press, 2003)

——'*Edward III*, Shakespeare, and Pembroke's Men,' *Notes & Queries* 210 (1965), 329–31

——'Linguistic Evidence for the Date of Shakespeare's Additions to *Sir Thomas More*', *Notes & Queries* 223 (1978), 154–6

——'Spurio and the Date of *All's Well that Ends Well*', *Notes & Queries* 48 (2001), 298–9

——*Studies in Attribution: Middleton and Shakespeare* (Salzburg: University of Salzburg, 1979)

James, Susan E., 'A New Source for Shakespeare's *The Taming of the Shrew*', *Bulletin of the John Rylands University Library* 81 (1999), 49–62

Johnson, Nora, *The Actor as Playwright in Early Modern Drama* (Cambridge: Cambridge University Press, 2003)

Johnstone, Keith, *Impro: Improvisation and the Theatre* (London: Faber & Faber, 1979; repr. Methuen, 1989)

Jones, G. P., '*A Burbage Ballad* and John Payne Collier', *Review of English Studies* 40 (1989), 393–7

Jones, John, *Shakespeare at Work* (Oxford: Clarendon Press, 1995)

Jowett, John, 'Henry Chettle and the Original Text of *Sir Thomas More*', in T. H. Howard-Hill, ed., *Shakespeare and 'Sir Thomas More': Essays on the Play and its Shakespearian Interest* (Cambridge: Cambridge University Press, 1989), 131–49

——'Johannes Factotum: Henry Chettle and *Greene's Groatsworth of Wit*', *Papers of the Bibliographical Society of America* 87 (1993), 453–86

——'New Created Creatures: Ralph Crane and the Stage Directions in *The Tempest*', *Shakespeare Survey* 36 (1983), 107–20

——'The Pattern of Collaboration in *Timon of Athens*', in Brian Boyd, ed., *Words that Count: Essays on Early Modern Authorship in Honor of MacDonald P. Jackson* (Newark: University of Delaware Press, 2004), 181–205

Kastan, David Scott, 'Killed with Hard Opinions: Oldcastle, Falstaff, and the Reformed Text of *1 Henry IV*', in Laurie E. Maguire and Thomas L. Berger, eds., *Textual Formations and Reformations* (Newark: University of Delaware Press, 1998), 211–27

——*Shakespeare after Theory* (London: Routledge, 1999)

——*Shakespeare and the Book* (Cambridge: Cambridge University Press, 2001)

Kathman, David, 'Field [Feild], Richard (*bap.* 1561, *d.* 1624)', *Oxford DNB*

Kathman, David, 'Grocers, Goldsmiths, and Drapers: Freemen and Apprentices in Elizabethan Theater', *Shakespeare Quarterly* 55 (2004), 1–49

——'Heywood, Thomas (*c.*1573–1641)', *Oxford DNB*

——'Reconsidering *The Seven Deadly Sins*', *Early Theatre* 7 (2004), 13–44

Keenan, Siobhan, *Travelling Players in Shakespeare's England* (Houndmills: Palgrave Macmillan, 2002)

Kermode, Frank, *Shakespeare's Language* (London: Allen Lane, 2000)

Kernan, Alvin, 'John Marston's Play *Histriomastix*', *Modern Language Quarterly* 19 (1958), 134–40

Kerrigan, John, *Motives of Woe: Shakespeare and 'Female Complaint': A Critical Anthology* (Oxford: Clarendon Press, 1991)

——*On Shakespeare and Early Modern Literature: Essays* (Oxford: Oxford University Press, 2001)

——*Revenge Tragedy: Aeschylus to Armageddon* (Oxford: Clarendon Press, 1996)

——'Revision, Adaptation, and the Fool in *King Lear*', in Gary Taylor and Michael Warren, eds., *The Division of the Kingdoms: Shakespeare's Two Versions of 'King Lear'* (Oxford: Clarendon Press, 1983), 195–245

King, T. J., *Casting Shakespeare's Plays: London Actors and their Roles, 1590–1642* (Cambridge: Cambridge University Press, 1992)

Kinney, Arthur F., ed., *A Companion to Renaissance Drama* (Oxford: Blackwell, 2002)

——*Humanist Poetics: Thought, Rhetoric, and Fiction in Sixteenth-Century England* (Amherst: University of Massachusetts Press, 1986)

Knapp, Jeffrey, *Shakespeare Only* (Chicago: University of Chicago Press, 2009)

Knight, G. Wilson, *The Crown of Life: Essays in Interpretation of Shakespeare's Final Plays* (London: Methuen, 1965)

Knowles, Edwin B., 'Thomas Shelton, Translator of *Don Quixote*', *Studies in the Renaissance* 5 (1958), 160–75

Knutson, Roslyn Lander, 'Histrio-Mastix: Not by John Marston', *Studies in Philology* 98 (2001), 359–77

——'Marlowe, Company Ownership, and the Role of Edward II', *Medieval and Renaissance Drama in England* 15 (2005), 37–46

——*Playing Companies and Commerce in Shakespeare's Time* (Cambridge: Cambridge University Press, 2001)

——*The Repertory of Shakespeare's Company, 1594–1613* (Fayetteville: University of Arkansas Press, 1991)

——'What if there wasn't a "Blackfriars Repertory"?', in Paul Menzer, ed., *Inside Shakespeare: Essays on the Blackfriars Stage* (Selinsgrove, PA: Susquehanna University Press, 2006), 54–60

——'What's so Special about 1594?', *Shakespeare Quarterly* 61 (2010), 449–67

Kozuka, Takashi, and J. R. Mulryne, eds., *Shakespeare, Marlowe, Jonson: New Directions in Biography* (Aldershot: Ashgate, 2006)

Lake, D. J., 'The Canon of Robert Armin's Work: Some Difficulties', *Notes & Queries* 222 (1977), 117–20

—— *The Canon of Thomas Middleton's Plays: Internal Evidence for the Major Problems of Authorship* (Cambridge: Cambridge University Press, 1975)

——'The Date of the *Sir Thomas More* Additions by Dekker and Shakespeare', *Notes & Queries* 222 (1977), 114–16

——'*Histriomastix:* Linguistic Evidence for Authorship', *Notes & Queries* 28 (1981), 148–52

Lamb, Charles, *Specimens of English Dramatic Poets* (Philadelphia, PA: Willis P. Hazard, 1857)

Lancashire, Anne, 'Annals of English Drama 975–1700 by Sylvia Stoler Wagonheim' (Review), *Shakespeare Quarterly* 42 (1991), 225–30

Lanham, Richard A., *A Handlist of Rhetorical Terms* (Berkeley: University of California Press, 1991)

Lawless, Donald S., 'Robert Daborne, Senior', *Notes & Queries* 222 (1977), 514–16

——'Some New Light on Robert Daborne', *Notes & Queries* 26 (1979), 142–3

Lennard, John, and Mary Luckhurst, *The Drama Handbook* (Oxford: Oxford University Press, 2002)

Lethbridge, J. B., ed., *Shakespeare and Spenser: Attractive Opposites* (Manchester: Manchester University Press, 2008)

Lievsay, J. J., 'Jacobean Stage Pastoralism', in Richard Hosley, ed., *Essays on Shakespeare and Elizabethan Drama in Honour of Hardin Craig* (London: Routledge, 1963)

Lippincott, H. F., 'Bibliographical Problems in the Works of Robert Armin', *The Library* 30 (1975), 330–3

Loewenstein, Joseph, *The Author's Due: Printing and the Prehistory of Copyright* (Chicago: University of Chicago Press, 2002)

Long, William B., 'Dulwich MS. XX, *The Telltale:* Clues to Provenance', *Medieval and Renaissance Drama in England* 17 (2005), 180–204

Lunney, Ruth, 'Rewriting the Narrative of Dramatic Character, or, Not "Shakespearean" but "Debatable"', *Medieval and Renaissance Drama in England* 14 (2001), 66–85

McDonald, Russ, *Shakespeare's Late Style* (Cambridge: Cambridge University Press, 2006)

McLuskie, Kathleen E., *Dekker and Heywood: Professional Dramatists* (London: Macmillan, 1994)

McMillin, Scott, '*The Book of Sir Thomas More*: Dates and Acting Companies', in T. H. Howard-Hill, ed., *Shakespeare and 'Sir Thomas More': Essays on the Play and its Shakespearian Interest* (Cambridge: Cambridge University Press, 1989), 57–76

——'Casting for Pembroke's Men: The *Henry VI* Quartos and *The Taming of A Shrew*', *Shakespeare Quarterly* 23 (1972), 141–59

——'The Ownership of *The Jew of Malta*, *Friar Bacon*, and *The Ranger's Comedy*', *English Language Notes* 9 (1972), 249–52

McMillin, Scott, and Sally-Beth MacLean, *The Queen's Men and their Plays* (Cambridge: Cambridge University Press, 1998)

McMullan, Gordon, 'Fletcher, John (1579–1625)', *Oxford DNB*

——*The Politics of Unease in the Plays of John Fletcher* (Amherst: University of Massachusetts Press, 1994)

——*Shakespeare and the Idea of Late Writing: Authorship in the Proximity of Death* (Cambridge: Cambridge University Press, 2007)

——'What is a Late Play?' in Catherine Alexander, ed., *The Cambridge Companion to Shakespeare's Last Plays* (Cambridge: Cambridge University Press, 2009), 5–27

——and Jonathan Hope, eds., *The Politics of Tragicomedy: Shakespeare and After* (London: Routledge, 1992)

Maguire, Laurie E., *Shakespearean Suspect Texts: The 'Bad' Quartos and their Contexts* (Cambridge: Cambridge University Press, 1996)

——and Thomas L. Berger, eds., *Textual Formations and Reformations* (Newark: University of Delaware Press, 1998)

——and Emma Smith, 'Many Hands: A New Shakespeare Collaboration?', *TLS*, 19 April 2012, 13–15

Malone, Edmond, *Inquiry into the Authenticity of Certain Miscellaneous Papers* (London: T. Cadell Jr & W. Davies, 1796)

Mann, David, *The Elizabethan Player: Contemporary Stage Representation* (London: Routledge, 1991)

Marcus, Leah S., *Unediting the Renaissance: Shakespeare, Marlowe, Milton* (London: Routledge, 1996)

Mason, Alexandra, 'The Social Status of Theatrical People', *Shakespeare Quarterly* 18 (1967), 429–30

Masten, Jeffrey, *Textual Intercourse: Collaboration, Authorship, and Sexualities in Renaissance Drama* (Cambridge: Cambridge University Press, 1997)

Maus, Katharine Eisaman, *Inwardness and Theater in the English Renaissance* (Chicago: University of Chicago Press, 1995)

Melchiori, Giorgio, '*The Book of Sir Thomas More*: Dramatic Unity', in T. H. Howard-Hill, ed., *Shakespeare and 'Sir Thomas More': Essays on the Play and its Shakespearian Interest* (Cambridge: Cambridge University Press, 1989), 77–100

Menzer, Paul, ed., *Inside Shakespeare: Essays on the Blackfriars Stage* (Selinsgrove, PA: Susquehanna University Press, 2006)

Metz, G. Harold, '"Voice and Credyt": The Scholars and *Sir Thomas More*', in T. H. Howard-Hill, ed., *Shakespeare and 'Sir Thomas More': Essays on the Play and its Shakespearian Interest* (Cambridge: Cambridge University Press, 1989), 11–44

Miola, Robert S., *Shakespeare and Classical Comedy: The Influence of Plautus and Terence* (Oxford: Clarendon Press, 1994)

Muir, Kenneth, *Shakespeare's Comic Sequence* (Liverpool: Liverpool University Press, 1979)

Munro, Lucy, *Children of the Queen's Revels: A Jacobean Theatre Repertory* (Cambridge: Cambridge University Press, 2005)

Murray, John Tucker, *English Dramatic Companies, 1558–1642*, 2 vols. (London: Constable & Co., 1910)

Nicholl, Charles, *The Lodger: Shakespeare on Silver Street* (London: Penguin, 2008)

Nielson, James, 'William Kemp at the Globe', *Shakespeare Quarterly* 44 (1993), 466–8

Norbrook, David, '"What cares these roarers for the name of king?": Language and Utopia in *The Tempest*', in Kiernan Ryan, ed., *Shakespeare: The Last Plays* (London: Longman, 1999), 245–78

Nosworthy, J. M., 'The Marlowe Manuscript', *The Library*, 4th series, 16 (1946), 158–71

Nungezer, Edwin, *A Dictionary of Actors* (Ithaca, NY: Cornell University Press, 1929)

Nuttall, A. D., *A New Mimesis: Shakespeare and the Representation of Reality* (London: Methuen, 1983)

Orgel, Stephen, 'The Renaissance Artist as Plagiarist', *English Literary History* 48 (1981), 476–95

Ostovich, Helen, Holger Schott Syme, and Andrew Griffin, eds., *Locating the Queen's Men: Material Practices and the Conditions of Playing* (Farnham: Ashgate, 2009)

Palfrey, Simon, *Late Shakespeare: A New World of Words* (Oxford: Clarendon Press, 1997)

——and Tiffany Stern, *Shakespeare in Parts* (Oxford: Oxford University Press, 2007)

Pavis, Patrice, *Analyzing Performance: Theater, Dance, and Film*, trans. David Williams (Ann Arbor: University of Michigan Press, 2003)

Pfister, Manfred, *The Theory and Analysis of Drama*, trans. John Halliday (Cambridge: Cambridge University Press, 1988)

Pigman, G. W., III, 'Versions of Imitation in the Renaissance', *Renaissance Quarterly* 33 (1980), 1–32

Potter, Lois, *The Life of William Shakespeare: A Critical Biography* (Oxford: Wiley-Blackwell, 2012)

Preiss, Richard, 'Robert Armin Do the Police in Different Voices', in Peter Holland and Stephen Orgel, eds., *From Performance to Print in Shakespeare's England* (Houndmills: Palgrave Macmillan, 2006), 208–30

Proudfoot, Richard, 'Marlowe and the Editors', in J. A. Downie and J. T. Parnell, eds., *Constructing Christopher Marlowe* (Cambridge: Cambridge University Press, 2000), 41–54

Quint, David, *Origin and Originality in Renaissance Literature: Versions of the Source* (New Haven, CT: Yale University Press, 1983)

Rappaport, Steve, *Worlds within Worlds: Structures of Life in Sixteenth-Century London* (Cambridge: Cambridge University Press, 1989)

Riddell, James A., 'Some Actors in Ben Jonson's Plays', *Shakespeare Studies* 5 (1969), 284–98

Roach, Joseph R., *The Player's Passion: Studies in the Science of Acting* (Newark: University of Delaware Press, 1985)

Rose, Mary Beth, *The Expense of Spirit: Love and Sexuality in English Renaissance Drama* (Ithaca, NY: Cornell University Press, 1988)

Rowland, Richard, *Thomas Heywood's Theatre, 1599–1639: Locations, Transactions, and Conflict* (Farnham: Ashgate, 2010)

Rudlin, John, *Commedia dell'arte: An Actor's Handbook* (London: Routledge, 1994)

Rutter, Carol Chillington, *Documents of the Rose Playhouse*, rev. edn (Manchester: Manchester University Press, 1999)

——'Playwrights at Work: Henslowe's, Not Shakespeare's, Book of Sir Thomas More', *English Literary Renaissance* 10 (1980), 439–79

Ryan, Kiernan, ed., *Shakespeare: The Last Plays* (London: Longman, 1999)

Salingar, Leo, *Shakespeare and the Traditions of Comedy* (Cambridge: Cambridge University Press, 1974)

Schmidgall, Gary, *Shakespeare and the Courtly Aesthetic* (Berkeley: University of California Press, 1983)

Schoenbaum, Samuel, *Internal Evidence and Elizabethan Dramatic Authorship* (London: Edward Arnold, 1966)

——*William Shakespeare: A Documentary Life* (Oxford: Clarendon Press, 1975)

Shapiro, I. A., 'The "Mermaid Club"', *Modern Language Review* 45 (1950), 6–17

Shapiro, James, *1599: A Year in the Life of William Shakespeare* (London: Faber & Faber, 2005)

——*Rival Playwrights: Marlowe, Jonson, Shakespeare* (New York: Columbia University Press, 1991)

Shapiro, Michael, *Children of the Revels: The Boy Companies of Shakespeare's Time and their Plays* (New York: Columbia University Press, 1977)

Sharpe, Kevin, and Steven N. Zwicker, eds., *Writing Lives: Biography and Textuality, Identity and Representation in Early Modern England* (Oxford: Oxford University Press, 2008)

Sharpe, Robert Boies, *The Real War of the Theaters: Shakespeare's Fellows in Rivalry with the Admiral's Men, 1594–1603*, Modern Language Association Monograph Series 5 (Boston, MA: D. C. Heath, 1935)

Shattuck, Charles H., *The Shakespeare Promptbooks: A Descriptive Catalogue* (Urbana: University of Illinois Press, 1965)

——'The Shakespeare Promptbooks: First Supplement', *Theatre Notebook* 24 (1969), 5–17

Simpson, Richard, *The School of Shakespeare*, 2 vols. (London: Chatto & Windus, 1878)

Sinfield, Alan, *Faultlines: Cultural Materialism and the Politics of Dissident Reading* (Oxford: Clarendon Press, 1992)

——'Give an account of Shakespeare and education, showing why you think they are effective and what you have appreciated about them; support your comments with precise references', in Jonathan Dollimore and Alan Sinfield, eds., *Political Shakespeare: New Essays in Cultural Materialism* (Manchester: Manchester University Press, 1985), 158–81

Skura, Meredith Anne, *Shakespeare the Actor and the Purposes of Playing* (Chicago: University of Chicago Press, 1993)

Small, R. A., *The Stage Quarrel, Between Ben Jonson and the So-Called Poetasters* (Breslau: M. and H. Marcus, 1899)

Smith, A. J., 'Theory and Practice in Renaissance Poetry: Two Kinds of Imitation', *Bulletin of the John Rylands Library* 47 (1964), 212–43

Smith, Bruce R., *Ancient Scripts and Modern Experience on the English Stage, 1500–1700* (Princeton, NJ: Princeton University Press, 1988)

Smith, Emma, 'Author v. Character in Early Modern Dramatic Authorship: The Example of Thomas Kyd and *The Spanish Tragedy*', *Medieval and Renaissance Drama in England* 11 (1999), 129–42

Smith, Irwin, *Shakespeare's Blackfriars Playhouse: Its History and its Design* (London: Peter Owen, 1966)

Smith, M. E., 'Personnel at the Second Blackfriars: Some Biographical Notes', *Notes & Queries* 25 (1978), 441–4

Snyder, Susan, *The Comic Matrix of Shakespeare's Tragedies* (Princeton, NJ: Princeton University Press, 1979)

Somerset, J. Alan B., ed., *Shropshire*, Records of Early English Drama, 2 vols. (Toronto: Toronto University Press, 1994)

Southworth, John, *Fools and Jesters at the English Court* (Stroud: Sutton, 1998)

States, Bert O., *Great Reckonings in Little Rooms: On the Phenomenology of Theatre* (Berkeley: University of California Press, 1985)

Stern, Tiffany, *Documents of Performance in Early Modern England* (Cambridge: Cambridge University Press, 2009)

——'"Whether one did Contrive, the Other Write, / Or one Fram'd the Plot, the Other did Indite": Fletcher and Theobald as Collaborative Writers', in David Carnegie and Gary Taylor, eds., *The Quest for Cardenio: Shakespeare, Fletcher, Cervantes, and the Lost Play* (Oxford: Oxford University Press, 2012), 115–79

——*Making Shakespeare: From Stage to Page* (London: Routledge, 2004)

——*Rehearsal from Shakespeare to Sheridan* (Oxford: Clarendon Press, 2000)

——'"A Small-Beer Health to his Second Day": Playwrights, Prologues, and First Performance in the Early Modern Theater', *Studies in Philology* 101 (2004), 172–99

Stopes, C. C., *Burbage and Shakespeare's Stage* (London: Alexander Moring, 1913)

Strachey, G. L., 'Shakespeare's Final Period', *The Independent Review* (August 1904), 401–18

Sutcliffe, Chris, 'The Canon of Robert Armin's Work: An Addition', *Notes & Queries* 43 (1996), 171–5

Sutcliffe, Chris, 'Kempe and Armin: The Management of Change', *Theatre Notebook* 50 (1996), 122–34

Syme, Holger Schott, 'The Meaning of Success: Stories of 1594 and its Aftermath', *Shakespeare Quarterly* 61 (2010), 490–525

Taylor, Gary, 'The Date and Auspices of the Additions to *Sir Thomas More*', in T. H. Howard-Hill, ed., *Shakespeare and 'Sir Thomas More': Essays on the Play and its Shakespearian Interest* (Cambridge: Cambridge University Press, 1989), 101–30

——'Divine [ ]sences', *Shakespeare Survey* 54 (2001), 13–30

——'Shakespeare and Others: The Authorship of *Henry the Sixth, Part One*', *Medieval and Renaissance Drama in England* 7 (1995), 145–205

——and John Jowett, *Shakespeare Reshaped: 1606–1623* (Oxford: Clarendon Press, 1993)

——and Michael Warren, eds., *The Division of the Kingdoms: Shakespeare's Two Versions of 'King Lear'* (Oxford: Clarendon Press, 1983)

Tennenhouse, Leonard, 'Family Rites: Patriarchal Strategies in Shakespearean Romance', in Kiernan Ryan, ed., *Shakespeare: The Last Plays* (London: Longman, 1999), 43–60

Thompson, Ann, *Shakespeare's Chaucer: A Study in Literary Origins* (Liverpool: Liverpool University Press, 1978)

Thorndike, Ashley H., *The Influence of Beaumont and Fletcher on Shakespeare* (Worcester, MA: Oliver B. Wood, 1901)

Tillyard, E. M. W., *Shakespeare's Last Plays* (London: Chatto & Windus, 1964)

Tilmouth, Christopher, *Passion's Triumph over Reason: A History of the Moral Imagination from Spenser to Rochester* (Oxford: Oxford University Press, 2007)

Traversi, Derek, *Shakespeare: The Last Phase* (New York: Harcourt, 1953)

van Es, Bart, 'Company Man', *TLS*, 2 February 2007, 14–15

——'Historiography and Biography', in Patrick Cheney and Philip Hardie, eds., *The Oxford History of Classical Reception in English Literature*, vol. II: *The Renaissance: 1558–1660* (Oxford: Oxford University Press, *forthcoming*)

——'*Johannes fac Totum*?: Shakespeare's First Contact with the Acting Companies', *Shakespeare Quarterly* 61 (2010), 551–77

——'Late Shakespeare and the Middle Ages', in Helen Cooper, Peter Holland, and Ruth Morse, eds., *Medieval Shakespeare: Pasts and Presents* (Cambridge: Cambridge University Press, *forthcoming*)

——'Michael Drayton, Literary History and Historians in Verse', *Review of English Studies* 58 (2007), 255–69

Velz, John W., '*Sir Thomas More* and the Shakespeare Canon: Two Approaches', in T. H. Howard-Hill, ed., *Shakespeare and 'Sir Thomas More': Essays on the Play and its Shakespearian Interest* (Cambridge: Cambridge University Press, 1989), 171–95

Vickers, Brian, *Appropriating Shakespeare: Contemporary Critical Quarrels* (New Haven, CT: Yale University Press, 1993)

——*Classical Rhetoric in English Poetry* (Carbondale, IL: Southern Illinois University Press, 1989)

——'Shakespeare and Authorship Studies in the Twenty-First Century', *Shakespeare Quarterly* 62 (2011), 106–42

——*Shakespeare, Co-Author: A Historical Study of Five Collaborative Plays* (Oxford: Oxford University Press, 2002)

——'*The Troublesome Raigne*, George Peele, and the Date of *King John*', in Brian Boyd, ed., *Words that Count: Essays on Early Modern Authorship in Honor of MacDonald P. Jackson* (Newark: University of Delaware Press, 2004), 78–116

——and Marcus Dahl, 'What is Infirm ... *All's Well that Ends Well*: An Attribution Rejected', *TLS*, 9 April 2012, 14

Wallace, Charles William, *The Evolution of the English Drama up to Shakespeare with a History of the First Blackfriars Theatre* (Berlin: Georg Reimer, 1912)

——'The First London Theatre: Materials for a History', in *University Studies of the University of Nebraska* 13 (1913), 1–297

——'Shakespeare and his London Associates as Revealed in Recently Discovered Documents', *University Studies of the University of Nebraska* 10 (1910), 261–360

——'Shakespeare and the Blackfriars', *The Century* 80 (1910), 742–52

——'Shakespeare's Money Interest in the Globe Theater', *The Century* 80 (1910), 500–12

——'Three London Theatres of Shakespeare's Time', *University Studies of the University of Nebraska* 9 (1909), 287–342

Walsh, Brian, *Shakespeare, the Queen's Men, and the Elizabethan Performance of History* (Cambridge: Cambridge University Press, 2009)

Weimann, Robert, 'Playing with a Difference: Revisiting "Pen" and "Voice" in Shakespeare's Theater', *Shakespeare Quarterly* 50 (1999), 415–32

——*Shakespeare and the Popular Tradition in Theater: Studies in the Social Dimension of Dramatic Form and Function*, ed. Robert Schwartz (Baltimore, MD: Johns Hopkins University Press, 1978)

——'Society and the Individual in Shakespeare's Conception of Character', *Shakespeare Survey* 34 (1981), 23–31

Wells, Stanley, *Shakespeare and Co.: Christopher Marlowe, Thomas Dekker, Ben Jonson, Thomas Middleton, John Fletcher, and the Other Players in his Story* (London: Allen Lane, 2006)

——and Gary Taylor, *William Shakespeare: A Textual Companion* (Oxford: Clarendon Press, 1987)

Welsford, Enid, *The Fool: His Social and Literary History* (London: Faber & Faber, 1935; repr. 1968)

White, Paul Whitfield, and Suzanne R. Westfall, eds., *Shakespeare and Theatrical Patronage in Early Modern England* (Cambridge: Cambridge University Press, 2002)

Wickham, Glynne, Herbert Berry, and William Ingram, eds., *English Professional Theatre, 1530–1660* (Cambridge: Cambridge University Press, 2000)

Wiggins, Martin, *Shakespeare and the Drama of his Time*, Oxford Shakespeare Topics (Oxford: Oxford University Press, 2000)

Wiles, David, *Shakespeare's Clown: Actor and Text in the Elizabethan Playhouse* (Cambridge: Cambridge University Press, 1987)

Withington, Phil, *The Politics of Commonwealth: Citizens and Freemen in Early Modern England* (Cambridge: Cambridge University Press, 2005)

Womersley, David, 'France in Shakespeare's *Henry V*', *Renaissance Studies* 9 (1995), 442–59

Worden, Blair, 'Shakespeare in Life and Art: Biography and *Richard II*', in Takashi Kozuka and J. R. Mulryne, eds., *Shakespeare, Marlowe, Jonson: New Directions in Biography* (Aldershot: Ashgate, 2006)

Young, William, *History of Dulwich College*, 2 vols. (London: T. B. Bumpus, 1889)

Index

Essex, Earl of, *see* Devereux, Robert,
  Second Earl of
Evans, G. Blakemore 278 n. 4, 283 n. 16
Evans, Henry 159, 199, 256–7
Everyman 14
expressive speech 62, 94

Fair Em 30, 54, 68
Faithful Friends, The 82 n. 9
Famous Victories of Henry V, The 14
feminist criticism 306; *see also* gender
  criticism; sexuality; women
Field, John 105
Field, Nathan 48 n. 36, 107 n. 36,
  126, 128–9, 169 n. 17, 177 n. 42,
  200 n. 15
Field, Richard 6 n. 19, 17 n. 56
Fitch, John 65
five-act structure 66
Fleay, F. G. 46 n. 30
Flecknoe, Richard 240
Fletcher, John
  as attached playwright 42 n. 11,
    107 n. 36, 129, 145
  as writer for children's companies 265,
    267–8
  co-authorship with Francis
    Beaumont 265, 268
  co-authorship with Shakespeare 23 n. 5,
    284 n. 18, 288, 291–5
  co-authorship with William
    Rowley 177 n. 43
  social origins 265
  style compared to Shakespeare's 265,
    269–77
  Faithful Shepherdess, The 265–8, 270–74,
    296–7
  Honest Man's Fortune, The 145 n. 64
  Humorous Lieutenant, The 114 n. 19
  Rape of Lucrece, The 300
  Tamer Tamed, The 62, 297
  see also Beaumont, Francis
Foakes, R. A. 186 n. 61, 290
fool, role of
  in early modern culture 171,
    173–4, 204
  in publications by Robert Armin
    164–5, 170–72, 191–93, 291
  Robert Armin roles 87, 167, 175–90

William Kemp 13 n. 43, 85 n. 20,
  163, 165
Ford, John 125
Forman, Simon 167, 254
Fortune playhouse
  accounts 11
  as licensed playhouse 101
  construction 160, 203, 242
  let out to Palsgrave's Men 47 n. 31,
    104 n. 24, 155 n. 24, 235 n. 15
foul papers 83, 95 n. 43, 278
Fuller, John 302 n. 2

Gabrieli, Vittorio 280
Garber, Marjorie 22
Gascoigne 15 n. 50, 59–61
gender criticism 305; *see also* chastity,
  female; sexuality; women
George-a-Greene 53 n. 56
Gesta Grayorum 58
ghosts 30 n. 27, 64–5, 72, 216 n. 67
Gieskes, Edward 212
gift and return 158
Globe playhouse
  as licensed playhouse 101
  Burbage family's controlling share 236
  construction and ownership 150,
    155–60
  first performance at 166, 209–10
  in competition with the indoor
    theatre 199, 222
Goldberg, Jonathan 253
Goldsmith, Robert Hillis 174 n. 31
Gosson, Stephen 8–9, 15, 39–40,
  59, 200
grammar schools 43, 51, 54
Gray's Inn 58
Grazzini, Antonio Francesco 59
Greenblatt, Stephen 265, 302 n. 2
Greene, Robert 2–3, 15, 23–4, 29–30,
  37–38, 40–41, 45, 48 n. 35, 52 n. 49,
  64, 74, 105, 125, 200
  dramatic style of 24–5, 30, 33 n. 34,
    37, 39, 56
  social origins 2–3, 38
  working conditions 38, 40, 45, 50, 125
  Alphonsus, King of Arragon 24–5, 30,
    33 n. 36
  Francesco's Fortunes 38 n. 1